Literature as Philosophy
Philosophy as Literature

# Literature as Philosophy

# Philosophy as Literature

*Edited by Donald G. Marshall*

University of Iowa Press   Iowa City

University of Iowa Press, Iowa City 52242
Copyright © 1987 by the University of Iowa
All rights reserved
Printed in the United States of America
First edition, 1987

Jacket and book design by Sandra Strother Hudson
Typesetting by G&S Typesetters, Inc., Austin, Texas
Printing and binding by Thomson-Shore, Inc.,
Dexter, Michigan

Library of Congress Cataloging-in-Publication Data

Literature as philosophy/philosophy as literature.

1. Literature—Philosophy.   I. Marshall, Donald G.,
1943–   .
PN49.L52   1987     801     86-25002
ISBN 0-87745-149-4

"Hölderlin's Poetry and the Persistence of the Self"
originally appeared, in modified form, in Stanley
Corngold's *The Fate of the Self,* © 1986 by Columbia
University Press; reprinted by permission. James
Mish'alani's "Kafka: Text's Body, Body's Text"
originally appeared in *Philosophy and Literature,*
published by Johns Hopkins University Press. "The
Hunchback in the Park" is reprinted by permission
of New Directions Publishing Corporation from *The
Poems of Dylan Thomas,* © 1943 by New Directions.

# Contents

v

*Donald G. Marshall*

# Preface

THE TWENTY-ONE ESSAYS gathered here explore the questions stimulated by the book's title, which joins, crosses, and yet holds distinct the terms "literature" and "philosophy." Neither field is fixed or unproblematic so as to be the measure of the other, but both are brought into complex and dynamic interaction. The contributors clarify similarities and differences between philosophy and literature both in matter and language and question acutely the imposition of disciplinary distinctions on texts which escape neat categorization. "Thought" and "language" are not hastily assigned to philosophy and literature respectively, but both issues are seen to be at stake in both kinds of writing. Analysis of language's simultaneous powers of productivity and deviousness converges with recognition of the challenge to traditional conceptions of thinking presented by moral philosophy, by awareness of the body and sexuality, and by political catastrophes such as the Holocaust and the threat of nuclear apocalypse.

An opening section of ten theoretical essays by philosophers and literary critics and theorists approaches issues from a range of perspectives, including analytic and moral philosophy and the traditions of phenomenology, existentialism, hermeneutics, and deconstruction. The section closes with a broad survey of contemporary philosophy and literary theory by Suresh Raval. A second part comprises eleven essays directed more specifically toward philosophical and literary texts, from Plato's *Ion* to seventeenth- and eighteenth-century English satire to works by Kant, Balzac, Hölderlin, Kafka, Virginia Woolf, Mishima, Jacques Derrida, Michel Tournier, Maurice Blanchot, and John Ashbery. Philosophical readings of literary texts and literary readings of philosophical texts bring out fresh perspectives and illustrate the emergence of a genuinely interdisciplinary approach to the textual interweaving of thought and language. The contributor's disciplinary affiliation would frequently be difficult to identify from the approach taken, the argument pursued, or the texts examined in the essays.

The papers were first presented at the Ninth Annual Meeting of the International Association for Philosophy and Literature, held on the campus of the University of Iowa, May 3–5, 1984. In making the selection for this volume, we sought papers that were both outstanding and representative of the range of literary and philosophical approaches and texts discussed at that conference. I have not preempted a reader's response by imposing any finer mesh of labeled categories on these papers than the broad division into those which take up the topic more generally and those which concentrate on particular texts. The latter are arranged in rough chronology of texts discussed.

At various stages before and after the conference, participants speculated whether the stated topic had deconstructive or Heideggerian or some other overtones. Such speculations overestimate the power of an organizing committee to pursue a hidden agenda. The only polemic undercurrent to which I can confess was a reminder that the association is for philosophy and literature, not philosophy and literary theory. Contemporary theory is so evidently involved with philosophy that much of the interest and tension implied in the association's name seems to evaporate unless the almost automatic shift to literary theory is, however mildly, resisted. Throughout its history, the association has been open to the widest variety within its stated interests, and it was gratifying to see that variety confirmed on this occasion.

When Plato recalled the ancient war between philosophy and literature, he spoke with regret and encouraged the defenders of literature to reply to his strictures in prose or verse. I would prefer to think of the relation as one of long and deep friendship, which certainly does not preclude moments of rivalry and disagreement. To vary Heidegger's well-known image, we are occupants of the same house, though one likes to have a room of one's own. The conviviality of our annual meeting gives the abstract notion of friendship embodiment, and it is a pleasure to find that presumptions of a local loyalty to philosophy or literature dissolve in a mutually sustained exploration of issues. The resulting high level of the exchange both of ideas and roles is a happy omen for the future of the International Association for Philosophy and Literature and for the indissoluble mutuality of the two fields, whose recognition first called the association into being.

Plato's strict separation of philosophy from imitative poetry in the training of wise rulers is balanced by the license he grants for hymns to the gods and praises of famous men; by the rulers' recourse to the noble lie or opportune fiction; and especially by Plato's own fashioning of extended images and fables to mediate between the souls of his auditors and the insights to which he would move them. Despite Plato's strictures against allegorical interpretation of poetry, his own myths, especially for the Neoplatonists, authorized what we, not they, called poetic "allegories," the imagistic and narrative shadows of higher things susceptible to "interpretation," not a point-for-point translation into dogma, but a socially sustained and regulated method of using images to keep ideas before the mind. The intertwining of thought and poetic image was again radically sundered in the wake of Descartes, when Alexander Baumgarten invented the term "aesthetica" and defined it as "clear and confused" (that is, fused together) ideas, in contrast to the "clear and distinct" ideas, which were, according to Descartes, the only reliable basis for thought. Even in the role Kant assigned the aesthetic—to bridge and harmonize the sensuous and the conceptual—this separation was maintained. Romantic aesthetics connected art simultaneously with the sensual and the transcendent, but despite the hospitable capaciousness of a system like Hegel's, dialectic and positivist philosophy both were not slow to see art as only a now-surpassed version of their own more authentic access to all that is "highest." What has enabled the entire problematic relation of literature and philosophy to be reconsidered in our century is not only the famous "linguistic turn" of philosophy, but also a thickening of the linguistic medium in modernist literature, which, from Artaud's "theatre of cruelty" to Wallace Stevens' "Supreme Fiction" to Borges' narrative puzzles, gives to literature the rigor, scope, coherence, and penetration of conceptual reflection and analysis, even when it defeats the abstractions of paraphrase. The emergence of this possibility is no guarantee of a fruitful marriage between Mercury and Philology, between ratio and oratio: that fruit must be forced and plucked by gardeners who can perceive the opportunity offered by the conjuncture. A discourse that mediates literature and philosophy, making a middle for them, may find an appropriate home in a university rooted both in the cultivated Middle West and in the tradition of the liberal arts, a university proud to have been the first to grant to the work of creative writers not simply the degree of Master of Fine Arts, but of Doctor of Philosophy.

The members of the Executive Committee who helped organize the 1984 meeting were Charles Altieri, Mary Ann Caws, James Edie, and Hugh Silverman.

Finally, on behalf of the participants and the association, I wish to thank Richard D. Remington, Vice President of Academic Affairs and Dean of the Faculties of the University of Iowa, for the support from his office and from the University of Iowa Foundation which made this meeting possible.

*Part One*

# Conjectures

*Anthony LaBranche*

# How Is
# Poetry Philosophical?

THE QUESTION of how poetry is philosophical is not a neutral request for information regarding something already taken to be
the case, that poetry really is philosophical in its own way. The tone of
the question is more challenging: How can poetry possibly be philosophical? The question implies that ordinarily poetry may not be philosophical and that even when it tries to be, we must adopt a lenient
attitude toward its efforts in order to bring them into line with the
transcendental concerns and manners of philosophy. So perhaps poetry has no business sounding as if it were philosophical, since it may
be doing so merely to manage a rhetorical effect. But this kind of quar-
reling continues an interminable vista of dispute, recalling for example the diatribes from classical times to the Renaissance upon
whether poetry is presentation or representation and why the supposed difference between the two terms should matter to poets and
philosophers. This dispute pitches two camps, the literary and philosophical, at each other's throats without due reflection. The one camp
says that what "sounds like" philosophy in poetry is surely as close as
one will get to philosophic thinking, and the other maintains that only
what *is*, not sounds like, philosophic thinking is philosophy. The professional enmity covers over strong similarities between the two vocations and does a great deal to raise each in its own self-esteem.

Without becoming embroiled in this bizarre contest between *sounds
like* and *is*, I would like to suggest some obvious traits which poetry
shares with philosophy, and then some further traits which sound poetically philosophic and some even philosophically philosophic. Fi-

3

nally, I will mention some similarities and differences between poets and philosophers in the light of how *poetry* is philosophical. Maybe these comparisons will begin to sketch what kind of benefit we are seeking from literature by opening the question of its philosophical ways in the first place.

## Some Obvious Similarities

BOTH POETRY AND PHILOSOPHY propose, then modify, statements of our relations to the world. Both disciplines use a variety of definitions in order to solidify their stance before concerns which it might benefit us also to contemplate. Definition often carries with it an aura of excitement and drama, definition by etymology, description, process, example, comparison and contrast, analogy, and even the formal definition of genus and differentia, which poetry might use for its complex and qualifying tone. Both disciplines reveal their thoughtful drift toward a final position, toward a definition of or a settling into a difficult or elusive insight. In order to accomplish this, both may resort to argumentative postures of paradox and ambiguity and of the dramatic Kierkegaardian figure, irony. But all these postures suggest that much remains unexpressed in the course of our attempt to reveal the essential in the particular. Something is always slipping away from our pursuit, and therein lies the heroic quality of each vocation. The vivid episodes of lyric poetry and of philosophical description alert us to the struggle between presence and absence, the speakable and the unspeakable. Their pedagogical end is to attune us to our reflective, struggling selves, and they also encourage us to listen for snatches of story beyond this struggle.

Poetry's statements and propositions are accompanied often by paradoxical or somehow not easily digested description. For that matter, so too are certain manners of metaphysical speculation, Heidegger's for example, which stress the dangers of their undertaking. The methodical virtue of indigestible description is that it alerts us to the disharmonies in the schemes we have imposed on the world by way of explaining it, and at the same time it alerts us to the valuableness of our persisting amid these disharmonies. Perhaps at a later date we will

discover deeper strains of harmony beneath them. We say that a metaphor is appropriate when it reflects a companionable disharmony,
one that we must learn to live with. This is often the case with Emily
Dickinson. In philosophy, the sensibility behind such difficult description may lead us, or drag us, toward sobriety or toward dialectic.
Dialectic stresses rather heavily that we must hold together contraries
and dissimilarities. In both poetry and philosophy, matters are not to
be taken at a first glance. We work into things snakily, sensitively, au-
tobiographically. We come to each recognition maturely. Frost's poem
"The Oven Bird" concludes with a lament for the passing of the world,
of nature, and of man, all reflected in the notes of the bird: "The question that he frames in all but words / Is what to make of a diminished
thing." This laconic comment upon the intonation pattern of birdsong
subverts the pedestrian surface of its statement. We are led beyond
words, where we can appreciate the unappreciable. No creature, man
included, can make much out of diminution, though much talk is
made of it, with little outcome. A poem, then, is a sufficiently excessive declaration to be compatible with the excessive dredging, turning, redirecting we find in philosophy. As in philosophy, there is
always "something more to be said" beyond the illumination of its current language, or something to be promised if not openly declared,
for that something is not likely to be captured soon. Both vocations, in
widely differing ways, collect these contraries and dissimilarities into
a fragile, temporary harmony. This reconciliation is an esthetic tour
de force, and it seems also to be the valuable *social work* of both poetry
and philosophy. This contribution is what criticism is most happy
with, although it may not be the most profound contribution to our
thinking and being. But at least by entertaining what might be a strange
new harmony of the world, we may achieve a deeper and more friendly
proximity to the world as it is. This is the hopeful social vision of
poetry and philosophy. Both disciplines disparage a literalistic or a
fatalistic view of experience and ask us to sense the hopefulness of
our sentient, thinking office in the world.

Poetry shares with philosophy an appreciation of temporality, not
merely as a fugitive topic of discussion but as the melody in which the
world unfolds before us. The "dramatic setting" alike of poetic and
philosophic narration—that is, their shaping of everyday occurrence

into a readable drama on which they in turn base their speculation—
encourages our sense of our temporalities and so of our importance
as observers and thinkers. Like poetry, philosophy occurs as a kind of
excessively refined commentary along the borders of our temporal experience; it shows off what human temporality is by redoing or retelling the events that settle themselves as our mundane histories. Our
postures of consciousness, our recognitions, recollections, wishing,
regretting, finding, and lacking are the background accompaniments
to philosophy's sober discourse, and they are the foreground subjects
of poetry's thoughtful retelling.

In terms of solid, practical headway, little is achieved in either vocation, because too much is undertaken. The penchant of each toward
imaginative, exemplary discourse is motivated by the impossibility of
its ideal. What is this impossible ideal? Poetry and philosophy invite
us to a sense of long-term-belonging-to, even to those areas which are
elusive and inexplicable and to which we cannot belong for long, nor
they to us. This invitation is generous and openhanded; perhaps it is
wasteful rather than an economical report which remains safely in
sight of its goal. Both poetry and philosophy ask us to consider that
our temporalities are not only historically particular but are particu-
larities, that is, a vivid appearance of destiny, of becoming.

In sum, poetry and philosophy present our life of attentiveness,
earthbound or speculative, through exceptional description, definition, and posture. To do so, both appeal to a sense of our temporal
being, whether the main attention be to the truth of our declarations
or to the truth of our striving toward declarations. Both efforts involve
us with an uncomfortable relation between our historical meaning
and the always blank urgency of our present being.

## Some Further Traits

WE CAN PASS BY the rhetorical postures which poetry and philosophy
share, in order to consider the occasion of their undertakings. Each
lets us know that something is at stake or at risk and requires an exceptional effort of us; each offers its kind of discipline as a response to
this call. Rather than allude to a common body of thought or aware-

ness, these two vocations meet in their efforts of expenditure. Each attempts to say something in the presence of a request. And so what each says becomes testimonial to this request. Each vocation is a model of generosity, and so we can find in each a vast, widespread economy, something worth preserving.

We first notice that this expenditure takes place, in both disciplines, in the figure of the concerned speaker who addresses his topic before us and so underscores the topic's presence in our presence. This setting both presents and represents the topic. How we witness the speaker struggle with his topic is central to the drama, and so to the definition of the topic. This is more basic than our argument over the presentational methods of each discipline. Poetry does not tell us in a fumbling, roundabout way to wake up to certain philosophical topics, as if they were the main focus of our living. It proposes a certain kind of attentiveness which can bring us before something that begs to be considered. A certain manner of speaking, of address, raises before us important, inalienable presences, even if partly uncapturable. What is this manner?

The concerned speaker whom I mentioned a moment ago is a speaker who feels he has a privileged access to events and to the meanings they offer him or solicit of him. This privileged or intimate access results in a testimonial erection of the speaker's attentiveness to his subject, rather than in a dispersing command of it. By *dispersing command* I mean an act of description which stands over against and at war with its subject, trying always to reduce the multiple life of the subject to the "diminished thing" of a single level of discourse. For *single level* we may also read *self-infatuated*.

The curious method of diction and imagery in a poem tells us that poetry's manner of philosophizing is not philosophy's and that we had better stop trying to locate philosophically respectable topics and locutions in poetry. Philosophy is not "in" a poem, whatever philosophical clichés a poem may impose on us. There is a deeper sense in which poetry is philosophical. The conduct of the poem opens our eyes to similarity and difference, to meaning and to things almost denuded of meaning, but in a poetic, not in a topical manner. The poetic manner repeats this world in a finer tone, as Keats has it, and the act of making philosophic propositions distills the world so that this repetition is no longer possible. There are two respects in which poetic philosophizing is both poetic and, if we follow Heidegger, philosophical. The first I have mentioned already—that the speaker should arrive concernfully on the scene and show how he has committed himself to reviewing prejudice and to letting the world stand revealed before him. He has delivered himself as a kind of familiarity with the world which is always a prior familiarity and yet which asks of him a repetition or rehearsal, and it is in this latter action that we discover that this familiarity also has seeds in us. The second respect is that poetry's manner of proceeding is narratively resumptive—I mean in its intimate attribution of meanings to events, not merely in its unfolding of an action. This narrative resumptiveness reflects the speaker's sense of his own autobiographical depth, the depth of his undertaking, and this sense is also philosophy's sense of a unity of understanding and of living.

Let me try to capture the narrative quality by offering the following poem by Dylan Thomas, "The Hunchback in the Park":

> The hunchback in the park
> A solitary mister
> Propped between trees and water
> From the opening of the garden lock
> That lets the trees and water enter
> Until the Sunday somber bell at dark
>
> Eating bread from a newspaper
> Drinking water from the chained cup
> That the children filled with gravel
> In the fountain where I sailed my ship
> Slept at night in a dog kennel
> But nobody chained him up
>
> Like the park birds he came early
> Like the water he sat down
> And Mister they called Hey mister
> The truant boys from the town
> Running when he heard them clearly
> On out of sound
>
> Past lake and rockery
> Laughing when he shook his paper

Hunchbacked in mockery
Through the loud zoo of the willow groves
Dodging the park keeper
With his stick that picked up leaves.

And the old dog sleeper
Alone between nurses and swans
While the boys among willows
Made the tigers jump out of their eyes
To roar on the rockery stones
And the groves were blue with sailors

Made all day until bell time
A woman figure without fault
Straight as a young elm
Straight and tall from his crooked bones
That she might stand in the night
After the locks and chains

All night in the unmade park
After the railing and shrubberies
The birds the grass the trees the lake
And the wild boys innocent as strawberries
Had followed the hunchback
To his kennel in the dark.

The death that inhabits each of us, fully emergent in the curled figure of the "old dog sleeper," is the cause or motive force of the narrative persistently resumed beneath the description of each stanza of
the poem. The poem moves forward by collecting the true directive of
what it has touched and left behind it as a temporal process, the evening bell, the baptismal water, the kennel, the mockery, the ideal figure fashioned to stand in the dark, beyond life. What is philosophic
*for this poem* is the working out of its events—and this is why there is a
strong timetable of daylight and darkness, holy day and everyday—
from everyday mortality to transformation of everyday mortality. The
peculiarity of its successive address to its events holds open the ques-
tionableness of those events. This particular poem winnows its descriptive detail from the chaff of commentary and explication which
usually accompanies our experience, and it substitutes reminiscence
and narrative action for that commentary. Particularly the last three

stanzas refine an internal narrative which accompanies the poem's external narrative-description, and so gives us the "second glance" which philosophy recurrently claims it means to give. But it enlists our joined labor toward this second glance; it does not issue it by fiat. The hunchback is narratively situated "propped between trees and water" rather than positioned among explicitly philosophical and theological terms as he might be in a treatise, and he drinks his water from "a chained cup" rather than "survives in spite of the constricting attitudes of the parkgoers." This narratively opaque unfolding encourages in us a deep watchfulness toward how meaning comes to light, a watchfulness deepened by the speaker's claim that he has witnessed this episode as a child. If we are encouraged to consider the human roots of philosophic discourse and of theological argument, perhaps it is because they are erected before us in the faultless form of the woman who stands beyond this event, into the night. This poem is philosophical precisely because it presents the "ingrainedness" of our acting, judging, suffering, not just the philosophic explicitness and ingrainedness of our water, trees, and chained cups. Both philosophy and poetry make an excessive yet necessary effort to uncover this ingrainedness and to preserve it from being dissipated into mere terminology or exclamation. Poetry's philosophical concern is apparent in its backward and forward collecting movement, which we misrepresent by such terms as "narrative association." The roots of narrative follow a passage underground. A consideration of the depth of this rootedness leads us to our inherence in our own autobiographies. This consideration is the philosophic act of poetry.

Both the selection of certain "themes" and their ever-increasing transformation into rooted narrative contribute to the philosophic action of a poem. Primarily it is the incremental transformation that accomplishes before us the movement toward philosophical thinking and invites us to participate in it—the eye's second glance at a too familiar landmark, reenvisioning the whole landscape. How severely we may wish to separate philosophy proper from this kind of action may depend on how literally or metaphorically we choose to read a particular philosopher's claims to truth-telling. Philosophy, too, is often considered a "second glance" at something, with varying claims to results. But how to read the claims and performance of Western philosophy is endlessly debatable.

The important correlation between the two vocations does not lie in some accommodation among their several logical and rhetorical procedures but in the saving awareness which those procedures, variously managed, promise us and try to promote in us. It is the élan, not the doctrine, that accomplishes philosophy. We are "put through" the narrative unfolding of the poem or of the philosophical commentary, an unfolding which I have called autobiographical in the sense that there is, at first, a stormy context or solicitation to which, next, we respond after our manner of speaking. Certainly the action of a poem lies in the poet's orderly response to the surroundings which for some time have been soliciting his or her speech. As there is some shelter for the hunchback in his kennel, so there is for man in his speakings. But poetry progressively gives us a sense of the strengths and weaknesses of this shelter of speech, which in protecting and expressing us shades us over. We can find this sense also in philosophy at times. In such instances, both lean away from our prosaically secularized discourse—one which does not bother to show the shadow obscuring us—and toward a sacredly secularized discourse which, like "the woman figure without fault," carefully shows our obscure geniture and manner of persistence. In alluding to our obscure autobiographical existence, the attitude and comportment of the poem or of the philosophical essay become a matter of concern for us.

## The Truth of the Difference between Philosophers and Poets

I WILL SUGGEST that philosophers, at their best, are specialized poets who are in turn specialized and highly attuned autobiographers. I am not comparing here the respective accomplishments of each, which can be variously appreciated. Traditionally we say that philosophers try to pursue, in creative ways, the rightness and wrongness of propositional statements. But beyond this activity, they attempt to revive a classical repertory of concerns. Poets try to imagine how it is that we live with rightness and wrongness, that is, with all our flawed acts of perceiving and judging, our childish misperception of the hunchback, disabused only in death. The targets of attention are nominally different but the efforts toward revivification and guardianship similar.

Philosophy offers propositions to aid our residential presence before ourselves and the world; poetry seems to dissolve what might be
propositions into descriptive details. In one of her stranger images
Dickinson describes the soul closing "the Valves of her attention / Like
Stone." Such poetic indirections dissolve the lurking philosophic
proposition into its rootedness—rootedness in how we address our
lives. What constitutes clarity for poetry is quite different from that
which does so for philosophy; the constituting intention of each bears
a different life-style. Poetry asks us to live with the proposition, to
suffer its presence rather than to depart with it hastily to the next step
of a logical summary. We do not merely apprehend and collect meanings. Meaning has been stalking us all the while in the things and
events of the world, but we do not admit to it until we see the poet
allow a familiarity, an exposure between meaning and himself, between meaning and ourselves. Then we sense how meaning is our
companion, how through it we are erected before events and events
before us in the detailed particularity of each event. We might say that
our best encounters are always poetic and narrative. In poetry the
next step is always sequential, narrative, temporal, rather mortally so;
even if it is logical it is not self-gratulatory in its logic. This is what is
philosophical about poetry, and at bottom about philosophy too. Both
vocations have a saving awareness of their next step, and this awareness of risk gives familiarity to their enterprise.

We speak about things and events in order to establish ourselves in
a spot where these things and events can find us out and address
themselves to us. We calculate that the sound of our voices will give
us, fortunately, away. The whereabouts of this spot philosophy sees as
a challenge in definition, poetry as an encounter to be perpetuated.
From here the poet launches the poem, the philosopher his or her
commentary. But poets and philosophers do not enjoy "public speaking" as our professional conferences, publications, and community
actions depict us enjoying it. They feel obliged to speak out privately.
This reluctant, obligatory speaking seems to be an important feature
also of our autobiographical narration. Listening to my own narration
readies me to listen to poets or philosophers in theirs. Of course they
are quite different from me because they have found the occasion,
which has found them out, and the idiom to speak, whereas I con-

tinue to look for the proper occasion and hope that it will find me out. But this difference is not decisive; if it were, I could not believe their words. Merely in listening to them, a part of me is saved and expressed. I often perform this kind of listening even without the benefit of philosophy or poetry—for example, in my recollection of childhood or of happy occasions and in my forward collection to me of my dying. Poetry and philosophy show a concern with my destiny and call me, in their particular ways, to attend to it. The inherence and faith they show in their particular ways render them philosophical.

*Kevin McGinley*

# The Hermeneutic Tension and the Emergence of Moral Agents

IT IS EVIDENT that every human situation is filled with questions of value. One expresses one's sense of meaning and values in terms of a story which one tells to oneself and to others about one's living. One relates the present moment to the myriad of past and future moments through the meaning expressed within stories. However, besides the stories which are expressions of one's lived meaning, humans characteristically tell stories and by this recitation of story expand the context of lived meaning beyond the narrow confines of actual experience. These stories, too, are carriers of meanings and values. Within this brief paper we will explore the moral significance of stories in terms of a tension that is created between stories which are told and stories which are lived. Both lived stories and literature emerge out of a mode of intentional consciousness which we shall term "narrative consciousness." Intentional consciousness as understood from a hermeneutic perspective is a cognitional/ontological structure which constitutes a world. Probing the nature of intentional consciousness will reveal in narrative consciousness the source both of stories and of the concern for what Lawrence Kohlberg understands as true human values.

## Intentional Consciousness

CONSCIOUSNESS is a difficult philosophical notion. The nature of consciousness and subjectivity in general has been rendered confused and opaque by modern philosophy and has only in recent times be-

gun to come clear, largely through the good agencies of the phenomenological and existentialist philosophers. The work of Bernard
Lonergan is particularly notable in this regard. Lonergan distinguishes
clearly between consciousness conceived as a content, reflexive self-
knowledge, and consciousness conceived relationally as the self-
presence of the subject to himself or herself co-posited with the given-
ness of any object to the subject. Consciousness must be primarily
conceived of as an awareness of self which makes possible any intentional presence of "world-objects" and only secondarily and deriva-
tively as reflexive self-knowledge.

As an act, consciousness is dynamic. The dynamism of consciousness is located in its self-transcendent orientation toward the real. Such
an orientation can be variously thematized as curiosity, questioning,
interest, and intentionality, but as the dynamism of consciousness
it transcends such thematizations. The dynamic orientation of consciousness opens up for the subject various horizons of meaning, or
intentional fields, which specify a set of operations on the side of the
subject and reveal a range of world objects with which the subject can
operate.[1]

Within the range of possible intentional fields which are open to the
subject, one can discern two characteristic orientations of consciousness: the theoretic and the primal. The primal intentional fields pattern experience in reference to the subject and his or her practical
concerns and projects. The only objects which are allowed into the
foreground of the subject's attention are those which have some plausible relevance to the practical subject, his or her concerns and projects. Within the general orientation of primal consciousness one can
distinguish various patternings of experience. In *Religion and Self-
Acceptance*, John Haught identifies four intentional fields within primal consciousness: the sentient, the interpersonal, the aesthetic, and
the narrative.[2] While all of these intentional fields operate in concert
within primal consciousness, it is possible to differentiate the characteristic patternings of experience which may dominate primal consciousness at any one time. Within the sentient intentional field,
meaning is revealed in one's feeling orientation toward and response
to the world. (Heidegger refers to such an intentional orientation as
*Befindlichheit*.) The interpersonal intentional field opens up the "other"
as a unique world object and specifies a set of intentional operations

which reveal to subjectivity the meaning of the other. Aesthetic consciousness orients the subject to a world of beauty and play. Meaning is revealed in the birth of form and symbol in a human artistry which liberates living from the tyranny of the merely biological. Among other things, the human subject exercises his or her artistry upon his or her own life, transforming it from the merely biological/organic to the human. Such artistry is exercised within the field of narrative consciousness in a dynamism which gathers together the moments of life and expresses their interrelationships in language, ritual, and symbol. Our primary concern, then, is with the narrative intentional field.

## Narrative Consciousness

ALL OF THE INTENTIONAL FIELDS have to do with meaning, and the characteristic manner in which meaning is expressed within the narrative intentional field is the story. Within the story one relates the moments of one's existence to each other. Further, personal stories are essentially social in their character. They serve to relate one's life to the lives of those with whom one lives. The personal story is lived and articulated within the larger context of cultural meanings and values.

In many of his works, and in particular in *The Birth and Death of Meaning*, Ernest Becker specifies the character of cultural meaning as a set of "hero myths" which serve to provide the members of the culture with a sense of primary heroism. Becker comments:

> When the child poses the question "Who am I? What is the value of my life?" he is really asking something more pointed: that he be recognized as *an object of primary value* in the universe. Nothing less. And this pointed question has ramifications immediately broad and embracing: He wants to know "What is my contribution to world-life?" Specifically, "Where do I rank *as a Hero*?"[3] [emphasis his]

Within the context of meaning specified by the system of cultural hero myths, an individual finds his or her status and role within society. Again Becker comments:

> One of the great and lasting insights into the nature of society is that it is precisely a drama, a play, a staging. . . . The child who learns the "I" and

begins to refer his action to those around him is trained *primarily as a performer*. His entire life is a training, preparation, and practice for a succession of parts in the plot—parts he can show himself worthy of filling, simply by handling them.[4] [emphasis his]

One's personal story, then, must be seen as a "part" within the cultural play.

Without the culturally derived and maintained context of meaning, life would be insupportable. The human person is, in Becker's view, filled with an overwhelming need to know the ultimate origin and destiny which define his or her place within the world. Without answers to the questions of origin and destiny, the individual is overwhelmed with a sense of his or her insufficiency, of doubt about his or her "worthiness to be," which is experienced as "existential anxiety." In the face of existential anxiety all action is paralyzed. Life depends upon the sense of cosmic meaning and worth which culture affords. Culture supports life, providing a context for action, spreading over the individual a "sacred canopy" (to borrow a phrase from Peter Berger). Only by virtue of the constant augmentation of one's self-esteem, of one's sense of one's "worthiness to be," which social intercourse under the aegis of culture provides, is individual action possible. The creation of such an action context is the product of one's socialization/inculturation.

In the process of inculturation the individual is transformed from a mere organism dominated by biological need into a social being living in a world of symbols. Having been inculturated, for all its obvious benefits, creates some difficulties for the individual. The problems resulting from socialization and inculturation stem largely from the "conventional" nature of cultural myths, and thus of personal stories. One is inculturated without having chosen the meanings which constitute the common context of action. Further, cultural and personal myths lack a critical component, for their function is not so much to articulate the "truth" about reality as to provide an arena for human action in the face of the radical contingency of human existence. The conventional nature of cultural meanings and values, and therefore of personal stories, has some important ramifications for morality.

Moral consciousness must be understood as unfolding in at least two stages. The first, represented by Lawrence Kohlberg's "conventional stage of morality,"[5] is familiar to us from the writings of Freud, Kohlberg, Becker, and others. Moral consciousness, expressed as "superego" and "guilt-consciousness," is to be understood as a product of cultural conditioning. It is, in Becker's terms, a manifestation of Oedipal dependency and is thus fraught with neurosis. To the extent that one finds oneself "out of step" with the meanings and values of the cognitive majority, one feels "guilty." One's "conscience" is largely one's internalization of the common meanings and values. One's need to manage one's anxiety about living holds one firmly in the "moral" context which culture establishes.

The second stage of moral consciousness emerges as a reversal of the first stage. It is marked by the emergence of the moral question "What ought I to do?"—which is more than simply an inquiry about conventional wisdom. The second moral stage is defined by a realization that one forms oneself by one's acts to be a person with a particular moral quality. One shifts, then, from the primal moral context in which one is formed *by culture* to the postconventional moral context in which one realizes that one freely forms oneself as a responsible moral agent. The second stage opens up to critical scrutiny the reality of one's inculturation. Such insights open up a new horizon for the subject and reveal a new sense of the human good. The criterion for one's actions ceases to be the culturally derived and maintained sense of "right" and "wrong." Rather, as Lawrence Kohlberg has identified, the postconventional level of moral consciousness in its highest development defines "right" moral action in terms of "the decision of conscience in accord with self-chosen ethical principles appealing to logical comprehensiveness, universality, and consistency. The principles are abstract and ethical. . . . At heart, these are principles of justice, of the reciprocity and equality of human rights, and of respect for the dignity of human beings as individuals."[6] Personal responsibility and the desire to avoid self-condemnation operate as primary motives for action in the postconventional stage of moral consciousness.

## Morality and Literature

AS ONE EXAMINES LITERATURE, one is struck by its existential character. Stories constitute a horizon of meaning and value into which the reader is invited to enter. To paraphrase Ricoeur, every semantics tends toward an ontology.[7] Stories are existential, then, in that they are fully concrete. The horizon of a story engages the subject completely, offering a *Weltanschauung* comparable in its breadth to his or her own personal story.

We have identified the moral issue in terms of the emergence of the question about postconventional human values. The goal of moral philosophy is to facilitate the emergence of such postconventional moral subjects, and literature can play an important role in this endeavor.

The moral significance of literature is greatly illuminated by Paul Ricoeur's work on biblical interpretation. His lucid analysis of parabolic discourse in the New Testament centers on the merger of the narrative with the metaphoric/poetic modes of discourse found in the New Testament parables. Metaphor, Ricoeur argues, involves a suspension of the "referential" nature of language. It juxtaposes two seemingly unconnected thoughts, establishing a "tension between all the terms in the metaphorical statement."[8] The tension is in truth not simply a tension between words juxtaposed, but a tension between two wholly different interpretations. For example, when the poet writes, "My love is like a red, red rose," he establishes a tension between love as commonly conceived, which includes no sense of flowers or color, and the experience of roses blooming in deep hues. Such a juxtaposition is a "semantic impertinence" on the part of the poet. But it is precisely in terms of this "absurdity" of juxtaposition that new, otherwise inexpressible poetic meaning emerges. For Ricoeur, the scriptural parable must be understood as a "mode of discourse which applies to a *narrative form* a metaphorical process."[9] Within the parable taken as a whole there is established a tension between two contexts of meaning, two interpretations, the "conventional" and the "eschatological" or "religious." The reader of these parables experiences within himself or herself the tension of these differing horizons. The reader's experience of the horizonal tension evoked by the parable calls him or her to *metanoia,* "conversion," for within this tension is exposed the conventional as "conventional," and she or he is opened up to the possibility of a religious understanding of life. The parable serves as a goad which constantly forces the religiously sensitive individual to reflect on whether he or she is living according to conventional meaning or according to religious meaning. We suggest that stories in general operate in a fashion analogous to the operation of scriptural parables.

As one begins to consider the nature of stories, one must differentiate between "stories" and "cover stories." As we noted, each individual elaborates a personal story line which provides him or her with a context for meaningful human action. However, as Marx, Freud, and Nietzsche (among others) have made painfully clear, human subjects are uniquely capable of alienation, and thus require a more or less elaborate scheme of self-deception to smooth over the lacunae in their stories which are the result of alienated subjectivity. Without such a smoothing over of inconsistencies in one's story, life's meaning is lost and human action is again insupportable. Even when the meaning is insincere, one still requires a context of meaning. The product of such self-deception is a "cover story." John Haught, quoting Herbert Fingarette's classic work on self-deception, comments upon the nature of "cover stories":

> In general, the person in self-deception is a person of whom it is a patent characteristic that even when normally appropriate he *persistently* avoids spelling-out some feature of his engagement in the world. . . . This inability to spell-out is not a lack of skill or strength; it is the adherence to a policy (tacitly) adopted.
>
> A self-covering policy of this kind tends to generate a more or less elaborate "cover story." For a natural consequence is the protective attempt on the part of the person to use elements of the skill he has developed in spelling-out as inventively as possible in order to fill in plausibly the gaps created by his self-covering policy. He will try to do this in a way which renders the "story" as internally consistent and natural as possible, and as closely conforming as possible to the evident facts. Out of this protective tactic emerge the masks, disguises, rationalizations and superficialities of self-deception in all its forms.[10]

All subjectivity is characterized to some extent by self-deception. Thus all personal story lines are a mixture of true "stories" and "cover stories." The cover story protects subjectivity from a truth which, if allowed conscious integration, would too radically upset the ego-integrity and psychic equilibrium which ward off anxiety. There is then implicated the necessity of an adequate hermeneutics and a comprehensive theory of alienation (a dialectics) to know whether any story is a true story or a cover story. While even a brief sketch of an adequate hermeneutics and dialectics is beyond our scope here, it is clear that one must be in a position to decide whether any given story is the product of authentic subjectivity, and thus expresses authentic human meanings and values, or whether it is the product of alienated subjectivity and thus functions as a cover story.

The problem of interpreting a story emerges when the horizon of meaning which underpins the text is different from the horizon of the interpreter. If the story simply exemplifies the type of discourse characteristic of the conventional mindset, the interpretation is not a problem. One simply and immediately understands the meaning of the text. Such stories, however, are all too readily simply cover stories elaborated to protect the individual from any need to question conventional wisdom. Such stories can be mere ideology elaborated to serve the subject's need to absolutize his or her cultural hero-myth system. However, as one reads a story whose horizon is different from one's own and attempts to understand the meaning expressed within the story, there is effected what Hans-Georg Gadamer terms a "fusion of horizons."[11] In interpreting the story, one enters into the story with a set of questions about the meaning of the text emerging out of one's own context of meaning. Understanding the text, however, is a process of coming to understand the *story's* horizon. The process of achieving such an understanding is a self-corrective process in which one begins the interpretation with a set of questions which thematize one's anticipations of the meaning of the text. In the encounter with the text and its horizon, the interpreter shifts his or her initial questions to others more pertinent to the horizon of the text itself. The self-corrective process is what is meant by the "hermeneutic circle," in which the meanings of the parts serve to interpret the whole and the whole contextualizes the interpretation of any of the parts. The tension between the horizon of the text and the horizon of the interpreter is never overcome. While this tension is especially operative in the interpretation of what are termed "classics," it is present in the interpretation of any text. This "hermeneutic tension" bears special importance for understanding the moral significance of stories, for essentially the tension of the interpretation mandates a change of horizon within the interpreter for the meaning of the text to be grasped. Such changes in subjectivity can contribute to the emergence of postconventional moral agents.

In the light of this hermeneutic tension we must understand all stories as written in an interrogative mode. Each story is a question posed to the reader which probes the limits of the reader's horizon. As the reader strives to interpret the text, the relation of reader and text becomes a mutual interrogation in which the horizons both of the text and especially of the reader are broadened.

Our reflections here have been wide-ranging. We began our inquiry by considering the nature of intentional consciousness and the various contexts in which intentional consciousness opens itself to the real and constitutes for itself a horizon. Of prime importance in the field of intentionality is narrative consciousness, which strives to express the meaning of living as a drama and understands each individual as a *dramatis persona*. Such individual stories are played out within the larger drama of culture, whose function is to provide an overarching meaning-context to support individual action. Cultural horizons, however, are not critically established, and thus both cultural and individual meaning are largely conventional in nature. Moral consciousness must be seen as developmental, culminating in the liberation of the moral agent from the conventional values of culture and the emergence of a critical, individuated moral agent acting upon his or her understanding of values which are universal and personalist. In light of this developmental view of moral consciousness it was necessary to distinguish true stories from cover stories.

Stories operate in a manner analogous to Paul Ricoeur's understanding of the way in which metaphors function. A metaphor is a semantic impertinence which establishes a creative tension between two contexts of meaning, two interpretations. The tension which the metaphor establishes is similarly operative within the clash of horizons characteristic of any interpretation.

Thus I argue that the understanding of most texts, and in particular those texts which can be called classics, requires a shift of perspective within the interpreter. The awareness of this shift of perspective alerts the interpreter to the possibility of an alternate way of viewing the world and, perhaps for the first time, raises the moral question "What ought I to do?" Only in glimpsing the possibility of another way of understanding the world can the moral agent inquire about postconventional human values. If one is locked into the conventional, then "what one ought to do" is already a settled issue. One ought always to do what a cultural hero ought to do. If, however, the conventional nature of one's horizon is revealed in the possibility of an alternate way of understanding self in the world, then one is capable of inquiring beyond cultural values toward true human value. In such an inquiry the emergence of moral agents concerned about truly human values becomes possible.

## NOTES

1. Bernard Lonergan, *Method in Theology* (New York: Seabury Press, 1972), pp. 235–37.

2. John Haught, *Religion and Self-Acceptance* (Washington, D.C.: The University of America Press, 1980), pp. 34–35.

3. Ernest Becker, *The Birth and Death of Meaning* (New York: Free Press, 1971), p. 76.

4. Ibid., p. 82.

5. Lawrence Kohlberg, *The Philosophy of Moral Development* (New York: Harper & Row, 1981), p. 19.

6. Ibid.

7. Paul Ricoeur, *The Philosophy of Paul Ricoeur: An Anthology of His Work*, ed. Charles E. Reagan and David Stewart (Boston: Beacon Press, 1969), p. 101.

8. Paul Ricoeur, "On Biblical Hermeneutics," *Semeia* 4 (1975): 77.

9. Ibid., p. 88.

10. Haught, *Religion and Self-Acceptance*, p. 152.

11. Hans-Georg Gadamer, *Truth and Method*, ed. Garrett Barden and John Cumming (New York: Seabury Press, 1975), pp. 273, 337.

*Steven Fuller*

# When Philosophers
# Are Forced to Be Literary

O NE WAY of marking the difference between philosophy and literature is to identify a kind of situation that forces the philosopher
to conceptualize his subject matter in the same way as, say, a novelist
naturally does his. The import of "forces" is to suggest that, in the
kind of situation we seek to identify, the philosopher is drawn away
from his usual pursuit of making and defending claims, and drawn
toward such intractably literary issues as whether things have been
given the right names and whether something has been described
from the right point of view. At the outset, it is important to distinguish our concern from the common observation that philosophers
have periodically found it effective to draw on literature, in some way,
to make their points. For example, philosophers regularly illustrate
complex mental states by citing passages from novels, and sometimes
they have even turned to writing novels themselves. Indeed, existen-
tialists do not seem to see much of a difference between these two
kinds of activities.

At the verge of our concern is the observation that philosophers
have often taken the pragmatic and semantic features of their own discourse to be so intertwined as to suggest that only one writing style
can convey what they have to say. Here philosophers have turned in
two quite different directions. On the one hand, in order to facilitate
philosophy's role as the conduit between otherwise isolated domains
of discourse, the American pragmatists (with the notable exception of
Peirce) have preferred a fluent prose style that demands little technical
knowledge from the reader. On the other hand, European thinkers of

a Marxist, hermeneutical, and deconstructionist bent have cultivated a difficult style both to heighten the self-referentiality of their claims and to force the reader to consider those claims very carefully. Yet despite this radical stylistic difference, the Americans and Europeans have typically intended to have much the same effect on their respective readers. Not only do both take their own styles as well suited for teaching the reader to see things in a new light, but they also regard their styles as especially designed to expose the vulnerability of what they have to say. Plain speaking allows the pragmatist's claims to be contested by the widest possible audience, whereas studied obscurity sensitizes the post-Hegelian reader to how the text conspires against the author's intention being adequately expressed. Not surprisingly, the Europeans tend to see the American style as an attempt to forestall criticism by capitalizing on easily understood—and hence uncritically accepted—turns of phrase (especially metaphors), while the Americans suspect the Europeans of retreating to a position of unassailability behind a veil of ambiguity. And so, considerations of style inevitably lead to questions of the philosopher's *authentic* voice, which become particularly vexed when the philosopher resorts to aphorism. In that case, a sufficiently few ordinary words are juxtaposed in an extraordinary-enough manner to render the text, in one reading, trivial, but in another reading profound. The result attracts a peculiar mix of popular and esoteric readers, as in the case of the later Nietzsche or of Adorno's *Minima Moralia*.

Yet having said all this, we have refused to *identify* the issue of philosophical style with the concern raised at the start of this paper. The reason is that literary critics usually characterize style as the feature of an author's discourse over which he or she has the most control. Admittedly, unless the author intends to write an experimental novel, he or she is forced to conform to the elementary rules of syntactic construction that we normally call "grammar." Within these initial constraints, however, the author has free stylistic rein. Discussions of authenticity are likewise tainted with this voluntaristic view of style: the philosopher is typically seen as exercising *moral* judgment in deciding the relative value of writing persuasively vis-à-vis writing truthfully. Calling such a judgment "moral" makes sense (at least in the context of a Christianized West) only if the philosopher's choice appears to be significantly unconstrained. And while no one denies that the philosopher has a choice in such stylistic matters, we propose that he does not have a choice as to when the choice will be made. If that is the case, then a shadow of suspicion is cast over the pursuit of authenticity, though the problem of the philosopher's stance toward his text still remains.[1]

Let us begin by considering a typical situation in which the philosopher does seem to have a choice as to when his or her stylistic choices are made. Analytic philosophers generally suppose that arguing a position is tantamount to explicating a concept. For example, to defend a claim about the nature of such dispositional properties as water solubility and linguistic competence, the analytic philosopher will isolate some significant sentences using the disposition-word, and then show how each of these sentences may be resolved into a set of intuitively less problematic sentences. What counts as "intuitively less problematic" may vary enormously, as in the case of Carnap's counterfactual analysis vis-à-vis Ryle's purely behavioral analysis of dispositions.[2] Furthermore, the intuitiveness may not stem from some Cartesian sense of self-evidence, but rather from the reducibility of the problematic concept to terms that the reader is already presumed to find acceptable. Thus, one cannot get much out of Carnap if one does not at least entertain the soundness of counterfactual analyses, nor can one get much out of Ryle if behaviorism is presumed dubious. In short, analytic philosophy cultivates a strong sense of what Carnap called *questions inside a framework*.[3] This sense has an important stylistic consequence, for, as the narratologists would say, in analytic works "story time is coextensive with writing time."[4] In other words, the author is presumed to tell the reader all and only all the reader needs to know for following the line of argument. Given an optimal piece of analysis, the reader should be surprised neither by the outcome nor by the particular moves made to get there. Indeed, any actual surprise or puzzlement would reflect either the reader's refusal to enter the author's framework or more simply his failure to follow the text closely. In short, once the analytic author decides to pose a question inside a framework, only incompetence can prevent him or her from being in complete control of the question's textualization.

It would seem, then, that tedious tales make for good analytic philosophy. But more to the point, philosophers who adopt an analytic style usually accord it the power to advance knowledge, if only by systematically clearing away conceptual errors. The style suggests this power once the analyst is taken to be doing something analogous to what a scientist does in the laboratory. Of particular relevance here is the Janus-faced concept of *constancy* in experimental condition. On the one hand, the scientist is said ideally to "hold constant" all factors that might interfere with the outcome of his or her experiment by eliminating them from the lab; on the other hand, he or she is presumed not to be interfering with the general physical laws that render the experiment intelligible and that are thus said to "remain constant," no matter what the outcome. And so, in order to determine the speed of an object moving in a vacuum, the scientist must eliminate all the air resistance that would normally be present, but he or she cannot assume that this artificial setting could somehow result in the suspension of Newton's laws. This dual sense of constancy constitutes the ceteris paribus clause implicit in the testing of a scientific hypothesis. It also informs the analytic stylist, who operates on the dual assumption that the outcome of his or her argument is determined exclusively by the terms he or she explicitly introduced for that purpose, and that the actual course of the argument does not alter the semantic framework of the language within which those terms were introduced. And so, if the analogy between experiment and analysis holds good, then we have a clear case in which the philosopher is not forced into making a stylistic decision, thus supporting the view that philosophy is *not* intractably literary.

But does the analogy hold good? I suspect not. In articulating this suspicion, we shall come still closer to the intractably literary situation that potentially besets the philosopher. One curious feature of analytic style that marks it off from ordinary discursive practice is the use of explicit definition as a means of stabilizing meaning. The aim, of course, is to focus the reader's attention on just the sense of the term that the author intended, and no other that the reader may have previously run across. However, very often the analytic author explicitly defines a term whose sense the reader would have understood as appropriate, even without the author's definition (because the author intends either ordinary or some canonical philosophical usage). Under those circumstances, following Grice's rules of conversational implicature, the reader seems forced to make a decision as to how the author intends the Quantity Maxim to be taken in the text. The Quantity Maxim stipulates that the speaker says *exactly* as much as the audience needs to know to understand him or her: the speaker neither repeats what the audience already knows, nor omits things that the audience would not know otherwise. Thus, when the analytic stylist gives an explicit definition of a seemingly familiar term, does the reader conclude (a) that the author has temporarily suspended the Maxim in order to conform to his or her self-imposed stylistic dictates (which would have the author make *everything* explicit), or (b) that the author has continued to obey the Maxim, and so what appears to the reader as a familiar sense of the term really involves some subtle variation that demands further scrutiny? In short, the reader must decide whether the analyst intends to have his or her specific stylistic practice overrule the general discursive practice. It is clear that this problem cannot be circumvented *within* analytic style, since, for any argument that the analyst may try to make, no unique set of definitions exists that would eliminate for *all* readers the analyst's ambiguous stance toward the Quantity Maxim.

If the history of analytic philosophy is any indication, it would seem that the reader has normally opted for (b). At least, such a conclusion would account for the fact that the lexicon of analytic philosophy consists almost entirely of ordinary words whose senses become more diverse and sophisticated as the trail of commentary in the journals lengthens. Two consequences may be drawn from this observation. First, in attempting to adopt a style that would permit the progress of philosophy through clarification, the analyst has unintentionally generated a new "jargon of authenticity," to borrow Adorno's phrase for a philosophical style (such as Heidegger's, allegedly) which claims to bring the reader closer to an extralinguistic truth but only succeeds in placing him or her in yet another hermetically sealed universe of discourse. Second, this new jargon has resulted from the reader's effectively subordinating the analyst's specific intention (which may indeed be progressive clarification) to the general intentional structure of the communicative act (which obeys the Quantity Maxim).

Moreover, the unwitting generation of this new jargon parallels the ironic use that is often made of a "realistic" sense of description in the course of "defamiliarizing" the reader from what is described. This point, first made by Viktor Shklovsky in "Art as Technique" (1917) and subsequently emblematic of Russian formalist criticism, highlights the fact that the text has an economy of its own, in terms of which all supposedly extratextual elements must be transacted.[5] The effects of this economy are especially striking when the information contained in an instantaneous glance is converted into discursive prose. Care for the kind of detail that could be registered in a glance may generate an exaggerated response in the reader: a sense of the grotesque (as in Gogol's protracted physical descriptions) or a sense of the belabored (as in Proust's protracted psychological descriptions). But in neither case does the reader's response in any way diminish the author's claim to realism. Rather, the reader's response simply *is* the product of the literary author's intended realism refracted through the medium of the text, just as the reader's tendency to sophisticate the analytic text is the product of the philosophical author's heightened sense of explicitness filtered through the Quantity Maxim, which the reader presumes the author to obey. Indeed, the phenomenon of defamiliarization in literature may be generally explicable in terms of an author's studied ambivalence toward the Quantity Maxim.

Can we also make sense of the philosopher's assuming this kind of studied ambivalence? If so, then our search is complete. As it stands, the analyst has generated a new jargon of authenticity as the unintended and *unforeseen* consequence of his or her choice of style. Nothing about the decision was *forced*, precisely because the analyst did not foresee that such jargon would be an inevitable outcome however he or she pursued the analytic style. What we need, then, is to describe a situation in which the outcome is the unintended, yet *foreseen*, consequence of some choice the philosopher made. This would be the analogue of a novelist, following Gogol's lead, intending the grotesque but, at the same time, realizing that the effect will not be brought about on the readers unless he or she intends the realistic (and hence meticulously attends to detail). As a result, the grotesque becomes the foreseen unintended consequence of the author's intending the realistic. This, in turn, constitutes the studied ambivalence he or she pays the Quantity Maxim. Moreover, following the Russian formalists, the need for such doublethink here reflects the refractive power of the text as a medium, a power that may also be seen as a source of the text's *literary* properties. I shall now argue that the philosopher engages in a similar doublethink when attempting to give what Robert Nozick has called *invisible hand* and *hidden hand* explanations.[6]

Although we normally associate the invisible hand with Adam Smith's account of how the market emerged as the unintended consequence of individuals pursuing their own interests, it first arose in the context of theodicy, as a means of explaining how evil could be a consequence of divine creation. Indeed, Smith's own source for the invisible hand, Bernard Mandeville, composed *The Fable of the Bees* (1714) in order to spell out the social consequences of Pierre Bayle's skeptical theology.[7] In cataloguing the public virtues that had resulted from the pursuit of private vice, Bayle effectively inverted the Old Testament lament, "How could evil things ever have been thought good?" to read, "How could such obviously good things ever have been thought evil?" Mandeville radicalized Bayle's observations to the point of arguing that, while not all private vices make for public virtue, all public virtue is the result of private vices. Mandeville followed Bayle in taking "private virtue" in the traditional Christian sense of self-abnegation. Moreover, he did not question self-abnegation as a cultivator of spirituality in the individual, but he did question it as a promoter of the welfare of society. Given this and the actual phrasing of Mandeville's thesis, it is clear that he did not intend to replace private virtue with private vice.

Yet all these points did not sit together well with a philosophical readership whose concept of rationality presupposed that good optimally arose as the foreseen, intended consequence of doing good. To think otherwise would present the classical rationalist with two unsavory possibilities:

1. If those acquainted with the truth of Mandeville's thesis wanted to promote the public good, they would have not only to pursue private vice but also to act inauthentically in the process (by giving others the impression that they intended to pursue vice when they really intended to pursue virtue).

2. In order to promote the public good authentically, one would have both to be ignorant of the truth of Mandeville's thesis and to pursue private vice. In other words, one would have to be a brute.

And so, two strategies arose for short-circuiting the effects of Mandeville's thesis. On the one hand, Hume and Smith decided that Mandeville had proven self-interest, not self-abnegation, to be the "real" private virtue; whence came the collapsing together of normative and instrumental rationality we now call *utilitarianism*. On the other hand, Kant concluded that Mandeville had shown real-world consequences to be entirely irrelevant to morality, since the most desirable state of affairs seemed to arise from the most morally suspect impulses; whence came the radical separation of normative and instrumental rationality we now call *deontology*. And theologians aside, virtually every major dispute in ethics conducted over the last two centuries has involved utilitarians and deontologists. As for Mandeville himself, he seems to have been a proto-Nietzschean who saw nothing wrong with the practice of self-abnegation, just so long as it was regarded as an *aesthetic* rather than as an *ethic*; for the latter term connotes, misleadingly, that somehow other people directly benefit from the practice.

And so, notice what has happened: Mandeville has, in effect, challenged the idea that the "Career of Reason" can be presented from a consistent point of view. From Mandeville's authorial stance, public virtue is the foreseen, unintended consequence of the pursuit of private vice. The fact that his consequence is "unintended" means that if Mandeville wants to keep the actions of his self-interested agents authentic, then he must presume that the agents are ignorant of the consequences of their actions. These consequences, whence comes public virtue, must thus be characterized from a different point of view—a distinctly literary maneuver.

It may appear unduly provocative to suggest that modern secular ethics is simply a by-product of the attempt by Kant and Hume to avoid the literary turn that Mandeville was forcing philosophers to take. But let us consider the claim more closely. Mandeville began his career as a translator of La Fontaine, another fabulist concerned with invisible hands, especially the ones that seem to be at work when someone unwittingly reinterprets his or her prior beliefs and preferences ex post facto so as to get them to cohere with the outcome of a decision he or she has made. Obviously echoing La Fontaine, Jon Elster has recently called this kind of invisible hand the "sour grapes" phenomenon.[8] It is curious that both La Fontaine and Mandeville turned to fables as their means of exploring the workings of the invisible hand. This move probably stemmed from the ease with which the narrator can widen his or her angle of vision in a fable, which is, after all, a story populated by animals whom the reader expects to be the unwitting exemplars of moral truths. In contrast, philosophical prose ideally presents its subject matter from a consistent angle of vision, which, if nothing else, impresses the reader as displaying a seamless view of things. And so, the analytic philosopher rarely draws on the syntactic resources available in natural language for shifting points of view and expressing referential opacity.[9] For example, rather than alternating between two roughly synonymous descriptions of an object, each of which accentuates one feature of the object at the expense of its other features, the philosopher normally prefers the object's proper name (or uniquely defining description), which gives the object a consistent identity throughout the piece. We see a similar kind of philosophical resistance to the literary in the Humean and Kantian responses to Mandeville. Hume effectively focuses on the end of the fable—public virtue—and redescribes the action of the characters as latently leading up to it; hence, a character's own view of his or her action as self-interested is overruled by Hume's view that it is really for the public good. Kant effectively returns to the start of the fable—private vices—and redescribes the actions of the characters so that it looks as though the characters would have altered their actions had they known any public benefit would result; hence, from Kant's point of view the virtuous end-state appears to be vitiated by the nonmoral impulses secretly motivating the characters.

Even neopositivists concerned with the problem of social scientific explanation, such as Edna Ullmann-Margalit, have recognized—if not actually diagnosed—the difficulties facing the philosopher who tries to give an adequate invisible-hand explanation of some social institution.[10] On the one hand, one is tempted to make the Humean move of casting the individuals now regarded as the founders of the institution as having had some preconscious awareness of the long-term role their actions would collectively play. This historically tenuous mode of explanation has the added disadvantage of leaving the false impression that social institutions can be freely engineered into existence. On the other hand, one can go to the Kantian extreme of stressing the arbitrariness with which private vices interacted to issue in a public good. The error here is somewhat subtler, for while this kind of explanation is likely to be faithful to the narrow horizons of the unwitting founders, it offers no indication of how this unintended public good managed to stabilize into an institution which has persisted beyond the original motivation of self-interest. Ullmann-Margalit's own solution involves, first, recognizing that invisible-hand explanations are intractably "story-like" and then proceeding to integrate aspects of what we have just identified as the Humean and Kantian points of view.

We have thus shown one philosophical task, the giving of invisible-hand explanations, that forces the philosopher (in spite of the proclivities of her school, in the case of Ullmann-Margalit) to think in terms of manipulating point of view, which is normally taken to be the province of the novelist. As mentioned earlier, a second philosophical task also having these features turns the invisible-hand explanation on its head: namely, the giving of an explanation in which a seemingly unintended end-state is shown to have been brought about intentionally—whence comes the name "hidden hand."

An explanation of this second type often appears as a conspiracy theory, which is in turn parasitic on an invisible-hand explanation. To illustrate this point, consider the following idealization of the conditions under which "the invisible hand" causes and maintains the market:

1. The complementary talents and desires of rational egoists unintentionally bring about the market. In short, each needs something that the other can readily provide.

2. The existence of the market increases the material well-being of all the egoists.

3. The egoists do not realize that the market emerged because of their complementary talents and desires.

4. Yet, since the egoists realize that the market benefits them, they try to maintain the market's existence, which, again unintentionally, leads them to maximize the required complementarity—say, through an increased division of labor.[11]

The conditions are idealized in that given a small-enough group of egoists who are able to observe the effects of their exchanges, it is unlikely that condition (3) would hold for long. But let us entertain the fiction—Adam Smith did—since a cause is more easily masked in the real world of large groups engaged in many exchanges. Enter now the conspirator, who wishes to turn this very condition (3) to his own advantage by eliminating the market's unintended cause, namely, the complementary talents and desires of the egoists. One strategy would be to eliminate the differences in upbringing and schooling that often produce such complementarity. However, since condition (4) also obtains, the conspirator must justify his strategy in terms that will appear *beneficial* to the market. Otherwise, the egoists will see through his ruse. With this in mind, the conspirator argues that standardization of the background of the egoists will make each person more versatile and hence his or her skills more marketable. Although the egoists find this argument persuasive, the conspirator knows that his policy will in fact undermine the market, since there will be nothing that an individual can do which another cannot do equally well. And instead of versatility, superficiality will be the net result, for to be somewhat good at everything is to be very good at nothing. Consequently, the egoists will be forced to depend on a tyranny of outside experts. But since the conspirator's hand remains hidden, the egoists never actually feel the coercion, since, from their point of view, the market has disappeared as mysteriously as it appeared. That is to say, condition (3) remains intact. The moral of the hidden hand—as told by the conspirator—could have been taken from La Fontaine: *Whatever is thought to have been gained by chance will not be regretted when lost.*

Now when does the *philosopher* tell conspiratorial tales? Answer: when he or she engages in *nonidentity thinking*. Consider Adorno's general remark about dialectics: "the name dialectics says no more, to begin with, than that objects do not go into their concepts without leaving a remainder, that they come to contradict the traditional norm of adequacy."[12] An identity thinker, such as Hegel, is committed to rendering the real rational, and so he or she proceeds by incorporating the "remainder" in a new set of concepts that hides the inadequacy of the old set. In contrast, Adorno's self-styled nonidentity thinker aims to render the real irrational (and the rational unreal). He or she does this by using the old concepts to reveal their own inadequacy in representing reality. And so, in short compass, we see the distinguishing feature of the Frankfurt School's "ideology-critique": namely, the pursuit of criticism as an end in itself. The strategy of subverting a conceptual scheme from within rather than from the vantage point of a master scheme betrays the conspiratorial nature of nonidentity thinking. But let us now examine the ruse close up.

As noted above, the hidden-hand explanation of the conspirator is parasitic on an invisible-hand explanation. And so, we shall start by attending to the latter. In our more unreflective moments, when we are thinking *with* concepts instead of *about* them, it is easy to be amazed at just how adequate these concepts are to the objects they represent—especially given the fact that, contrary to some analytical fantasies, no decision was ever made either to forge or to monitor the concepts. Idealists are in fact so amazed that they doubt there is a real difference between concepts and objects. Even the sober pastime of ordinary-language philosophy is predicated on such identity thinking. And no less a thinker than Niels Bohr has taken the fine fit between concepts and objects in the "midworld" as a guarantee that the counterintuitive results of quantum mechanics will never be part of our everyday discourse.[13] This collective amazement from diverse quarters no doubt reflects our inability to give a clear causal account of why identity thinking actually works. In short, our unreflective intuitions point to an invisible hand. Consequently, when our conceptual scheme does begin to yield a "remainder," as in the case of quantum indeterminism, we are caught by surprise. However, it is a stoical surprise, since we never knew why our conceptual scheme worked so well in the first place, and so it is only fitting that we do not anticipate its subsequent poor performance.

It sounds as if we are making a case for *the objects themselves* conspiring against our concepts. But stripped of its anthropomorphisms, the claim becomes rather mundane, since conceptual anomalies are a matter of course in at least scientific encounters with objects. What, then, does Adorno add to this picture? Quite simply, he replaces the anthropomorphisms with human thinkers—as befits a hidden hand. In other words, the nonidentity thinker aims to *simulate* the objects that the identity thinker aims to *represent*. And as we have suggested, the way to simulate objects in one's own thinking is by subverting the concepts with which one thinks; for only then do the objects reveal themselves to be something different from the concepts: hence, the "nonidentity" of the thought. This all probably seems either quite obvious or quite obscure. Assuming the latter for the moment, we can make the same point by borrowing some of Adorno's favorite tropes and, in a considerably simplified manner, laying out some of his conspiratorial tactics for subverting our conceptual scheme.

Adorno regards a concept as simply a scholastic universal, which "universalizes" by canceling out the difference in the particular objects it subsumes. For example, regardless of their many differences, all humans are conceptualized under "humanity." Although philosophers from Plato to Hegel have identified the pursuit of universals with the growth of knowledge, Adorno more readily likens the universal to Marx's "commodity," whose defining characteristic is that intrinsic (use) value has been reduced to some common (exchange) value.[14] And so, for Adorno, something is always lost in conceptualization. The question, then, is how to recover the loss. Hegel would have us adopt an omniscient perspective, with its ultimate conceptual scheme. But Adorno objects: the very essence of conceptualization is the canceling out of differences, and so, to speak of a conceptual scheme that "perfectly represents" objects is to utter a self-contradiction. Thus, Adorno does not forge an artificial master language in the Hegelian mold. Rather, as the early Wittgenstein would say (in a somewhat disgruntled tone), Adorno wants to use language to articulate its own limits. At this point two tropes enter: *pleonasm* and *oxymoron*. I would be pleonastic if I spoke of a "manly man" and oxymoronic if I spoke of an "effeminate man." From a strictly logical point of view, the former utterance is tautologous and the latter self-contradictory. Yet, Adorno's texts are peppered with these forms.[15] And while Wittgenstein might take the tropes as evidence that Adorno's discourse has been rendered senseless, the looser logical standards of literary and ordinary language permit us to render these tropes significant. A pleonastic utterance normally conjures in the reader's mind the archetype of the repeatedly mentioned concept. Interesting arguments may ensue about whether the archetype represents an *average* or an *ideal* instantiation of the concept, but in either case some kind of paradigmatic use of the concept comes to mind. In contrast, an oxymoronic utterance usually causes the reader to consider a deviant case of the contradicted concept. Again, interesting arguments may ensue about whether the deviation constitutes an *improbable* or a *pathological* instantiation of the concept, but in either case the reader is forced to think about the limits he or she would place on the concept's use.

It is unfortunate that Adorno always chose to conspire (and hence to write pleonastically and oxymoronically) rather than to teach conspiracy. As a result, *Tractatus*-inspired readers have measured his prose against the standards of representation—that is, the standards of the identity thinker. And by those standards, Adorno does fall short. However, as we have argued, they are not Adorno's own, for he would rather provoke us—perhaps against our logical instincts—to think that our conceptual scheme is not as "amazingly accurate" as it might first seem. The first lesson for the apprentice conspirator, then, is to adopt the point of view of the objects that escape our concepts and that are articulated in the pleonasms and oxymorons.[16] But perhaps this lesson has already been learned. Cognitive psychologists have recently developed an experimental paradigm based on *pictures* for studying the difference in conceptual schemes between, say, adults and children, and Europeans and non-Europeans, which forces the subject to simulate the nonidentity thinking needed for defining the limits of his or her concepts. Although a bat is certainly an unbirdly bird to most, it is not nearly as unbirdly as an ostrich—unless, of course, one is an educated European adult.[17] Obviously the scientists have yet to appreciate fully the revolutionary—or at least critical—potential of this paradigm. The trick now is for *us* to realize that potential.[18]

## NOTES

1. We would use the term "implied author" for "philosopher's stance toward his text," were it not for Wayne Booth's moralizing overtones.

2. Rudolf Carnap, "Testability and Meaning," *Philosophy of Science* 3 (1936): 419–71, and 4 (1937): 1–40. Gilbert Ryle, *The Concept of Mind* (Totowa, N.J.: Barnes & Noble, 1972).

3. Rudolf Carnap, "Empiricism, Semantics, and Ontology," in *Meaning and Necessity* (Chicago: University of Chicago Press, 1956), Appendix A.

4. Oswald Ducrot and Tzvetan Todorov, *Encyclopedic Dictionary of the Sciences of Language*, trans. Catherine Porter (Baltimore: Johns Hopkins University Press, 1979), s.v. "Discursive Time."

5. Viktor Shklovsky, "Art as Technique," in *Russian Formalist Criticism*, ed. and trans. L. T. Lemon and M. J. Reiss (Lincoln: University of Nebraska Press, 1965). See also Ducrot and Todorov, *Encyclopedic Dictionary*, s.v. "The Discourse of Fiction."

6. Robert Nozick, *Anarchy, State, and Utopia* (New York: Basic, 1975), chap. 2.

7. Bernard Mandeville, *The Fable of the Bees*, ed. F. B. Kaye, 2 vols. (Oxford: Clarendon, 1924). Much of the information on Mandeville's career and effect on moral theory comes from the excellent introduction by F. B. Kaye.

8. Jon Elster, *Sour Grapes: Studies in the Subversion of Rationality* (Cambridge: Cambridge University Press, 1983), chap. 3.

9. Ducrot and Todorov, *Encyclopedic Dictionary*, s.v. "Reference."

10. Edna Ullmann-Margalit, "Invisible Hand Explanations," *Synthese* 39 (1978): 263–91.

11. The following idealization is patterned on Jon Elster, *Explaining Technical Change* (Cambridge: Cambridge University Press, 1982), chap. 2.

12. Theodor Adorno, *Negative Dialectics*, trans. E. B. Ashton (New York: Seabury Press, 1973), p. 5.

13. One of the few philosophers to have noted (and criticized) this similarity between ordinary-language philosophers and quantum physicists has been Paul Feyerabend. See his "An Attempt at a Realistic Interpretation of Experience" (based on his Ph.D. dissertation), in *Realism, Rationalism, and Scientific Method: Philosophical Papers* (Cambridge: Cambridge University Press, 1981), vol. 1, chap. 2.

14. Cf. Gillian Rose, *The Melancholy Science: An Introduction to the Thought of Theodor W. Adorno* (New York: Columbia University Press, 1978), chap. 3.

15. Cf. Rose, *The Melancholy Science*, chap. 2. Also, Theodor Adorno, *Against Epistemology*, trans. Willis Domingo (Cambridge: MIT, 1982), "Translator's Note."

16. Adorno, ever the aesthete, would probably compare the Tractarian treatment of his texts with an attempt to judge surrealism (pleonasm) and cubism (oxymoron) by the classical standards of the French Academy. For an interesting account of Adorno's aesthetic way (via Walter Benjamin) to nonidentity thinking, see Susan Buck-Morss, *The Origin of Negative Dialectics* (New York: Free Press, 1977), esp. pp. 78–81.

17. See, for example, Eleanor Rosch, "On the Internal Structure of Perceptual and Semantic Categories," in *Cognitive Development and the Acquisition of Language*, ed. Timothy E. Moore (New York: Academic, 1973), pp. 111–44. An extremely difficult problem facing anyone who intends to pursue nonidentity thinking is the prospect that two syntactically and semantically identical languages may be incommensurable because they do not share the same archetypes.

18. This paper continues a line of thinking initiated in my "A French Science (with English Subtitles)," *Philosophy and Literature* 7 (1983): esp. 6–12.

*Stephen H. Watson*

# The Philosopher's Text

The "rationality"—but perhaps that word should be abandoned for reasons that will appear at the end of this sentence—which governs a writing thus enlarged and radicalized, no longer issues from a logos. Further, it inaugurates the destruction, not the demolition but the desedimentation, the de-construction, of all the significations that have their source in that of the logos. Particularly that of truth.
—Jacques Derrida, *Of Grammatology*[1]

Cf. The Darwin Upheaval. One circle of Admirers who said, "Of course," and another circle (of enemies—R) who said, "Of course not." Why in the Hell should a man say "of course"?
—Ludwig Wittgenstein, *Lectures on Aesthetics*[2]

IT IS A COMMONPLACE that one can (or at least that one must) clearly delineate the philosophical and the literary—that one can say once and for all that philosophy clearly does one thing and literature does something else. As a result, philosophers would, among other things, not be constantly plagued by the danger that they merely weave webs of belief (*doxa*), stringing the reader along without making him or her confess the belief's truth or falsity, virtue or vice. On the contrary, the philosopher's text would be *justified* and would once and for all signal the *exclusion* of mere opinion from the tribunal of reason. And its author (and likewise the demand for the philosopher's authorship) would be just as decisive, cut loose from the realm of shadows and the opinable, again once and for all.

The text is Platonist, of course, perhaps not without just cause. Plato was in any case clearly and consistently able to delineate it already:

40

The man who cannot by reason distinguish the Form of the Good from all others, who does not, as in a battle survive all refutations, eager to argue according to reality and not according to opinion, and who does not come through all the tests without faltering in reasoned discourse— such a man you will say does not know the Good itself, nor any kind of good. If he gets hold of some image of it, it is by opinion, not knowledge; he is dreaming and asleep throughout his present life.[3]

Plato's text is perhaps extreme—ideal, certainly the exemplar or "idealization" of the philosophical text. And yet, this *agon* of Reason which demands of the philosopher that he or she survive all refutations perhaps reaches from Plato's dialectic to "the battlefield of metaphysics" of Kant's first *Critique*, Wittgenstein's "battle against bewitchment," and beyond.[4] The need to *exclude* here is absolute: the dogmatic, the unreal, the fictional, the imaginary, and ultimately their text, the literary. And Plato, as is known, is consequently strict in the need to regulate this *eros* of the literary: "One should be cautious in adopting a new kind of poetry and music, for this endangers the whole system."[5] That there is such a threat to the philosophical "system" seems innocuous, perhaps. The philosopher, after all, is the one who sees the *things themselves,* as Plato was the first to say with the force of that reflexive autoclitic which indicates his certainty.

AND YET equally commonplace is the assertion that philosophy and literature do mutually threaten one another. It is perhaps a recent claim, but not without ancient roots, a claim involving a controversy, as Plato manifests, which is as commonplace as philosophy itself. The controversy between the philosopher and the poet in the *Republic* is already described as "an ancient quarrel" whose threat involves a certain "grudge" that Homer himself had already felt.[6] One might even argue that the very foundation of philosophy necessitates this threat. The philosopher's text is, after all, a writing, a transformation or set of transformations in the system of signs. It is one text among others, one genre among others, with its own stylistic variants and good and bad stylists. In accordance, then, with the most ancient meaning of the word "literature," philosophy is an architecture of signs, of letters.

It is, in short, literature, a text whose lexemes are in fact idiomatic, "philosophemes." Moreover, this practice, the philosopher's *writing*, is a practice among other practices with all the accompanying conditions, contexts, permutations, and perhaps dependencies. Still, the philosopher's text claims to be more than one text about others; it claims to be their meta-text, the text which provides the axis of their intelligibility and which orders and evaluates. Rather, it would institute a critical tribunal which itself *claims* to distinguish, to justify, to adjudicate: the real and the unreal, the true and the false, ·the literal and the fictional.

The problem has always been, however, that bad philosophical texts have often looked retrospectively like bad novels. The battlefield of metaphysics has always been a place of "mock-combat" (*Spielgefecht*), as Kant, again, put it.[7] Hence the response of empiricism and positivism committing all these bad novels to the flames. Artists, it is claimed, because of their logical-shortsightedness, do better and more openly that to which metaphysicians won't admit. And at least artists have the good *taste* not to couch their delirium, their *focus imaginarius*, in the language of truth—or so went the response.

THE THREAT, however, is the return of the constitutive difference between philosophy and literature. While philosophy is built upon particular classificatory schemata and strategies—those regarding the methodology for the differentiation and exclusion of the false, the imaginary, the fictional—literature affirms them. Unlike the irreal of the literary, the philosopher's text truly builds into *its world* the requirement that there be both logical and ontological order (*ratio*), that as Kant put it in the construction of the Transcendental Ideal of *metaphysica rationalis*, only "one òf every pair of *possible* predicates must belong to it."[8]

The literary, on the other hand, turns all disjuncts into possible syntheses. That is, rather than excluding, the possibility of the literary *admits*. As Bloom declares in the midst of the Walpurgisnacht episode of *Ulysses*, that "metaphysics in Mecklenburg street," a night of illusion, of unreason, or to use Joyce's words, "woman's reason"[9]—a declaration made precisely in relation to that *aporia* of *aporiae* for Western thought, the problem of time, of presence, and immutability:

I wanted then to have now concluded. . . . Hence this. But tomorrow is a
new day will be Past was is today. What now is will then tomorrow as
now was be past yester.[10]

Fully cognizant perhaps of an *epos* and a *historia* and the archive of its
overdetermination from Aristotle's own *aporiae* to Augustine's "thought
which cannot be comprehended"—and beyond, Joyce's text differs.
Joyce refuses to choose between theses, between affirmation and
negation, real and irreal, refuses to assume the propositional attitude.
Rather he affirms, without stopping short, the phantasmagoria of
time as dispersion, as contradiction, one before which "the center of
gravity is displaced," as Stephen states.[11] The contradiction introduces, as Harold Bloom and Jürgen Habermas, among others, have
argued, a certain notion of the sublime and perhaps, thereby, a certain gnosticism which would dominate art of this century.[12]

This is not to say that all literature is built upon "disjunctive syntheses," as Deleuze calls them,[13] or that there have not been times
when literature was thought to be "good" precisely when it avoided
such possibilities—though, as Adorno quite rightly points out, one of
the distinctive features of art of this century is that "many modern
works simply defy the question of how good or bad they are."[14]
Rather, nothing "fictional" excludes those possibilities. Literature, it is
said, not without a certain risk, forges its own possible world. And
(apparently unlike the philosopher's text) even if this should be an impossible world, it is still "*fictive*," a commonplace that is perhaps forgotten when philosophers look at texts other than their own. When,
for example, philosophers attempt to delimit this margin by simply
denying that the literary constitutes a world, that there is strictly
speaking no world at all to the literary, they still must face the response of the margin itself: does one speak literally or figuratively
here?[15]

The literary text occurs on that margin produced in bending language beyond the confines of strict reference, a *meta-phora* which
demonstrates in its "turning," in its extending if not its extensionality,
the inherent "meaningfulness"—the overdetermination—of language
itself, a *Sinn* which surpasses *Bedeutung*. Kant was the first to make
truth a problem of meaning, a problem of *Sinn und Bedeutung*.[16] That

signs were true only when they had *Sinn und Bedeutung* meant only
that they could be cashed out in sensible intuition. Before Kant,
Hume had not made it strictly a question of meaning, perhaps. Certainly all the signs of those old metaphysical *phantasmagoriae* remained
"meaningful" for him even when they were not true or even if their
truth-value could not be decided—which is what both Hume and
Kant meant by the rejection of metaphysics. Hume even believed that
"a criticism of the fictions of the ancient philosophy" could be useful
in the same way that we "recollect our dreams in a morning," [17] its history being something like Joyce's "nightmare from which [we] are trying to awake." [18] This word, "meaningful," and its vagaries both linguistic (for example, "grammaticality") and epistemic (for example,
"adequacy," that is, meaning*ful*ness) nonetheless have proven especially recalcitrant in current discussions in literary criticism, as
has been shown in the exchanges between John Searle and Jacques
Derrida. [19]

For Hume himself it was hardly a question of "meaning" in any but
a conflated sense. We could still *read* all those "fictions of the imagination" even if we could not validate them. If truth were to be limited,
indeed *had* to be limited, what could limit the fictional? We can after
all, as Kant would admit, "think whatever we please." [20] And if, as
Descartes before him argues, imagination is limited and it is only the
will which "indicates to me that I am made in the image and likeness
of God," still that act of willing presupposes a re-presentation, that is,
an image of the intentional object. [21] Confronting the issue of the
"meaningfulness" of the literary, we come not to a problem of limits
but to the problem of margins. In the Kantian idiom, we come to the
problem of extension *in indefinitum*.

NOW, in a sense all of this seems less than obvious. Recognizing the
unlimited spontaneity of the imagination, the *libera facultas concipiendi*
and its *virtus fingendi*, as Nicholas of Cusa had already put it in
broaching the site of aesthetic modernism, Kant was quick at the same
time to ground the link between spontaneity and receptivity. In the
*Anthropology*, the text in which he most fully probes this faculty, admitting again that "imagination is creative, and being less subject than
other powers to the constraint of rules [is] more apt for originality," [22]

Kant was likewise quick to assure, to reintroduce order and perhaps even the realist's text: "Imagination, however, is not so creative as we pretend. We cannot think of any form other than that of man as suitable for a rational being. So a statue or a painting of an angel or of a God always depicts a man."[23]

John Searle's recent work claiming that fictional discourse is always parasitic on the ordinary, the normal, the real, seems to concur. What distinguishes the fictional from its opposite is the illocutionary stance of the author. Doyle, for example, not only pretends to make assertions in his text but pretends to *be* John Watson, M.D. What obliterates the threat of the literary for Searle is the fact that what lies behind these assertions is already categorically distinguished—the intention to pretend and that upon which it is in turn parasitic, serious intentions.

Moreover, the imaginary is likewise equally *derived*, a fictive variation on an original pre-text.

> But how is it possible for an author to "create" fictional characters out of thin air, as it were? . . . Again, if Sherlock Holmes and Watson go from Baker Street to Paddington Station by a route which is geographically impossible, we will know that Conan Doyle blundered even if he has not blundered if there never was a veteran of the Afghan campaign answering to the description of John Watson, M.D.[24]

And just as the author's fiction is parasitic upon normal usage—pretending upon serious usage—so his or her success is measured by how the text "figures" vis-à-vis its real commitments, here its "London." That is, the fictional text finds its intelligibility outside itself, in its coherence with the primitive, original text of the serious.

> To the extent that the author is consistent with the conventions he has invoked or (in the case of revolutionary forms of literature) the conventions he has established, he will remain within the conventions. As far as the *possibility* of the ontology is concerned, anything goes: the author can create any character or event he likes. As far as the acceptability of the ontology is concerned, coherence is a crucial consideration.[25]

Like Kant, Searle looks almost as if he is willing to allow the fictional text the creative—that is, originary—function that he has subtracted from the realist's text. And yet "acceptability" and "coherence" still receive "regulative employment" in this discourse, as do even the revolutionary "forms" of literature. Still, he admits as well that "coherence," when it comes to the fictional text, remains an abstract criterion and—as Kuhn had discovered with science—somewhat problematic:

> However, there is no universal criterion for coherence: what counts as coherence in a work of science fiction will not count as coherence in a work of naturalism. What counts as coherence will be in part a function of the contract between author and reader about the horizontal conventions.[26]

While the text remains internally unregulated, Searle again appeals to the illocutionary practices of author and reader to introduce a homogeneity into the play of fictions. That is, the realm of the fictional and the imaginary again *derives*—at least in its acceptability—from the real. "Acceptable" fiction will not challenge that from which it ontologically derives. Still, the nature of this derivation and what it ultimately implies concerning the intentional relations between the literary and fictional, and more specifically, the imaginary and the serious intentions that underlie them, is not further elucidated. What Searle does acknowledge, once more, is the ambiguity in the distinctions themselves. Literal meaning, for example, is not to be construed as the simple, classical, realist text. While the distinction remains in force, the literal is in a sense itself in flux—relative to a background of assumptions and a context "which are not and in most cases could not also be completely represented as part of or as presuppositions of the representation."[27] While literal meaning is thus relative, Searle stands fast: "Literal meaning, though relative, is still literal meaning."[28] And yet, in the midst of these shifts, what orders, what differentiates and adjudicates—perhaps still—remains the meanings, the "*Protokollsätze*," constituted within the "*Urtext*" of intentionality.[29]

THIS MORE "obvious" view is, in one regard, still not without its own strangeness. It is perhaps a strange view of language, after all, as univocal and well ordered, which rules discourse by *one* of its texts.

And it is perhaps a strange view in this regard of "reality" and the realist text it stands on. It is strange that the play of signs, that fictive variations, that the *dis*order—the Babel—of language, in the end is a chimera. After all, it is a fact that there are competing accounts (*logoi*)—discourses, theories, practices, and literatures. Can one read Kafka in terms of coherence and decidability, as an example of deductive-nomological feigning—the way one reads Doyle, the philosopher's novelist par excellence, perhaps?[30] It is strange, in any case, that in the midst of this play of differences one could seek a route back to an initial baptism (or intention) that would be clearly and distinctly nonlinguistic: an *Ursprung*, and its theory, and its observation. It is, after all, a curious thing "to put into words," this *Wovon* of which humans speak but which itself remains silent. This brute index, this given, this tabula rasa of discourse seems anything but "given," seen from this side, seen as a figure of speech, if you will. For it is, *qua* linguistic, *literature* too.

This *chimaira*, this labyrinth that refuses a pure "taking," that refuses to separate the Same from the Other, as Joyce aptly caught, is a kind of "she-monster" within the philosopher's text, a certain Greek variety of sphinx with all its mystery, its "otherness" intact—the other perhaps to all that is Greek and that constitutes the philosopher's text. This discursive monster, the labyrinth of fiction, is akin—in fact essentially related, perhaps—to that other monster Plato guards against, which is uncontrolled because uncontrollable and which, in the ninth book of the *Republic*, must be governed, won over. This multiheaded beast threatens Reason from the other side, from below.[31] It is known, however, from the first book of the *Republic*, and will appear again and again thereafter, the threat which Socrates incessantly combats—namely, that we will only *seem* to be convinced, that the discourse, a mere *image* of *epistēmē*, would have been through and through an endless and uncontrollable "banquet of words."[32] And Gorgias would in the end then be right: words are inspired incantations, in their wizardry capable of saying or affecting anything, a sophistic precursor of the principles of expressibility.[33]

And finally, it is strange that confronted with this chimera the philosopher feels compelled to refute, to survive intact this battle with "Otherness." It is strange perhaps that this difference does not com-

fort, that, as Nietzsche would have it, it not be "welcomed" as the philosopher's proper destiny, or even, as Wittgenstein put it at the end of
a similar confrontation, that "ordinary language is all right." [34] Or to
invoke a reference that is more archaic, it is strange that the philosopher does not affirm Plotinus' assertion made still within the ease of a
certain metaphysical enthusiasm: "Difference everywhere is good." [35]
The philosopher's text nonetheless needs to *appropriate*, to set language straight, to reduce its difference, to domesticate: if nothing else
to *fix* a reference, to bestow a meaning, and finally, to express an idea.

LIKE SEARLE, but within a different context and perhaps a different notion of science, Edmund Husserl saw the problem of intentionality as
the clearinghouse of meaning and truth. Husserl in many respects
perhaps more directly faces (already) the problems inherent to the realist and here Cartesian text. The problem again is the content of the
imaginary, the phantasm, and its incursion upon the text of philosophy. For Husserl, as for Descartes (and for Searle, implicitly), it is a
question of science, truth, and the rational tradition from which both
emerge in the mind's "intentions."

> Now one will say that in the sphere that interests us here—that of sci-
> ence, of thinking directed toward the attainment of truths and the avoid-
> ance of falsehood—one is obviously greatly concerned from the start to
> put a stop to the free-play of association. In view of the unavoidable sedi-
> mentation of mental products in the form of persisting linguistic acquisi-
> tions, which can be taken up again at first merely passively and be taken
> over by anyone else, such constructions remain a constant danger. [36]

The danger for Husserl, the phenomenologist of essences, is that
language will get used without attending to the meanings, the essences it conveys—a failure of re-collection in all its senses. Rather
than reactivating the original sense of a sign it will be used in a way
that "makes sense" without attending to all that went into its original
meaning; so, for example, geometry gets leveled off to a mere play of
signs which *constructs* semantic grids, rather than holding its original
position in its emergence within conscious experience and the life-
world (*Lebenswelt*). The danger is that the *essence* of geometry, that

which regulates its origin, its intelligibility, its order, its truth, and thereby its meaning, will be lost.

This is a late text, "The Origin of Geometry" (1936), in which Husserl explicitly affirms that rational practices are constituted within a certain facticity, notwithstanding all that he had attributed to their ideality. Still, as early as the *Logical Investigations* (1900), the danger of the potential for transformation inherent in usage, its *Spielbedeutung*, had already been the subject of analysis. And Husserl had categorically distinguished it as a parasitic or surrogate function, as the "operational function" in which meaning is not "determinate," not, that is, intentionally "fixed."[37]

This question has by now a long history of interruptions. Sellars perhaps put forward the most direct challenge to its position in science, saying just point-blank that Husserl had got it wrong: science does not retrieve the life-world; its "essence" is not to recapture conscious experience but to surpass it.[38] And unlike Mach, who shortly after the invention of the spinthariscope (which made it possible to detect alpha-ray scintillations) affirmed the existence of atoms,[39] there is little evidence that Husserl would have regarded atoms as anything but theoretical entities *derived* from the "original" ontological types of the life-world, from a typology and its theory that remained "classical" (Western/Greek). Derrida, on the other hand, had demonstrated the problem of arriving either at an unbound ideality or a pure origin (the intention, or a pure index) once the issue of the factuality of the rational (linguistic) tradition has been raised, one which inevitably conditions meaning.[40] The situation regarding meaning and intention is perhaps more like the one Wittgenstein described:

> The fundamental fact here is that we lay down rules, a technique for a game, and that then when we follow the rules, things do not turn out as we had assumed. That we are therefore entangled in our own rules.
>
> This entanglement in our own rules is what we want to understand (i.e., get a clear view of). It throws light on our conception of meaning (*Meinung*). For in those cases things turn out otherwise than we had foreseen.[41]

Far from being the repository of perceptual and intentional acts which would precede it, *founding* language and making all *imaginary* derivations parasitic, language and "perception" are in this regard already intertwined: "Uttering a word is like striking a note on the keyboard of the imagination."[42] Language and our rational practices offer not a simple reflection of the real but a route, or a schema, which no more belongs to the actual, to *the* real, than to *the* possible, *the* imaginary. But this is precisely what the philosopher *needs* to deny, it seems— that the real, the "essences," are somehow infused with the imaginary, their contrary, that they are in some respect "fictive." In *Ideas I*, Husserl had faced the comparison head-on:

> The comparison with our fiction-constructing consciousness might raise still another doubt, in respect namely of the "existence" of essence. Is not the essence a fiction as the skeptics would indeed have it? It is true that as the coordinating of fiction and perception under the more general concept "intuiting consciousness" casts a doubt on the existence of objects given in perception, so the comparison drawn above renders suspect the "existence" of essences.[43]

Husserl, in fact, "coordinated" fiction and perception and their faculties under the concept of "intuiting consciousness," but he fought with his whole philosophical archive the attempt to do anything but *co*ordinate. Imagination simply belongs to the acts of consciousness, to perception, ultimately to the intending of real objects. There is no fantasy to perception. No real danger, no real fictions. The danger is perhaps defused a priori, and that is perhaps why it has failed to convince those who have followed in Husserl's wake, wondering whether the phenomenological experience ever fully escaped its imaginary margins.[44]

AND WHAT IF that "Other" be admitted? What if the "real" were in fact an effect or as much a product as a cause, the result of a figuration and a figurative synthesis? What if "imagination [were] a necessary ingredient of perception itself?"[45] The words, innocuous enough within the economics of his thought, are again Kant's. But perhaps they should be reread. *Per-ceptio*, the strict "taking" of the real, the thing-in-itself, never takes place. It is, it might be said, in some ways a postmetaphysical view. And yet the Kantian text, too—at least the first *Critique's* Analytic—remains seemingly unthreatened by this "mixture." And this remains true even if the imagination, the *synthesis speciosa*, is defined as "the faculty of representing in intuition an object that *is not present*."[46] Still, Kant remains strict about the coordination between perception and imagination. Imagination is not unleashed—nor does it threaten as it would Husserl, who separated perception and imagination. It is not, as the earlier cited text indicates, "so creative as we pretend," our imagination being tied to "real" origins in its manipulations. While one might be tempted to align these products with the empirical or reproductive imagination, in the *Anthropology* the contrary is the case. "Fantasy" is an "unintentional play of productive imagination."[47] "The imagination run riot," as Kant put it in one of those assertions that almost anticipate Nietzsche. And yet Kant, again, remains strident about the nature of this rioting. While genius gives the rule to art, it does not for all that, *pace* romanticism, become ruleless or lawless. Kant is specific, specific about the nature of genius's world, if not his own regulation of it:

> The offenses (*vitia*) of imagination consist in inventions that are either merely unbridled (*Blosszugellos*) or down right lawless [*regellos*] (*effrenis aut perversa*). Lawless inventions are the worst fault. Unbridled inventions could still find their place in a possible world (the world of fable); but lawless inventions have no place in any world at all, because they are self-contradictory. . . . Unbridled fantasy can always be bent [to the artist's end] (like that of the poet whom Cardinal Este, when presented with the book dedicated to him asked: "Master Ariosto, where the deuce did you get all these absurdities?"). It is luxuriant because of its richness. But lawless fantasy comes close to madness.[48]

Despite its downfall here, the "schema" of the Ideal, of *metaphysica rationalis*, in a sense still carries its own weight. Fiction (*phantasia*) must remain consistent for Kant, though it need not be consistent with our world. Still (again like Searle), fiction remains consistent as an imaginary "bending" (*Einbeugen*)—the classical word for this transgression—from our world. Kant will not open up the riot further. The imagination cannot (should not?) give birth to fantasies that contradict. The lawless is not the realm of the fantastic. It is, apparently, the realm of the insane. This notwithstanding, both fantasy and insanity remain *vitia* within the philosopher's text (contrary to the view of Nicholas of Cusa, stated above), occurring either by association off of the primal ground of the real or by a letting down of the rational guard. "Mere *play* is in keeping with the weakened state of our powers after the day's work, while business suits a man strengthened and, so to speak, reborn by a night's rest."[49] The "turning" here is a turning away from business, the philosopher's business, *Sinn und Bedeutung*. "Imagination is richer and more fertile in ideas than sense (*Sinn*)."[50]

And yet, as many who may have lost Kant's realist commitments may wonder (regarding aesthetics, in any case), he was not above using the predicate "lawless" to describe things other than the insane. In fact, he provides again a quaint example whose discussion is over-determined. In reference to boring social conversations he states, "A lawless, vagrant (*herumschweifende*) imagination so disconcerts the mind by a succession of ideas having no objective connection that we leave a gathering of this kind wondering whether we have been dreaming."[51] Discourse itself, it seems, does not parse out easily into the imaginary and the real.

ONE COULD PERHAPS SAY many things about Kant's entrance into the realm of "ordinary" discourse. Having just talked about the *vitia* of the imagination, Kant himself, nostalgic as ever for the Platonic text, states, "An artist in the political sphere, like one in the aesthetic, knows how to guide and rule the world by dazzling it with images in place of reality."[52] Consistently, to end the matter it might have sufficed for him merely to reinvoke the categorical distinction between the subjective and the objective underlying his account of *Sinn und Bedeutung* (as would Husserl after him, as has been seen). Kant nonetheless does not make this return to the "objective." Instead, he immediately adds the following rider to this discourse, without objective connection (or apparent connection) with the understanding and its truth:

> Whether in silent thought or in conversation, there must always be a theme on which the manifold is strung, so that understanding too must be operative in it. In such a case the play of imagination still follows the laws of sensibility, which provide the material, and this is associated

without consciousness of the rule but still in keeping with it. So the association is carried out in *conformity with* understanding, though it is not
derived from understanding.[53]

Even here the manifold is gathered. There is a "thema," a "schematism," even if Kant must appeal to "associative," or reproductive,
or empirical imagination, as he described it in the first *Critique*—
against his earlier outburst concerning its productive but "unintentional play." And yet, this "schematism" is not derived from the *understanding*. Recall that Kant's example, nonetheless, remains discursive,
that is, categorical, a particular significative "running along" to appeal
to the significative past of "ratio."

When Kant proceeds to explicate the relationship further, it is not
through recourse to the dichotomies of the constituted and the received, the sensible and intelligible, the orderly and the disorderly,
the lawless and the lawful. Rather, what emerges is that mystery, that
common root at the basis of the Kantian system,[54] that third faculty
which is the mediation between the other two. But here it emerges in a
simply "formal" fashion.

> The word affinity (*affinitas*) suggests the chemical term: when under-
> standing combines ideas in this way, its activity is analogous to the inter-
> action of two specifically different physical elements working intimately
> on each other and striving toward a *union* that produces a third thing,
> with properties that can be generated only by the union of two dissimilar
> elements. Understanding and sensibility, for all their dissimilarity, join
> together spontaneously to produce knowledge, as intimately as if one
> had its source in the other, or both originated from a common root.[55]

Since its emergence (perhaps, its "re-emergence," as has been seen),
philosophers have had trouble in grasping this unwieldy event. Hegel—logician without arguments, it has been said—would speak of
affinity as an "external" relation, a relation to the outside, a relation of
transformation from the quantitative (the Same) to the qualitative (the
Other), a "neutralizing" which is mediated through a third.[56] This
third occurs in Kant's text by means of the spontaneous intertwining
of sensibility and understanding through imagination, that indispensable element in perception. This "play of imagination," when agree-

able, would provide the "schematism" for the third *Critique*'s narrative about the Beautiful, the sensible depiction of the infinite. It arises then as the degree zero of meaning, a syntax, a *thema*, which cannot be derived from the laws of understanding but rather from the "laws of sensibility," the "semantics" of a finite rational intellect.

The problem of the discourse in question, then, is not that the discourse is "lawless," as Kant first stated, but that it submits to that other *vitia*, that wandering that departs from everything to which *Sinn* had become bound by Kant. It has the best that Kant can do, granted the oppositions which organize the *Critique*'s code, *another* law, the "laws of sensibility." Kant is fast, almost determined to move to the understanding's opposite here. An appeal to this "other" law, classically that "other" to understanding, can involve no simple opposition.[57] It is not a question of opposition: "Understanding too must be operative in it"—since there is a *thema* that is present. And yet this *thema* no longer simply *derives* from the understanding, which is merely *"in conformity"* with it—that is, which merely *participates* in it. If it is still pertinent here to appeal to a *logos*, an appeal must be made to a point at which this "logos" in question, no longer derived from the understanding, proceeds on its own way, a meaningful—but for Kant boring—extension beyond the limits of *Sinn und Bedeutung*. And Hegel, still at a loss for proof if not exposition, was perhaps right to call the faculty of this spontaneity, the imagination, this third which externalizes both roots in their other, the faculty of speculation[58]— though wrong to think that this externalization could be harnessed, that this faculty of *ex-stasis* and the archaic threat it posed before the philosopher' text, could be reduced and returned from its "vagrancy" to harmony or ultimate adequacy—in short, that this *logos* could ever simply be made a determinate *ratio*—this "logos," pre-text of *Sinn und Bedeutung*, of which the latter is, if not by the transcendentalist *de jure*, then *de facto* but one *thema*, one conceptual form, one mode, perhaps one idiom or genre. And its play remains uncircumscribable, unencompassable, and inexponible by means of a transcendental category or *Aufhebung*. Hegel's affinity is itself followed in the *Logic* by the "incomprehensible" externalized "leaps" of nodal lines.[59] If it remains an event which is difficult to make conceptually determinate, it is perhaps apparent that this *logos*—itself without ultimate grounds—

was in some sense a *conditio sine qua non,* a primitive possibility of what Kant called the *facultas signatrix,* and in this sense even the possibility of *Sinn und Bedeutung,* the possibility of grounds. Its introduction would always enforce a certain undecidability within the play of significative practices, making their "origins" irreducible to a pure or transcendental logic, concept, or possibility—introducing thereby a contingency which left their engagement always ultimately ungrounded and open-ended, and the rationality involved in their participation always in a sense at risk. Wittgenstein perhaps said little else, if in saying it he "says" as well that his text is post-Kantian, the text of a certain *Lebensphilosophie:*

> You must bear in mind that the language game is so to speak something unpredictable. I mean: it is not grounded: neither rational nor irrational. It is there—like our life.[60]

All of which should not forestall the recognition that this "logos" from which Kant demurs cannot be *read* if it cannot be "understood" (adequated) in the full sense. In fact, its "readability" is flagged with the same analog that Hume's rejection of metaphysics had been—the rejection of the dream discourse. The difference is that fiction and fantasy are seen here not only as parasites, derivations of the real, but as *haunting* its *possibility,* the *archē,* the "common root" of "transcendental synthesis."

THIS UNPREDICTABILITY, this elusive heterogeneity, would be ineradicable. And it would perhaps elude the grids of philosophical modernism and its strict commitments concerning the foundational, the rational, and the determinate—perhaps even its *virtù*—as MacIntyre on other grounds has argued, invoking Machiavelli's *Fortuna,* goddess of unpredictability on the margins of scientific modernism.[61] Moreover, if Machiavelli completes accounts like MacIntyre's about reason and virtue here, we would not be wrong perhaps to look for the symptoms of regulation and closure within the same epoch and similar protocols. If Kant is in fact the most direct about the "regulative employment," to use his term, of the problem of *Sinn und Bedeutung,* perhaps opening up a conceptual grid which will inform linguistic inquiry after him, he was not the first (nor would he be the last) to assign the loss of and the impenetrability of the failure of *Sinn und Bedeutung* to the asylum. Kant's position is in this regard complex, and needs to be seen as the presentation of a certain inversion of—and perhaps even the "reaction formation" against—a claim made on behalf of reason against madness that Hobbes could be seen already representing. Hobbes in fact claimed that the madness affecting the social discourse which struck Kant blind belonged only to the philosophers, the "Schoole-men" to be precise. An empiricist and yet a Platonist through and through, he again classified their discursive extravagances as unruly passions—reiterating, as has been seen, an assignment that returns once more upon Plato and an exclusion of the sacred which was equally overdetermined.

> The common sort of men seldom speak Insignificantly and are by those other Egregious persons counted Idiots. But to be assured that their words are without anything correspondent to them in the mind, there would need some Examples: which if any man require, let him take a Schoole-man into his hands, and see if he can translate any one chapter concerning any difficult point; as the Trinity, the Deity, the nature of Christ; Transubstantiation; Free-will, etc. into any of the moderne tongues, so as to make the same intelligible; or into any tolerable Latine, such as they were acquainted withall, that lived when the Latine tongue was Vulgar. . . . When men write whole volumes of such stuffe, are they not Mad, or intend to make others so? . . .
>
>    So that this kind of Absurdity, may rightly be numbered amongst the many sorts of Madnesse.[62]

In all of this, Hobbes claims, the speaker "will find himself entangled in words."[63] It was precisely this entanglement, as has been seen, that Wittgenstein believed we had to get clear of. And yet for him (unlike Hobbes) this entanglement was the lot of all that was "ordinary" and "alright," while for Hobbes and those after him it involved a fateful loss, a failure (intentional or not) "to remember what every name [the speaker] uses stands for."[64] As has been seen, Husserl claimed that a similar recollection needed to be invoked to preserve language against the usurpation and surprise of *Spielbedeutung*. And this view that we are entangled in words not only stresses, as Gadamer has said, the negative side of language, but limits language's "positivity" and its epistemic role to the domain of the determinate and the strictly demonstrable. Moreover, "it condemns as heresy all knowledge that does not allow for this kind of certainty."[65]

What connects Kant and Hobbes and those who follow them here, their "opposition" notwithstanding, is precisely the "modernist" version of the philosopher's text to which Hobbes appeals and the system of exclusions that it underwrites. It is a version which is in fact as "modern" as the languages into which Hobbes demands the "old" philosophical concepts must be "translatable." Like the story concerning translation to which it appeals (unlike the stories about translation that preceded it and those that have followed it since Quine and Derrida), it rests upon the dream of a discourse that would be univocal. It would require a discourse that was scrutable, and ultimately grounded; an *ordo* capable of standing its ground before all that escaped, all that remained underdetermined, unpredictable, merely conditional, undecidable, or incommensurable—all that undercut the attempt to provide an ultimately adequate account of the real, its re-presentation, an image purged of all that exceeded the concept, enabling the construction of an epistemic *picture*, an *Abbildung* in the most literal of senses purified into facts that were de facto "logical."

The failure of representation, on the contrary, forced a confrontation with the problem of deciphering all that exceeded simple adequation, requiring a discursive practice capable of encountering that for which there could be no simple rules of correspondence. It was a confrontation which the Wittgensteinian text (perhaps no less than the Gadamerian) disclosed in terms which were archaic, a confrontation involving a failure regarding the irreducibility of what it called "the variety of interpretation."[66] The ensuing indeterminacy involved a threat, as the text states more directly, of *anders gedeutet werden;* and its effect radically, inevitably, displaced the marginal status of interpretation within the text of philosophy. Beyond the ideal of simple representation, of univocal adequacy, provoked instead by what Wittgenstein called (as had Kant before him) the "play of imagination,"[67] it outlined a domain in which justification would be more akin to the aesthetic than the ideals of classical rationality had decreed.[68] And as a result, its provocation forced (as Wittgenstein's text, along with others,

perhaps manifests) the question of style, genre, and form, to promi-
nence, a provocation in which the propositional function of representation was turned back upon itself, forcing it to rejoin its rhetorical
past, to turn subjunctive, submitting its "logical space" to a "labyrinth" which undermined the clarity of simple assertion.[69]

FAR FROM BEING a mere appendage to the truth, the problem of interpretation must be seen then to arise necessarily out of the failure of
the classical *recherche de la vérité,* the search for strict objectivity, for
what Kant had called "determinate judgments." It thus called forth a
*Vor-urteil* which turned its predecessors into fictions, and their accounts, as Descartes half-saw, into "fables."[70] The domain which
emerged thus was more akin to Kant's domain of the reflective: un-
determined, justified only by its practices, by its "task," as Kant put
it, but perhaps equally by Wittgenstein's "use" and perhaps also by
the experience accompanying it. It was a domain in which the force of
imagination could not be denied, nor the productive character of its
syntheses, nor finally the effect of imagination upon the extensions of
the literal—the *Einbeugen* of metaphor, to use Kant's word. But Quine
has perhaps said little else:

> It is a mistake to think of linguistic usage as literalistic in its main body
> and metaphorical in its trimming. Metaphor, or something like it, gov-
> erns both the growth of language and our acquisition of it. What comes
> as a subsequent refinement is rather, cognitive discourse itself, at its
> most dryly literal. The neatly worked inner stretches of science are an
> open space in the tropical jungle, created by clearing tropes away.[71]

The account of literal usage as a rigorously delimitable set of propositions must be devalorized of its honorific privilege.[72] Even if it is true
that recognizing the "conditional" past of the literal does not end the
discourse of the literal—if it is true, as Searle put it, that the literal,
though relative, is still literal—it remains equally true that it is never
*fully* literal—as Derrida said—never unquestionably literal, not literal
in the privileged, classical sense, not demonstrably and timelessly or
"strictly" real, and so on. The literal is never in the classical sense "objective" or well founded; that is, it cannot necessarily come through

the philosopher's *agon* of refutation unscathed. As Michel Foucault put it in his study of madness (and reason) in the Classical Age, the latter account would have fortuitously provided "a serene division which makes truth possible and confirms it forever."[73] Within this account, what escaped could no longer threaten—either as simple "disease" or as the "Homeric" poetic truth against which philosophy seemingly always struggled. Rather, in accord with its paradigm, all that escaped the grids of simple representation and its evaluative methods—what showed, consequently, no promise of strict and univocal decidability—could have nothing to do with truth or its representational equivalent, "truth-value." It could arise then only as a domesticated state of nonbeing: "unreason"—like the transcendence of "nature," the imagination and discourse subdued.[74] And yet, the breach opened up by Kant's text differs. In a sense, faced with all that made up what he himself called an abyss (*Ab-grund*) here, Kant no longer *believed* the metaphysics of Bacon, Descartes, Hobbes, and their successors, even if he still tried to justify it. But in fact he did so only by opening up at the same time another account of (reflective) judgment which undercut—by surpassing—all that had been excluded in committing the canons of rationality to the *more geometrico*, acknowledging, thereby, an event whose extension (*Erweiterung*) forced him precisely to admit the free play of imagination and, ultimately, the necessity (as well as the risk) of seeing even judgment itself as an art (*ars inveniendi*).

ONE MIGHT BE TEMPTED, as were many of Kant's followers, from Schelling to Foucault (at least in *Madness and Civilization*[75]), to claim that classical reason's altern, the affinity of the imagination, the locus of this abyss between genius and madness, indicates an *originality*, a primordiality, and the divine madness of Plato himself—a domain that was more than just "other," but privileged. In fact it is perhaps not without a certain inspired madness that Schelling attempted to prove not only the excess but the priority of the poetic (and what he as well termed its surprise, its *Überraschung*, before the idealist version of the cognitive) over the philosophical text in a *Deduktion* within his 1800 *System of Transcendental Idealism*.[76] One might be led to believe, then, that fictions are not only stranger than facts but more true, the sign of a *poiēsis* more primordial than the philosopher's, instead of the locus of an Other that eludes all strict grounds, all *homoiosis* or *adequatio*. Then one could simply place the philosopher's text *sous rature* and send the positivist to art school. One would then have the Romantic's text, perhaps as well the text of the avant-garde, the ultramodernist text. But the point is that both fail, for the same reason. The affinity, this "logos," belongs to "taste" no more than it belongs to "reason." The philosophers' text no more accounts for this exceeding than does the artist's attempt to coincide with it. Rather, it is what puts this simple version of adequacy in question and forces the indeterminacy and the *agon* of interpretation—and what is specific to its rationality—upon both. It is true: "Interpretations by themselves do not determine meanings."[77] But equally, it is precisely the failure of meanings to stand their ground—beyond interpretation—that ruptures all ultimate determinacy, all strict foundations, and all attempts to surpass, thereby, the finitude of interpretation itself. Within the discourse of this *ex-stasis*, instead, philosophers no less than poets—and those who would intervene between them—all share the same fate, the inevitable straying to which Plato condemned his other, the interlocutor of the *Ion*. They are, that is, "interpreters of interpreters (*hermēneōn hermēneis*)."[78]

## NOTES

1. Jacques Derrida, *Of Grammatology*, trans. Gayatri Chakravorty Spivak (Baltimore: Johns Hopkins University Press, 1976), p. 10.

2. Ludwig Wittgenstein, *Lectures and Conversations*, ed. Cyril Barrett (Berkeley: University of California Press, 1967), p. 26.

3. *Plato's Republic*, trans. G. M. A. Grube (Indianapolis: Hackett, 1974), p. 185 (534c).

4. Immanuel Kant, *Critique of Pure Reason*, trans. Norman Kemp Smith (London: Macmillan, 1933), p. 21 (B xv). Ludwig Wittgenstein, *Philosophical Investigations*, trans. G. E. M. Anscombe (New York: Macmillan, 1953), p. 109.

5. Plato, *Republic*, p. 90 (424c).

6. Ibid., p. 251 (607b). See also Homer, *The Odyssey*, trans. Walter Shewring (Oxford: Oxford University Press, 1980), p. 9 (I 346).

7. Kant, *Critique of Pure Reason*.

8. Ibid., pp. 488–89 (A573/B601).

9. James Joyce, *Ulysses* (New York: Vintage, 1961), pp. 432, 504.

10. Ibid., p. 515.

11. Ibid., p. 589.

12. On the sublime in modern art, see, for example, Jean-François Lyotard, "Presenting the Unpresentable: The Sublime," trans. Lisa Liebman, *Artforum* 20 (April 1982): 64–69, and Theodor Adorno, *Aesthetic Theory*, trans. C. Lenhardt (London: Routledge, 1984), pp. 28off. On the gnostic in modernism see, for example, Jürgen Habermas, "Modernity versus Post-Modernity," *New German Critique*, no. 22 (Winter 1981): 3–14, and Harold Bloom, *Agon: Towards a Theory of Revisionism* (Oxford: Oxford University Press). Neither of these concepts can be borrowed from their classical sites unchanged, however.

13. See, for example, Gilles Deleuze, *Logique du sens* (Paris: Minuit, 1969), pp. 325ff.

14. Adorno, *Aesthetic Theory*, p. 470. Examples at the extreme are works such as Cage's "silent" compositions, Reinhardt's black paintings, and Dadaist writing. But there is a sense as well in which "good" and "bad" are derivative questions for modern art.

15. See Nelson Goodman, "Fiction for Five Fingers," *Philosophy and Literature* 6 (Fall 1982): 162–64.

16. Kant, *Critique of Pure Reason*, p. 163 (B149).

17. David Hume, *A Treatise of Human Nature* (Oxford: Oxford University Press, 1968), p. 219.

18. Joyce, *Ulysses*, p. 34.

19. Derrida, in fact, at one point suggested that their entire disagreement rested upon equivocations on this point and the implications of the relations obtaining between its grammatical-institutional sense and the possibilities of epistemic "incommensurabilities" (between traditions but also between speaker's meaning and language meaning, to use Gricean terms). See Jacques Derrida, "Limited Inc. a b c . . . ," trans. Samuel Weber, *Glyph* 2 (1978): 203.

20. Kant, *Critique of Pure Reason*, p. 27n (B xxvi).

21. René Descartes, *Meditations on First Philosophy*, trans. Laurence J. Lafleur (Indianapolis: Bobbs Merrill, 1960), p. 55.

22. Immanuel Kant, *Anthropology from a Pragmatic Point of View*, trans. Mary J. Gregor (The Hague: Martinus Nijhoff), p. 93.

23. Ibid., p. 53.

24. John R. Searle, "The Logical Status of Fictional Discourse," *New Literary History* 6 (Winter 1975): 329–31.

25. Ibid., p. 329.

26. Ibid., p. 331.

27. John R. Searle, "Literal Meaning," *Erkenntnis* 13 (1978): 219.

28. Ibid., p. 220.

29. Compare Searle's discussion of the question of the character of the intentional origin of the speech act, "What Is an Intentional State?" *Mind* 78 (1979): 89.

The mind imposes Intentionality on the entities that are not intrinsically Intentional by intentionally transferring the conditions of satisfaction of the expressed psychological state to the physical entity. The double level of Intentionality in the speech act can be described by saying that by intentionally uttering something with a certain set of conditions of success, those that are specified by the essential conditions for the speech act, I have made the utterance Intentional, and thus necessarily expressed the corresponding psychological state.

30. In this regard, Michel Serres has remarked that the classical novel has the same history as the physics of this age: "The classical novel is determinist and determined. It is a system with a hierarchy, a closed narrative, homogeneous, open to evaluation on all points, regulated locally as it is globally" (*Jouvences sur Jules Verne* [Paris: Minuit, 1974], p. 241, my translation).

31. Plato, *Republic*, p. 235 (588).

32. Ibid., p. 27 (354b).

33. Gorgias, "Encomium of Helen," trans. George Kennedy, in *The Older Sophists*, ed. Rosamund Kent Sprague (Columbia, S.C.: University of South Carolina Press, 1972), p. 52.

34. Ludwig Wittgenstein, *The Blue and Brown Books* (New York: Barnes & Noble, 1969), p. 28.

35. Plotinus, *Enneads*, trans. Stephen MacKenna, V.7.3.

36. Edmund Husserl, "The Origin of Geometry," in *The Crisis of European Sciences and Transcendental Phenomenology*, trans. David Carr (Evanston, Ill.: Northwestern University Press, 1970), p. 362.

37. Edmund Husserl, *Logical Investigations*, trans. J. N. Findlay (London: Routledge & Kegan Paul, 1970), vol. 1, p. 305. And yet in the same text Husserl admitted the failure of the project, the impossibility of carrying out the task of determination: "Strike out the essentially occasional expressions from one's language, try to describe any subjective experience in unambiguous, objectively fixed fashion: such an attempt is always plainly in vain" (vol. 1, p. 322). Nonetheless, not having yet made the transcendental-subjective turn, he does not see the Platonist research program of the *Investigations* threatened by this failure in the theory. Later, in *Formal and Transcendental Logic* (trans. Dorion Cairns [The Hague: Martinus Nijhoff, 1969]), Husserl would describe the earlier attempt to ground phenomenology in the ideal of nomological sci-

ence precisely as a "prejudice" and would be compelled to abandon Bolzano's notion of a simply objective "truth-in-itself," which both he and Frege shared. See my "On the Agon of the Phenomenological," forthcoming in *Philosophy of the Social Sciences.*

38. See Wilfred Sellars, *Science, Perception, and Reality* (London: Routledge & Kegan Paul, 1963), pp. 25–28.

39. See John T. Blackmore, *Ernst Mach: His Work, Life, and Influence* (Berkeley: University of California Press, 1972), pp. 319f.

40. See Jacques Derrida, *Edmund Husserl's "Origin of Geometry: An Introduction,"* trans. John P. Leavey (Stony Brook, N.Y.: Nicolas Hays, 1978), pp. 101ff.

41. Wittgenstein, *Philosophical Investigations,* p. 50e, sec. 125.

42. Ibid., p. 4e, sec. 6.

43. Edmund Husserl, *Ideas,* trans. W. R. Boyce Gibson (London: Collier Books, 1962), p. 83, sec. 23.

44. See, for example, Maurice Merleau-Ponty's discussion of essential intuition and the problem of induction in "Phenomenology and the Sciences of Man," in *The Primacy of Perception,* trans. John Wild (Evanston, Ill.: Northwestern University Press, 1964), pp. 68ff., as well as Jacques Derrida's similar reservations (*Edmund Husserl's "Origin of Geometry,"* pp. 133ff.).

45. Kant, *Critique of Pure Reason,* p. 144n (A120n).

46. Ibid., p. 165 (B151).

47. Kant, *Anthropology,* p. 55.

48. Ibid., p. 56.

49. Ibid. This reference to the business of the philosophical, the cognitive, and the serious also makes a crucial entrance in the third *Critique* in defusing the play of imagination in poetry and rhetoric. See Immanuel Kant, *Critique of Judgement,* trans. J. H. Bernard (New York: Hafner, 1968), p. 165:

> The arts of speech are *rhetoric* and *poetry. Rhetoric* is the art of carrying on a serious business of the understanding as if it were a free play of the imagination; *poetry,* the art of conducting a free play of the imagination as if it were a serious business of the understanding.
>
> The *orator,* then, promises a serious business, and in order to entertain his audience conducts it as if it were a mere *play* with idea. The *poet* merely promises an entertaining play with ideas, and yet it has the same effect upon the understanding as if he had only intended to carry on its business.

50. Ibid., p. 55.

51. Ibid., p. 52.

52. Ibid., p. 56.

53. Ibid., p. 52.

54. Kant, *Critique of Pure Reason*, p. 61 (A15, B29).

55. Kant, *Anthropology*, pp. 52–53.

56. G. W. F. Hegel, *Hegel's Science of Logic*, trans. A. V. Miller (New York: Humanities Press, 1969), pp. 354ff.

57. Cf. Kant's statement in the *Anthropology:* "Unreason (which is not mere lack of reason but something positive) is, like reason itself a mere form into which objects can be fitted, so that both reason and unreason are ordered to the universal" (87–88).

58. G. W. F. Hegel, *Faith and Knowledge,* trans. Walter Cerf and H. S. Harris (Albany: State University of New York Press, 1977), p. 80.

59. Hegel, *Hegel's Science of Logic*, p. 368.

60. Ludwig Wittgenstein, *On Certainty,* trans. Denis Paul and G. E. M. Anscombe (New York: Harper & Row, 1972), p. 73e, sec. 559, translation altered. See P. M. S. Hacker's related discussion in *Insight and Illusion: Wittgenstein on Philosophy and the Metaphysics of Experience* (Oxford: Oxford University Press, 1967), pp. 167f.

61. Alasdair MacIntyre, *After Virtue* (Notre Dame: Notre Dame University Press, 1981), p. 89.

62. Thomas Hobbes, *Leviathan,* ed. C. B. Macpherson (Baltimore: Penguin, 1968), pp. 146–47.

63. Ibid., p. 105.

64. Ibid.

65. See Hans-Georg Gadamer, *Truth and Method,* ed. Garrett Barden and John Cumming (New York: Seabury, 1975), pp. 313, 433.

66. See Wittgenstein, *Philosophical Investigations,* secs. 28, 215.

67. Ibid., sec. 216.

68. The position emerges at least as early as the *Brown Book's* declaration that "what we call 'understanding a sentence' has, in many cases, a much greater similarity to understanding a musical theme than we might be inclined to think" (167). While obviously difficult to explicate, what is at stake here is a judgment which cannot be objective, cannot be ultimately grounded, ending in a practice and its description. What is at stake then is a form of justification akin to that of the aesthetic in precisely the way that these are features as well of what Kant, for example, called "reflective" rather than determinate judgments, as is manifest from the text:

—"But surely when you play it you don't play it *anyhow,* you play it in this particular way, making a crescendo here a diminuendo there, a caesura in this place, etc."—Precisely and that's all I can say about it, or may be all that I can say about it. For in certain cases I can justify, explain the particular expression with which I played it by a comparison, as when I say "At this point of the theme, there is, as it were, a colon," or "This is, as it were, the answer to what came before," etc. (This by the way, shows what a "justification" and an "explanation" in aesthetics is like.). . . . This doesn't mean that suddenly understanding a musical theme may not consist in finding a form of verbal expression which I conceive as the verbal counterpart of the theme. . . . What we call "understanding a sentence" has in many cases, a much greater similarity to understanding a musical theme than we might be inclined to think (166–67).

69. Compare Ludwig Wittgenstein, *Tractatus Logico-Philosophicus*, trans. D. F. Pears and B. F. McGuiness (London: Routledge & Kegan Paul, 1961), sec. 1.13, p. 31, and *Philosophical Investigations*, sec. 203, p. 82. See Gadamer's discussion of what he calls "the interpenetration of interpretation and rhetoric" in "On the Scope and Function of Hermeneutical Reflection," in *Philosophical Hermeneutics*, trans. David E. Linge (Berkeley: University of California Press, 1977), pp. 21ff.

70. René Descartes, *Discourse on Method*, trans. Donald A. Cress (Indianapolis: Hackett, 1980), p. 2.

71. W. V. O. Quine, "A Postscript on Metaphor," in *On Metaphor*, ed. Sheldon Sacks (Chicago: University of Chicago Press, 1978), p. 201.

72. See Wolfgang Stegmuller, *The Structure and Dynamics of Theories* (New York: Springer-Verlag, 1976), pp. 170–80, and Richard Bernstein's discussion of this issue in *Beyond Objectivism and Relativism* (Philadelphia: University of Pennsylvania Press, 1983), pp. 56ff.

73. Michel Foucault, *Madness and Civilization: A History of Insanity in the Age of Reason*, trans. Richard Howard (New York: Pantheon Books, 1965), p. 110.

74. Ibid.

75. See Foucault, ibid.

After Sade and Goya and since them, unreason has belonged to whatever is decisive, for the modern world in any work of art. . . . [T]hrough madness, a work that seems to drown in the world, to reveal there its non-sense, and to transfigure itself within the features of pathology alone, actually engages within itself the world's time, masters it, and leads it. . . . (285, 288).

76. F. W. J. Schelling, *System of Transcendental Idealism* (1800), trans. Peter Heath (Charlottesville: University Press of Virginia, 1978), pp. 219ff.

77. Wittgenstein, *Philosophical Investigations*, sec. 198.

78. Plato, *Ion*, trans. Lane Cooper, in *The Collected Dialogues* (Princeton: Princeton University Press, 1963), p. 221 (535a). In effect, then, the charge brought against Ion can be seen among other things as one of not having unequivocal, stipulatable principles by which to represent and explain his practice, hence of being without "rules of art" (*technē*) (534), proof perhaps of the extent to which Plato maintains an intellectualist account of practice. On the other hand, when Schleiermacher, whose work is often thought to be the origin of contemporary hermeneutic theory, developed his position within the breach in Kant's text, speaking of interpretation as an "art," he had a very different conception of art and the technical in mind, one modeled after Kant's notion of reflective judgment, one which works with given appearances so as to bring them under concepts "not systematically, but technically, not just mechanically, like a tool controlled by the understanding and the senses, but artistically" (see *First Introduction to the Critique of Judgement*, trans. James Haldane [Indianapolis: Bobbs-Merrill, 1965], p. 18). Nonetheless, in claiming as well that this act ultimately resolved itself in a divination restoring the identity of subject and object, that is, in objectivity, Schleiermacher perhaps also misunderstood its advance, one which allowed both for revision and clarification, if not ultimately decidability. See my account of these developments in "Between Truth and Method: Gadamer and the Problem of Justification in Interpretative Practices," Collected Papers from the University of Dayton's 11th Annual Philosophy Colloquium on Hermeneutics, *The University of Dayton Review* 17 (Spring 1984): 21–31.

Louis Nicholas Raphael

# The Philosophy of Hidden Rhyme

WITHIN THE CONTEXT of the post-structuralist discussion of metaphor, the question of the philosophical value of poetry is an
eminently topical question, in both the Aristotelian and ordinary
senses.[1] As a *topos*, the question is the age-old chestnut, ever available
for scholastic disputation, which asserts that poetry presents in a
living way what philosophy presents abstractly. Contemporary debate
has so questioned and complicated this role of illustration for poetry
that an interest in it may seem merely antiquarian. But a living interest
can abide in this formulation of the topic in virtue of the humble but
insuperable requirements of pedagogy. In pedagogical treatment, poetry is constantly used as an illustration, indeed as *a* philosophy, by
being framed in the terms of the more commonly shared notions
which are already available to those whom one teaches, including
oneself. Such issues as the value of love, the meaning of life, and the
aporias of deconstruction, *because* they are hackneyed, provide a
means of access to more sophisticated concerns. Banality assures a
common currency of exchange which, practically speaking, amounts
to the indispensable popular metaphysics from which philosophical
discourse itself emerges. As Derrida says, there are no concepts which
are in themselves metaphysical, but rather only metaphysical movements of concepts; whence the specifically metaphysical value of the
unrecognized use of clichés, no matter how derivative they are in an
absolute sense. So used, clichés are a priori ontological syntheses, immediately intelligible and unquestionably referential and/or pertinent.

Now it is undeniable that such translation of poetry into a more
ordinary language occurs when the poetry concerned is of that con-
stitutively hermetic variety which defies any immediate comprehen-

sion. But it must also be admitted that such translation occurs with respect to that more accessible variety of poetry which has allowed philosophers such as Heidegger to grant it the function of the first uncovering of the world: a kind of concrete philosophy of Wordsworthian man speaking to men.[2] But however philosophical such poetry, as immediately moving it is precisely not a conceptualization. The ambition to *understand*, whether it makes the hermetic first accessible or whether it allows us to contain an all-too-immediate feeling, always presupposes a translation of some kind into the currency of an ordinary language, both before and after the poetry is read. Even the hermetic, whether experienced or discursively determined as hermetic, does not escape this translation. And so the chestnut can always stand a little more roasting.

Thus, on the other hand, the question is a topical one, even an urgent one. This might seem to be a paradoxical topicality. In the past fifteen years, spectacular efforts have been directed at showing not how poetry is philosophical but how philosophy is poetic.[3] The supposed effect of these endeavors has been to unmask conceptual discourse as a kind of insane sanity under the spell of a poetry or of a primal poeticity of language called *écriture*. In this perspective, the philosophical dimension of poetry is the paradoxical philosophy of the overcoming of philosophy. Thus, indeed, Geoffrey Hartman openly argues for a literary literary criticism and Derrida, in *Glas*, addresses philosophical issues in a hybrid of poetry and philosophy.

But if the function of understanding is thus constantly undercut, it is by no means simply obliterated. How else could the escape from the insane lucidity of the concept be erected as a project, instead of rejected as mere bungling? The program presupposes that the undoing of understanding recognize itself as such, and recognition takes the form of conceptual judgment. The assertion of the priority of poetry over philosophy unavoidably reproduces the priority of philosophy over poetry. This is indeed what Derrida never tires of stating, but it is also what he is too often accused of denying. One must agree, for instance, with Paul Ricoeur, when he asserts that even deconstruction presupposes conceptual discourse or what he calls speculative discourse. One must disagree with him, however, when he couches this observation in the form of a reproach, as if Derrida had not made this very same observation in the first place. Why is it that Ricoeur can see only the *act* of the presupposition of the philosophical and not its clear statement? It is in the light of this strange dialectic of act and statement that I wish to address the question of how poetry is philosophical. If it is the case that the poetic makes possible and inevitable the (re)appearance of the philosophical as an autonomous standpoint, how does this poetically constituted philosophy nevertheless retain a philosophical value in the eminent sense? How does it grant me a true understanding? This question divides into a series of consecutive questions. What is poetry that it should undermine philosophy? What is philosophy if, thus undermined, it nevertheless reemerges as a presupposed standpoint? And finally, and most ambitiously, what is the philosophical value of a philosophy that is thus poetically and paradoxically reproduced?

To pursue these questions, I shall present Ricoeur's conception of the role of metaphor. The essay relevant to my purposes is study 8 of *The Rule of Metaphor*.[4] Ricoeur first defends what he calls living metaphor against a scientific kind of philosophy in the name of another, ontological kind of philosophy. He then turns around to defend the autonomy of this ontological philosophy against the all-too-powerful threat of metaphor. The crux of his problem is to distinguish the poetic ambiguity of the metaphor from the philosophical ambiguity of the ontological concept.

Let me address first what Ricoeur means by poetic ambiguity. For Ricoeur, the metaphor is both improper and proper—improper with respect to customary categories but proper with respect to a new region of entities. As specifically a living metaphor, it is unparaphrasable into the customary concepts while at the same time uniquely compelling. It is, therefore, like an immediate perception of the same in the different: an originary presence and unaccountable truth. Together, these two dimensions make for a nonconceptualizable ambiguity which, far from being a weakness, is the very basis for what Ricoeur calls the metaphor's dynamism or "ontological vehemence."

Metaphor's dynamism, however, is capable of philosophical import only if the philosophy concerned is not that of the customary categories. The perspective of customary categories is the perspective of what Ricoeur calls, following Heidegger, representational thinking.

Representational thinking offers only an ontology of already constituted, mere objects. This is why Ricoeur argues that a philosophical
value for poetry presupposes a knowledge of the whole of things in
respect of their own dynamism (297). It is from this perspective that
poetry has ontological value. By its dynamism, poetry produces the
feeling of belonging to the whole. It opens up the life-world, rather
than merely a new realm of potentially scientific objects. Correspond-
ingly, only a philosophy of "being-in-the-world" can account for this
more fundamental dimension of human existence.

   Such a philosophy, however, is no longer a univocally conceptual
one. The problem concerns the apparently indissoluble link between
the concept and the function of understanding. Only that which is
knowable in its finite, distinctive traits can be grasped by a univocal
concept with a determinate meaning. By contrast, the whole which is
being-in-the-world is precisely the always presupposed infinity which
makes conceptualization possible but which no one concept, other
than itself, can grasp (306). Philosophy is then faced by a double
threat (268). On the one hand, the threat to understanding is tautology
and circularity. This tautology is indeed a kind of test for the speculative insofar as, absolutely simple, it cannot be divided into any
elements. But if only infinity adequately conceives infinity, it says
everything and nothing. Speculative discourse forms a closed system
hovering above existence, informing existence without, however,
being reducible to such existence. Therefore, on the other hand, philosophy must come down to earth and use different, determinate concepts. The difficulty here is that, in seeking to think and understand
infinity under this or that concept, philosophy both falls into a circle
(defining the to-be-defined by what it makes possible) and pushes the
concept beyond its limits, asking the definite and determinate to account for the undividedly simple. When Thales said "All is water," insofar as he was a philosopher he had to avoid two pitfalls, that of the
subject and that of the predicate. Firstly in the subject, to avoid tautology he cannot depend on any prior, implicit predetermination of the
all *as* water. Secondly, in the predicate, water cannot be meant in the
ordinary, literal sense, but must be varied in view of according with
the all. The concept "water" thus acts in this context like a metaphor
because of this double ambiguity. But, for Ricoeur, this ambiguity

must be philosophical as opposed to poetic (272, 277, and *passim*). That is, it must rest not upon a similarity as in living metaphor, but upon an as yet unexpressed identity (301). This is where the defense of poetry becomes for Ricoeur a defense of philosophy and its speculative discourse against poetry.

Poetic ambiguity is all well and good as metaphor's dynamism. But the dynamic, living metaphor, being beyond any paraphrase into conceptual discourse, is also this side of understanding. Thus the ambiguity of any one concept of totality should nevertheless allow us not to *feel* but to *think* our belonging to the whole (303). To be sure, in any one particular example Ricoeur cannot show that the ambiguity of speculative discourse is such a philosophical, temporary ambiguity. But, he argues, the distinctness of philosophical ambiguity from poetic ambiguity must nevertheless be retained. As seen earlier, because of the paradox of any negation of philosophy, its standpoint is both something I always already possess in a preontological understanding and, correlatively, the task of making this preontological understanding explicit.

It is on this matter that I must part company with Ricoeur.[5]

The question is this: How is speculative discourse brought home to me such that I understand and use it right now? Here, in spite of the inevitability of the structure of presupposition, Ricoeur's Heideggerian answer of preontological understanding is simply not enough. For what is brought home to me is speculative *discourse* and not some ineffable spiritual activity (let it be recalled that the ineffable must be so designated to be what it is). But I control discourse as much as it controls me. As soon as I enter the realm of discourse for the origin of the speculative, I am asking that something I have given myself give itself to me without my participation. This, far from Heidegger's hermeneutic circle, is quite simply a vicious circle whereby I grant myself from the start what is supposed to be demonstrated.[6] The question of the philosophical ambiguity is then the question of the conflict between these two circles.

For my purposes, this conflict arises in Ricoeur's text most productively in connection with his polemic against Derrida's thesis that all definitions of metaphor are themselves metaphorical. As is well known, Derrida replied to the polemic in *"Le retrait de la métaphore,"*[7] and many of my remarks are indebted to him. I will not, however, simply paraphrase him; instead, I will argue that the value of metaphor should not be attributed to a differential novelty, but rather to its absolutely hidden, tautological circulation of the old. For me, the issue of the truth-value of a poetically conditioned philosophy is the issue of the truth-value of a tautology or, as I have said in my title, of a hidden rhyme.

Now, Ricoeur attempts to refute the thesis of the metaphoricity of the definition of metaphor. To safeguard the concept of the metaphor as a speculative concept, Ricoeur must show that any apparently metaphorical definition is at bottom a conceptual one. He argues this in a variety of ways,[8] but preeminently by appealing to the notion of the lexicalization of metaphor whereby the metaphor is the first step in the creation of a new proper term. Ricoeur writes: "That there are philosophical terms at all is due to the fact that a concept can be active as thought in a metaphor which is itself dead. . . . 'Comprendre' [to understand] can have a proper philosophical sense because we no longer hear 'prendre' [to grasp] in it" (293). How, then, does *comprendre* become a proper term and meaning? How do I stop hearing *prendre* in *comprendre*?

In order to follow such a lexicalization, let us assume that, as Ricoeur suggests, *comprendre* actually derives from *prendre*. Moreover, let it be kept in mind that the lexicalization, although authorized by the effect of a preontological understanding, must in fact be entirely a discursive operation. I cannot here go into any greatly detailed analysis of the lexicalization. I will say only as much as is needed to fill out the concept of hidden rhyme.

*Prendre* must never simply not be heard in *comprendre*, for otherwise I would not recognize the sign. In the lexicalization, not the sign *prendre* itself but its recognizability must disappear. In the same way, a cliché becomes an honest and sincere expression when I do not recognize it as a cliché. Insofar as I *do* hear the cliché, I hear not the expression of a thought but the reiteration of a formula, the repetition of a refrain—in short, a rhyme in which the utterance refers me not to a thought but to the type for which the utterance is a token. The same holds in the coining of *comprendre*. Insofar as *comprendre*'s meaning derives from *prendre* without any other independent semantic source, *comprendre* refers me not to a thought, nor to a thing, but to the linguistic elements giving rise to it. This too is a rhyme in the sense that the utterance refers me to a linguistic model for its meaning rather than to a referent. Furthermore, still in the absence of the referent, I can produce a context in which nothing will draw my attention explicitly to the sign *prendre* when I utter *comprendre*. For example, in a discussion of the topic "acts of mind" where I take it for granted that there are such things as distinct mental activities, nothing will remind me of my remembering; or, say, in a discussion where I console a friend for the loss of a car by uttering "Je comprends." In such contexts, I will not thematically hear *prendre* in *comprendre*, because *prendre* is not my theme. But without having a relation to its referent, the coinage *comprendre* must still refer to *prendre* for its meaning. There is still a rhyme, but the rhyme has been dampened; it is a distant echo.

But how is the rhyme absolutely silenced? It is silenced when *comprendre* refers not to *prendre* but to the act it would designate, and indeed to a singular instance of the act of comprehension it would designate. *Comprendre* becomes a proper speculative term when it functions as a true concept corresponding to the speculative reality it would designate. However derived initially, then, its sense would be authorized by the referent. For this, a special difficulty faces the metaphor *comprendre*. Unlike the catachreses "leg of the table" or "male and female plugs," *comprendre* intends an invisible, transcendental act which I can perform but cannot publicly view; for, because of its transcendentality, it is an act I can never know directly. It is either an act I always presuppose and thus know only as something I must have performed, or else an act I experience empirically, without the benefit of transcendental experience, since this is precisely the possibility of mine that is under dispute. At the same time, this singular act of mine which will serve as the referent to *comprendre* must also be everybody's act from the start. One cannot appeal to an intentional or an ontological sense of the identity of myself with the other, since this is precisely what is under dispute. Now, as both Husserl and Heidegger say respectively, ego and Dasein are always mine. But if they are always mine, the speculative cannot escape solipsism. The singular act to which *comprendre* is enabled to refer must be both mine and everybody else's from the start; that is, it must be a discursive operation accomplished in me, but which all can similarly inhabit.

*Comprendre* is true under these requirements when it does two things. First, in the context of the distant echo suitably predetermined and then forgotten in its predetermination, *comprendre* must refer to itself. This self-reference will be a metalinguistic predication where I recognize the implicit *comprendre* as identical to the explicit *comprendre*. But the self-reference's profound resource is still the rhyme on *prendre*. Indeed, what other discursive resource is there? This rhyme, however, is now definitively drowned out by the recognition of the implicit *comprendre* by the explicit *comprendre*. This self-identification of the implicit by the explicit is thematically a comprehension in the sense that it explicitates its object *as* the sign *comprendre*. But—and this is the second requirement—the self-identification is also *operationally* a comprehension in that making it explicit is indeed, as a perceived repetition, a conceptualization, even though, as the determination of an empirical event, the grasping resembles mere clutching. Thus indeed, no sooner is *comprendre* produced as a sign referring to itself than it can refer to this act of production as an instance of itself. The produced and the producing, the cause and the effect, may thus appear identical. What is noteworthy here is that what is produced has the form of an infinite self-identity: *comprendre* refers to *comprendre* and to this very reference as to the sources of its meaning. At the same time, the self-identity is absolutely empirical and so is both determinate and capable of variation in content from person to person while retaining an identical tautological institution and inscription.[9]

This somewhat subtle analysis is more familiar in the form of the ontological proof of God's existence. The key to this proof, as well as to the lexicalization, is to suppress a vicious circle while employing its irreplaceable resource. In this suppression, God's existence is both thematically and operationally proved in that I remember what is indeed the predicate of existence, but having forgotten my predetermination of perfection as containing existence, I experience this remembering as a passive reception of the truth, and this passive reception is then the operation of the existing of God. This is the philosophy of hidden rhyme.

I have presumably reached my goal. It seems, of course, to be a joke, at least in relation to the seriousness of the question I started out from. All I have done, one might say, is to deconstruct Ricoeur's argument. Deconstruction, however, is not a rejection but a reinscription.

As already noted, speculative concepts are everywhere at work in the notion of hidden rhyme. And, indeed, the question of the philosophical value of poetry remains, but now it is posed in the following terms: What is the growth in understanding brought about by the hidden rhyme effected by metaphor?

As can be seen, this is a difficult, perhaps impossible question. But an answer must nevertheless be sought. This is, as Ricoeur states, our task. I will therefore hazard a short answer. In the eminent sense, the philosophical value of metaphor is its power to allow me to communicate to myself and to others an understanding of common, but both transcendent and transcendental speculative concepts. As we have seen, however, the experience and act of understanding are not a sufficient condition for philosophical value in the eminent sense. Therefore, the communicated understanding must be both a growth with respect to what is already known and a true understanding. But truth, as true understanding, can be nothing less than a truth of correspondence. I will leave aside the criterion of novelty, although it goes almost without saying that the dimension of the speculative is as much invented as discovered. I concentrate on the truth condition as a shared self-reflexive correspondence. How can hidden rhyme be the basis for a truth? Some frustrating answers come readily to mind. First, we can see how such a rhyme would have a pragmatic truth. As a matter of practical necessity, people need *some* kind of understanding of primary concepts in order to live. But serviceable truth is not necessarily of value to the goal of universal truth. Is there a way in which truth as hidden rhyme contributes to absolute truth? Instead of the pragmatic answer, the more ethical, imperative answer offers itself again. Truth is a task. The metaphor grants me a new tool, but since metaphor's rhyme must be hidden, part of what allows me to understand must remain beyond my immediate grasp. Accordingly, there always remains more for me to articulate. This task, then, is infinite, but in the sense of being endless and without a goal. Is there no explicit access *now* to absolute truth?

Presumptuously but dutifully I suggest a third answer, the one implicit in this paper. The concept of hidden rhyme seems to proceed from a semiotic perspective. It designates a semiotic or rhetorical mechanism. Would semiotics be the answer? Would that hidden rhyme which thinks hidden rhyme be an absolute truth regarding the speculative? It seems that semiotic explanation would succumb to the act of preontological understanding while thematizing it as the hidden rhyme or semiotic process it is essentially. To be sure, hidden rhyme is the essence of this process only to the same extent that, in the above example of the predetermined context of the distant echo, the making explicit is a comprehension. There, the making explicit was indeed a comprehension, but only empirically, not essentially, since it is the dimension of essentiality that is always absent, precisely on account of the matter of hidden rhyme. The "comprehensiveness" of the comprehension was precisely not the entire content of its *empirical* reality. Hidden rhyme may itself name the process that cancels its own essentiality; it nevertheless cannot pretend to any value other than, at best, that of an empirical concept. Indeed, in general, the kind of semiotic explanation aimed at can never more than provisionally designate the particular inscription actually operating in any one particular context, while at the same time it only provisionally describes the general structure of the effect of self-identity made possible by the inscriptions.

We are back to a serviceable truth, even though this semiotics is self-consciously serviceable. Its critical, negative function is all too clear. The inscribed identity is the very stuff of the pseudo–self-evidence for which I have, presumably, provided a genealogy. But lest one get carried away with this suggested genealogy of truth, one must not forget one's own dependence upon an empirical operation whose content by definition must never be possessed: that hidden rhyme which one must never thematically hear. The object of the semiotics in question would thus indeed be an absence, a determinate but indeterminable absence of this semiotics' concrete condition of possibility. And what about the truth of the inscribed identity making the semiotics possible? The truth of this serviceability? Because of the empirical nature of the inhabiting of the inscribed identity, its truth, as a self-identity, is indeed always metaphorically mediated. Accordingly, sometimes it will be right and sometimes it will be wrong. What I hope to have shown is that, in the face of the dismal poverty of this result, the concept of hidden rhyme grants an understanding, no matter how provisional.

## NOTES

1. The basic text is of course "White Mythology" in Jacques Derrida's *Margins of Philosophy*, trans. Alan Bass (Chicago: University of Chicago Press, 1982), esp. pp. 268–71. The specificity of metaphor, as independent of any *telos* of conceptuality and identity, is tied to its nonspecularity. The remarks regarding the *other* self-destruction of this metaphor that does not confirm its tenor but explodes its limits (see p. 270) cannot fail to be recognized as the capital of the closed economy of many an article.

2. See Martin Heidegger, *The Basic Problems of Phenomenology*, trans., intro., and lexicon by Albert Hofstadter (Bloomington: Indiana University Press, 1982), pp. 171–73, and *Being and Time*, trans. J. Macquarrie and E. Robinson (New York: Harper & Row, 1962), p. 205.

3. Of all the works one might here mention, I cite only Jean-Luc Nancy's *Le discours de la syncope* (Paris: Aubier-Flammarion, 1976), because of its study of the production of the transcendental standpoint.

4. Paul Ricoeur, "Metaphor and Philosophical Discourse," in *The Rule of Metaphor*, trans. Robert Czerny, with Kathleen McLaughlin and John Costello, S.J. (Toronto: University of Toronto Press, 1979). All numbers in parentheses in the text refer to pages in Ricoeur.

5. See "Miroirs rhétoriques: Sept ans de réflexions," in *Rhétorique générale*, Groupe $\mu$ (Paris: Editions du Seuil, 1982; 2d ed.), pp. 212–16, esp. p. 216, where, in response to Ricoeur's critique, the whole granted by poetry is qualified as mythic in a pejorative sense, and rhetorical analysis is characterized as deconstructive. My point, against both Ricoeur and Groupe $\mu$, is that myth is inevitably ontologized.

6. See in particular Derrida's "The Ends of Man," in *Margins*, p. 126, the remarks on the vicious circle and Heidegger's defense against the charge. See also pp. 134–35, Derrida's discussion of a deconstructive "strategic bet" on a "change of terrain," where one of the risks taken is "the autism of the closure." What I am trying to pursue is a nondialectical change of terrain *within* the autism of the closure.

7. Translated by the editors as "The *Retrait* of Metaphor," *Enclitic* 2 (Fall 1978): 4–33. The issue of tautology is a thorny one. If sterile confirmation of the classical philosophemes remains the legitimate bugbear, even their deconstruction, which is to say their reinscription, seems to require the restricted economy within the open economy, by the same token as the inverse. Moreover, if rhetoric rests on the *retrait* (125), the *retrait* itself, as naming its own truth and limit, has as much merely tactical as strategic value. And tactics are rhetorical. Thus, for instance, *entame* names itself as an *entame* (123),

but this self-reference is as much its limit as its truth. By the same token, rhetoric is rhetorical. This structure of paradoxical self-reference has a teeming host of more or less topical embodiments.

8. There are at least three other ways in which Ricoeur attempts to reduce metaphoricity to the conceptuality he would have it presuppose. First, in the discussion of dead metaphor following the discussion of lexicalization, Ricoeur claims that the metaphoricity of *epiphora* in Aristotle's definition of metaphor is "qualified conceptually by its insertion in a network of significations, where the notion of *epiphora* is bounded by the primary concepts *phusis, logos, onoma, semainein,* etc" (293). But from what does the conceptuality of the primary concepts derive? The circularity of this argument is patent and Ricoeur recognizes as much (perhaps a bit too implicitly) with regard to Aristotle's ontology of potency and actuality (307).

The second way is effected indirectly through a hierarchization of disciplines that gives the problem of the relation of language and being to philosophy over linguistics. Although to be expected, given Ricoeur's phenomenological bias, this devaluing of linguistics is surprising in a book whose self-claimed key (4) is Benveniste's preference of semantics to semiotics (68–70). Nevertheless, Ricoeur claims that "semantics can only allege the relation of language to reality but cannot *think* this relation as such" (303). The difference between allegation and thinking rests on the validity of phenomenology.

Indeed, this outcome of the drama between semantics and philosophy is justified in terms of the paradox of language's self-reference. This is the third way. Ricoeur acknowledges that "there is no standpoint outside language" (304). "Yet," he continues, "speculative discourse is possible, because language possesses the *reflective* capacity to place itself at a distance and to consider itself, as such and in its entirety. . . . This [reflective] knowledge articulates the reference postulates in a discourse other than semantics, even when the latter is distinguished from semiotics" (304). But if the speculative follows from language's possession of a capacity for reflection, in virtue of which kind of knowledge can I say language possesses this capacity: speculative or linguistic, phenomenological or empirical? What is the difference between presupposition and allegation, since the former in fact rests upon the allegations of natural consciousness recognized as such? Any particular answer to this question can only be, as Derrida says, a bet, to the extent that it could only be primally stupid to deduce the invalidity of inference.

9. It must be borne in mind that the explicitation presences as a conceptualization only to the extent that on the one hand I predetermine its schema as a kind of grasping and on the other I actually and actively hear similarities

from out of the noise of actual speech. For universal, self-identical phonemes are never actually heard, because of their sheer relationality. Thus, Umberto Eco makes all decoding dependent on a prior abduction (see *Semiotics and the Philosophy of Language* [Bloomington: Indiana University Press, 1984], sec. 1.11, esp. p. 41 and the notion of "overcoded abduction").

*T. R. Martland*

# Quine's "Half-Entities," and Gadamer's Too

I TAKE IT to be axiomatic that language has meaning only insofar as it communicates information about something.

I take it to be intuitively reasonable that this something must meet certain identity and individuation conditions in order for us to communicate information about it. That is to say the following: in order for us to communicate information about something to others we must assume that we are talking about the same thing; for "we cannot know what something is without knowing how it is marked off from other things."[1]

From this, I conclude that in order for language to communicate information about something or to refer to something, there must be rules for the identification and individuation of the entity to which these words refer. There can be no referring without these rules; that is, no information is being communicated about anything, there is no meaning.

I am sure that E. D. Hirsch, for one, would be quite happy with what I have said so far. In expressing his dissatisfaction with what he understands to be a hermeneutic relativism, Hirsch argues that if there is no identified entity, only an ambiguous text and that always in process, ambiguous but nevertheless *necessary*, no external evidence,[2] then there can be no interpretation of that text which is fair or unfair, because there is no identifiable authority to prove or disprove any statement's claim first to be an interpretation of that text, second to be a fair interpretation of that text.[3] But Hirsch insists interpretations do communicate information, so there must be prior identified entities.

His thesis is that that about which information is communicated is "whatever an author wills to convey by his use of linguistic symbols and which can be so conveyed," that is, the author's intention.[4]

Certainly Hirsch's move from recognizing the logical need for a proper identity to asserting the independent and necessary existence of this proper identity is common. Quine notes the same progression with the problem of attributes. He tells us the positing of attributes to substance "is accompanied by no clue as to the circumstances under which attributes may be said to be the same or different. This is perverse, considering that the very use of terms and the very positing of objects are unrecognizable to begin with except as keyed in with idioms of sameness and difference." Accordingly, he continues, this "lack of a proper identity concept for attributes is a lack that philosophers feel impelled to supply; for, what sense is there in saying that there are attributes when there is no sense in saying when there is one attribute and when two?"[5]

There is something to say in favor of such a move as this. It does not introduce a verification procedure. It does not argue that we *must* validate a particular utterance's knowledge claim by verifying whether it designates or refers to an entity other than itself which we know from elsewhere. It simply assumes that identity conditions are logically prior to verification conditions, that they are not identical. Wittgenstein's familiar argument for the dismissal of private language is a case in point. Wittgenstein did not rest his case on the view that sentences about subjective states are not verifiable because they are subjective— that is, because they do not refer to something we know from elsewhere—but rather on the view that they are not verifiable because there are no identity conditions the satisfaction of which could be verifiable. To suppose that I could verify that I am in pain is to suppose that the connection between "pain" and its putative referent is a steady one and that the term makes the same reference whenever I use it. This is just what Wittgenstein argues is absent in the case of "pain."[6]

From the above I think this much is clear. In order for language to refer there must be rules for properly identifying that entity to which the language supposedly refers. Verification comes afterward. But let us now consider the negative consequences. If the intended entity does not meet these identity and individuation conditions, must we interpret Quine's "identity is thus of a piece with ontology" (cited in the first note) to mean that a failure to meet these conditions of reference implies the intended entity does not exist? I dare say this conclusion has some intuitive support. Is it at all meaningful to say something exists when all we can say of it is that it is something to which we cannot refer?

In response to follow-up questions such as these, Hirsch and Quine part company. Whereas we noted they both insisted upon identity and individuation conditions, so much so that Hirsch proposes the author's intention to be such an entity, we now discover that in the face of certain philosophical problems, Quine is willing to rethink that upon which he previously insisted. In effect, whereas both Hirsch and Quine encourage us to think about what constitutes the entity to which reference is allegedly being made, we have seen that Hirsch argues from the need for identity and individuation conditions, while we will see that Quine argues from acknowledging the failure of already proposed identity and individuation conditions to satisfactorily demark what it is that we actually know. By doing this, Quine not only undercuts Hirsch's argument for the logical *need* for identity conditions and therefore for the need to accept the author's intention as bearer of the meaning of a literary work, but he also encourages a receptivity to speculative elements in the definition of what constitutes entities to which references are being made. I am thinking of the kind of speculative elements Gadamer introduces with his consideration of "occasionality" or his "analysis of effective-historical consciousness."

After Quine observes that certain philosophical solutions to the problem of identity of attributes and of propositions are "discouragingly artificial," his openness to such moves as Gadamer's becomes apparent when he suggests that "perhaps, after all, we should be more receptive to the first and least premeditated of the alternatives. We might keep attributes and propositions after all, but just not try to cope with the problem of their individuation." Then he adds the most interesting point of all.

> The precept "No entity without identity" might simply be relaxed. Certainly the positing of first objects makes no sense except as keyed to identity; but those patterns of thing talk, once firmly inculcated, have in

fact enabled us to talk of attributes and propositions in partial grammatical analogy, without an accompanying standard of identity for them. Why not just accept them thus, as twilight half-entities to which the identity concept is not to apply?

What can we say of these "twilight half-entities to which the identity concept is not to apply?" Quine himself speculates, this "idea of accommodating half-entities without identity . . . some day . . . may . . . end up half vestigial and half adapted, within a new and as yet unimagined pattern beyond individuation." [7]

The one thing we have already noted about this relaxed world is that there is no logical need for those referential a priori rules of identification and individuation which in the third paragraph of this article I concluded were necessary. If we press further and take seriously Quine's words "keyed to identity" in the above passage, there is something else we might say. To posit twilight half-entities which are "keyed to identity," though not meeting rules for identity, is to provide oneself with that which leads into or opens up talk of identity and things "in partial grammatical analogy." In other words, to be "keyed to" is to be a step away from, to have a key to a door or threshold which when open and passable allows us to see that which is different from what lies on this side of the threshold. To the extent that these keying entities allow us to talk as if there were a standard of identity for them, they are identifiably half-entities fitting our expectations of thing talk on this side of the threshold, yet also passing us over to the other side of the threshold, so that we can talk our way into a different world in which the identity concept does not apply.

Let me use an analogy from painting in order to point out the importance of "keying" even more clearly. Insofar as Quine's half-entities allow us to talk of attributes and propositions, they are similar to the painter's use of light when that light gives existence to the things the painter paints. If the light does not show, the objects never appear. In fact they do not exist. So it is, if the "keying" half-entities are not considered or if they fail to serve as thresholds, those particular identifiable world experiences on the other side of the threshold never occur, they never appear. They, too, do not exist. Gadamer seems to agree: "The object appears truly significant only in the light of him who is able to describe it to us properly. Thus it is certainly the subject that we are interested in, but the subject acquires its life only from the light in which it is presented to us."[8]

The contrast to the painter's use of light which gives existence to the object is chiaroscuro, that technique so marked in the works of Caravaggio and Rembrandt whereby light becomes a theatrical lighting of objects out there, bestowing clarity on what was previously only obscure. In this case there is no "keying to identity." The identities already exist in the darkness in keeping with the rules of identification and individuation. The threshold now is merely the light which allows us to point them out. That which was in the dark is now in the light. If by chance the light goes out or the threshold no longer serves as a passage and these entities to which we refer are again in the dark, they continue to exist, though at the moment no information about them is being communicated.

I think Archibald MacLeish plays with these two kinds of light to which I am referring. He does so with his now familiar fragment

> A poem should not mean
> But be.

In one sense, the chiaroscuro sense, he is correct. The poem points to the fact that since poems do not refer to something existing elsewhere which meets identity and individuation conditions, they do not mean. But of course this poem is itself a poem and it does mean what it says. Thus, by its very existence as a poem it refutes itself. In effect the poem also sheds that other kind of light or talk, which enables us to see or talk of that which has not previously existed. By keying to itself, the poem turns itself into a half-entity which opens the way into itself in which it means by being. Like the painter's light, which gives existence to the things the painter paints, the poem fragment gives existence to a poem which gives meaning to poems.

Whereas MacLeish the poet actually creates half-entities, the philosopher Gadamer, like Quine, acknowledges their existence. He does so with his insistence that "understanding is, essentially, an effective-historical relation." What we actually understand is not an object which meets identity and individuation conditions, but a relationship of these lighted-up identities in their contexts. The "effective-history" of this relationship "determines in advance both what seems to us worth enquiring about and what will appear as an object of investigation, and we more or less forget half of what is really there—in fact, we miss the whole truth of this phenomenon when we take its immediate appearance as the whole truth." [9]

Though Gadamer speaks of these objects of investigation being led *from* their "twilight region" by means of history's light, that they nevertheless remain lighted half-entities in Quine's sense is indisputable. Gadamer writes: "It is the progress of events that brings out new aspects of meaning in historical material. Through being re-actualised in understanding, the texts are drawn into a genuine process in exactly the same way as are the events themselves through their continuance. . . ." [10] The consequence is, of course, "that after us others will understand in a different way. And yet it is a fact equally well established that it remains the same work." [11] It seems that so far as these objects of investigation remain "the same work," they meet the identity concept. So far as they are illuminated or "reactualized in understanding," they have incorporated a "character of occasionality" which contributes to their meaning, so much so "that [an artwork] contains more [meaning] than it would without this occasion." [12]

The important thing for us to remember with these entities or objects of investigation, half immediate appearance and half occasion, is that their occasionality is part of what the work itself is saying and is not something forced onto it by an interpreter. For example, consider a portrait which actually is a portrait—that is, which represents a particular person, even if we do not know the person represented. Here is the "occasionality" of the picture, which is not necessarily fully realized by the viewer and which goes beyond the picture's immediate appearance. Gadamer would insist this is part of the picture's total meaning, constituting part of its ontology. Examples which more clearly have to do with questions concerning the nature of art are drama, dance, and music, art forms which need the occasion or performance in order to exist and find their form. It is the work itself which "takes place" in the performance. As with the painter's use of light when that light gives existence to the things the painter paints, so the performance makes the dance appear and brings out what it means all at once.

With Gadamer I think these examples of what I am relating to
Quine's half-entities can be extended to include painting and sculpture. Their differences from the previous examples might be that
though here the occasion is no less essential to what constitutes the
half-entity which is the work of art, the occasion itself involves more
completely the "horizon" of the interpreter. I am thinking of the fact
that painting and sculpture are displayed to different interpreters
under different conditions. So long as the interpreters look at them as
works of art, these different interpreters working under different conditions not only see the paintings and sculpture in a different way,
they see different things.

In any case, rather than argue that in fact the interpreter's perspective is more evident in appreciating the fine arts than in appreciating
the performing arts, I really wish to argue the more basic point that
the interpreter's perspective, provided by what Gadamer calls the dimension of occasionality, is applicable to all works of art, that in effect
all works of art are functioning half-entities. Consider, for example,
this familiar passage:

> Caesar: Let me have men about me that are fat;
>            Sleek-headed men and such as sleep o'nights.
>            Yon Cassius has a lean and hungry look;
>            He thinks too much; such men are dangerous.

On the most obvious level, the chiaroscuro level, the level which
meets identity and individuation conditions, we discern something
about Caesar's preference for how his associates should physically
look, something about Cassius, and generally something about fat
and sleek-headed men as against lean and hungry men. This is that to
which Shakespeare's language refers. To this extent Shakespeare's passage is propositional, probably something which can be stated more
clearly, and certainly something which can be tested as to its truth
value by finding evidence for Caesar's preference, for Cassius's looks,
and for cases in support of what Caesar asserts about the nature of fat
and lean men. Toward this end we could begin by contributing North's
version of what Plutarch had to say about Caesar and Cassius.

Caesar also had Cassius in great jealousy and suspected him much; whereupon he said . . . to his friends, "What will Cassius do, think ye? I like not his pale looks." Another time, when Caesar's friends complained unto him of Antonius and Dolabella . . . he answered them again, "As for those fat men and smooth-combed heads," quoth he, "I never reckon of them; but these pale-visaged and carrion lean people, I fear them most."

Ah, so we say, there *is* some truth in what Shakespeare asserts. Caesar *does* have his preferences. But notice that we can ask again, is it absolutely clear that yon Cassius, pale though he was, was one of those pale-visaged and carrion lean people Caesar so feared? We can go on indefinitely with questions of this sort, but quite frankly, they and their answers have nothing at all to do with why we read Shakespeare. Instead of trying to prove the passage's claim by looking elsewhere for supporting evidence, we stay with the passage and journey back to a rereading of it for what *it* says. Thus to appreciate "Yon Cassius has a lean and hungry look; / He thinks too much," is to see it not as pointing to something about Cassius but rather as operating like the painter's light, a statement illuminating itself.

But what does this mean—a statement illuminating itself? And how does it come about? We should have asked this question of MacLeish's fragment but did not, because at that time we had not yet considered this dimension of occasionality as a part of the artwork itself. It will help us now to provide an answer. At first we might be content to say the statement that Shakespeare's lines illuminate themselves means they provide the light by which they themselves appear and mean. For instance, this would suggest that we should appreciate the lines for their rhythm and perhaps try to point out how their meter is effective for lyricism and/or for argument. This is no foolish move. We certainly can look at Pound's *Cantos* in this way, as well as many of the works of Samuel Beckett and Gertrude Stein.

But it is not enough. Although this kind of reading presents a legitimate dimension of the text's occasionality, it ignores that aspect of occasionality to which I referred when I mentioned the interpreter's "horizon." This latter dimension becomes evident only when we acknowledge that Shakespeare's lines clearly mean something else, that a mental or thought component is signified. On this level I can only say that what is illuminated is a current understanding of the lines themselves, that is, a current understanding of introspective lean and hungry men. I suggest that this then constitutes the whole of the occasion through which the lines do their work. The occasion has to do with what the lines themselves say *as an interpreter understands them.* The lines illuminate themselves so long as there are current "external" understandings of introspective lean and hungry men and so long as these lines illuminate for contemporary interpreters what they already know about introspective lean and hungry men. So long as they and texts like them so function, they are half-entities to which the identity concept does not apply. They are *half*-entities because "external" understandings are no longer external to them; they are *entities* because the lines themselves are identifiable. With Quine we might say they are "keyed to identity" because they enable us to talk of statements illuminating themselves in partial grammatical analogy.

I conclude that there are "twilight half-entities" and suggest that works of art, all of them, are examples. But Quine also spoke of an "as yet unimagined pattern beyond individuation." Based on what we have here discovered, I will contribute three observations.

1. Shakespeare's lines communicate information not only because the interpreter's attention is directed to the lines themselves, which do meet identity and individuation conditions, but also because of what the interpreter already knows. As such, Shakespeare's lines function as half-entities keyed to bringing out "more" meaning only so long as there are qualified interpreters who are what we might call connoisseurs, that is, interpreters who possess a certain knowledge capable of being so illuminated. Another way of putting it: Shakespeare's lines are half-entities keyed to illuminate new understandings only sometimes, only so long as they actually do illuminate new understandings, only so long as they function within a tradition or history which includes individuals who are prepared and qualified to take them seriously. This may only be another way of pointing out that the identity concept does not apply, that in fact half-entities function in a haze of *more or less* rather than in the clear atmosphere of *yes* and *no*.

2. To say Shakespeare's lines communicate information about them-

selves—that is, about a current understanding of lean and hungry men—is to say this current understanding is always current; that is, it undergoes change or, in Gadamer's words, it is constantly being introduced "to new aspects of meaning." In words that we have been using, it seems that half-entities are keyed not only to that onto which doors and thresholds open but to the thresholds themselves.

Consider, for example, the plight of a listener trying to understand that half-entity, twentieth-century music. The connoisseur's understanding is structured the way it is because she or he has been listening to Debussy, Schönberg, and Berg. Appreciating them is an integral component of understanding the more advanced music. The older, more familiar music, what the listener already knows, illuminates his or her understanding of the newer, more advanced music. But now, in keeping with this second observation, the process of understanding goes in the other direction as well. Not only does the necessary background contribute to our understanding twentieth-century music, but the twentieth-century music contributes to our understanding the necessary background. In actually listening to and understanding Debussy, Schönberg, and Berg, the connoisseur comes to understand the more complicated modern music in such a way that Debussy, Schönberg, and Berg actually do become a part of the history of that understanding leading up to the advanced pieces. In other words, not only does understanding Debussy, Schönberg, and Berg affect the connoisseur's understanding of the advanced pieces, but listening to these advanced pieces affects the understanding of Debussy, Schönberg, and Berg.

What occurs seems to go as follows: (1) There is an already partly known relevant and required background which the connoisseur brings to the work of art and which necessarily contributes to his or her artistic understanding of that work. (2) The connoisseur comes further to understand this relevant background the way she or he now understands it because of current understandings which themselves were made possible in part because of it. This is to say, although the background is required for understanding the piece, the understanding reflects back onto the background.

This may be no unusual matter. To say, for instance, "This act is justified," a statement which ostensibly says something about the act in front of me, is also to say something about the term "justified," thereby revising our current understanding by extending or modifying the term's meaning. As attention to Shakespeare's lines illuminates our prior understanding of lean and hungry men, as listening to contemporary music illuminates our prior understanding of Debussy, Schönberg, and Berg, so pointing out that this act is justified illuminates our prior understanding of "justified." But unusual or not, it does seem clear that even the half of the half-entity which we already know does not fulfill identity and individuation conditions.

3. Although Shakespeare's lines require attentive interpreters who already possess a certain knowledge of lean and hungry men so that they can communicate their information, that certain prior knowledge and the communicating of new information are achieved independently of whether there is a single example of a lean and hungry man available for evidence. It seems the prerequisite knowledge did not, and the power of the lines to illuminate does not, need concrete evidence for support. Yet it would be unfair to claim that all is fantasy. I would suggest that though there is no entailment, there is inference. The assurances are not evidential but rather intuitive. There is no logical certainty, but there is a certainty which coheres with what the interpreter knows from elsewhere.

But if fantasy is inappropriate, what then? Wittgenstein, in response to the objection that he concluded "the sensation [of pain] is a nothing," said, "Not at all. It is not a something, but not a nothing either." [13] We have argued that half-entities exist. Do we dare say, then, with my colleague Kenneth Stern, to whom I owe so much in this paper, that they exist in that netherworld halfway between thing and nothing, that they exist but simply are not real, the way dreams exist but are not real? Of course Stern's point is to stress their mind-dependency. But our findings regarding the nature of half-entities make clear a difficulty with too easily identifying the likes of dreams with Shakespeare's lines, which do here and now illuminate the meaning of "lean and hungry men." Whereas Stern would say dreams are indeterminate in that they have no identity with a meaning shared by other people, that they spin out their existence in no place and at no time other than in the mind that gives them their existence, our findings suggest that half-entities like Shakespeare's lines, though indeterminate, do shed a shared light here in this place at this time with a whole host of we's who are their particular interpreters. As such, what they say is "independent of the vagaries of you and me," and can in principle be validated.

I have one final suggestion to make. It should come as no surprise for Quine. In this presented pattern of ours of half-entities beyond individuation, our observations 1 through 3 suggest an ontology of process. Half-entities are half-entities only so long as they contribute meaning, in the process of which they change. The background required for them to do their work is a tradition which itself is also constantly open to change. I suggest, then, that John Dewey might be the appropriate guide into Quine's "as yet unimagined pattern beyond individuation." His work is an extensive attack on appeals to identities beyond change. He insisted philosophers must shift their interests from how changes serve or defeat concrete purposes, to the idea of particular intelligences shaping things here and now. Philosophy must take into account the experience of insecurity and reject the classical claim that the world in which we live is fundamentally one of a fixed order, significance, and worth. In fact, the form that remains unchanged to sense, "the form of seed or tree, is regarded not as the key to knowledge of the thing, but as a wall, an obstruction to be broken down." [14] Of course, all of these directives are quite appropriate for the study of "twilight half-entities to which the identity concept is not to apply."

If this appeal to John Dewey and to the experiences of insecurity works out, perhaps we might call the study of "twilight half-entities" an ontology of event.

### NOTES

1. Quine adds that "identity is thus of a piece with ontology" (W. V. O. Quine, *Ontological Relativity and Other Essays* [New York: Columbia University Press, 1969], p. 55).

2. I derive "external" from William K. Wimsatt and Monroe C. Beardsley's article "The Intentional Fallacy," reprinted in Wimsatt and Beardsley, *The Verbal Icon* (Lexington, Ky.: University of Kentucky Press, 1954), pp. 3–18, especially p. 10. The authors define "internal" evidence as that which is "discov-

ered through the semantics and syntax of a poem, through our habitual knowledge of the language, through grammars, dictionaries, and all the literature which is the source of dictionaries, in general through all that makes a language and culture." They define "external" evidence as that which is "not a part of the work as a linguistic fact: it consists of revelations about how or why the poet wrote the poem. . . ." We shall see that Gadamer is not at all willing to insist with Wimsatt and Beardsley that "external" implies irrelevance to the meaning of a text. He would say some of what they consider to be "external" evidence falls into their third kind of evidence, that which becomes part of "the word's history and meaning."

3. E. D. Hirsch, *The Aims of Interpretation* (Chicago: University of Chicago Press, 1976), pp. 75–85. We can extend the validity of what Hirsch is insisting upon when we consider claims about what culture contributes to textual understanding. In order to make such a claim, Hirsch would say we must be able to identify and individuate not only the nature of texts, but what is and is not a cultural contribution. To be able to make such a distinction presupposes that a noncultural perspective can be attained.

4. E. D. Hirsch, *Validity in Interpretation* (New Haven: Yale University Press, 1967), p. 49. "Verbal meaning is, by definition, that aspect of a speaker's 'intention' which, under linguistic conventions, may be shared by others. Anything not shareable in this sense does not belong to the verbal intention or verbal meaning" (218). In effect, Hirsch is insisting first that there must be a determinate object in order to interpret; second, that this cannot be defined as the text because from it many disparate meanings can be construed. See pp. 1–67.

5. Quine, *Ontological Relativity*, p. 19.

6. Ludwig Wittgenstein, *Philosophical Investigations* (Oxford: Blackwell, 1953), paragraphs 253–62. Incidentally, this is the reason Hirsch's thesis of the author's intention as the bearer of meaning is sometimes seen to be a recommendation or a proposal rather than an assertion. He proposes his thesis as the necessary prerequisite to verification procedures.

7. Quine, *Ontological Relativity*, pp. 23, 24.

8. Hans-Georg Gadamer, *Truth and Method*, ed. Garrett Barden and John Cumming (New York: Continuum, 1975), p. 252. Could we also say the object appears only in the light of the word which describes it? In this the word resembles the painter's light.

9. Ibid., pp. 268, 269.

10. Ibid., p. 336. "Effective-historical consciousness is something other than enquiry into the effective-history of a particular work, as it were, the

trace a work leaves behind. It is, rather, an awareness of the work itself, and hence itself has an effect" (305).

11. Ibid., p. 336.

12. Ibid., p. 127.

13. Wittgenstein, *Philosophical Investigations*, paragraph 304.

14. John Dewey, *Reconstruction in Philosophy* (London: University of London Press, 1921), p. 113. See also T. R. Martland, *The Metaphysics of William James and John Dewey* (New York: Greenwood Press, 1969), especially chap. 4.

*Walter Glannon*

# Why There Is
# No Fact of the Matter
# about Meaning in Fiction

How is it that the meaning one reader explicates from a work of fiction is incompatible with the meaning discovered by another reader? Is it merely a matter of the first reader deciphering something that the second reader misses, or are disparate meanings functions of readers with asymmetrical, interest-relative points of view? Just what the meaning of a work of fiction is and whether it is to be found in the author, text, reader, or the linguistic community to which all three belong are questions that I shall address and attempt to answer in this paper. These same questions have been the focus of an ongoing debate within literary criticism since Wimsatt and Beardsley's seminal article on the intentional fallacy, which generated the school of literary formalism and the grounding of meaning in the language of the text.[1] Subsequently the plot thickened, first by virtue of Hirsch's identification of meaning with authorial intention,[2] and later with reader-response criticism and the notion of interpretive communities, whereby meaning was relocated within the domain of readers.[3] The appeal of these theories notwithstanding, I shall pursue a different tack, adopting a more strictly analytic approach to the problem of meaning in fiction.

In the late nineteenth century, Gottlob Frege, the founder of modern mathematical logic, reacted against the psychologism that had permeated philosophy since Descartes. What psychologism amounted to was the thesis that the meanings of words could be given by appeal to the ideas which speakers and hearers associated with these words. Frege's major work, *Die Grundlagen der Arithmetik* (1884), marked a shift in the philosophical tradition from the mental to the sentential; meaning thereby became a function of truth-values of the sentences in a language.[4] According to this semantic theory, the truth-value of a sentence depends upon the reference (*Bedeutung*) of the components of the sentence. Frege's work has been carried on by such philosophers as Tarski, Davidson, and Quine insofar as all have eschewed couching "meaning" in psychologistic terms, opting instead for an extensionalist account. Roughly construed, on such a theory the meaning (extension) of a term or expression is the object or set of objects to which the term refers. Consequently, an austere empirical notion of meaning has eclipsed the vague psychologistic one.

How can this enable us to understand a text such as *Don Quixote?* Provided we are working from a referential base with *"Don Quixote"* at the source, we can employ such predicating expressions as "was written in 1605 (part 1) and 1615 (part 2)," "contains 126 chapters," "was written by Miguel de Cervantes," and the like to get an extensionally pure notion of meaning; for all of these expressions are intersubstitutable *salva veritate*. In other words, the truth-value of an expression with a constant subject-term (*"Don Quixote"*) is maintained when substituting one predicate for another. Although far from being sufficient for our purposes, the extensionalist view is necessary to the extent that it provides a criterion of identity, since the predicates supply empirically verifiable features that enable us to individuate the *Quixote* from other literary artifacts. Yet such truth obtains only trivially and amounts to no more than a platitude in deciding what *Don Quixote* means to its readers. The concept or proposition (intension) we believe the fictive narrative to express is what we ordinarily take to be the meaning of a given text. This is usually conveyed by the properties of characters occurring within the fiction. Nevertheless, Frege, Russell, and Strawson take names such as "Don Quixote" and "Sancho Panza" to be empty singular terms, owing to their failure to denote existing individuals. The fact that these constitutive elements of fiction lack reference renders an extensionalist account inadequate in literary interpretation, a point illustrated by a story from Borges.

In "Pierre Menard, Author of the *Quixote*," Menard intends to accomplish the impossible task of composing *Don Quixote,* or more precisely, "to produce pages which would coincide—word for word and line for line—with those of Miguel de Cervantes."[5] The result is that "the text of Cervantes and that of Menard are verbally identical, but the second is almost infinitely richer" (101). In other words, the texts are extensionally equivalent. Yet what makes Menard's "almost infinitely richer"? Is the greater richness a measure of such factors as authorship and readership? Apropos of Borges's distinction between the *"visible* part" of Menard's work and something more obscure, or "subterranean" (99), it is suggested that two literary works can be linguistically identical but different in some other sense. It is in light of this that my skeptical thesis will take shape, for it turns on the belief that certain thoughts are separable from language. That is, there are particular thoughts that are intractable to linguistic expression; their contents cannot be articulated. I take Borges to be alluding to this in saying that there is something "richer" about Menard's *Quixote.* By refuting the thesis that language is an accurate purveyor of mental thoughts, I shall resurrect something of a Cartesian point of view from the linguistic morass. What might appear initially to be a contentious claim will become more plausible once indexical thoughts are introduced into the discussion.

I have already claimed that we must introduce intensions, commonly construed as concepts or propositions, into literary interpretation because presumably the meaning of a text is the proposition, or complex of propositions, a reader believes the text to express.[6] For example, "reading too many books causes one to go mad" is the proposition corresponding to what some readers take to be the point of the fiction when reading *Don Quixote.* But because of the presence of such semantically deviant terms as "Don Quixote" and "Sancho Panza," there does not seem to be any direct access to such a proposition. One could even make the rather bold claim that nothing is asserted in the narrative, since sentences containing vacuous names are devoid of truth-value. The possibility of a determinate meaning could thus be summarily dismissed on this score, for there is nothing in the fiction which could be *known.* Consideration of the alternatives is in order.

Literary formalism is unavailing in this matter.[7] Imagine a situation in which a reader interprets *Don Quixote* as a romantic novel, expressive of the critical proposition "assiduously pursuing the dictates of one's will gives value to life," or something to that effect. Contrariwise, a second reader interprets the text as suggestive of the critical proposition "the actions of Don Quixote are a parody of the romantic ideal."[8] If meaning is something heterogeneous by virtue of an inexhaustible power of textual signifiers, then seemingly no interpretation can be excluded. But this results in a contradiction, given that the romantic and parodic views exclude each other. How can the semantics of the same sentences in the same shared language (be it the original Spanish or an English translation) allow for such radical divergence? What in the sentences themselves of, say, Don Quixote's first sally from La Mancha, adjudicates between the two interpretations and determines which is in the right?

It may seem more plausible to contend that the meaning of a fictional text is assigned relative to distinct interpretive communities, each having its own conception of a work of literature and all generally agreeing on the concept or proposition expressed by the fiction. What fictional sentences mean, then, is relative to how members of an interpretive community use them. In this way, critical propositions of the type "*Don Quixote* is a romantic novel" can be ascertained by members of the community, for the content of the proposition derives from the conventionally determined senses of the words used to express the proposition. However, such senses cannot yield a procedure any more satisfactory for establishing the correct reading of a text like the *Quixote* than can literary formalism. The communal practice of specifying an interpretation for a given text is suspect because there is no independent criterion to which the community can appeal its decision. On this account, meaning is simply what each community says it is, a function of the community's own internal standard of interpretation. Yet if the standard is internal, the interpretation of one community is just as "correct" as that of any other; none can be wrong. This type of literary relativism is found wanting because it is self-refuting. That is, in the absence of external criteria, extreme internal relativism implies that the statement "*Don Quixote* expresses the critical proposition p relative to community c" is itself relative in sense and therefore rests on shaky semantic ground.[9] One might attempt to dispel this concern by claiming that fictional meaning amounts to an open set of interpretations with respect to a particular text. Insofar as each interpretation underdetermines the sense of the whole, there is no "correct" reading. Nevertheless, something is badly amiss when the same language generates not merely different but disjunctive interpretations. Accordingly, endorsement of an "anything goes" attitude toward interpretation runs the risk of reducing "meaning" to an empty notion.

The tendency in literary formalism and reader-response criticism is to relegate the author to the periphery, if not to banish him or her altogether and rest content with such absence. But the inadequacies of these two theories make obvious the need to bring the author back from exile. Indeed, the very fact that interpretation amounts to filling in the semantic gaps resulting from nondenoting singular terms (for example, "Don Quixote," "Sancho Panza") underscores the propriety of positing an author who creates such gaps. Owing to the reference-failure of these terms, there is something essentially subjective about the introduction of them into the fiction by an author. Thus, the occurrence of the names of fictional characters is indistinguishable from the intentional attitudes an author has when introducing such names. Surely we can imagine Cervantes thinking about some state of affairs and having propositions like "reading too many books causes one to go mad" or "letters cannot exist without arms" strike him in such a way that they impel him to write the fiction. Presumably, the author's intention in writing is to get the reader to grasp the same concept or proposition that the author entertains. But the occurrence of vacuous fictional names implies that the author only alludes to and hence does not directly express the proposition via the fictional narrative. This seems to preclude the reader from knowing just what the author had in mind. Given only an indirect means of expression from which to work, the reader can only speculate about the nature of the author's thoughts.

Cervantes' own propositional attitudes make it impossible to grasp a general proposition suggested in *Don Quixote*. "Reading too many books causes one to go mad" is really a disguised form of "I believe that reading too many books causes one to go mad," where "I believe" designates the attitude of the author vis-à-vis the proposition in question. Furthermore, the fictional names that are taken to be vague

markers of propositions are at bottom idiosyncratic; they are reflections of subjective ideas and as such constitute what Leo Spitzer calls
Cervantes' "linguistic perspectivism." [10] Thus the proposition the author wants to express through his fiction is not semantically transparent but rather is infected by his peculiar manner of thinking about
the proposition. Put another way, the attitude conveyed by "I believe"
controls what is no longer a neutral content of the "that"-clause following the attitude-type. What Frege calls a "mode of presentation"
on the part of a particular subject intrudes into the propositional content, and so there is no separating *what* is presented from *how* it is
presented to the individual—in this case, the author.[11] Concepts have
become much more oblique. What is clear, however, is that once the
beliefs, desires, and intentions of the author become paramount,
pragmatics eclipses semantics (word-world and sentential relations)
as the standard for a theory of meaning.

For Frege, an oblique context is one in which there is failure of sub-
stitutivity of co-referential expressions within "that"-clauses following an attitude-type such as "believes." Truth is not retained because
the clauses (as *ungerade Rede*) contain names with only an indirect reference, or a sense. For our purposes, what is oblique results from a
shift in focus from the proposition to the propositional attitude. Indeed, "opaque" may be a more appropriate term, since the force of
the attitude blocks the proposition from being sent to and taken up by
an audience. Consequently, the content of the proposition is no longer
publicly accessible. If x is the author of a work of fiction, then all intensional contexts of the form "x believes that . . . ," where the words
in the "that"-clause express a proposition, are opaque because they
are affected by *how* the proposition is presented to x. Moreover, since
the senses of the proper names we draw upon to make inferences to
putative propositions are idiosyncratic, we do not have readily available any semantically transparent (extensional) terms that might justify such inferences. This point derives from the view that our most
basic propositional knowledge is grounded in reference.[12] The upshot
is that the meaning of a fictional text, defined in accordance with the
author's attitudes or mode of presentation, is inaccessible to readers.
Meaning thus becomes narrower in scope, for semantics has been
supplanted by psychology.

What justifies these claims? Although I am unable to give a perspicuous rendition of the contents of an author's thoughts, my own experience enables me at least to infer, by analogy, that the author has the same type of thoughts as I. Just as I can imagine Cervantes being struck by a proposition in a unique way, so too is it unproblematic to conceive of a reader thinking about what he or she is reading under a certain mode of presentation. Thus "*Don Quixote*" can be taken as an abbreviation for "the book that I am thinking about in this way." A more straightforward formulation is "I believe that *Don Quixote* expresses the proposition that reading too many books causes one to go mad." If a certain belief-type is operative when I read *Don Quixote*, I can assume (again by analogy) that the author Cervantes had a similar belief-type in mind when writing the novel. The problem is that there is no transparent route to the cognitive content of the author's thoughts, no infallible means of specifying how he thinks of a given state of affairs.

Why is it that the reader and author cannot share the same mode of presentation and thus have the same sense of a text? It is plausible to say that the seventeenth-century context in which the *Quixote* was written and the twentieth-century context in which it is read may be responsible in great measure for the differences in the assignment of meaning. Yet even if authorship and readership shared the same historical context, there would still be a divergence of sense, owing to the indexicality of perspective in author and reader. The indices from which both think about a state of affairs are radically distinct.

Thus far I have construed the thoughts of reader and author in terms of the same type of attitudinal expression, "I believe that . . . ," contending that the sense of the resultant clause is opaque, its content accessible only to the individual having the attitude. The explanation is that "I" is not amenable to formal semantics; nor can its sense be relativized to the practices of a linguistic community. It is the one word whose meaning or sense, understood as the cognitive content of a person's thoughts, is inscrutable. Deference once again to Frege should underscore the problem.

Having shifted his concern from truth-value in his early writings to the vexing possibility of variable individual senses in his later work "The Thought," Frege suggests the same sort of inscrutability to which I have been alluding in the example of the wounded Dr. Lauben:

Now everyone is presented to himself in a particular and primitive way, in which he is presented to no-one else. So, when Dr. Lauben thinks that he has been wounded, he will probably take as a basis this primitive way in which he is presented to himself. And only Dr. Lauben himself can grasp thoughts determined in this way. But now he may want to communicate with others. He cannot communicate a thought which he alone can grasp. Therefore, if he now says, "I have been wounded," he must use the "I" in a sense which can be grasped by others, perhaps in the sense of "he is speaking to you at this moment," by doing which he makes the associated conditions of his utterance serve for the expression of his thought.[13]

Furthermore, Husserl's remarks in *Logical Investigations* buttress the incommunicability thesis: "The word 'I' names a different person from case to case, and does so by way of an ever altering meaning."[14] In addition, "each man has his own I-presentation (and with it his own individual notion of I) and this is why the word's meaning differs from person to person" (316). In light of this asymmetry of "I"-thoughts, the following argument can be advanced: if that state of affairs or proposition an author entertains when writing a fictional text is shaped by his or her indexical mode of presentation, and if the proposition the *reader* believes the text to express is infected by *his or her* indexical mode of presentation, and further, if the meaning of the indexical "I" varies from person to person, then the sense or meaning of the text is variable, relative to the incommunicable thoughts of author and reader. Given the identification of meaning with an author's propositional attitudes and the inability of readers to accurately explicate the contents of those attitudes, it is impossible to posit a fact of the matter as to the determinate meaning of a work of fiction.

Even if an author from the same language community to which I belong were to express directly what he might call "the meaning" of his fiction, I still would not be able to grasp it because the indexical element in a token utterance such as "I believe that letters cannot exist without arms" would be unique to him. There is no method available to purge such a concept of its subjective element; for deleting the attitudinal prefix from the locution occurring in the "that"-clause cannot alter the fact that the author must be thinking in a peculiar way about the proposition he is trying to express. Language cannot account for the content of one's mental state when writing fiction, since it is possible for different token expressions of the same sentence-type to have distinct senses when uttered by different speakers. Insofar as each instance of an utterance containing the pronoun "I" involves thinking about oneself in a privileged way, "I believe that *Don Quixote* expresses the proposition that reading too many books causes one to go mad" can have a distinct meaning, or sense, for each of two interpreters. Following the lead of Frege and Husserl, what John Perry and David Lewis have labeled "self-locating beliefs" and "attitudes *de se*," respectively, demonstrate that first-person indexical modes of presentation are unique in that no one can make an utterance containing the indexical "I" and have the same first-person attitude that I myself have toward a literary text.[15] I alone know how the text is presented to me. Only the person with "I"-thoughts has access to them.

The notion of a first-person perspective imposes constraints upon the reader, for his doxastic limitations—he can only speculate—vis-à-vis the author's thoughts fall short of the epistemic access requisite to claim "I know that p," where p is the proposition that impelled the author to write the fiction. Here we can see how an analysis of meaning akin to Grice's theory would fail to bridge the gap between distinct "I"-thoughts. There are similarities between what I have presented and Grice's attempts to reduce conventional sentence meaning to the content of the speaker's intentions.[16] Yet his program entails a communicability thesis, whereby a speaker can succeed in his intention to get an audience to grasp some proposition that he believes. It is assumed that the proposition derives from some salient object or truth with respect to which speaker and audience are in agreement. In the case of fiction, however, the uptake intended by the author is not effected. What the author intends to communicate is not just that he or she has a certain attitude but more importantly the contents of that attitude, which cannot be conveyed through the vacuous names of fictional characters. The result is that communication fails by virtue of the asymmetrical indices that are entirely subjective in nature. There is no interface between author and reader and hence nothing capable of linking their indexical thoughts.

It seems that only an omnipersonal, God's-eye point of view encompassing all indices could infallibly specify the thoughts of all individuals, authors and readers alike. But without access to an author's attitudes, the reader is left to interpret the text relative to his or her own interests. This results not in intensional isomorphism, or the assignment of equivalent senses to all readings of a text, but rather in closure. If meaning is to be located anywhere, it must be in the head.

Returning to the Borges story, it is Menard's "style" (102) that makes his text "almost infinitely richer" (101) than that of Cervantes, to answer the question posed at the outset of this discussion. Commenting on the same story, Kendall Walton claims that the seventeenth-century context determines the style of Cervantes' *Don Quixote*, on the one hand, and that a twentieth-century context affects the style of Menard's *Quixote*, on the other.[17] I am inclined to think of style as defined by one's indexical mode of presentation, that is, how a text strikes a particular author or reader. It is because of this view of style that Menard can inscribe the same sentences as Cervantes and yet have a text with a different sense. The distinction comes with the secondary qualities—for example, romanticism, parody, tragedy, humor—which Menard ascribes via the relation of the text to his first-person attitudes. Such qualities are relational rather than intrinsic to the text, the latter category encompassing such defining textual characteristics as language and sequence of chapters. Menard's unique ascription of secondary qualities to the text lends it a nominal essence and thus only a contingent identity.[18] For this reason, as Borges tells us, "*Don Quixote* is unnecessary," and that is why Menard can "write it without incurring a tautology" (100). In other words, the meaning Menard assigns to the text from his first-person point of view is for him part of the nominal essence of the fiction, an essence incomplete prior to his act of writing.

The same sort of nominal essence is ascribed to other fictional texts by other readers similarly limited by their own subjective perspectives. Moreover, just as the clauses "truth, whose mother is history, who is the rival of time . . . and warning to the future" from Menard's opus are "shamelessly pragmatic" (102), likewise the meaning of a fictional text is not intrinsic to the text but is what the reader believes that meaning to be. Therefore, meaning in fiction is relational, interest-relative, and inseparable from how individual authors and readers view a particular text in their own privileged way.

I have argued that formalist and communal theories of meaning in literary matters are undercut by indexical modes of presentation. Because each indexical or "I"-thought is unique to each person, the contents of an author's or reader's thoughts are unspecifiable. Since I have defined meaning in fiction as a function of such inscrutable thoughts, there can be no empirically verifiable fact of the matter about this meaning. Nevertheless, it is this very inscrutability of an author's thought-contents which makes fiction the allusive, evocative medium that it is. In light of this, my remarks should not be construed as advocating a thoroughgoing nihilism, but instead as pointing toward a principle of interpretive charity. For if meaning in fiction were not as obscure as I have made it out to be, then perhaps we would have nothing to write about.

## NOTES

1. "The Intentional Fallacy," *Sewanee Review* 54 (1946): 468–88.

2. *Validity in Interpretation* (New Haven: Yale University Press, 1967).

3. The reference I have in mind is Stanley Fish's *Is There a Text in This Class? The Authority of Interpretive Communities* (Cambridge, Mass.: Harvard University Press, 1980).

4. Michael Dummett traces the development and significance of Frege's philosophical thought in "Frege's Philosophy," in *Truth and Other Enigmas* (Cambridge, Mass.: Harvard University Press, 1978), pp. 87–115.

5. "Pierre Menard, Author of the *Quixote*," in *Borges: A Reader*, ed. Emir Rodriguez Monegal and Alistair Reid (New York: E. P. Dutton, 1981), pp. 96–103. Page references follow in parentheses.

6. Intensions are not to be confused with intentions. "Intension" indicates a concept or proposition, usually occurring after such prefixes as "Necessarily . . . ," "Possibly . . . ," and "S believes that. . . ." The content of a "that"-clause is thus an intension. See the glossary to Susan Haack's *Philosophy of Logics* (Cambridge: Cambridge University Press, 1978), p. 246.

7. I advert to the following remark by Paul de Man as representative of literary formalism: "The reading is not 'our' reading, since it uses only the linguistic elements provided by the text itself." "Semiology and Rhetoric," in *Textual Strategies*, ed. Josué Harari (Ithaca: Cornell University Press, 1979), p. 138.

8. For an example of disjunctive interpretations with respect to the *Quixote*, compare Anthony Close's *The Romantic Approach to Don Quixote* (Cambridge: Cambridge University Press, 1978) with Miguel de Unamuno's *Our*

*Lord Don Quixote,* trans. Anthony Kerrigan (Princeton: Princeton University Press, 1979).

9. I am drawing upon Hilary Putnam's arguments against relativism here. See *Reason, Truth, and History* (Cambridge: Cambridge University Press, 1982), p. 121.

10. Leo Spitzer, "Linguistic Perspectivism in the *Don Quijote,*" in *Linguistics and Literary History* (New York: Russell and Russell, 1962).

11. The expression "mode of presentation" is taken from Frege's essay "On Sense and Reference," in *Translations from the Philosophical Writings of Gottlob Frege,* ed. Peter Geach and Max Black (Oxford: Basil Blackwell, 1970), p. 57.

12. Cf. Keith S. Donnellan: "When a name is used and there is failure of reference, then no proposition has been expressed—certainly no true proposition. If a child says, 'Santa Claus will come tonight,' he cannot have spoken the truth, although, for various reasons, I think it better to say that he has not even expressed a proposition." "Speaking of Nothing," *Philosophical Review* 83 (1974): 20–21.

13. Gottlob Frege, "The Thought: A Logical Inquiry," trans. A. M. and Marcelle Quinton, in *Philosophical Logic,* ed. P. F. Strawson (Oxford: Oxford University Press, 1967), pp. 25–26.

14. Edmund Husserl, *Logical Investigations,* trans. J. N. Findlay (London: Routledge, 1970), p. 315.

15. See David Lewis, "Attitudes *De Dicto* and *De Se,*" in *Philosophical Papers* (Oxford: Oxford University Press, 1983), vol. 1, pp. 133–59; and John Perry, "The Problem of the Essential Indexical," *Nous* 13 (1979): 3–21. A more general discussion of indexical thoughts is given by Colin McGinn in *The Subjective View* (Oxford: Clarendon Press, 1983).

16. See H. P. Grice, "Utterer's Meaning and Intentions," *Philosophical Review* 78 (1969): 147–77.

17. Kendall Walton, "Style and the Products and Processes of Art," in *The Concept of Style,* ed. Berel Lang (Philadelphia: University of Pennsylvania Press, 1979), pp. 45–66.

18. My use of "secondary qualities" derives from Locke's *Essay Concerning Human Understanding,* ed. A. D. Woozley (London: Fontana, 1964), *passim.* See especially bk. 3, chap. 3, sec. 15 of the *Essay* for Locke's discussion of "nominal essence."

*James LeRoy Smith*

# Meaning and Poetic Expression

How is poetry philosophical? This question can be approached by drawing together ideas and lines of ideas from Rainer Maria Rilke, John Searle, Samuel Levin, and Richard Hugo. My point of departure is a signal comment by Rilke; the philosophical framework is originally John Searle's; suggestions for refinement come from Samuel Levin; and the poet of reference is Richard Hugo. I work toward the sense of this admonition: to poeticize is necessary if we are to wear the full fabric of our possibility as speaking beings—though I do doubt that any *one* mode of creative activity is sufficient for acquiring that full fabric. In the end I am not sure we will be forced to say that poetry *is* philosophical, but then, since I think that there exist no theory-neutral conceptions of philosophy, I think we could attach the delineated philosophical predicate to poetry as a reward for our having drawn together these lines of ideas.

What goes on when we use language? It behooves us to reflect on *that* first, to straighten a few shelves at *that* level before getting more acquisitive. First a logical (because presuppositional) point: language use *is* presuppositional. To respond to the question about poetry being philosophical presupposes that we know what we should mean by both "poetry" and "philosophy." The general point, of course, is that "How is X Y-ical?" presupposes that we have a clear grasp of the sense and reference of both X and Y. One option is to slip into sociology and attempt an "ostensive sum" of how we use these terms "poetry" and "philosophy." But ostensive definitions will differ according to where we look, and there is no statistical calculus capable of integrating such data, even if the latter were compatible. Let us first focus on the predicate: I will present a conception of philosophy and compare it with a specific poetic expression. This will illuminate the boundaries of both philosophy and poetry. With a topic such as this, there is nothing to be gained by being timid.

What is philosophy? What does it mean to be philosophical? Philosophy is not the gathering (hypothesizing, testing, confirming, or falsifying) of empirical knowledge. Some might think so because of the time-honored dictum that philosophy is the love of wisdom, and fact-gathering would seem to increase our wisdom. But it is a different sort of wisdom that philosophers seek.[1] We find that conceptual and normative matters are the main concerns of philosophy. That is, if we excise factual claiming insofar as routine gathering and authentication are concerned, and if we excise the kinds of linguistic activities that carry us through our normal day (greeting, informing, reporting, asking, telling, hinting, entertaining, joking, and so on[2]), then we are left with the other kinds of claiming, those that fall outside the natural and social sciences proper, namely, *conceptual* and *normative* claiming. A short example and we will return to the main road.

We might assert (make the claim) that the right to privacy in a given circumstance takes precedence over a right to life because life-continuance necessitates an invasion of privacy.[3] Were that to be our view regarding a circumstantial relationship between some two parties, clearly that view is not established as a matter of *fact*. It is a *moral* claim, a species of *normative* claiming. The criteria whereby we judge its acceptability are *not* the same criteria we would use in the ascertaining of a fact, in the accepting of a factual claim. Moreover, we might well need a conceptual claim (a definitional clarification) of the sort "A *right* is . . ." before we could satisfactorily conclude on the acceptability of the original moral claim. Thus, this is an example of both how conceptual and normative (moral) claims go hand in hand *and* how neither is constituted by factual matters—though they may be *related* to crucial facts in some way or other.

What has all this to do with poetry? Again, unless we have the sense and reference of *Y*, we cannot satisfactorily assert *X*'s *Y*-ness.

We are working toward a notion of Y (philosophy) so as to intelligently ask if X (poetry) is philosophical. Let us now generalize this conception of philosophy.

*Philosophy is the assertion and clarification of adequate and consistent normative and conceptual claims to the end of satisfactorily establishing the meanings and their criteria that we would be willing to take as constitutive of self and world.*[4] While pages could be written both in defense of and in critical response to such a stipulation, I will resist the temptation to defend the conception in vacuo and will lay out some lines along which we can do some observing. It is still too soon to turn directly to poetry. More timely here is the reference I wish to make to one of Rilke's expressions.

Rilke writes: "At bottom one seeks in everything new (country or person or thing) only an expression that helps some personal confession to greater power and maturity. All things are there in order that they may, in some sense, become pictures for us."[5] This is a curious pair of statements, especially in light of our analysis above regarding claiming. We have to take great care in identifying both the kind of speech act being made (whether claiming or some other linguistic act), and *if* claiming, what kind of claiming it is. The first statement might appear to be an empirical claim. We might say that it is either true or false that people do this, that whether or not people do this could be tested with an appropriate experimental design, and so forth. Taken as a sociological claim of this sort, that first statement is surely false. Yet Rilke was a serious person, and one would not want to think that he indulges here in such obvious falsities. We should be cautious in these two senses: first, the statement might be hortatory—Rilke might well be admonishing us to do such seeking ourselves; second, perhaps he intends that we take "confession" as a variable that would track a person's scope, ability, and limitations—varying degrees of power and maturity are reflected as people plant young flowers, buy new tools, pick up or even write new books!

In the former case, what looked like an obviously false empirical claim would then be seen as a fairly subtle, yet understandable normative claim admonishing us to greater achievement of expression. In the latter case, the obviously false empirical claim gains respectability through a refining of the concept of "confession," the respectability generated through our imagining the widespread, even universal, actions of people to improve their worlds in their own respective ways and certainly with varying degrees of power and maturity. In this latter case, we see an implicit conceptual claim concerning "confession," a claim that (if we were to accept it) would extend our sense—and therefore the reference—of "confession." We would see both confessional activities and our activities of improving our surroundings in a new, related light. Clearly, the point is that certain manners of expression—here Rilke's—lend themselves to our active, extensional (and I mean the pun) reflection. I intend that you see my analysis here as one wherein we are unpacking the implications of Rilke's expression in terms of the direct as well as the indirect claims his expression could intelligently be said to state or imply. I am not impressed with the counterclaim that I am reading all of this into Rilke's language. On the contrary, all of this comes to be through a close attending to *exactly* what Rilke wrote. The proof is in the conviction one gains from the analysis. The manner of Rilke's expression—brief, compact—conveys a richness (we often say *depth*) of meaning that my analysis is intended to track and highlight. But it is, I think, *his* meaning and not originally mine.

Thus, I am concerned with the kinds of claims that Rilke's expression conveys and with their acceptability. His manner is not to assert within a typical argumentative framework, as philosophers would do and have come to expect. Yet his expression, as translated into the normative admonition given above and into the conceptual clarification of "confession," carries with it the capacity to convince, to motivate, to move to action. This latter characteristic is certainly one philosophers would wish to claim for their arguments. A contrast emerges between poetry and philosophy: Rilke's expression is *poetic*—it declares a motivating depth and richness of meaning that explicit claiming, whether philosophic or scientific, cannot accomplish (see his whole letter in note 5, below); yet our analysis of his utterance is *philosophic*—we examine possible lines of coherent intention to the end of classifying and deciding on the acceptability of that intention (Rilke *does* admonish rather than only describe). We therefore respond to the manner of his expression in terms of a depth and richness of meaning with a stronger consequent motivation to think, to experience, and to act than any explicit claiming of comparable duration would usually have elicited.

Let us examine his second statement to see if a similar grist is available for the philosophic mill. When Rilke writes, "All things are there in order that they may, in some sense, become pictures for us," he is, I think, intending to say something which is *true*. We should be inclined to agree that the utterance is an empirical claim. But we must resist the impatient urge to test and falsify such a short, sixteen-word package, cut off and isolated from its birthright. The intended meaning here is inaccessible apart from a wider context. What Rilke means by "pictures," "things," and even "there" cannot be fully understood without the statement which immediately precedes. Further, those two statements taken together are not as understandable as would be the entire letter, nor the letter as understandable as would be his letters and poems taken together.

If one were to respond here that "apparently, then, each word that Rilke uttered would help clarify every other word he ever uttered," I would suggest that such a response would be symptomatic of an impatient zeal, a zeal shared by many philosophers and natural and social scientists, a zeal brought to the light of day through the lack of extended, direct experience with prose and poetic literature. Such an attempted reductio would be singularly unhelpful.

The grist that Rilke gives us here is an embodiment of the suggestion that we conceive of the world as a constant, complex source of motivations for the process of continuing, through our creative use of language, our articulation of the meanings by which we constitute self and world. His "there" is thus never a passive "there," his "things" not only objects for us to manipulate and move about, his "pictures" never mere passive renderings placed for our passing appreciation of their inert composition. At bottom, our analysis, if carried on to proper proportion, would show in greater detail than can be suggested here that Rilke conveys in his statement a concept of self and world which, once we grasp it, would put us in the contextual position to make the judgment as to whether the utterance—yes, an empirical claim well wrought, once we understand operational definitions of its central concepts—was *true-to* our experiences or possible experience. Through such analysis of this and other statements as we find them conveyed by the expressions in Rilke's prose and poetry, we would come to the end of deciding on the ultimate acceptability of his manner of constitution (the adequacy of his *true-to* . . .) for ourselves. We would decide that his character was either worth emulating or not, or to what degree. Surely this would take us beyond testing procedures with sixteen-word, isolated expressions! The broader and more genuine approach would involve examining the possible lines of coherent intention (philosophical analysis) as expressed and consequently discovered in his letters and poems (poetic expression). Thus, it seems, poetry is not so much itself philosophical as it is evocative of philosophical analysis as philosophical analysis takes on the role of assertion of necessary and proper canons and directions for criticism.

Still, it is too soon to state conclusive findings. Let us broaden the circles of our conception of philosophical analysis by referring to the work of John Searle more explicitly than we have heretofore and look to Samuel Levin's thought for even further insight.

Philosophers have in this century been widely concerned about the meaning of utterances. In this paper, for instance, I have argued that the meaning of one and another of Rilke's utterances could not be gathered outside their context, that his expressions were not singular propositions the truth or falsity of which could be gleaned in their isolated settings. In short, I have argued that we could neither verify/falsify nor accept/reject his claims without an extended understanding (and certainly no common dictionary-meaning) of the operational definitions of the central terms in his claims. All of that seems correct. Expression and meaning are difficult ducks to capture and train. Such training is a philosophical task, and my paper up to here concurs with that view while being an example of it. I am also asserting that poetic expression seems to provide help in that task, grist for that mill, and so forth, by both allowing a test for what we think "expression" and "meaning" *mean* while at the same time giving us expressions and meanings.

Without the poet, I am coming to think, the philosopher runs the risk of fabricating categories of linguistic use that are too thin, too unmolecular, and that consequently fail to bond in the actual chemistry of language use where it operates best. Also, perhaps, without the philosophers, the poets run the risk of not being able to articulate why they say what they do, however glad they may be that they have said it, or—at the very least—of not being sufficiently interested in such articulation. Either way, the fabric of our possibility as speaking beings falls frayed. I turn to Searle and Levin to further this point.

John Searle writes as follows in his engaging book *Expression and Meaning:*

> One of the most obvious questions in any philosophy of language is: how many ways of using language are there? Wittgenstein thought the question unanswerable by any finite list of categories. . . . But this rather skeptical conclusion ought to arouse our suspicions. No one I suppose would say that there are countless kinds of economic systems or marital arrangements or sorts of political parties; why should language be more taxonomically recalcitrant than any other aspect of human social life? I argue in "A Taxonomy of Illocutionary Acts" that if we take the illocutionary act (that is, the full blown illocutionary act with its illocutionary force and propositional content) as the unit of analysis . . . then we find there are five general ways of using language, five general categories of illocutionary acts. We tell people how things are (*Assertives*), we try to get them to do things (*Directives*), we commit ourselves to doing things (*Commissives*), we express our feelings and attitudes (*Expressives*), and we bring about changes in the world through our utterances (*Declarations*).[6]

Searle states that he has arrived at this list in an empirical way, looking about to see how it is that we use language. He declares that the justification of these categories in terms of the nature of mind must await a longer work on the nature of human intentionality. He also asserts that many utterances are obviously of one category but also indirectly of another. He announces as the main theme of his collection of essays the relations between literal sentence meaning and the speaker's utterance meaning, where utterance meaning differs from the literal meaning of the expression uttered.[7]

Obviously, then, our analysis of Rilke concludes commensurately with Searle's distinction: surely the extended reach of the needed operational definitions that we briefly tracked indicates that Rilke's "utterance meaning" differs from the literal meaning of the expression uttered. Thus, the expressions were not only Expressives but probably Assertives, Commissives, Directives, and perhaps even Declarations as well! The main point is that the philosophical analysis of Rilke's expressions would lead us to the logic of his intention in uttering the expressions. Moreover, just as Searle's philosophy of language must be tested against the richness of Rilke's expression, Rilke's intentions must pass the rigorous scrutiny of the logic of his intentions, a scrutiny made possible by the parameters of Searle's categories.

In short, the reciprocity that would come about both through applying Searle's categories to poetic expression and through testing the logic of the poet's intention with those categories would be healthy for both poetry and philosophy. Moreover, we note again that poetry is not itself so much philosophical as it is a home companion to philosophy. Additionally, we now begin to see that although literary criticism could not avoid many of the canons and criteria of the philosophy of language, Searle's approach shows us that philosophers of language have other intentions—taxonomic in nature—than the specific criticism of literary works. And thirdly, we see again and now with more refinement how poetic expression left unexamined by philosophical analysis as well as philosophy of language left untested against the richness of poetic expression both run the risk of becoming a less than adequate linguistic fabric.

More specifically, and while looking further into Searle's work, his eight principles for the clarification of the dynamics of metaphor do indeed allow further comparative analysis. Moreover, the poetic expression chosen might reflect shortfalls in Searle's program. Searle says, for example: "The expressive power that we feel is part of good metaphors is largely a matter of two features. The hearer has to figure out what the speaker means—he has to do that by going through another and related semantic content from the one which is communicated."[8] We can see here more clearly the reciprocity value of studying and evaluating Searle's categorial scheme as he develops it and comparing it to the expressions wrought by the poet. Indeed, the "other and related semantic content" is what was needed to understand the full impact of the lines quoted from Rilke.

Before applying this conception of philosophical analysis to one of Richard Hugo's poems, I wish to deepen our commitment to such analysis by contrasting Searle's phrase "going through another related

semantic content from the one which is communicated" to a procedure characterized by Samuel Levin. Levin states:

> We have concluded that deviant sentences in poetry are to be taken
> literally, that, so taken, they have meaning and thus express truth condi-
> tions. This conclusion is enabled by a shift in world orientation. Instead
> of attempting to construe the expression, i.e., make it conform to a sen-
> tence that has truth value in this world, we as it were construe the
> world—into one in which the deviant sentence is no longer deviant.[9]

If Levin's suggestion is accepted, then Searle's "another and related semantic content" would be parsed as a different possible world—the
one of the poem—for the sake of emphasizing that content. Such a
construal would have the beneficial effect of opening us to alternative
content, disarming any tendency to refer too commonly, and so
forth—but, shouldn't we ask, at what cost?

Levin goes on to develop what he calls "phenomenalistic construal,"
whereby that possible world of the poem develops. But then he states:
"Where the extensional semantics is concerned, the linguistically construed sentences may be true or false, depending on conditions in the
actual world. For the phenomenalistically construed sentence, on the
other hand, those occurring, namely in (lyric) poems, we stipulated
that they are all true."[10] With this transfer, Levin concludes that by
attributing credibility to the poet, we thus accept that whatever the
poet (or his or her persona) says is true. Thus, "going through another and related semantic content," as Searle would have it, has become with Levin a truth-oriented question, at bottom one of the poet's
credibility.

While a certain stance is thus available with Levin's approach, it
seems that our earlier approach, with emphasis on the normative-
conceptual aspects of the poet's expression, concludes more strongly
by stressing the need to take a stand with or else reject the poet's
articulated possible world. Because poetic expression is assertive,
even directive, we must make such conclusions: this obligation is why
we love or else remain unmoved by particular poets. While Levin's
suggestion is consistent with Searle's philosophy of language, he
stops short of insisting that we grapple with the credibility question.

The grappling is also consistent with Searle's framework and is a necessary condition for benefiting from the reciprocity that can occur between poetic expression and this kind of philosophical analysis—that reciprocity, in turn, being necessary if we are to wear the full fabric of our possibility as speaking beings. In short, while there is some consistency among the statements of Searle and Levin, it appears that Searle's track gives us a more unavoidable mandate for applying philosophy of language to poetry.

Let us now consider Richard Hugo's "Open Country":

> It is much like ocean the way it opens
> and rolls. Cows dot the slow climb of a field
> like salmon trawls dot swells, and here or there
> ducks climb on no definite heading.
> Like water it is open to suggestion,
> electric heron, and every moon
> tricky currents of grass.
>
> 　　　　　　　Let me guess;
> when you repair the damaged brain
> of a beaten child or bring to a patient
> news that will never improve, you need
> a window not a wall to turn to.
> And you come back here
> where land has ways of going on
> and the shadow of a cloud
> crawls like a freighter, no port in mind,
> no captain, and the charts dead wrong.
>
> 　　　　　　for George [11]

There are five utterances in this poem; initially, all would be classified as *assertive*, empirical. Of course, we have neglected the title. In entitling the expression "Open Country," Hugo identifies, initially at least, the referent of the first word of the poem, thus clarifying the first assertive to a degree: it is a descriptive factual claim. A parcel of country is assimilated to the ocean, cows to salmon trawls, a field to the opening and rolling of a swell as the description becomes more specific. Through his word choice, through the strength of the similes and the implied metaphors, Hugo pushes through the walls of assertion and out into transactions which are expressives, even declarations (as Searle defines these categories).

With the fourth utterance we gain the pronoun "you" and understand that the poem is dedicated to George, whoever George is. But moreover, through the power of the similes, we are ourselves introduced to George's tasks of repairing and informing. We share in his ability and in his frustration, his accomplished disappointment. The empirical aspects of the fourth and fifth assertives reach over out of description into prediction and away from the universality of a common actor toward the demand that *we* take up George's context, that we hold it as our own. In this transition, the assertive use moves through the expressive to the directive and to the stage of declaration. Finally, if we accept Hugo's stance—the stance conveyed by the voice of the poem—he gives us the *commissive* of the poem and asks us for that same commitment. That is, because of this commissive, we see the "voice" of the poem culminate in an utterance which *commits* the speaker (and asks the reader for the same commitment) to the specified stance.

When Ted Cohen writes that "a potent metaphor does not abbreviate its paraphrase, it generates it," he refers, I think, to the very kind of track that we have just sketched.[12] A poem, in this case one that is itself a compound metaphor, clearly does not abbreviate its paraphrase but rather generates it. The proper paraphrase, I am saying, is the extended analysis of the logic of the poet's intention—an analysis philosophical in nature in that it begins with the classification of utterance and utterance meaning and extends into the refinements of speaker meaning. As descriptive assertion passes over into declaration and the concomitant commitment, we come to a context impossible to generate other than with poetic expression, and either we accept the implicit constitution of such a self in such a world or we do not. What Levin says may apply, but Searle's analysis demands that philosophic elaboration accompany poetic expression. This is poetic criticism fostered by the framework of philosophy of language. It is philosophical analysis made personal by the contributions of poetic expression. It is a mature use of language to the end of constituting the semantic content of self and world. Never again would we enter open country quite the same.

Some conclusions:

1. Poetic expression contains a richness and depth of meaning which is conveyed in concise, evocative manners which prompt the reader to an active uptake of that intended richness and depth.

2. That uptake is best accomplished through a philosophical analysis which leads to decisions concerning the ultimate acceptability of the semantic content thus availed and, through that content, to commitments about the credibility of the poet's constitution of self and world. This analysis proceeds by classifying the kinds of utterances, the nature of any claims made, and consequently determining and evaluating the logic of the poet's intention. Through comparisons of utterance meaning and speaker meaning, we develop a kind of literary criticism, but one fueled by the spirit and direction of contemporary philosophy of language. The result is a putative articulation of the sense and reference of the poet's intentionality as that intentionality rests waiting in the poet's written accomplishments.

3. Seeing the nature of the poet's intention through a phenomenalistic construal (Levin), whereby what is stated is simply taken as true in a possible world, is a useful idea, but the crucial question concerns how the actual world of the reader is thus revised by the poet's making and by reader uptake. We must return to that actual world to judge the adequacy of the "true-to," regarding our experience or what we would wish that experience to be. Should we revise or not revise our lives?

4. Poetic expression is thus self/world-generating in this manner, provided that we take seriously both the original reach of the poet and the need to push poetic expression through the analysis of utterance classification, concept clarification, and the normative evaluation allowable as a consequence thereto. Thus, poetry is not so much itself philosophical as it is the primary proof of the human need to cultivate the claim that philosophical analysis and poetic expression are importantly symbiotic.

5. Because our ultimate goal as reflective human beings is to be sure that what we commit ourselves to is credible and tenable, we cannot

wear the full fabric of our possibility as speaking beings unless we poeticize. This kind of making, too, is loving.

## NOTES

1. This is *not* to say that the determination of what counts as a factual claim, as authentication of such claims, and how such claims function in scientific explanation are not philosophical questions. The history of the philosophy of science is of course constituted by such questions.

2. As with factual claims, talking *about* the character of such speech acts, what their force might be, how such utterances are to be classified and seen to interact and so on—all of that and more is of course part of the philosophy of language. Such investigations would involve claiming of nonempirical sorts.

3. This circumstance is relevant in, for example, discussion of abortion. The implicit view is compatible with that developed by Judith Thomson in her widely anthologized article "A Defense of Abortion," originally published in *Philosophy and Public Affairs* 1 (Fall 1971): 47–66.

4. I do not mean to assert that empirical truths are irrelevant to such constitutive acts. Still, empirical claims themselves must contain clear operational definitions (conceptual claims).

5. *Letters of Rainer Maria Rilke 1892–1910*, trans. Jane Bannard Greene and M. D. Herter Norton (New York: W. W. Norton, 1945), vol. 1, pp. 31f., "To Frieda von Bülow, May, 27, 1899, from St. Petersburg, Russia." Here is the letter in its entirety:

> An intention to write never turns into a letter. A letter must happen to one like a surprise, and one may not know where in the day there was room for it to come into being. So it is that my daily intentions have nothing to do with this fulfillment of today. They were concerned with much that I am now saving up to tell personally. For the many experiences and impressions are still heaped up in me in such disorder and chaos that I do not want to touch them. Like a fisherman who comes home late at night, I can only guess vaguely at my catch from the burden of the nets and must wait for the morrow in order to count it and enjoy it like a new discovery. As I think over the immediate future, it seems to me that it will be in Meiningen that the sun will first rise on my wealth. Accordingly you will be able to witness my greater or lesser prosperity, and I do well to be silent about it before I can show it fully.

Only this much: I feel my stay in Russia as a strange complement to that Florentine spring of whose influence and success I have told you. A friendly Providence led me to the next thing, further into the depths, into a greater simplicity and toward an ingenuousness that is finer. Florence seems to me now like a kind of prefiguration of and preparation for Moscow, and I am thankful that I was permitted to see Fra Angelico before the beggars and supplicants of the Iberian Madonna, who all create their God with the same kneeling power, again and again, presenting him and singling him out with their sorrows and with their joy (indefinite little feelings), raising him in the morning with their eyelids, and quietly releasing him in the evening when weariness breaks the thread of their prayers like rosaries. At bottom one seeks in everything new (country or person or thing) only an expression that helps some personal confession to greater power or maturity. All things are there in order that they may become, in some sense, pictures for us. And they do not suffer from it, for while they are expressing us more and more clearly, our souls close over them in the same measure. And I feel in these days that *Russian* things will give me the names for those most timid devoutnesses of my nature which, since my childhood, have been longing to enter into my art!

6. John Searle, *Expression and Meaning* (Cambridge: Cambridge University Press, 1979), pp. viiff.

7. While it is the case that Searle is in a sense doing something empirical, his analysis is hardly what we should call empirical linguistics.

8. Searle, *Expression and Meaning*, p. 114.

9. Samuel Levin, *The Semantics of Metaphor* (Baltimore: Johns Hopkins University Press, 1977), p. 127.

10. Ibid., p. 138.

11. See Richard Hugo, *White Center* (New York: W. W. Norton, 1980).

12. Ted Cohen, "Notes on Metaphor," *The Journal of Aesthetics and Art Criticism* 34 (Spring 1976): 251.

*Carl Rapp*

# Philosophy and Poetry: The New Rapprochement

And even if works of art are not thought or the Concept, but a development
of the Concept out of itself, a shift of the Concept from its own ground to
that of sense, still the power of the thinking spirit lies in being able not only
to grasp itself in its proper form as thinking, but to know itself again just as
much when it has surrendered its proper form to feeling and sense, to
comprehend itself in its opposite, because it changes into thoughts what has
been estranged and so reverts to itself.
—G. W. F. Hegel, *Aesthetics*

A NYONE who tries seriously to understand the relationship between poetry and philosophy—being convinced that there *is* a
relationship and that the two must, in some sense or in some instances, coincide with or overlap each other—must sooner or later
face the objection that "poetry" and "philosophy" are the names of
two essentially different enterprises, which properly ought not to be
confused. Nothing used to be more common than to hear, from poets
and critics alike, that poetry is corrupted when it is forced to bear the
burden of a philosophical content or, as William Carlos Williams so
eloquently put it, when it is "enslaved, forced, raped, made a whore
by the idea venders."[1] Poetry, according to this view, is a way of doing
something with words, not a way of saying something important
about reality. The content of a poem—what it *says* about this, that, or
the other—must therefore never be obtrusive. When it is obtrusive,
one feels constrained by this view to argue either that the poem in
question is inferior as poetry or that its content is a mere smoke

screen ("a mere pretext," as Williams calls it[2]) for something else which is more intrinsically poetical. By the same token, it has been equally common in the past for philosophers to insist that there is a fundamental difference between the search for truth to which philosophy is committed and the pursuit of other goals such as the aesthetic goals of poetry. From Plato on, the complaint, when it has been made at all, has always been more or less the same: poetry, when it seeks to be more than a pleasing diversion, is mythmaking; and myth, however much it appeals to the imagination, is ultimately erroneous and misleading. From the very beginning, poets have attributed great importance to their activities by preferring them to the search for truth or, in some instances, by claiming for themselves a wisdom made possible through deep insight or visionary power, whereas, in fact, access to genuine wisdom is available only to those who are capable of critical thinking. Indeed, one way to characterize the history of Western culture would be to say that in the course of that history philosophy has sought to purify itself by divesting itself as much as possible of the trappings of poetry, while poetry, especially in recent times, has likewise sought to identify itself and even justify itself by becoming increasingly independent of philosophy.

Although there would certainly be a large grain of truth in such a characterization, in the sense that philosophers and poets often have felt themselves to be in opposition to each other, nevertheless it is equally certain that a rapprochement between poetry and philosophy was effected relatively early in the history of their mutual relations, that it has persisted and, indeed, continues to persist, despite attempts to undermine it. Formerly, the main condition of this rapprochement was that poetry should play the rather obvious role of junior partner, accepting the tasks assigned to it by philosophy. Now, however, this condition has changed. Poetry in the modern period has declared its independence, produced its own credentials, and in general given the impression of being quite autonomous, although, as I intend to argue, philosophy remains as vigorous as ever behind the scenes, covertly active in its original capacity as senior partner. The new rapprochement, in other words, depends on maintaining the impression, which seems to me to be false, that philosophy has retired altogether from the firm.

Let me try to sketch very briefly the history of these developments. Poetry, as everyone knows, came first, before what we now think of as philosophy had yet appeared. In Greece, Homer and Hesiod produced poems which, in part, serve a philosophical function in that they purport to give true knowledge of why things are as they are. By virtue of their inspiration, these two poets professed to show how history and nature constitute a revelation of the divine will. Even before Plato, however, their wisdom was opposed by the first philosophers, the Ionian cosmologists, so that Plato can speak in the *Republic* of "an ancient enmity," "an ancient quarrel between philosophy and poetry."[3] Interestingly enough, in the *Laws* Plato implies that the poets came closer to the truth than the philosophers did, since the philosophers mistakenly assigned the causes of all things to lifeless material substances. This, says Plato, "gave rise to much atheism and perplexity," so that "the poets took occasion to be abusive—comparing the philosophers to she-dogs uttering vain howlings."[4] But if the Ionians were wrong to deny the priority of mind or soul in the universe and so, to some extent, deserved the contempt hurled at them by the poets, the case, Plato says, is now reversed. It is the philosopher—the Platonic philosopher—who now emerges as "a true worshipper of the Gods" in contrast to the superstitious, ignorant poets. Not only do the poets fail to understand properly the things they describe or imitate in their verses; they cannot even understand the verses themselves, as Socrates learns when he asks some of them to explain to him the meaning of a few of the more elaborate passages in their own writings. Their inability to do so, as he reports in the *Apology*, leads him to conclude that they possess no wisdom. "Then I knew," he says, "that not by wisdom do poets write poetry, but by a sort of genius and inspiration; they are like diviners or soothsayers who also say many fine things, but do not understand the meaning of them."[5]

Plato's description of poetry as a sort of crude approximation of the genuine insight attainable by philosophy established the superiority of philosophy in such a way that philosophy's preeminence has never been seriously shaken, despite some appearances to the contrary. Hegel, for example, after two thousand years of post-Platonic philosophy, echoes the Platonic judgment when he observes that "for us art counts no longer as the highest mode in which truth fashions an existence for itself"[6]—the highest mode being, for Hegel as it was for Plato, the mode of philosophical reflection. And even Martin Heidegger, concerned as he is to outflank the tradition that leads to Hegel, admits that the truth of Hegel's judgment against art "has not yet been decided."[7] Nevertheless, we know that a rapprochement between philosophy and poetry *did* occur to the extent that poetry found it possible to accept a subordinate role in the relationship. Plato himself concedes that certain kinds of poetry can be useful in the life of reason; for example, hymns to the gods and praises of famous men may very well foster the piety and patriotism necessary to the security of an ideal state. It is Aristotle, however, who rescues poetry from the almost total banishment Plato intended for it, by suggesting that it has the power to represent or embody truths which are determined for it in advance by philosophy. Poetry may not be capable of determining the truth from scratch, so to speak, but it is capable of presenting for contemplation certain general truths having to do with human nature and behavior. In this respect, says Aristotle, poetry is "a more philosophical and a higher thing than history."[8] In other words, Aristotle conceives of poetry not as a groping towards truths inaccessible by other means, but rather as a vehicle for expressing truths which have already been grasped and appropriated, at least by the poets themselves. Poetry, for Aristotle, is the product not of inspired or hysterical soothsayers but of intelligent makers who know what they mean to say (and why), and who design their poems in accordance with that knowledge.

It is impossible, I think, to exaggerate the significance of this maneuver, for it constitutes a justification of poetry's claim to intellectual respectability which has remained valid until almost the present time. It permits us to regard the great poems of Western culture as a deliberate, conscious reflection in story and verse of ideas, attitudes, sentiments, and beliefs which are clearly derived from a previously established commitment to religion or philosophy. This is true not only of explicitly "philosophical" poems like *De rerum natura*, the *Divine Comedy*, *Paradise Lost*, or the *Essay on Man*, but also of works less explicitly or openly didactic, such as the *Canterbury Tales* or the plays of Shakespeare. There is a sense in which all this poetry is a kind of clarification or re-presentation of thoughts and feelings, or even whole

schemes of thought and feeling, which are familiar to us outside the
poetry and which the poetry exists to convey. As Sidney put it in his
*Apology for Poetry*, "Any understanding knoweth the skill of the ar-
tificer standeth in that idea or foreconceit of the work, and not in the
work itself."[9] Indeed, Sidney goes so far as to defend the very poets
Plato excoriates, on the ground that they themselves did not invent
the wrong opinions of the gods which Plato found outrageous, but
instead received them from "the very religion of that time." These
poets, says Sidney, "did not induce such opinions, but did imitate
those opinions already induced."[10] Finally, of course, Sidney gives a
higher place to poetry than to philosophy, but he does so only because it seems to him that poetry communicates more effectively than
philosophical treatises what philosophy itself has to teach us. As "the
right popular philosopher," the poet, according to Sidney, "yieldeth to
the powers of the mind an image of that whereof the philosopher be-
stoweth but a wordish decription: which doth neither strike, pierce,
nor possess the sight of the soul so much as that other doth."[11]

This conception of poetry as a sort of splendid vehicle for conceptions which originate elsewhere in belief-systems or thought-systems
of one kind or another is, of course, a conception that has been under
attack now for about two hundred years. In the period running from
Blake and Wordsworth to the present day, something like a poetic reformation has been under way whose principal aim is to liberate the
Muse from her Babylonian captivity to philosophy. We can see this
reformation at work, for instance, in Blake's angry reaction against the
dominant empirical philosophy of Bacon and Locke, against the enlightened skepticisms of Voltaire and Rousseau in religious matters,
and against Newton's physical theories of nature. Indeed, much of the
time Blake sounds exactly like those "abusive" poets Plato speaks of
who dared to compare the materialist philosophers of their own time
to "she-dogs uttering vain howlings." Blake does essentially the same
thing, because he believes the prevailing philosophy of his day to be
wrong-headed and atheistical. Moreover, since he also believes that
the genuine truth of the Bible has been radically misrepresented by
Christian institutions and Christian theology, he feels obliged to
create his own system based entirely on the strength of his own autonomous imagination, instead of on the symbolism handed down by

tradition. In this respect, Blake is hardly more radical than Wordsworth. It is Wordsworth, after all, who claims to find in his own mind, within his own experience, and without the benefit of any mythology, the substance of the highest, most epical, most philosophical poetry. It is Wordsworth who claims access, in "life's every-day appearances," to "worlds / To which the heaven of heavens is but a veil." This is still, I think, the most extraordinary claim in the whole of modern poetry, that we can have it all—"Paradise, and groves / Elysian, Fortunate Fields"—as the fruit of our daily intercourse with real things expressed in "words / Which speak of nothing more than what we are" (Preface to *The Excursion*). Poetry *can* start from scratch, in other words; poets *can* arrive at the profoundest truths, not by accepting conclusions already propounded but by ransacking the materials of their own personal experience. Hence, Wordsworth's observation that "One impulse from a vernal wood / May teach you more of man, / Of moral evil and of good, / Than all the sages can" ("The Tables Turned"). Properly understood, this is not nature-worship but self-reliance; it is a declaration of intellectual independence, of intellectual self-sufficiency.

The Romantic poets, by and large, refuse to go to philosophy (unless it be on their own terms) because they think they can get everything they need at home. Passionate experience is what they seek rather than the preestablished truths to be found in books. Very quickly, in fact, passionate experience becomes an end in itself, not just the means by which to acquire true ideas. The ultimate goal is not to arrive at correct theories about Paradise and groves Elysian and Fortunate Fields but to experience these things in the things around us and, further, to experience this experience itself by writing about it. The production of poetry wherein one can endlessly experience and reexperience one's experiences becomes the highest thing of all. In such poetry we find presented, not re-presented, the self (the mind as "lord and master," to use Wordsworth's phrase) constructing itself objectively to itself; we find self-thinking thought. After that, who needs philosophy? After that, philosophy itself would be mean descent.

It seems to me that we are still not finished working through the implications of this reversal of what I have called Aristotle's maneuver.

And it makes little difference whether we are considering the art-for-art's-sake or "pure poetry" school at one end of the spectrum or the "mythmaking" school at the other end. Poets who cultivate the aesthetic experience as an alternative to what they regard as the vulgar pursuit of truth are as much affected by the Romantic reversal as the seemingly quite different poets who cultivate poetry because they see it as the absolutely indispensable means to truth. Both groups have largely abandoned the didactic procedures and intentions formerly associated with conventional narrative and argument, and they have done so for the simple reason that these procedures and intentions now seem incompatible with the essence of poetry. Poetry must be permitted to develop according to its own laws, whether it comes to you, as Pater says, "proposing frankly to give nothing but the highest quality to your moments as they pass, and simply for those moments' sake," [12] or whether it comes proposing to offer "a way of controlling, of ordering, of giving a shape and a significance to the immense panorama of futility and anarchy which is contemporary history." [13] The claims for poetry in our own day, whether they be pitched as high as possible or as low as possible, whether they be based on the assumption that poetry can completely absorb the whole enterprise of philosophy within itself or on the assumption that it can completely expel philosophy from itself as an altogether alien enterprise, have this much in common: the belief that poetry cannot exist in a subordinate relation *with* philosophy without betraying its own essential nature.

I would like to suggest that this belief is wrong, or rather, I would like to suggest that it is simply untrue to say that modern poetry has succeeded either in absorbing philosophy into itself or in expelling philosophy out of itself. In spite of the pervasive illusion that it has gained its independence, poetry remains subordinate to philosophy. I do not mean, of course, that most poets spend their time giving overt expositions or transparent allegories of the philosophical ideas they find most attractive. I mean that the kind of poetry poets now produce almost invariably seems to originate from, or to have its raison d'être in, philosophical considerations which make certain kinds of poetic activity appear to be especially desirable or even vitally necessary. Virtually every modern poet is full of theories—theories about language, theories about history and society, theories about consciousness and perception, indeed, theories about all sorts of things. Fortunately for the bewildered student, these theories are almost always expressed in essays and letters, in notebook jottings and other writings, which, however obscure and unsystematic, serve as an indispensable vade mecum for the reader who is seriously trying to understand modern poetry. Simultaneously, these same theories assume an implicit form in the shape of actual poems. Thus, if a poet holds a certain view concerning the nature of experience or of language, that view is likely to dictate both the matter and the manner of his or her poems. Particularly with respect to modernist poetry and a good deal of post-modernist poetry as well, if one encounters an especially odd manner or method of organization, one can be sure that one is looking at the poetic corollary of a theory.

Interestingly, one of the most pervasive theories governing modern poetry is the theory that poetic language is somehow deeper or purer or more original than other kinds of language. Philosophy, because of its discursiveness and because of the abstractness of its conceptions, can thus be denied direct expression in poetry, which paradoxically excludes it on principle, that is to say, as a result of philosophical consideration. Such poetry—imagist poetry, for example, or objectivist poetry—supersedes or transcends philosophy, but only at the behest of philosophy and with the license of philosophy, which grants it the illusion of autonomy. The best description I know of how the new relation between poetry and philosophy was implemented by the symbolist poets is given by Paul Valéry in the following passage, which may be taken as applicable not only to the generation just preceding Valéry's own but also to that of the modernists themselves.

> It was a time of theories, curiosities, commentaries, and passionate explanations. A young and somewhat stern generation rejected the scientific dogma which was beginning to be unfashionable, without adopting the religious dogma which was not yet so. In the profound and scrupulous worship of the arts as a whole, it thought it had found an unequivocal discipline or even a truth. A sort of religion was very nearly established. . . . But the works of that period did not themselves positively disclose these preoccupations. Quite to the contrary, one must note carefully what they prohibit and what ceased to appear in poems during the time of which I am speaking. It would seem that abstract

thought, formerly admitted even into verse, having now become almost impossible to combine with the immediate emotions that it was desired continually to arouse, being banished from a poetry that was endeavoring to reduce itself to its own essence, and dismayed by the multiple effects of surprise and of music demanded by modern taste, had betaken itself to the preparatory phase and to the theory of poetry. Philosophy, and even ethics, tended to shun the actual works and take their place among the reflections preceding them. This was a very real *progress*.[14]

The kind of "progress" Valéry is describing here is quite explicitly recommended by a modern poet I have already mentioned, one who would seem to be very different temperamentally from Valéry and the symbolists, namely, William Carlos Williams. With characteristic bluntness, Williams advises, in a letter to the editor of the magazine *View*: "Brilliant articles cry out to be written. Why bother? No one would read them. The thing is, make the things that such world shaking deductions would imply and OMIT the deductions."[15] Or, as Williams once remarked to his friend and publisher James Laughlin, poetry gains immensely by having thought taken out of it and made instead into "the spring-board for what the setup it indicates induces objectively in things." In other words, he says, "if you think this way, then it should induce you to see a hog or a wife or a fifty cent piece *that* way—whatever that way would be. That would be poetic creation."[16] Which means, of course, that, if we reverse the procedure, we can take poems about hogs or wives or fifty-cent pieces and work backward until we reach the thought that has served as the "springboard." This is precisely what contemporary critics have learned to do with increasing skillfulness. Even the most refractory poetry can be made to yield up its springboard of thought if the critic will steadfastly pursue the question "Why has *this* poet chosen to use language like *this?*" A proper answer leads straight to the heart of the poet's philosophy. Thus the style of a good deal of modern poetry is seen to be not only that which conceals but also that which reveals the thought that governs the character of this poetry. Moreover, further reflection seems to suggest that, if philosophy is in a certain sense the beginning of this poetry, it is also the end of it, since the transaction that occurs between the poem and the reader is not over until the poem has been translated, as it were, back into its philosophical presuppositions. Indeed, a truly postmodern criticism can be said to have begun with the discovery that the work itself is perhaps a terminus for the poet who produced it, but not at all for the reader whose task it is to appropriate the work. This task (which may be evaded or rejected for a number of reasons, some of them philosophical) is a philosophical task by its very nature, and it invariably serves to illustrate that philosophy remains the senior partner in its relationship with poetry.

This leads me to the final point I wish to make. One of the respects in which modern poetry is most philosophical is its apparent (but only apparent) repudiation of, or superseding of, philosophy. Nothing could be more in keeping with the spirit of modern philosophy itself. Over the last hundred years or so, the most philosophically interesting development in both poetry and philosophy may very well have been the growing suspicion on both sides that philosophy in the traditional manner is no longer possible, that philosophy is finished, played out. If metaphysics is defunct, if the science of knowledge is really no science at all, if ultimate truths are ultimately elusive (or illusive), then perhaps poetry can show us the way by providing what we need to get by in such a situation. On the throne left vacant by the willing abdication of philosophy, poetry comes to sit with its momentary stays against confusion, its acts of finding what will suffice, its supreme fictions. This is not a situation philosophers generally deplore; it is one they approve of. It is, so to speak, philosophically sanctioned.

There is neither the space here nor the need to rehearse the various self-immolations philosophers have engaged in since Hegel. It is enough perhaps to remember that while Wittgenstein regarded with thinly disguised condescension the prospect of G. E. Moore standing in the garden and saying to himself, with philosophical tenacity, "I know that's a tree," he was profoundly impressed by the seemingly antiphilosophical implications of Piero Sraffa expressing Neapolitan revulsion by ever so concretely and, as it were, illogically "brushing the underneath of his chin with an outward sweep of the finger-tips of one hand." [17] In their eagerness to declare philosophy's bankruptcy, philosophers from Nietzsche to Richard Rorty have made explicit the philosophic grounds, the philosophic justification, of what they take to be poetry's cultural ascendancy. And the latest trick is to pretend that philosophy itself lacks the ability to account for this odd paradox. It is a new version of the old modernist doctrine that poetic uses of language are superior to other uses. As Rorty says in his essay "Nineteenth-Century Idealism and Twentieth-Century Textualism":

> The *weakest* way to defend the plausible claim that literature has now displaced religion, science, and philosophy as the presiding discipline of our culture is by looking for a philosophical foundation for the practices of contemporary criticism. That would be like defending Galilean science by claiming that it can be found in the scriptures, or defending transcendental idealism as the latest result of physiological research. It would be acknowledging the authority of a deposed monarch in order to buttress the claims of a usurper. The claims of a usurping discipline to preside over the rest of culture can only be defended by an exhibition of its ability to put the other disciplines in their places.[18]

In other words, instead of trying to demonstrate that literature or poetry, as I have been calling it, is better or truer or more powerful or more successful than the old-fashioned demonstrative techniques collectively known as philosophy (a demonstration which would, of course, be self-contradictory), the shrewd critic will permit his or her criticism to become an exhibition of techniques associated with literature. Criticism, which used to be philosophically rigorous after a fashion, must now, in order to be as powerful as possible, become poetically playful. Instead of accounting for poetry's ascendancy, we can exhibit its ascendancy by giving it free rein in our own critical practices.

In another essay, Rorty argues that this is precisely the significance of Derrida's contribution: it is not that Derrida has discovered the truth about texts (for example, that they are irreducibly poetical in their richness or complexity of meaning) but that he has learned how to play around poetically with the texts he chooses to "interpret." Thus, according to Rorty:

> Derrida regards the need to overcome "the book"—the notion of a piece of writing as aimed at accurate treatment of a subject, conveying a message which (in more fortunate circumstances) might have been conveyed

by ostensive definition or by injecting knowledge straight into the brain—as justifying his use of any text to interpret any other text. The most shocking thing about his work—even more shocking than, though not as funny as, his sexual interpretations of the history of philosophy—is his use of multilingual puns, joke etymologies, allusions from anywhere to anywhere, and phonic and typographical gimmicks. It is as if he really thought that the fact that, for example, the French pronunciation of "Hegel" sounds like the French word for "eagle" was supposed to be relevant for comprehending Hegel. But Derrida does not want to comprehend Hegel's books; he wants to play with Hegel. He doesn't want to write a book about the nature of language; he wants to play with the texts which other people have thought they were writing about language.[19]

I myself will try to resist the temptation to go round and round in a circle by not arguing, as I would like to argue, that this is a preference shared by a growing number of critics, which has philosophical motives as well as philosophical implications. I will merely suggest that it is a preference which has already been comprehended and thus circumscribed by the philosophy of Hegel, wherein it is identified as the characteristic preference of what Hegel calls "the romantic artist." Particularly in the last stages of his development, this "artist," according to Hegel, abandons all belief in the objective validity of that which presents itself to him and adopts an ironical stance towards the world according to which the creative and destructive power of his own ego alone has absolute validity. Although Hegel sees in this stance an affinity with the idealism of Fichte,[20] it might also be argued that his description of "the romantic artist" applies to poets like Pound and Williams, to critics like Bloom and Barthes, and to such recent post-philosophers as Derrida and perhaps even Rorty. Thus, when Hegel speaks in the following passage of art and artists, it is both plausible and tempting to think of "philosophy" and "philosophers" or "criticism" and "critics" as appropriate contemporary synonyms.

Bondage to a particular subject-matter and a mode of portrayal suitable for this material alone are for artists today something past, and art therefore has become a free instrument which the artist can wield in proportion to his subjective skill in relation to any material of whatever kind. The artist thus stands above specific consecrated forms and configurations and moves freely on his own account, independent of the subject-matter and mode of conception in which the holy and eternal was previously made visible to human apprehension. . . . The great artist today needs in particular the free development of the spirit; in that development all superstition, and all faith which remains restricted to determinate forms of vision and presentation, is degraded into mere aspects and features. These the free spirit has mastered because he sees in them no absolutely sacrosanct conditions for his exposition and mode of configuration, but ascribes value to them only on the strength of the higher content which in the course of re-creation he puts into them as adequate to them.[21]

It is from the point of view of "the romantic artist," then, that red wheelbarrows or the broken bits of a green bottle can assume a tremendous importance while the whole of Western metaphysics can be dismantled by joke etymologies and multilingual puns. That this point of view is now dominant in many circles would seem to indicate that poetry has indeed carried the day. That it can be recognized as such and even appreciated for what it is must be seen, however, as a tribute to the persisting power of philosophy.

## NOTES

1. William Carlos Williams, "The Simplicity of Disorder," in *Selected Essays of William Carlos Williams* (New York: New Directions, 1969), p. 96.

2. See Williams' letter (June 25, 1919) to Alva N. Turner in *The Selected Letters of William Carlos Williams*, ed. John C. Thirlwall (New York: McDowell, Obolensky, 1957), p. 44.

3. *The Dialogues of Plato*, trans. B. Jowett (New York: Random House, 1937), vol. 1, p. 607 (607b).

4. Ibid., vol. 2, p. 701 (967c).

5. Ibid., vol. 1, p. 405 (22bc).

6. G. W. F. Hegel, *Aesthetics: Lectures on Fine Art*, trans. T. M. Knox (Oxford: Oxford University Press, 1975), vol. 1, p. 103.

7. Martin Heidegger, "The Origin of the Work of Art," in *Poetry, Language, Thought*, trans. Albert Hofstadter (New York: Harper & Row, 1975), p. 80.

8. Aristotle, *The Poetics*, trans. S. H. Butcher, in *Aristotle's Theory of Poetry and Fine Art* (New York: Dover Publications, 1951), p. 35.

9. In *Criticism: The Major Texts*, ed. Walter Jackson Bate (New York, Harcourt, Brace, 1952), p. 85.

10. Ibid., p. 100.

11. Ibid., p. 89.

12. Walter Pater, "Conclusion," in *The Renaissance: Studies in Art and Poetry* (New York: New American Library, 1959), p. 159.

13. T. S. Eliot, "*Ulysses*, Order, and Myth," in *Selected Prose of T. S. Eliot*, ed. Frank Kermode (New York: Harcourt, Brace, 1975), p. 177.

14. Paul Valéry, "A Foreword," in *The Art of Poetry*, trans. Denise Folliot (New York: Vintage Books, 1961), pp. 43–44.

15. Letter to Charles Henri Ford entitled "Surrealism and the Moment," *View* 2 (May 1942): [19].

16. Letter to James Laughlin (Sept. 18, 1942), *The Literary Review* 1 (Autumn 1957): 16.

17. For Wittgenstein's reaction to G. E. Moore's quest for sure foundations, see Ludwig Wittgenstein, *On Certainty*, ed. G. E. M. Anscombe and G. H. von Wright, trans. Denis Paul and G. E. M. Anscombe (New York: J. & J. Harper, 1969), *passim*. For the anecdote concerning Sraffa, see Norman Malcolm, *Ludwig Wittgenstein: A Memoir* (Oxford: Oxford University Press, 1962), p. 69.

18. Richard Rorty, *Consequences of Pragmatism (Essays: 1972–1980)* (Minneapolis: University of Minnesota Press, 1982), p. 155.

19. Richard Rorty, "Philosophy as a Kind of Writing: An Essay on Derrida," in Rorty, *Consequences of Pragmatism*, p. 96.

20. See Hegel's discussion of "the closer connection of Fichte's propositions with one tendency of [romantic] irony" (*Aesthetics*, vol. 1, pp. 64–69), according to which

> the *ego* can remain lord and master of everything, and in no sphere of morals, law, things human and divine, profane and sacred, is there anything that would not first have to be laid down by the *ego*, and that therefore could not equally well be destroyed by it. Consequently everything genuinely and independently real becomes only a show, not true and genuine on its own account or through itself, but a mere appearance due to the *ego* in whose power and caprice and at whose free disposal it remains. To admit or cancel it depends wholly on the pleasure of the *ego*, already absolute in itself simply as *ego* (64–65).

Here is one explanation, at least, of the currently fashionable free play with texts which exhibits what Derrida calls, in "Structure, Sign, and Play," "the joyous affirmation of the play of the world and of the innocence of becoming, the affirmation of a world of signs without fault, without truth, and without origin which is offered to an active interpretation" (*Writing and Difference*, trans. Alan Bass [Chicago: University of Chicago Press, 1978], p. 292).

21. Hegel, *Aesthetics*, vol. 1, pp. 605–6.

*Suresh Raval*

# Philosophy and the Crisis of Contemporary Literary Theory

THERE IS currently great anxiety among literary critics and theorists about literary criticism's loss of identity, both as an identifiable, coherent discipline with a recognizable set of problems and as a body of authoritative and well-founded convictions about literature and its history. Part of the reason for this anxiety is that everything that was until recently considered relatively unproblematical has now been rendered problematical. The hermeneutic of suspicion emerges as an interpretative strategy, pitting itself against the hermeneutic of belief; radical indeterminacy of meanings challenges the certainty of traditional epistemology which authorized the objectivity of meaning, text, and context; and the whole of the Western metaphysical tradition is "inscribed" in any piece of writing which undermines the traditional notions of canon-formation, evaluation, and responsible criticism. Traditional literary theory assumes literary works to be structures of determinate meaning accessible by objective critical procedures.[1] This assumption, and along with it a number of critical practices, are challenged by the contemporary interest in the indeterminacy of meaning. In deconstruction, the thesis of indeterminacy takes its most radical and thoroughgoing form, so that all modernist critical stances from New Criticism to phenomenological, psychoanalytical, structuralist, Marxist, and reader-response criticisms are put into question.[2] This renders the scene of contemporary criticism and its theory highly volatile, since every theoretical claim or critical practice has become vulnerable to the deconstructive critique, even if this critique itself requires some form of certainty to question any critical theory or practice.

The trajectory of structuralism from its inaugurating premises to its later attempts at historicizing its concepts captures dramatically the crisis of contemporary literary theory, indeed of all those projects in the human sciences inspired by structuralism's reflections on language, mind, and society.[3] Structuralism's original ambition to articulate universal conditions of meaning and of the permanent, invariant properties of language had to be abandoned in favor of a deeper grasp of meanings as conventions anchored in history and of the changing nature of conventions themselves.[4] This was structuralism's historicist insight that it was itself a product of history and therefore could not hope to acquire an Archimedean leverage in order to provide a universal, ahistorical, and neutral matrix or grid in terms of which to render everything intelligible once and for all. This has not prevented at least some structuralists from seeking to formulate a general theory of the ways in which conventions undergo change.[5] This project returns structuralism to its universalist ambitions, though it also falls prey to a more radical critique which culminates in post-structuralism. Gadamer's hermeneutic, too, in many ways a theory free from the limitations of structuralism, faces problems which it cannot resolve at the level of its own general reflection about the linguisticality and historicity of understanding.[6] The proliferation of literary interpretations has led Jonathan Culler to separate primarily interpretative activity from a study of literature which would go beyond interpretation.[7] Geoffrey Hartman, shortly after worrying over whether our age would be able to "save the concept of art,"[8] embraced the position that at first had prompted this worry—a position which first blurs and then eliminates the boundary between literature and criticism. This position would have outraged Hartman in his earlier stance, since this altered conception of criticism would make the idea of appreciating Milton's or Shakespeare's art strangely antiquarian. For his later stance the critic, on the occasion of reading *Paradise Lost* or *Hamlet*, becomes the creator of the work.

Hartman means to underline the importance of our historical moment when the reader has sought to take back the authority traditionally vested in the work of art.[9] The logical point, however, of the reader's critical authority, in at least some versions of this theory, amounts to his capacity for praising his own self for making works of art appear and disappear, a gift dramatized with great rhetorical resourcefulness by Stanley Fish. Since the narcissism of this stance becomes embarrassing when it is indulged in public, one makes a tactical retreat by praising the whole community of readers who are collectively able to bestow praise on their own creative powers.[10] The community, on this view, not only creates, say, *Paradise Lost*, but holds the credentials for legitimizing its sense of its artistic creations. Hartman, of course, wants to celebrate the indeterminacy of meaning as articulated by Derrida, but he also wants to endorse the Konstanz School of *Rezeptionsaesthetik*, which is in part a theory of the history of reader-responses.[11] Hartman's stance involves a fatal self-contradiction, for the commitment to radical indeterminacy makes impossible any conception of the history of reader-response. Such a history must postulate both the possibility of determinate meaning and at least a relatively objective analytical apparatus to make that meaning available to posterity.

Such a contradiction makes this stance, along with other related stances in contemporary literary theory, suspect in the eyes of those who believe that without the distinction between literature and criticism, neither the concept of art nor that of criticism can be saved. Without pausing to worry over whether there is a way out of this difficulty, and if there is, whether it would make various versions of radical theories intelligible, I should like to stress the importance of the insufficiently explored notion that criticism is an institutional activity.[12] The institutional nature of criticism is a mixed blessing, since what is unfortunate, ill-conceived, preposterous, or downright silly in the institution cannot be easily eliminated without sometimes endangering what sustains the power and interest of criticism itself. One is reduced to hoping, piously, that those who contribute to shaping the institution of criticism will have a capacity for the kind of self-criticism which requires the skeptical examination of one's own grounds. For if we can plausibly argue that the institution of criticism is inevitably embroiled in academic as well as real politics, such politics would be as often as not self-serving, self-aggrandizing, and potentially or actually harmful to those whose pursuit of criticism and its theory, however morally intense, may be more scrupulous.

The fanaticism with which some forms of contemporary literary theory project a sense of crisis betrays a desperate situation; these theories seek to impart a sense of danger, and argue that there is just one choice: either to be orthodox and objectivist, condemned to a powerless rationality, or to self-consciously embrace unreason and chaos as the very principles of vital response to art and cultural thought. Much contemporary criticism that flaunts its radical nature makes the latter choice, and considers its choice necessary because of the desperate nature of the interpretative situation. Thus if traditional epistemology took reason as the basis of all intelligent thought, radical theory takes unreason or negative reasoning as the strategy by which to deprive criticism of its self-confidence. Thus the hermeneutic of indeterminacy, when it is completely radicalized, results in what Hayden White has aptly called the "absurdist moment" in contemporary criticism.[13] There is no reason, however, to accept traditional epistemology and epistemological skepticism—and their corollaries in criticism, objectivism and radical indeterminacy—as genuine and unavoidable alternatives. The hermeneutic of indeterminacy is, in its moderate version, quite compelling, since it would abandon the ideal of absolute objectivity of meaning across historical periods, while granting determinacy within specific historical contexts.

The conflict between deconstruction and other modernist literary theories can be seen to center on the question of meaning as discussed in various forms of contemporary philosophy. Deconstruction questions all rival theories because of their conviction that there are particular determinate meanings in terms of which to interpret literary works. Gadamer's historicist thinking, however, shows a way out of what has surely become an orthodox philosophical opposition between the determinacy and indeterminacy of meanings. By characterizing meanings as historical, contingent, and therefore changing, Gadamer shows literary meanings as products of a complex cultural transaction within interacting historical horizons.[14] Consequently, if literary meaning is not determinate in the sense of being available to a presumed objective critical reader, it is not indeterminate either, since the act of criticism allows for and indeed requires a projection of meaning through the process of dialogue the critic engages with a literary text. Hartman could of course adopt Gadamer's resolution of the problem of meaning, but that would require a substantive shift from his Derridean observations about meaning and interpretation. For Gadamer, particular literary meanings are dispensable in the sense that they cannot be binding on critics in another era employing a more or less radically different conceptual and analytical apparatus.

We need to see, nevertheless, how and why the interest in determinate meaning arose and continues to hold sway over all kinds of theorizing in the humanities. The idea that with sufficient ingenuity and care we could discover, and state clearly, the essential nature of literature and the legitimate function of criticism, arose in a complicated historical context in the late seventeenth century in England and became dominant in the eighteenth century. The idea that we can specify once and for all the framework for interpreting literary works is a corollary of the notions of literature and criticism developed in the eighteenth century. These notions are, at least in part, the products of the new conceptions of science and philosophy which emerged in the late seventeenth century. The notion of what it was to be scientific was in the process of emerging in the seventeenth century, and it was closely connected to the new notion of what it was to be a "philosopher." As Ian Hacking and Richard Rorty have in different ways explained, there occurred during this period a shift from metaphysics to epistemology.[15] The insistence on precision, clarity, probability, and naturalness in science and philosophy began to influence debates in criticism. If in the sixteenth century poets and critics like Sidney had to deal with attacks on poetry for its inferior status to logic and religion, in the mid- and late seventeenth century poets and critics had to face the question of whether poetry could deal with truth at all. While some of these attacks were no doubt deeply antagonistic to poetry, the more important criticism was leveled against the rhetoric and poetics of literary art, and the consequence of this criticism was a certain fundamental reform in both poetry and poetics, best exemplified in the works of Dryden, Addison, and Pope. Increasingly, the concern with matters of fact and reliable testimony, initially characteristic of discussions in religion, spread to science and philosophy, and thence to history, literature, and criticism. From Abraham Cowley, John Dryden,

John Locke, and Addison, we have a fairly sustained demand for a mode of expression purged of the rhetorical excesses and elaborate stylistic devices of Donne, Andrews, and Milton. Among the emerging new genres of writing, fiction began to present itself as fact, as feigned history, because of the new interest in history-writing concerned with the presentation of factual truth and accurate reporting. The three new genres of writing which became dominant in eighteenth-century England were travel narratives, newspapers, and the novel. These took their impetus from Lockean epistemology, self-consciously rejecting romance as a form of literary writing.[16]

These scientific and philosophic ideas were, of course, challenged by both romantic poetry and poetics, but they by no means went underground. They have in fact continued to develop in the form of historical and biographical criticism. Such criticism has, from the nineteenth century to the present day, sought to interpret literary works either in terms of their writers' historical contexts or biographies. The use of psychoanalysis for historical and biographical scholarship has as often as not deepened practitioners' confidence in their methods of research and analysis, while opening up a dimension of life previously closed to them. E. D. Hirsch has defended a conception of objective interpretation by arguing that the meaning of a work is identical with what the author meant by it, though he tries to escape the difficulties involved in this theory by developing a notion of the "intrinsic genre" of the work. The intrinsic genre is essentially the conventions of writing and interpreting which govern the author's meanings at the time of his or her writing, and is thus a theory of historical context as the arbiter of legitimate objective interpretation.[17] In the works of the best New Critical theorists, William K. Wimsatt and Monroe C. Beardsley, we have an anti-intentionalist theory of interpretation which construes poems on the analogy of physical objects. The conception of objectivity underlying their theory contrasts radically with that underlying Hirsch's theory, though the latter allows that a reader is free to interpret a literary work in terms of a normative structure completely different from that available to scrupulous historical investigation. For Hirsch, then, the historical context structures the dimension of meaning in a literary work, whereas for Wimsatt and Beardsley the work frees itself, at its very inception, from

both its author and its historical context. However different these theories are from neoclassical theory, the epistemology underlying all of
them is essentially Lockean, especially in their concern with objective
meaning.

The conception of objectivity underlying traditional historical criticism, New Criticism (at least in its theoretical claims), and Hirsch's
hermeneutic theory cannot withstand the critiques leveled against it
from a variety of perspectives. Gadamer's characterization of the historicity of all understanding and interpretation radically questions
any transhistorical notion of objectivity. Modern philosophy of science, as developed in somewhat different versions by Thomas Kuhn
and Paul Feyerabend among others, acknowledges both theory and
history as among the important constitutive elements of scientific inquiry. The point of these critiques is that there is no permanent, neutral conceptual or disciplinary matrix within which criticism must
elaborate its various practices and theories, that critics and theorists
cannot provide a final theoretical structure in terms of which to define
the nature and function of both literature and criticism. A recognition
of these insights will make it easier for critics and theorists to engage
in dialogue and conflict over what constitutes interesting and relevant
new problems in our current cultural context (however it may be defined), and to write critical narratives that dramatize literature's vi-
tality and usefulness in our cultural life.

The conflict among contemporary literary theories, on the one
hand, and between modernist and traditional theories, on the other,
is, in the final reckoning, a conflict over preference for one vocabulary
over another. This does not make the conflict merely terminological or
verbal and therefore superficial and empty, for one's preference will
inevitably involve profound conceptual, aesthetic, and attitudinal
issues in one's critical practice. It is simply to say that neither side rests
on something stronger than felt intuitions or insights. Traditional literary theory tries to legitimize a vocabulary and a host of concepts
which have become shopworn and need considerable rethinking and
refinement if they are to make themselves available to an altered dialectical context. Even so, its notions of objectivity, determinate meaning, and critical practice are positivist and are founded on a concept
of scientific inquiry dictated by objectivist philosophy rather than by

an effective grasp of scientific practice. Some theorists worry that the rejection of the positivist conceptions of meaning and objectivity would result not only in the neglect of criticism's history, of the particular attitudes and insights that have informed the works of thinkers as diverse as Plato, Aristotle, Sidney, Johnson, Coleridge, Schiller, Valéry, and T. S. Eliot, but also in the attitude that traditional critical practice, in all its forms, is irretrievably false because it belongs to the past. I am making, however, the historicizing point that you will not understand the romantics, the neoclassicists, or the medieval writers unless you also understand what it is that obsessed them as writers and why they were obsessed by it. We need to explore these questions because modern literary critics and theorists as well as artists are free, as René Wellek has said, to "reach into the remotest history" and exploit the resources of form, technique, and thought.[18] (In philosophy, Nietzsche's and Heidegger's interest in the pre-Socratics is a comparable case.)

Our interest in writers' obsessions and in the reasons for these obsessions is not meant to reestablish traditional criticism and its theories, though it is likely to enable us to grasp the ways in which various versions of foundationalist philosophy influenced, more or less directly, the theories and practices of traditional criticism. The historicizing interest can help us to acquire a better grasp not just of the past but of the present, by showing how traditional insights, often in fragmented forms, continue to help and sometimes hinder our current practices. And it can enable us to articulate the context in which we can keep fragments of traditional criticism's insights and rethink them. For the whole of what traditional criticism did could be abandoned only if one held the self-defeating view that one could continue to use the language we use without the encrustations of meanings our literary and philosophical past has built into it. This may even help us to question the past, and hence the present, in a way with which we are not yet familiar. For while we have learned to talk about the need for historicizing questions of cultural inquiry, we do not quite know what this historicizing practice would be (except whatever it is that we do in our critical practice), nor how to carry it out consistently on a host of problems in criticism. To say this is to admit that while the received forms of theory and practice could be questioned on many specific grounds, not all of them could be put in jeopardy without making us completely incoherent and unintelligible. Such an admission may take the wind out of those who always strive for strident, thrilling rhetoric, but it will in fact make the possibilities for more serious thinking more genuinely exciting.

The course of literary and critical history, then, is a course shaped, altered, and complicated by many forces in cultural traditions as well as in the social-historical-political arenas of a given society. It is in such a difficult context of interacting forces that new and sometimes better theories and practices of criticism emerge. These will be *new* in that they will try to play literary theories and practices against each other, generating at times very productive and fruitful vocabularies and thus provisional, historically determined concepts. But they will *not* be better in the sense that they fulfill some previously known standard or criterion which all previously known practices and theories failed to meet. They will be better in the rather pragmatist, historicist sense that they appear to be better than their predecessors, that they minister to the needs and demands we have come to feel are urgent in our altered context. Whether they do indeed minister to our currently urgent needs and demands is, however, a question that cannot be decided in advance, without further debate; and that question, too, will be complicated by further questions about what constitutes our current cultural context, what our currently urgent needs are, and what would constitute an intelligent response in the absence of a general consensus on solutions to these questions. Whether we want to assert certain literary propositions, or tell ourselves certain narratives about literature and criticism, or develop certain commentaries to tell ourselves and others what is important to us—these things make up our ways of dealing with what we consider worth exploring or saying. That some of our narratives or commentaries are, or are found by our contemporaries or by a later generation of critics to be, silly or impoverishing is something we must live with. It is because we will eventually live with our own ways of doing things that we must be critical of even our most cherished theories.

It was Hegel who first taught philosophers and cultural theorists alike how to historicize philosophical and cultural problems. He established, however, a simple parallel between history and philosophy, one in which history concretized the systematic form of his own philosophy. For Hegel the failure of systematic philosophy would have meant that history itself had failed. Hegel, in other words, could not have entertained the idea that philosophy and history did not exist in some form of systematic accord or a preestablished harmony, that systematic philosophy itself was the product of a conception of logic which decided in advance the kind of relation philosophy would have to the world or history. There are, of course, numerous ways in which philosophy becomes abstracted and alienated from the world it hopes to make intelligible, and systematic philosophy, like positivism, is one way in which the world and history are streamlined and removed from the threat that the contingencies of history present to all systematic thought. Critical philosophy is, as it were, abolished by the completion of Hegelian thought.

Similarly, positivism drains philosophy of its critical function. The consequence of both positivism and the Enlightenment is the loss of subjectivism, since both declare, at different levels of intention, that essences neither exist nor matter, that appearance coincides with reality. Wittgenstein, in *Tractatus Logico-Philosophicus*, claimed to have brought philosophy to its end. The later Wittgenstein, however, came to recognize that the task of philosophy is endless, that it never reaches finality, except in systematic thought whose finality only masks its own exhaustion. Wittgenstein does not mean, of course, to revive philosophy's traditional quest for ultimate foundations, but shows rather the ways in which this quest engenders its problems. As Richard Rorty has argued in a number of essays, Wittgenstein's later philosophy, the work of Heidegger, Gadamer, Foucault, and Derrida, Dewey's pragmatism, the work in the philosophy of science by Thomas Kuhn and others, and the implications of the work of W. V. O. Quine and Wilfrid Sellars lead us away from philosophy's Cartesian as well as Kantian interest in providing a permanent, neutral, and unambiguous grid for making and validating knowledge-claims.[19] All of these thinkers force us to consider the features that attend various forms of cultural practices, and they show us the ways in which these practices are grounded in the shifting contexts of a discipline's history. Contemporary historiographical explorations, especially by Hayden White and Quentin Skinner, also contribute to a shift in intellectual history, from epistemology to rhetoric and hermeneutics, thus deepening the interest in the poetics of various cultural disciplines.

This altered self-image of philosophy and cultural history has, for those of us who find it compelling, important consequences for criticism and its theory. For we come to see that theoretical certainties will not provide foundations for criticism, just as epistemological skepticism itself will not undermine what foundations the activity of criticism may possess or require. Epistemological skepticism will at best show either that we must learn to do without epistemology or that what epistemology we do need does not require the foundationalist assumptions that sustained traditional epistemology. I think literary criticism and its theory will benefit more from the second alternative. This alternative is in fact compatible with what appears to be the first alternative, which is essentially a rejection of traditional epistemology. Criticism's foundations, then, must be seen as historically shifting, and in a complex age such as ours they must be seen as comprising a number of disjunctive practices which, though they may occasionally intersect and overlap, are often enough juxtaposed against each other, or are simply separate. The rejection of foundationalism for the theory and practice of criticism means only that we are no longer in the sway of skeptical worries, but it is not a rejection of theory as such. Ours is a skepticism which simply gives up faith in foundationalism, while still being interested in the fascination that foundationalism exercised in a variety of ways in philosophy, literature, and criticism. This form of skepticism acknowledges theories as provisional instruments that seem to be compelling in particular historical contexts; the legitimacy of theories resides for it in the practices they sustain, clarify, and perhaps deepen. The insights such theories provide no doubt continue to be felt as powerful in later periods, but in altered contexts and in revised, modified, or dialectically renewed formulations. The skepticism underlying such a stance differs fundamentally from the traditional dialectical context in which absolute doubt required absolute certainty if knowledge-claims were to hold.

The altered conception of inquiry which gives primacy to historical-conceptual investigation does not require us to pursue the search for a general philosophical theory of justification, meaning, or language. For historical inquiry, with its interest both in the network of forces that give rise to particular conceptions and in the manner of their emergence, is likely to tell us what we need to know about our critical and cognitive contexts in order to pose and address our normative problems. This recognition, too, calls in doubt the possibility of objective analysis which may hope to eliminate conflict and disagreement by fixing once and for all the conditions of critical discourse. But it can call in doubt neither a whole structure of procedures which make possible intelligent discriminations nor the fact that conflict and disagreement do not impose an insuperable barrier to serious debate and mutual understanding. Only an ideal of consensus as transcending our historically situated context of problems can make us feel bewildered about conflict and dissent.

My discussion so far has sought to question the strong prescriptive force that theories of criticism have come to acquire in recent times. No doubt there is much banal structuralist, reader-response, Marxist, and deconstructionist criticism which takes literary theories to be strictly a priori structures which determine the kinds of things a critic can say and do in his or her dealings with literary works. This, I think, is a fundamentally erroneous view. But I do not mean to say that criticism is free from elements of theory, or that it is some sort of preconceptual, intuitive activity. Indeed, any conception of criticism as a theory-free activity is itself a theoretical stance against theorizing and naively idealizes criticism's unmediated contact with literature. This fact of our theoretical consciousness is complicated, as Frank Kermode says, by the fact that our hermeneutic encounters are "in a measure, historically conditioned."[20] The critical problem, then, is one of making difficult but necessary adjustments between theoretical interests which often seek to cut across historical contexts, and historical as well as institutional forces which require a rethinking of our theoretical interests.

But there is no reason for deconstructionists as well as adherents of other methods to deceive themselves that they can do better what, according to them, the New Critics did badly—that is, arrive at some incontrovertible propositions about literature and criticism. They will do well not to assume that their critical practice will be better because it is based on the latest theories. The fact that deconstruction and several other forms of criticism have given centrality to textual analysis suggests that supposedly newer forms of criticism may not be necessarily more compelling than the ones provided by the New Critical practice at its best. But it is a mistake to think, as some critics do,[21] that because New Criticism and deconstruction pursue close textual analysis, there are no inherent or profound differences between them. Such an argument attends to external resemblances and ignores the internal dynamics of each critical practice. The interest of the best deconstructive critics, such as the late Paul de Man, lies in pursuing theoretical analysis and reflection in order to offer what is known, in Continental philosophy, as critique. Though in de Man's work the critique has considerable analytical power and force, literary theory conceived primarily as critique has its severe limitations, especially if it drains criticism and its theory of their positive function, which is that of interpretation of and reflection on literature in a variety of ways. Hegel, we may recall, formulated the notion of critique as a form of negative dialectic aimed at exposing the inadequacies in the empirical world. His goal was to pave the way, by means of such a critique, for possibilities of change. De Man's negative critique is, to the extent that it exposes the internal inconsistencies of literary theories and interpretations, extremely important for further reflection on criticism. But de Man remains too thoroughly committed to negative thinking in this useful but limited sense to break out into the sort of things that those interested in post-structuralism admire in Nietzsche, Foucault, and Derrida.

As for New Criticism, it was the result of a slow institutional revolution, some of whose premises were abstractly formulated long before critics knew how to make them fruitful in critical practice. Indeed, the New Critical practice, in the works of T. S. Eliot, William Empson, R. P. Blackmur, Cleanth Brooks, Robert Penn Warren, and John Crowe Ransom, among others, made possible a thorough rethinking of the rather austere premises of Kantian aesthetics and resulted in the work of Wimsatt and Beardsley, particularly their two essays on the affective and intentional fallacies. Wimsatt and Beardsley tended to assume that criticism could be given a relatively strict logical and conceptual foundation, and that all sorts of conceptual errors and confusions could be eliminated by disclosing what they construed as logical fallacies that threatened criticism. It is erroneous to think, however, that if the New Critical theory is conclusively wrong in at least some of its theoretical claims, the New Criticism is therefore wrong or refuted. To the extent that New Critical practice, like any other serious critical practice, is able to engage a process of reflection and rethinking in the context of important contesting practices, it can continue to produce compelling criticism. We need to think, then, more about the relations between theory and practice, and about the power and limits of theory as such.

The crisis that is supposed to have engulfed literary theory today is a crisis only from the perspective of a belief that it is possible to have some sort of unified theory that will unproblematically define and control critical practice, one that will also eliminate or dialectically overcome all rival theories and practices in the domain of criticism. The crisis of contemporary literary theory consists not in the fact that no single theory has emerged as the true foundational theory on which to build all future criticism, but in the fact that contemporary literary theory is unable to come to terms with the implications of a loss of an Archimedean position from which to talk about literature and society. It is indeed no reason for dismay to think that contemporary literary theory is in crisis. What should provoke some dismay is that this sense of crisis is not informed by an historical grasp of criticism and its theory in a way that can help us develop a sense of how criticism's problems today are different from what they used to be in the past. To see some of criticism's problems as belonging to its past requires a grasp of the ways in which some of these problems continue to underlie our current critical preoccupations, however conflicting and various these preoccupations might be. The absence of historical, analytical investigation of these problems has resulted in the use of critical methods as strict analytical instruments which predetermine everything many critics say in their literary interpretations. These interpretations, moreover, endlessly repeat themselves while endlessly confirming the same limited premises.[22]

We should not ask philosophy to perform a task it cannot perform, nor should we expect cultural or literary theory to perform it either. What theories we hold and defend are the theories *we* hold in our specific critical culture, under *our* specific historical conditions. This is no reason to lose self-confidence or to allow our sense of the possibility of rich cultural and literary criticism to become impoverished. For to let that happen would be to believe, without grounds, that we can gain a transcendental or universal perspective on our tradition, one that will enable us to stand not only outside that tradition but outside our cultural present. Once foundationalism, the epistemological quest for foundations, loses its power, we will need to know what the cultural criticism that developed in the era of epistemology would now look like. In other words, when the distinctions of unhistorical philosophy are no longer available, what can we say about the notions of literature and criticism which emerged under the aegis of that philosophy? What can we say about our literary past and present without seeming silly or preposterous? And what sort of distinctions can we possibly make if we are to continue our conversation with the past and present? Answering these questions will depend in part on our ability to avoid abstracting theory from practice, and in part on seeing that practice includes features not fully contained or comprehended by theory.

## NOTES

1. See, for instance, E. D. Hirsch, Jr., *Validity in Interpretation* (New Haven: Yale University Press, 1967).

2. The works of Jacques Derrida do not concern themselves primarily with literary texts, though they are no doubt the master texts for deconstructive theory and practice. See also Paul de Man, *Allegories of Reading: Figural Language in Rousseau, Nietzsche, Rilke, and Proust* (New Haven: Yale University Press, 1979).

3. See, for instance, Claude Lévi-Strauss, *Structural Anthropology*, trans. Claire Jacobson and Brooke Grundfest Schoepf (New York: Basic Books, 1963), and Jonathan Culler, *Structuralist Poetics: Structuralism, Linguistics, and the Study of Literature* (Ithaca, N.Y.: Cornell University Press, 1975).

4. See, for instance, Derrida's criticism of Saussure and Lévi-Strauss in his *Of Grammatology*, trans. Gayatri C. Spivak (Baltimore: Johns Hopkins University Press, 1976), pp. 27–73, 101–40.

5. For some implications along these lines, see Jonathan Culler, *The Pursuit of Signs: Semiotics, Literature, Deconstruction* (Ithaca, N.Y.: Cornell University Press, 1981), chap. 2, pp. 18–43.

6. Hans-Georg Gadamer, *Truth and Method,* ed. Garrett Barden and John Cumming (New York: Seabury, 1975). The difficulties in Gadamer arise especially in the context of his notion of the interpreter engaging in a dialogue with a text and in the context of determining what constitutes the truth of a tradition and how to arrive at an understanding of it.

7. Culler, *Pursuit of Signs,* pp. 3–17.

8. Geoffrey H. Hartman, *The Fate of Reading and Other Essays* (Chicago: University of Chicago Press, 1975), p. 107.

9. Geoffrey H. Hartman, *Criticism in the Wilderness: The Study of Literature Today* (New Haven: Yale University Press, 1980), p. 162.

10. Stanley Fish, *Is There a Text in This Class? The Authority of Interpretive Communities* (Cambridge, Mass.: Harvard University Press, 1981). Fish's early essays make up a subjectivist reader-response theory, whereas his later essays develop the notion of interpretive communities.

11. Hartman, *Criticism in the Wilderness,* p. 270.

12. For a discussion of this, see Frank Kermode, "Institutional Control of Interpretation," *Salmagundi* 43 (Winter 1979): 72–86.

13. Hayden White, "The Absurdist Moment in Contemporary Literary Theory," *Contemporary Literature* 7 (Summer 1976): 378–403.

14. See Gadamer's discussion of the fusion of horizons, *Truth and Method,* pp. 267–73 and 310–41.

15. Ian Hacking, *The Emergence of Probability* (New York: Cambridge University Press, 1975); Richard Rorty, *Philosophy and the Mirror of Nature* (Princeton, N.J.: Princeton University Press, 1979), esp. chap. 1, pp. 17–69 and chap. 3, pp. 131–64.

16. The scholarship on seventeenth-century literature is extensive. My own discussion in this paragraph is indebted to Barbara J. Shapiro, *Probability and Certainty in Seventeenth-Century England: A Study of the Relationships between Natural Science, Religion, History, Law and Literature* (Princeton, N.J.: Princeton University Press, 1983), pp. 257–66.

17. Hirsch, *Validity in Interpretation,* pp. 78–89.

18. René Wellek, *The Attack on Literature and Other Essays* (Chapel Hill: University of North Carolina Press, 1982), pp. 143–44.

19. See the essays collected in Rorty's *Consequences of Pragmatism: Essays 1972–1980* (Minneapolis: University of Minnesota Press, 1982). In *Philosophy and the Mirror of Nature,* Rorty probes the implications of several of Sellars' essays, esp. on pp. 167–88, and of Quine's work, esp. on pp. 169–75, 192–204, and 217–30.

20. Frank Kermode, *The Genesis of Secrecy: On the Interpretation of Narrative* (Cambridge, Mass.: Harvard University Press, 1979), p. 39.

21. See, for instance, Gerald Graff, *Literature against Itself: Literary Ideas in Modern Society* (Chicago: University of Chicago Press, 1979), p. 145.

22. I make this argument in *Metacriticism* (Athens, Ga.: University of Georgia Press, 1981), pp. 227, 234. For a similar recent argument, see Frank Kermode's prologue to his *The Art of Telling: Essays on Fiction* (Cambridge, Mass.: Harvard University Press, 1983), pp. 5–7.

*Part Two*

# Circumscriptions

*Joel F. Wilcox*

# Cross-Metamorphosis
# in Plato's *Ion*

Eric a. havelock's seminal work, *Preface to Plato*, ascribes Plato's treatment of the poets and of poetry to the transformation of Hellenic civilization from a largely oral to a largely literate culture. For Havelock, Plato's rejection of the oral traditions as the educational standard was inevitable in the growth of the collective Greek mind. As the written word came to replace the oral tradition as the means for memorializing and transmitting culture from one generation to the next, the Greeks were able to objectify data and at the same time internalize the review of those data and thereby create science and abstract thinking.[1]

For Plato, according to this argument, poetry, as a vestige of the oral *paideia*, would have existed only under definite negative conditions. Hence the polemic against poetry in the *Republic*. Readers, however, are still apt to sense at some stage of their reading of Plato a peculiar inconsistency between his rejection of the poets in the *Republic* and his clear affection for them elsewhere in his dialogues, or even in the *Republic* itself. George Chapman criticized his otherwise-revered Plato for "dealing with them [Poets] like a Politician indeed—use men and then cast them off."[2] Most readers probably feel the justice of Chapman's remark, and yet most probably also believe that Plato's particular argument in the *Republic* necessitated an unremitting attack on the poets because of the educational role people had traditionally accorded them. In circumstances where the issues concerning the poets were less complex, Plato might express or imply more favorably his estimation of their accomplishments.

Whether one believes that Plato ultimately rejected the poets or embraced them or settled for some gesture of compromise, a little dialogue like the *Ion* can be shuffled about to suit the purposes of one's larger interpretive sweep. If one needs to make the case that Plato's rejection of poetry and poets was hard-and-fast throughout his long career, Socrates' alleged attempt to show Ion for a fool, a pompous ass, and an ignorant braggart[3] will support the position that Plato was right to expel the poets because, as enthusiasts, they had no discipline for gaining understanding and yet had a high opinion of themselves—a lethal combination. But if one wishes to argue that Plato was proposing a positive account of poetry, Socrates' analogy of the magnet and rings explains poetic truth as a chain of inspiration—a chain which might be associated with the daimonic offices of Love in bringing divine knowledge to men, as we read in the *Phaedrus* and the *Symposium*. Socrates' analogy, however, proves nothing decisively, for it may be read both as damaging to the poets in showing their natural ignorance and as flattering in making them the spokesmen of gods.

I am no different in seeing the *Ion* as helpful for understanding concerns about poetry in other dialogues, but I hope to do justice to the *Ion* in itself. If we look at the *Ion* alone, Plato's shaping of Socrates' role and character in the dialogue is the primary focus of interest. With a special dramatic irony (as distinct from the so-called Socratic irony normally associated with the historical Socrates), Plato makes Socrates and Ion into transmogrified images of each other. In doing so, Plato points toward a union of the philosophical and poetic traditions which fulfills the ideals of both.

IF A READING of the *Ion* is to do justice to the dialogue's serious literary content, a number of objections against the dialogue must be put to rest. In their prefatory note to the dialogue, Hamilton and Cairns suggest a number of these, saying that in the *Ion* "Plato is amusing himself." The real interest of the dialogue is Socrates' insistence that inspiration, not knowledge, is responsible for poets, rhapsodes, and their enthusiastic appreciators. Above all, this hypothesis carries a political message. "The balance of opposites which made the Periclean Age possible was passing away . . . to such a degree that the greatest of the Athenians had to put his effort into counteracting the rapidly growing disorder in a state ruled more and more not by the mind, but by the emotions."[4] The dialogue's serious content resides in its sociopolitical implications rather than in its depiction of Ion, with whom Plato merely amuses himself.

The twentieth-century penchant for political allegoresis provides Hamilton and Cairns with a convenient overlay through which to sort out primary and secondary concerns. While there is no denying Plato's interest in politics, their treatment of the dialogue rates the conversation between Ion and Socrates low and rates Socrates' analogy about the magnet and rings high, but only when placed ultimately in a context suggested by nothing in the dialogue itself. Hamilton and Cairns are merely typical in this regard, and all of this goes to show that the most probable cause of misunderstanding the *Ion* is the uncertain interpretation of its irony.

Readers will often assume that the presence of irony undercuts serious content altogether. At first view, Plato seems content in the *Ion* to thwart what we would naturally suppose are his own philosophical purposes in order to present an unusual picture of his mentor engaged in a sometimes hilarious conversation[5] with an accomplished man who nevertheless argues like everyone's little brother. Is not Socrates' irony palpable from the first page? He says he feels "envy" (ἐζήλωσα) for rhapsodes "on account of their craft" (τῆς τέχνης)[6] (530b), but he goes on to explain that his interest in the rhapsode's business has in part to do with the accoutrements of the profession: "For it is always necessary for you to beautify your bodies for the sake of your craft and to appear as fine as possible." This is a familiar enough ploy of Socrates the εἴρων: praising the characteristics he was sensible had their strongest effect on the masses but to which he had made himself ultimately indifferent.[7]

Socrates' disposition to practice irony, however, can easily be exaggerated. It would be absurd, for instance, to think that Socrates practices irony on Ion in order to refute him. For one thing, Ion never really engages in anything but a parody of philosophical argument. We can see that, compared to more sophisticated interlocutors, Ion is foolish and incapable of anticipating the point of Socrates' proofs, but our assessment is not the same thing as Socrates' refuting him. In fact, even when Ion steps into the quicksand of elenchus and states that his training as a rhapsode would prepare him to be a fine general, his claim is so desperately illogical that Socrates himself must resort to an ad hominem argument to refute him: if Ion knew how to be a great general, he would be one; but he is not a general; *ergo*, he does not know how to be one (541c–e). If one is truly amused by such things, it is at least as amusing to watch Socrates searching for every possible means to make Ion realize that he understands very little as it is to laugh at Ion's logical difficulties.

The suspicion that Socrates' approach toward Ion is all ironic is also quelled by Socrates' more serious assessment of rhapsodes. In his words, they are "conversant about the many excellent poets and especially about Homer—the best and most divine of poets—and to learn his thought, not just his words, is enviable" (530b–c). Socrates quickly shifts from the trappings of the rhapsodic craft to what ought to be closer to the essence: knowing the "thought" (διάνοια) of the poet as a means of giving life to his "words" (τὰ ἔπη). Socrates further implies that the best of poets ought to have some connection with the "divine" (θεῖος), suggesting that there is a correlation between a poet's thought and divinity. For this reason, when Socrates finally gets Ion to accept that his business is a matter of the divine, and not of his being a great craftsman, he has made his point and the dialogue comes to an end.

There may well be irony in Socrates' glib reference near the beginning of the dialogue to Ion's business as a "craft" (530b), when the actual doubts about its being a craft at all form the centerpiece of the dialogue. But because this reference occurs on the first page of the dialogue, it is most likely no more than an example of Plato's using terms in their natural, if imprecise, way before examining that use more closely. Though it is clear by the time Socrates delivers his analogy of the magnet and rings that he has not believed at any time that poetry and her attendant arts are "crafts" like other crafts, his use of the term at the beginning of the dialogue merely indicates that he is approaching his subject in an informal, conversational way. Ion, on the other hand, is forthright in his conviction that the rhapsode's "greatest task" (πλεῖστον ἔργον) is to be an "interpreter" (ἑρμηνέα) (530c), and Socrates respects Ion's claim enough that he never challenges it or Ion's boast that he has finer thoughts than any other interpreter of Homer (although the validity of Ion's claims to having "thoughts" about Homer is obviously connected to the central issue of the dialogue). Unlike the *Apology*, where Socrates claims that he tested the wisdom of the poets and found them wanting, Socrates here seems to go along with Ion's self-assessment, which is supported credibly enough by his competitiveness in the festivals and by wide public acclaim. Again, Socrates' deference could be ironic. Yet, Ion does indeed "know" his business, and Socrates congratulates him on his taking a crown in the Epidaurian festival and expresses his hope that "we win the Panathenaia, too" (530b). If Socrates does deny later that Ion's skill is a craft like other crafts, he does not deny that Ion has a gift, rare and divine.

The discussion of art as craft is sometimes assumed to be ironic because it does not lead to a satisfying conclusion. It serves as an introit to Socrates' analogy of the magnet and rings, and many readers are distressed that Socrates and Ion have to cover the same ground after Socrates' recitation. The two discussions of art as craft have important differences, however, and a clear sense of Plato's shaping of the dialogue's structure helps to enrich our appreciation of what otherwise seems like a clumsy development of theme. The assumption that Socrates' argument against art as craft is straightforwardly conclusive is incorrect, but this assumption contributes a great deal to the minimization of Ion's character and to Socrates' treatment of him.

Although Socrates and Ion's specific discussion of the rhapsode's business centers on its likeness to a craft (τέχνη), it is worth the reminder that Socrates' analogy of the magnet and rings applies not only to the writing of poetry but to all of the interpretive arts which mediate the artist's "thought" to the general public. In the Platonic canon, the most extensive discussion of the likeness of knowledge to the crafts comes in the *Republic*. To find the exact nature of the just man, Socrates and his interlocutors look to the analogy of the state. The just state would be one in which every member did his or her own work in contribution to the good of the whole and did not usurp responsibilities which properly belonged to someone else. Indeed, Socrates' whole argument on the need for well-educated guardians and philosopher-kings hangs upon this argument. Nevertheless, the discussion of the crafts in the *Republic* does not help us with the *Ion* because there is a basic and ultimately insoluble problem with the discussion. If justice demands that each craftsman know and practice only one craft, what must the rulers of this city know in order to see that the craftsmen are doing what they are supposed to be doing? Clearly, Plato does not expect his philosopher-kings to "moonlight" at all of the crafts in order to know how to make decisions regarding each and every one of them. He must presuppose that the rulers will have enough general understanding of the crafts to make correct decisions for the good of the city. How will they attain this general information? Probably no differently from the way the poets attained it— not by practice but by observation.[8]

A distressing feature of the *Republic*, then, is that Plato gives to his rulers a knowledge of the crafts which they could not have had any more than the rhapsodes and artists to whom he would seem to deny such knowledge in the *Ion*. The point is that the development of the discussion about who should know the crafts in the *Republic* is no clearer than in the *Ion*, and it should perhaps be the more perplexing in the *Republic* because there it is philosophy ultimately, not poetry, which falls short of the mark. If the issue of knowing the crafts is one which Plato would not or could not resolve in "print" by the time he wrote the *Republic*, the open-endedness of the issue in the *Ion* should not count against consideration of the *Ion* as a serious piece of work.

One other point of similarity between the *Ion* and the *Republic* is perhaps more germane. Socrates remarks in the *Republic* that the man who in the present, corrupt state of society comes to a good character is blessed by the "Fate of God" (μοῖρα θεοῦ) (493a), exactly the same power to which Socrates attributes Ion's talents as a rhapsode (542a, *passim*).[9] In the early part of the conversation with Ion, Socrates intends to show Ion that Ion's own talent as a rhapsode is no more assured as this world goes than a man's character is, spawned as it must be amidst the corruption of men and states. The wonder, apparently, is not that men, whether poets or kings, do or say evil but that they sometimes do and say something good.

As such, Ion's self-satisfaction is his chief fault. More to the point, in his state of *hybris* he has failed to give the inspiring gods their due. He has the typical blindness of the self-made man to those favorable circumstances which have conditioned his success. Knowing Homer well, he says, "seems to me enough" (ἱκανὸν γάρ μοι δοκεῖ εἶναι) (531a). When Socrates takes this claim and shows that Ion, as a result of knowing Homer well, must also know "those who speak worse and the fact that they speak worse" (532b) about any subject common to all of the poets, Ion follows Socrates' reasoning, but without much conviction: "So it seems" (ἔοικέ γε), he says. Ion finally objects only when Socrates forces the issue to the point of claiming that Ion's expertise on Homer (if it really were expertise) would make him an expert on the other poets as well. "Then whatever is the reason, Socrates, that whenever someone discourses about another poet, I pay no attention and I am not able to offer anything worth a word?" (532c). Why, indeed? Socrates' argument ought to have the devastating effect of a reductio ad absurdum, but Ion does not miss being tripped up simply because he does not blush as easily as Thrasymachus. He actually has the experience, so he thinks, of knowing Homer well, so that he is truly perplexed as to why Socrates' reasoning does not seem altogether true for him.

Socrates' explanation of Ion's perplexity more or less proves that Socrates' ulterior motive in questioning him has been to show that Ion does not really *know* anything as a result of his enterprise or success as a rhapsode, and Socrates for the first time explicitly identifies "craft" (τέχνη) with "science" (ἐπιστήμη).[10] If Ion actually *knew* something about Homer, he would know about other poets as well because, as he says, "the poetic craft is in some way a whole thing" (ποιητικὴ γάρ πού ἐστιν τὸ ὅλον) (532c). Socrates' contention that the poetic craft is a "whole thing" means that to be master of one part of the craft entails one's understanding of the craft as a whole.[11]

This line of reasoning might not have withstood rebuttal by a more skillful interlocutor than Ion. Socrates infers from Ion's interest in Homer and lack of interest in other poets that Ion does not derive his skill from craft. Using analogies to the plastic arts, Socrates defines his experts as those who are competent to judge the virtues or vices of all practitioners in painting or sculpture (532e–33b). This reasoning is, of course, false. Lack of interest is not the same thing as ignorance, certainly not to the extent that one can argue that their opposites—interest and knowledge—are somehow identical. Or perhaps the conversation is still at the stage in which Socrates has not quite figured out what Ion really thinks: Ion believes that Socrates has proved that he (Ion) has knowledge about poets who interest him very little, but Socrates is only beginning to discover how greatly Ion's "knowledge" is devoid of dialectical props. Whatever Ion's deficiencies in word or deed, his failure to detect a deity outside himself quickening his feebler capabilities begins to emerge as his deepest defect. Socrates' determination to get Ion to accept his dependence becomes the driving force of the dialogue.

CRUCIAL TO OUR DISCOVERY of Plato's purposes, however, is the cross-metamorphosis which begins to take place between Ion and Socrates. When Socrates asks if Ion needs further explanation of the analogies among the crafts, Ion replies enthusiastically: "Yes, by Zeus, I do indeed! I welcome hearing from you wise men" (532d). Is this a parody of the Socratic irony? The word for "wise men" (σόφοι), of course, has seamy connotations in this period.[12] Because the "sophists" made claims to wisdom which were not always valid, writers of the period used the term σόφος ironically at times. The ignorant, after all, often call merely clever or cynical people "wise." Socrates taught the paradoxical truth that the claim to wisdom does not admit of proof, only of disproof.[13] One can prove one has wisdom only to whoever has the wisdom already to see it, and in such a case that person will see wisdom without what we ordinarily mean by proof.

Therefore, Socrates' reply to Ion represents more than Socrates' habitual personal irony. He says: "I only wish you were speaking the truth, Ion. But you rhapsodes and actors and the ones whose poems you sing are the wise ones, while I say nothing more than the truth, like an ordinary man" (532d–e). The exasperating feature of this courteous exchange is that we believe Ion is right to call Socrates wise but that he does not know what the term means. Similarly, we doubt that Socrates could really mean that rhapsodes and actors are wise, except in some qualified sense (no doubt related to their commerce with the gods) which has yet to be specified. But the dramatic significance of the moment is that after this polite intercourse Socrates and Ion effectually shift places: Ion plays the auditor as Socrates recites.

Socrates' analogy of the magnet and rings is mythlike in its aetiological purport—evidence, surely, of Plato's "playful seriousness" in shifting about the roles of Socrates and Ion.[14] Here is Socrates, the "ordinary man," giving an account of divine inspiration. But more to the point, Socrates' own extraordinary struggle for wisdom enables him to recognize not just ignorance but also wisdom in the poets, wisdom which they cannot account for themselves. His analogy, therefore, is like a unique form of philosophical "poetry": how else could Socrates presume to divulge the mysteries of the poets and their inspiring god? The man who claimed to know nothing becomes a philosophical Hesiod. Ion likes Socrates' story, saying that it "touches somehow into the λόγοι of my soul" (535a3–4). It sounds very much as though Socrates has been "inspired." Has he not been seized himself by the god of philosophy?[15]

To explain the nature of the interlinking of wisdom and power through poet, rhapsode, and auditor requires at least as much inspiration (if I may quantify such a term) as that demanded by the poet and his followers. As for what divine inspiration is in itself, this is never defined in Socrates' analogy. Plato tempts his readers to suppose that the analogy of the magnet and rings is a *via positiva* to an understanding of divine inspiration, but it is instead a *via negativa:* wisdom must first be identified as an enigma, indescribable and quite separate from the confusion of ordinary experience. My application of these theological "paths" to Plato is not merely ingenious, if it even seems that. Wisdom, as Socrates never tires of telling us, is the province of the gods.[16] Socrates did not lay claim to wisdom, because he understood that human wisdom can be evaluated only by reference to divine and intelligible things. The analogy of the magnet and rings "explains" only the fact that the existence of poetry entails certain truths which depend more upon the gift of a divine revelation than upon human power or cunning. By implication, however, philosophy, like poetry before it, makes its partisans intermediaries between God and man, between wisdom and the chaos of human experience. Men shall not become true poets until they have communed with the gods, and whereas this had been the task of poetry to perform, for Plato it is philosophy which must answer the calling. In revealing the god, Socrates becomes the mediator between the god and men. Therefore, as important as anything Socrates says is Plato's depiction of him. He is at once the witness and the example to the life he describes.

ASIDE FROM THE larger conceptual framework of the dialogue, the cross-metamorphosis of Socrates and Ion helps us to understand the problem of the dialogue's structure. We have already seen that the problem of how one individual might comprehend all of the crafts was not satisfactorily resolved even by the time Plato had written the *Republic*. Instead of complaining that Plato, after Socrates' analogy, lets the dialogue degenerate into a silly sort of bantering until Socrates finally badgers Ion into admitting his basic ignorance of everything, we can now see that Plato is giving, in the attitude of Ion, a living example of precisely the kind of educational failure which those who had looked solely to the traditional sort of poetic "inspiration" had suffered. Whether Ion has any λόγοι in his soul or not, he clearly has not learned anything from Socrates, because his response is a relatively undisciplined emotivism. To this point in the dialogue, the idea of poetic creation has been jarred loose from the concept of craft; inspiration must now be credited as a viable means of "creating." The problem now is that we can no longer be satisfied with Ion as the example of the inspired man. Can a picture of the inspired man which will satisfy philosophy be constructed from this dialogue? Can this picture be shown to fit within the frame of Plato's canon as a whole?

As I have already hinted, Socrates' example in "playing rhapsode" in the analogy of the magnet and rings is both a dramatic and a cognitive presentation of the dialogue's core meaning. In placing Socrates in the role of philosophical rhapsode, Plato points toward the blending of philosophy and art (not precisely the same thing as the blending of reason and emotion, but close enough) to the better purposes of both. The blending obviously parallels the cross-metamorphosis of Ion and Socrates, at least to the extent that poetry's special task in bringing human qualities into relation with the divine is shown in a kind of concrete perfection in Socrates. This symbolic role is developed more significantly in the *Phaedrus* and the *Symposium*, but Plato's use of it in his earlier *Ion* differs only in degree, not in kind.

We must pause to consider what it means to say that philosophy and art (or reason and emotion) may be blended to the better purposes of each. As often occurs in Plato, a proper study of the particular gives insight to the whole. In this case, the purposes of both philosophy and art may be approached through the analysis of individual consciousness.

Every event of experience is a simple, single thing, but one which we are forced inevitably to describe in terms of such categories as reason and emotion. If our total collective consciousness of a single event were merely a sum of differing points of view, each private consciousness as distinct from another as snowflakes, it would be impossible to say that one reaction was more nearly the correct reaction than another. Some may believe that this relativism is exactly the situation with consciousness, especially the consciousness of moral or aesthetic events, but experience implies otherwise. Everyone has had the experience of witnessing someone else's incorrect reaction to, say, a work of art and has *known* this person's reaction to be incorrect and not just different from his or her own. Similarly, we have all experienced "growing into" a work of art; we call it "acquiring taste." The consciousness of individual reactions to events necessarily internalizes and isolates us as individuals. On the other hand, the attempt to clarify or correct our responses ultimately initiates an externalization, unification, and universalization of mind. "Acquiring taste" shows that, through experience itself, some corrective faculty (call it reason) chastens raw awareness and fosters the capacity in consciousness for clearer, finer emotional response.

Plato's difficulty with the poets and poetry comes not from the fact that poetry and philosophy seek different ends but that they minister to the same shaping purpose of consciousness. If we may judge from the dialogues in which Plato measures poetry and philosophy against each other, his design is certainly not to reject poetry but, properly understood, to fulfill its better purposes. There are two stages in this process of transmutation which are also analogous to the stages of emotional clarification in the consciousness which I have just described. The first stage is like the bifurcation of reason and emotion which occurs when consciousness becomes aware of itself. Though Plato often analyzes claims made through the old *paideia* and shows through his interlocutors how the previous tradition falls short, just as often he shows how the poets have sometimes been right. Furthermore, everyone is familiar with those instances in which Plato follows a stretch of careful dialectical analysis with what I will call a synthetic construct—a myth, if you will. In its way, this mythologizing is analogous to the rejoining of clarified emotion to experience in the human consciousness. This synthetic, poetic quality certainly becomes manifest in Plato's occasional use of heightened language and imagery. At its most profound, it manifests itself in such mythlike, talismanic symbols as the charioteer and horses, the philosopher-king, or Love begetting spiritual offspring. I say "talismanic" symbols because I wish to emphasize the power of these images to present concepts in as concrete a manner as possible while still fostering in the consciousness an increasing refinement of the mind's own clarity and purpose.

These talismanic symbols are always comprehensible to some extent as concrete images. Unlike poetic figures in Homer, which must be rationalized through allegoresis (for example, Circe as the witch of sensuality or Zeus and his golden chain as representing God and the chain of being), Plato's talismans are at once open-ended and yet self-disclosing. They may be discussed as examples or illustrations, and in this way they may have relatively literal meanings in the context of their discussion. But they are also larger than their context, focusing both reason and emotion upon a single thing and drawing the unified and increasingly refined consciousness onward. This, I would submit, is the finest of Plato's various gifts and the reason we come back to him continually. The myth of the soul's journey in the *Phaedrus*, for example, can be paraphrased in part, and it is right that we should attempt to express its meaning as clearly as we can. But the myth's compelling quality is linked to what may not be expressed by paraphrase. In fact, the Neoplatonists are right in assuming that the grasping of truth involves principally a metamorphosis of the comprehending soul by which the soul becomes, in a manner of speaking, a shadow to the shaping force of that truth. By such a response to Plato's philosophical poetic, the individual consciousness is unified, silently and ineffably, in response to some otherwise undisclosed truth.

In the *Ion*, the talisman of implied philosophical-poetical meaning is Socrates as a rhapsodizing and mythologizing philosopher. While I would not argue that this talismanic expression is one of Plato's profoundest, it is better than is often credited. Certain difficulties of the dialogue are resolved because of it, principally the problem of having to account for Ion's often absurd demeanor in order to justify the assumption that Socrates might be serious about the things he has to say. Despite Ion's stupid moments, his failings help us to see that Socrates is not Ion's opposite. Socrates is rather a transfigured type of the inspired man which Ion slowly—very slowly—sees that he himself must be if he is to be counted among the interpreters of Homer's "thought."

I have mentioned several instances in which Socrates' dialectical moves fail to trip up Ion. Ironically, it is in his role as rhapsode rather than as ironist or logician that Socrates triumphs over Ion. His Janus-faced analogy traps Ion in a way that his reductio ad absurdum argument could not. His analogy is not only mythlike but explains myth, and in so doing it paints a setting from which Ion can scarcely extricate himself. In applying this new philosophical-poetical schema to himself, Ion will have to accept the consequences of the new self-consciousness. (That Ion does not at once see these consequences is one reason a rehash of the earlier discussion must follow Socrates' performance. The point is that someone like Ion—that is, a pretender to poetry and the arts—cannot say he understands Socrates' analogy without accepting its pedagogical implications.) Acceptance would entail the pursuit of a new relationship to the gods. The *Ion*, therefore, is propaedeutic to a philosophical, religious, and perhaps even mystical initiation.

Although Ion is not hostile to Socrates, he is in a technical sense a hostile witness to Socrates' ideas about inspiration. For dramatic purposes, Plato exemplifies through Ion the complacency embedded in the old educational traditions. Ion reacts to art as one would react to flattery. Art either "interests" him or it does not, which is little different from saying that he likes what he likes because it says what he is prepared to hear. Ion's self-congratulatory interpretation of Socrates' analogy repels the thoughtful reader, who is then driven to interpret the analogy in some new way. Being forced to reject the belief that art is produced by a knowledge identical with craftsmanship, the reader nevertheless is impressed simultaneously by the power which enables Socrates to explain something of the purposes of divine inspiration and its effects in unwitting agents like Ion. Ion himself is a living example of Socrates' suggestion that the gods use fools to manifest themselves so that there can be no mistaking who is the cause of the wisdom they articulate (534e).

With Socrates' suggestion, however, the cat, so to speak, is out of the bag. Socrates' act of explaining inspiration and his manner in doing so mark the transition from the old to the new *paideia*. As representative of the new, Socrates brings human qualities into relation with the divine, bearing witness by word and deed to the true divine inspiration (ἔνθεοι ὄντες καὶ κατεχόμενοι) (533e). If bringing human qualities into relation with the divine is an acceptable definition of inspiration, then the gods inspire more profoundly by means of a philosophical poetic.

Finally, there is at least one more way in which the cross-metamorphosis of Socrates and Ion allows us to see that the ending of the dialogue is less farcical than it is often made out to be.[17] Socrates pushes Ion mercilessly to the point where Ion must admit that to be the kind of interpreter of Homer he thinks he is, he would have to know every craft. This is patently impossible, even for the philosopher, as I have argued. Still, when Socrates asks Ion which of the crafts Homer writes about seems peculiarly related to the rhapsode's skill, Ion persists in his uncomprehending way, saying, "All of them" (539e). If pushed to it, Ion would like to say that the rhapsode has at least as comprehensive a view of the world as any philosopher because the world is clearly Homer's province (as, in fact, we can see from the passages the "rhapsode" Socrates quotes[18]). And driven by Socrates' imperious logic to the point where he must decide what he does know of the world and what he does not, Ion claims all the crafts for his own—a comprehensive knowledge which would surpass that of the greatest lover of wisdom.

Ion's assessment of the rhapsode's universal comprehension cannot stand long as Socrates forces him to abandon one by one his claims to the crafts. In a last-ditch effort to fortify himself against the Socratic onslaught, Ion culls a parody of the philosopher-king (if we may be allowed to look back to the *Ion* from the *Republic*) out of his Homeric world view. If the rhapsode cannot have understanding of all the crafts, he has at least an understanding of the craft of generalship! And when Socrates forces him to choose between being known as an unjust man for lying or a man divine for being inspired, Ion chooses the man divine, accepting his fate, as Socrates had accepted his, that he knows nothing. The cross-metamorphosis is now complete on both sides.

The bud of inspiration in the *Ion* comes into full leaf and flower in the *Symposium* and especially in the *Phaedrus*. In these later dialogues, we see a fully developed philosophical poetic in which the oral *paideia* has been transformed, internalized, and objectified onto the canvas of experience as a means for directing reason and emotion in proper subordination to the divine.

All of this I believe can be deduced from Plato's depiction of Socrates' words and deeds and from the equally telling portrayal of Ion. If Plato never gives a fully articulated statement of the nature of inspiration per se, the dialogue points us in the proper direction for ascertaining some sense of the meaning and importance of inspiration. The view I hold is consonant with the interpretations of the Neoplatonists generally, who believed, at least, that inspiration was a serious matter. The alternative—that inspiration is a random, feckless affair, somehow unworthy of the philosopher—is sometimes the reading which is found attractive. Ironically, this is in essence Ion's own erroneous construction of the meaning of Socrates' analogy.

Furthermore, inspiration is probably central to both the content and the method of Plato's creation. We ought not to confine the doctrine of inspiration to the early Plato or to regard it as a side issue among Plato's major themes.[19] If we may take seriously Plato's statement that he never disclosed his doctrines in the dialogues,[20] then the teachings he kept out of his writing probably pertain to that dogma which he allowed to appear here and there throughout his works: the gods are the measure of all things. It is not unreasonable to assume that Plato's unwritten teaching may have included something like a negative theology. If so, a positive force like divine inspiration would have to be part of the path to true wisdom as taught by Plato. The idea of Love as it evolves in the *Symposium* is not far from such a concept.[21]

Finally, the assumption that Plato had a genuine interest in divine inspiration is supported by his adapted use of drama and the poetic arts generally. The importance of Socrates as an intermediary agent in the *Ion* suggests that Plato found the authentic presentation of a life to be most important for the incipient stages of moral and theological education. A propaedeutic cannot merely be stated; it must be made compelling. If art for Plato is essentially mimetic,[22] then art teaches best when it gives the best pattern that may be followed. Socrates is at once our equal and our superior. His ability to know the weaknesses of his fellows is brought into harness with his extraordinary sense of the otherness of that world in which he and those who love wisdom must find their happiness. I have no wish to vindicate the excesses of the Neoplatonists in turning everything in the direction of mysticism, but there can be no doubt that in the dialogues the mundane and material world is judged according to a standard which, while immanent to it to a degree, is increasingly shown to be beyond the pale. Plato was able to use the drama of the dialogue to clarify the immanent and point toward the transcendent. This process of clarification is also a drama of self-discovery and self-disclosure; the example of Socrates is Plato's finest creation to the purpose.

## NOTES

1. Eric A. Havelock, *Preface to Plato* (Cambridge, Mass.: Harvard University Press, 1963).

2. George Chapman's *Homer*, ed. Allardyce Nicoll, 2d ed. (Princeton: Princeton University Press, 1967), vol. 1, p. 20.

3. By the time of the writing of the dialogue, rhapsodes had a reputation for being foolish, so that even Ion's success at his profession would not necessarily have been grounds for Socrates' being impressed with him. Cf. W. J. Verdenius, "L'Ion de Platon," *Mnemosyne*, 3d ser., vol. 2 (1943): 239. Verdenius thinks, for example, that the dialogue attacks rhapsodes rather than poets. But why should Plato compose a dialogue merely to discredit a group which was already discredited? Furthermore, Socrates' analogy of the magnet and rings implies the interlinking of poet, rhapsode, and audience.

4. *Plato: The Collected Dialogues*, ed. Edith Hamilton and Huntington Cairns (Princeton: Princeton University Press, 1961), p. 215.

5. A case in point: at 536e3–7, Socrates asks Ion what things of Homer he is able to speak about well.

ION: Socrates, mark me: all, without exception.
SOC: Surely, not about what you don't know anything about, but about

those things which Homer speaks about?

ION: What sort of things is it Homer actually speaks about? I don't know.

6. "Craft," or sometimes "skill," is the translation I use for τέχνη. "Art" is a somewhat more common translation, and "trade" might do just as well. I avoid "art" in particular because it carries with it the baggage of our own conceptions of art. Plato almost always wishes to analyze "art" in terms of crafts or trades. Further translations, unless otherwise stated, are also mine.

7. Socrates strikes a similar pose in the *Menexenus* where he describes how, after hearing a good patriotic speech, he is overcome by a great "consciousness of dignity" which "lasts more than three days, and not until the fourth or fifth day do I come to my senses and know where I am." (Jowett's translation. Socrates always treats his opponents to this sort of baby-talk; and some, like Thrasymachus or Callicles, call him on it, even though they still fall to his argumentation in the end. We should learn from this fact that Socrates' reputation for irony was so well known that Plato could not have wished his readers to think that Socrates actually triumphed solely by means of it.)

8. R. G. Collingwood (*The Principles of Art* [London: Oxford University Press, 1938]), who held the view that art is a language of emotion as opposed to a discipline of representation, stated that Plato's distrust of poetry was confused by his likening of poetry to a craft even though he had demonstrated elsewhere that he considered poetry to be useful (or dangerous) for rousing certain emotions. Collingwood argues that Plato, in *Republic* X, had examined the nature of representational or mimetic poetry without stopping to ask the Socratic question "What is the nature of poetry itself?" Instead, if art is likened to craft, one must inevitably presuppose that in its use some sort of form is applied to some sort of matter by means of a scheme or practical understanding of how to attack a certain problem (that is, ἐπιστήμη). The theory of art as craft, therefore, implies a representational or mimetic intent on the part of the artist which exposes art to all of the criticisms aimed at it in *Republic* X (*The Principles of Art*, pp. 42–52). If art is like craft in this sense, then Plato would be right in thinking that all art looks to a lower species of knowledge, one which is inferred from visible objects rather than deduced from intelligible ones.

9. The appearance of this phrase in several other Platonic contexts is discussed in R. Hackforth's *Plato's "Phaedrus"* (Cambridge: Cambridge University Press, 1972), pp. 60–61. Insofar as μοῖρα θεοῦ implies both μανία and ἐνθουσιασμός, Hackforth argues that "it is in the *Phaedrus* alone that we find unqualified commendation of the poets' μανία, commendation which

almost goes to the length of saying that the inspired poet is all the better for
his lack of knowledge" (61). I would argue that commendation of the poets'
μανία in the *Ion* is qualified only by the stupidity of its representative in the
person of Ion. But inasmuch as Socrates will become the cross-metamorphosis
of Ion, as I explain later, Plato commends the chain of inspiration by means of
dramatic irony.

10. Ἐπιστήμη suggests a method or scheme for gaining knowledge. Διάνοια is connected with intelligible entities in *Republic* 599ff. Socrates does not
question that the poets have διάνοιαι or that these "thoughts" entitle them to
the epithet θεῖος, but he proves only that there is no ἐπιστήμη for achieving a
grasp of a poet's thought through the "crafts" associated with the chain of inspiration. The implication, since he explains this by philosophy, is that philosophy is the only way to grasp a poet's thought. This would also explain why
Plato loved Homer but expelled the poets from the ideal state.

11. Thus Paul Friedländer, *Plato*, trans. Hans Meyerhoff, Bollingen series
49 (New York: Pantheon, 1958–64), vol. 2, p. 130. In the context of the whole
argument, Socrates' logic is interesting here. At least a part of the purpose of
the argument is to discover the nature of the poetic craft. With that definition
in doubt, Socrates can nevertheless argue that, as a "whole thing," certain
characteristics can be assumed about it, one of which is that it is *like* other
"whole things," especially other crafts. The groundwork for Socrates' whole
argument is laid with this rather frail assumption.

12. W. K. C. Guthrie, *The Sophists* (Cambridge: Cambridge University
Press, 1971), pp. 27–34.

13. Cf. *Apology.*

14. I call Socrates' explanation of divine inspiration an "analogy" rather
than a "myth" in order to distinguish it from Plato's more profound extra-
philosophical explanations. R. Hackforth (*Plato's "Phaedrus"* [Cambridge: Cambridge University Press, 1971], p. 72), citing P. Frutiger's *Les mythes de Platon*,
calls the great speech of Socrates in the *Phaedrus* a "parascientific myth" in its
design "to complete the results of λόγος, to extend them beyond the limits of
pure reason, to take the place, by way of δεύτερος πλοῦς, of dialectic when it
comes up against some impenetrable mystery. . . ." Put this way, the *Ion* cannot be said to contain a myth. As I argue below, however, the analogy of the
*Ion*, coupled with the cross-metamorphosis of Socrates and Ion, suggests poetic consciousness in Plato which returns fully expressed in the *Phaedrus*.

15. Socrates had a reputation for being "seized" by the god of contemplation, something which is remarked upon twice in the *Symposium*, among
other places.

16. *Laws* 906b, *Symposium* 204a, *Theaetetus* 176b, and *passim*.

17. For a summary of the *Ion's* critical fortunes and misfortunes (the allegation of farce goes back at least to Goethe), see E. N. Tigerstedt, "Plato's Idea of Poetical Inspiration," *Commentationes Humanarum Litterarum*, no. 44 (1970): 18–20.

18. In the concluding section of the *Ion*, Plato is hinting at the description of mimesis he makes explicit in *Republic* X, 598ff. Where does an imitator get his imitations? He "works up" (ἀπεργάζεται) "tid-bits" (σμικρόν τι) from each thing he lights upon. The problem with mimesis can be inferred from comparison of the imitation of a chair with the chair itself (598a). Somehow, for Plato, a physical chair, insofar as it is known to be a chair itself, entails the whole structure of its existence and reality. A representation of the chair, however, fixes upon only a perspective of the chair, which cannot express anything of the chair's reality. This analysis is surprising, because if we remember the whole discussion of book X, we will recall that the physical chair is not a real object either; but mimesis (as the process of artistic representation) is suspect not because of its failure to entail the eternal Form of chair but because of its simple failure to entail the complete physical characteristics of the crafted chair, the physical likeness of the Form. Similarly, in the *Ion*, Socrates is intent to show that the best judges among the "tid-bits" of life as drawn up in poetry are the craftsmen, not the philosophers.

Though Plato is silent on the subject, can we not infer the possibility of a nonmimetic poetry—a poetry in which the poet looks beyond the physical crafts and their objects toward the construction of myths and stories which direct one out of physical existence and into eternal life? I think that Plato simply leaves this pathway open, implying by his own example that philosophy can direct new interpretations of the old "texts" as well as provide subject matter for the new myths.

19. Although the later ontological dialogues seem less integrally associable with this early rhapsodic strain, I think that it is a mistake to read them as though they cease to be works with a bearing upon art in the same way as the *Ion*, *Phaedrus*, or *Symposium*. I am not just thinking of moments like that in the *Sophist* where the Stranger mentions the battle of gods and giants (245e–246e). I would like to suggest that this dialogue's focus on resemblance, even with its implications for the profoundest ontological discoveries, is fundamentally poetical-philosophical: with this discussion we locate a point at which metaphor and denotation serve a common end. Similarly, the *Parmenides*, with its discussion of ways to talk legitimately about the One, was read by the Neoplatonists as a text which showed that the profoundest specu-

lations concerning ontology must necessarily be presented in terms of analogy and metaphor. F. M. Cornford discusses this interpretation in *Plato and Parmenides* (rpt. Indianapolis: Bobbs-Merrill, n.d.), p. 131.

20. Letter 2, 314c1–4.

21. Marsilio Ficino's *Commentary on the Symposium* (trans. Sears R. Jayne, *University of Missouri Studies* 19 [1944], no. 1) interprets love explicitly in this way. Love is the highest of the inspired gifts, and Socrates claimed love as his specialty, having learned it not from any philosopher but from the priestess Diotima. The light and beauty of God are the object of love's ultimate longing. Ficino aptly sees in Alcibiades' speech at the end of the dialogue the allegorical implication that Socrates is himself the very image of Love described throughout as the child of poverty and plenty, a trickster, and an enchanter suspended, as it were, between wisdom and ignorance. Thus, Ficino sees Plato as having made Socrates both the conduit of this wisdom concerning Love and the example of the wisdom he describes. Socrates plays the same role in the *Ion*.

22. *Laws* 668a ff., *Republic* 595ff. This is the way Plato explicitly defines it, although I have taken some pains to argue that Plato's own practice and his doctrine of inspiration inchoately suggest a philosophical poetic in addition to a technical theory of art. Collingwood argues that mimesis in Plato's sense means art as amusement and as magic. As amusement, it is simply frivolous and should be rejected. As magic, however—which means that it stirs up emotions, whether base or noble—art can be useful, and Plato seems to have this particular utility in mind in *Republic* III and in the *Laws*. For Collingwood, art proper separates our consciousness of things from raw awareness. This bifurcation of common experience is potentially purifying. Plato's own writings apotheosize the divine gift of poetry by both teaching and employing purified consciousness.

*Kevin L. Cope*

# Satire: The Conquest
# of Philosophy

SATIRE is the only literary genre which is enthusiastically philosophical. From other genres critics may distill lessons pertinent
to every branch of philosophy, but only satire openly esteems truth
more than art. Only the satirist claims to declare truth without worrying about beauty. Even long, didactic works like Lucretius' *On the
Nature of Things* or Herbert's *Temple* are sanctioned by the need to
squeeze truth into entertaining or enticing forms. Satire, though, al-
leges its disgust with an accommodating art, relinquishing, whenever
a choice is necessary, literary elegance and ease to philosophical truth
and moral struggle.

The claim of satire to philosophical rigor—its preoccupation with
truth at the expense of feeling or beauty—has seduced its major critics into a misunderstanding of the service it performs for philosophy,
of the type of truth it announces, and of the reasons for its efflores-
cence in the seventeenth and eighteenth centuries. The foremost critics of satire have stumbled into a naive philosophical and literary realism which defeats and devalues the ethical and philosophical project
of the satirist. Whether we believe with Ellen Leyburn and Alvin Ker-
nan that a satire observes definite generic rules, rules which represent
and report the confidently held ideals of a culture, whether with
Northrop Frye and Edward and Lillian Bloom we reduce satire to a
procedure for attaining an elusive ideal, or whether we are drawn to
some compromise between these critical poles, we still attribute to
satirists a philosophical optimism that they lack. We grant them an accurate knowledge of experience, even though they may distort that ex-

perience as greatly as Rabelais distorts France, and we allow them a happy certainty of their ethical ideals, even though they may, like Samuel Butler, sink these ideals in a "dirty pond." Critics as dissimilar as W. H. Auden and Patricia Spacks unite in the hope that satirists know—or worse, believe that they know—both ethical and natural truth.

These theories of satire should startle us. Even if we shy away from Robert Elliott's vision of satire as a form of magical exorcism, as an artful means to smash the physical reality of an enemy and the spiritual reality of his or her gods, then certainly the modern history of satire should exorcise these critical opinions. The two great waves of English satire, beginning in the early and late seventeenth century, are propagated along with fashionable skepticism. Donne's well-known third satire provides a fine example, from the first wave of the genre, of a satiric recognition of the remoteness of knowledge. Our subject, the second great wave of satire, swells atop tracts on doubt such as Jeremy Taylor's *Ductor Dubitantium*, Joseph Glanvill's *Vanity of Dogmatizing*, and Robert Boyle's *Sceptical Chymist*. This satire crowns no Restoration cultural consensus; instead it meters the aftershocks of the tentative assertion of any values at all against historical forces which had clearly demonstrated their fragility. This wave of satire rises on the pleas of Thomas Sprat and Abraham Cowley to steer philosophy away from unknowable absolutes; it passes through Dryden's attempt to introduce academic skepticism into literary criticism; and it rolls into an "empirical" philosophy which dams our conduits to nature and God. Let us ask, then, whether the confident genre of satire relies on something as flimsy as the Restoration notion of truth, then consider its natural affinity with the literary philosophy of the early empiricists.

THE RESTORATION inherited from the earlier seventeenth century a conception of the world as dualistic. The elements of this ontology were usually spiritual and corporeal substance, though nature and grace or monarchy and democracy provided apt religious and political analogues. However distorted, the vocabulary of dualism yielded the basic language of satire. While an author like Descartes aimed to seal a truce between the two factions of reality, the Restoration satirist sets mind and body, ideal and real, at war with one another. He works against the formation of any objective or absolute order, for the outrage which identified his genre depends, ironically, on a conflict between explanation and experience. While an optimistic critic like Sidney regards ideal and actual as two more or less perfect renderings of the same reality, the very language of the Restoration satirist is scarred by the war of philosophy on nature and of ethics on experience. Consider these two examples from Butler's *Hudibras:*

> 'Twas *Presbyterian* true blew,
>
> . . . . . . . .
> Such as do build their Faith upon
> The holy text of *Pike* and *Gun;*
> Decide all Controversies by
> Infallible *Artillery;*
> And prove their Doctrine Orthodox
> By Apostolick *Blows* and *Knocks.*
>                     (I.i.189–98)

> What makes a Knave, a Child of God,
> And one of us?—*A Livelyhood.*
> What renders beating-out of Brains,
> And murther Godliness?—*Great gains.*
> What's tender Conscience?—*'Tis a Botch,*
>
> . . . . . . . . . . .
> What makes y'encroach upon our Trade,
> And damn all others?—*To be paid.*
>                     (III.i.1263–72)

Butler's "nature" is relentlessly abstract; experience is filtered through the senses and sieved through prejudices. A rendering of the process of perception, Butler's world converts objective events and uncompromising ideals into the immediate experience of error. On the one hand, the simple experience of religious faith splits into its apparently opposed components, whether *"Pike* and *Gun"* or "Infallible *Artillery";* on the other, these sets of contraries define both one another and the whole to which they contribute, much as two hemispheres define a sphere. Like two hemispheres, the oppositions defined by the dualistic philosophy belong to a single whole, yet intersect at no point. So in the second passage Butler sprinkles the dashes midway through his sentences not only to emphasize the conceptual boundary dividing the two halves of every phenomenon, but also to remind us of the control we can assert over the process of conceptualization. Placing cognition under the government of the will, he tells us that experience and its companion, epistemology, belong to ethics.

Butler, then, asks satire neither to vindicate any absolute ideals nor to condemn any segment of experience; he depends on it instead to knit together the edicts of a philosophical system with the rendering of experience that those edicts tend to produce. Satire is especially adept at fleshing out hypocrisy for just this reason, for it welds together experiences and ideals which both contradict and define one another. In *The Plain Dealer*, a dramatic satire, Wycherley's femme fatale, Olivia, has no more in common with that world "where men devour one another like generous hungry lions" than the "cordial drop heaven in our cup has thrown" has for Rochester with the empty flask of love. But both Rochester and Wycherley interlock the ideal conception of experience with experience itself in order to show them both opposite and inseparable. Satire warns philosophy that the very process of explanation will define the contradictions which make explanation impossible.

Satire never sparks a simple argument between defective experience and unreachable ideals, but sews them together on an infinitesimal seam, where they may touch but never intersect. Once he has secured this tentative bond of rigid philosophy with intractable experience, however, the satirist wonders what he should *do* with his hybrid image of reality. Although this mixture of philosophy and nature offers a fair image of the dualistic conception of reality, the satirist notices that this image of complete knowledge was produced artificially, not by copying some real archetype but by willfully stitching together antitheses. The power to create such a model of reality suggests to him the power to dismantle or expel it. Inadvertently, the artificing power overrules the philosophic, for only art can bind ideas to their contrary experiences so that reason may decide to reject both together.

Dryden, for example, regularly relies on the satiric character to extract from chaotic experience the principles which must inform that experience. Dryden's poetic characters bind philosophical ideas to the countervailing facts that they create and criticize, thus allowing Dryden to expel both halves of this perverse duality together. After this process is complete, only Dryden, his artifact, and his conviction remain to fill the void left by expelled idea and object. When, for example, Dryden decides, in *Absalom and Achitophel*, to exhaust rhetorically the character of Shaftesbury, he vibrates his victim through a series of positive ideals and contrasting "crimes." He clinches the character when the earl permits the condensation of natural chaos, the crowd, to "shake the Tree" of absolute authority. The image of natural error and the image of absolute truth cancel one another, Dryden's moral outrage hounding both beyond the margins of intelligibility (*A&A*, 203). When Shaftesbury later tries to seduce Monmouth, he offers the misguided bastard no theoretical argument at all, but only a series of facts intended to counteract the philosophical truisms which he casually satirizes at the end of his speech (244–302). "God were not safe, his Thunder cou'd they shun / He shou'd be forced to crown another Son" (*Medall*, 215–16); no metaphor is too daring when the subject is the link between a realistic version of truth and the real error such a version produces. "True or False" may serve for Rochester as man's main "subject of debate," but only when debate shows art driving the dichotomy of ideal and real into the void of "Nothing"—into an anti-realistic genre like satire ("Upon Nothing," 32).

A philosophy which stresses the objectivity of truth is thus as much the victim of satire as are the repugnant features of experience. Both depend on a decision to treat conceptualizations of experience as though they were objective. Both surrender to a voluntary rejection of this naive philosophical faith. Once the Restoration satirist has jettisoned both ideal and real, how does he fill the vacuum created? When Archilochus satirically expelled his adversary Lycambes, Lycambes and his daughter killed themselves, leaving nothing behind but depression. But when a writer of Arabic *hijà* satirically repulsed an enemy, the conquering tribe cast their arbitrary values into the relenting social void. So Johnson, in "The Vanity of Human Wishes," fills the chasm dug by the erosion of both wishes and rewards with an illogical and unrealistic call to prayer. The furious energy which ejected the factious fraternity of ideal and real now replaces them with ethical exhortation. For lost virtues and forgotten vices it substitutes a pattern for living which, being only a pattern, an artifact, submits to neither logical analysis nor empirical verification, but instead presents a constructive method for governing both activities. Often feared as a destructive genre, satire is thus constructive. It frees us from the tyranny of a disappointing reality and helps keep the philosophical idea of that reality at bay. Yet it also forces us to avoid the contrasting tyranny of subjectivity, for it asks us to manage and express publicly those ideas and experiences that we have subordinated. Satire demonstrates the conquest of ontology by ethics.

The process of satiric conquest, so much more congenial to modern philosophy and to the ritual origins of satire than the belief that satire mimics popular truisms or quasi-Platonic ideals, is most manifest in the odd—and critically troubling—structure of most Restoration satires. We have mentioned the satires of Rochester, Wycherley, Butler, and Dryden; each of these authors characteristically ends his bitter indictments with an unexpectedly positive vision:

> All this with indignation have I hurled
> At the pretending part of the proud world
> Who, swollen with selfish vanity, devise
> False freedoms, holy cheats, and formal lies
> Over their fellow slaves to tyrannize.
>                     (*Satyr*, 114–18)

So Rochester concludes his assault on theory and experience. He concludes his *poem*, however, by wondering, in an interrogative mode exempt from analysis and verification, whether we might at least imagine a perfect courtier or a "churchman who on God relies." Indeed, Rochester self-consciously added this inquiry long after his satire had been completed. Wycherley preempts the relentless satire of *The Plain Dealer* with a fairy-tale ending in which poetic justice triumphs over all probability; Dryden ends all his political satires with a prophetic "nod" from the "divine," a nod which retires all the false theories and events that he has defeated; even Butler tops his late third part of *Hudibras* with the artfully irrelevant literary experiment of the *Heroical Epistle*. And many other satirists, whether Halifax or Congreve, Buckinghamshire or Shadwell, arrest the arrows of satire, which fly through the void between pedestrian experience and impractical ideas, with an artificial target held beyond the bounds of reality.

ALONG WITH SATIRE, the seventeenth and early eighteenth centuries nourished a philosophy loosely designated as "empiricism." The nominal dependence of this philosophy on experience seems to disqualify it as a colleague of a highly artificial genre like satire. Similarly, the intractable subjectivity usually credited to the systems of Locke and his posterity seems to obstruct the parade of confidently held ideals alleged to characterize our genre. The project of the empirical philosophers, however, is precisely the same as that of the satirist: the substitution of an artificial moral pattern of experience for both an accurate rendering of "reality" and the objective truth behind it. One of the longest (and most satirical) stretches of Locke's *Essay Concerning Human Understanding* is his demonstration that both material and spiritual substance, both nature and mind, are absolutely unknowable and therefore should be expelled from the field of human knowledge (2.23.23–27). Locke allows us, of course, representative ideas of these two realms. More than mere sensual impressions of unknowable worlds, these ideas spring from an intermediary process of "observation" which, by scanning both internal and external worlds, generates ideas, or "the materials of thinking" (2.2.2). While Locke butts the notion of spiritual or corporeal substance with the same vigor that Butler tramples the "dark-lanthorn of the spirit" or the accompanying *"ignis fatuus"* of matter, he wonders with Rochester whether the very process of stitching together and then discarding the two halves of reality might yield true ideas. When we squeeze the notion of "idea," we find that the basic elements of human knowledge never represent objective reality at all, but that they betoken "the Power to produce an Idea in our Mind" (2.8.8); knowledge is a currency in which one can express the relative values of the forces which contribute *to* reality. "Simple *Ideas*" are "all real and true because they answer and agree to those Powers of Things, which produce them in our Minds" (2.30.2); the only false estimate we could make of reality would accrue from compounding ideas with objective "things" rather than powers.

Locke thus quells the zeal for objective knowledge first by tightening the alliance between objectivity and subjectivity and, secondly, by discarding subject and object in favor of an artful system of "observation" and "thinking" which manages and occludes both. Like the satirist, he vests more faith in the products of art than in those of reality. Dryden brought together an "anarchy" of data about a "man so various" as Zimri in order to consolidate and expel his character; so in the philosophical analogue of the literary character, the theory of identity, Locke convenes a welter of experiences in order to prove that identity abides in none of them, that the idea of the self emerges from "the same continued life" as it asserts its "ownership," its authority, over the experiences in memory (2.27.6). Similarly, the "property" which results from participation in an artificial system like the economy quitclaims the real soil seized by a real native isolated in the American woods (*Second Treatise of Government*, sec. 48), while

> the Truth and certainty of *moral* Discourses abstracts from the Lives of Men, and the Existence of those Vertues in the World, whereof they treat: Nor are Tully's Offices less true, because there is no Body in the World that exactly practices his Rules, and lives up to that pattern of a vertuous Man, which he has given us, and which existed no where, when he writ, but in *Idea.* (4.4.8)

The most interesting ideas in Locke's system are the most abstract. For these ideas make manifest his tendency to frown on anything approaching reality or objectivity, even to lose interest in the more sensual components of his system, and to favor programmatic ideas like "justice" which organize experience and which create "truth" by vanquishing irregular experience with order and coherence. Whether of "property" or "virtue," abstract ideas coordinate the finest of satires on the unintelligibility of objective experience and realistic philosophy.

Not surprisingly, those philosophers who followed Locke fancied themselves literary artists, even satirists. Writing in the interrogative mode characteristic of the happy conclusions to Restoration satires, Locke's pupil Shaftesbury converts a branch of satire into a root of truth:

Now what rule or measure is there in the world, except in the considering of the real temper of things, to find which are truly serious and
which ridiculous? And how can this be done, unless by applying the
ridicule, to see whether it will bear? But, if we fear to apply this rule in
anything, what security can we have against the imposture of formality
in all things? (I:11)

Shaftesbury counsels an aggressive interrogation of the idea of "reality" lest we succumb to its tyranny, lest we open our philosophy to
satire. Ridicule, or satire, cultivates the "serious," the ethical purpose
which transcends and expels the real obstacles to its fulfillment. Satirists guard against "the imposture of formality." They insure that the
Drydenian prophecies or Rochestrian characters which counteract
ideals or experiences are truly coherent—or, as Locke would say, true
because coherent. "Now since there are several opinions concerning a
superior Power . . . the consideration is, how many of these opinions,
or this want of opinion, may possibly consist with virtue or merit, or
be compatible with an honest or moral character" (II:231). For nothing
is a "fairer matter of speculation than that of a beautiful, propor-
tioned, and becoming action" (I:97); indeed nothing is more true than
the "good humour" which Shaftesbury identifies as the chief feature
of Christ!

Berkeley, who concluded his sequence of satires against the naturalistic theory of knowledge and its accompanying ethics with an
artful character of tar-water, comes to the same conclusion: "I had
rather my wife and children all believed what they had no notion of,
and daily pronounced words without a meaning, than that any of
them should cut his throat, or leap out of a window" (*Alciphron*, 113).
Berkeley addresses the naturalistic ontology of the libertine and the
fideistic philosophy of the theologian with equal severity, for both
systems define one another, and both systems value an accurate presentation of either the corporeal or incorporeal worlds more than they
value the expulsion of error and the artful construction of a model of
moral character. Even in an early work, the *New Theory of Vision*,
Berkeley replaces an objective model of "space" with an ethical description of "distance" as a sensual shorthand for the actions we must

take to reach an object. By the late work *Siris*, however, he warns against taking even sense too seriously, suggesting that we conceive of sense as only a vehicle for the formal instructions of ethics. Nature bows to a "language of Nature" which converts experience itself into a satire against remote ideals and mind-independent matter. Satire becomes reality itself. As Adam Smith, the last disciple of Berkeley and a self-styled empiricist, was to exclaim, "the most perfect knowledge" must be "supported by the most perfect self-command"; but the "self" doing the commanding should be no real person but an artificial identity, a Swiftian persona, an "impartial spectator" who artfully represents the moral attitude behind philosophy and who, by asserting that attitude against any objective reality, proves more real than real people or real satirists (*Theory of Moral Sentiments*, 237). Like another great satirist, Blake, Smith dubs this powerful satirist the "real" man.

Neither the horn of confidently held ideals nor the image of bitter experience, satire is less a factor in than a founder of the relationship between literature and philosophy. The satire of the seventeenth and eighteenth centuries frees both philosophy and literature from the obligation to imitate truth directly. Philosophy it frees from the impulse to objectify ideals, which also tend to objectify their antitheses, and literature it frees from the duty to portray life accurately. The satire of this period converts philosophy and literature into matched instruments for asserting a moral, and ultimately groundless, conviction against antagonistic experience *and* paralyzing speculation. Satire directs value and beauty against evidence and disorder. It saves fact and fiction from too plodding a definition. In search of the objective nature of satire, the Elizabethans found it the ugliest of genres; in search of its philosophical purpose, the Augustans revered satire as the weapon of order and elegance against too literal an idea of truth.

*Claudia Brodsky*

# Knowledge and Narrative in Kant's *Logic*

WHEN HEINRICH VON KLEIST wrote precipitously to Wilhelmine von Zenge in 1801, "Mein einziges, mein höchstes Ziel ist gesunken, und ich habe keines mehr" ("My only, my highest goal has sunken, and I have none left"),[1] it was not to some reversal imposed upon their formal engagement to which he referred, nor to any personal disillusionment on his part with the romantic attachment between them. The reason Kleist gave Wilhelmine for the sense of purposelessness he had come to suffer was his reading of the critical philosophy of Immanuel Kant. "Wenn alle Menschen statt der Augen grüne Gläser hätten . . ." ("If all men had green glasses instead of eyes . . ."),[2] is Kleist's famous attempt to formulate, for the benefit of his fiancée's understanding, the radical equation of all cognition with the formation of mental representations set forth in Kant's deduction of the only possible knowledge reason may claim. The image Kleist employs of vision through colored glass may seem, in its reference to distinctly physical circumstances, a particularly inadequate or inappropriate analogy for the founding of a philosophical system concerned with a reconception of reason itself. The purely intellectual nature and purpose of Kant's *Critique* may in fact be seen to be conveyed most accurately by Kant's own chosen metaphor for his endeavor: that of a "revolution" in metaphysics most closely resembling the Copernican in physical sciences for its power to change not the objects but the very *Denkart*, the "way of thought," of philosophy.[3] For the particular status quo or the state of things to be affected by Kant's "revolution" were the mental procedures which we ourselves conceive of as governing speculative thought. Yet, any further acquaintance with Kleist's life should serve to remind us that the experience his image compares to the consequences of "Kantian philosophy"[4] is no more physically concrete than the specific course of action, attributed to reading Kant, that image is used to explain. For Kleist's letter announces his impending departure on a needed diversionary excursion through Germany to France from which as a writer, and as Wilhelmine's intended, he will to all intents and purposes never return.[5]

In employing Kleist as a means of introducing Kant within the context of a critical investigation of narrative, the present study leaves aside the question, certainly of related interest in itself, of whether Kleist's reference to Kant at this pivotal instance of communication did not provide him with an effective intellectual fiction serving to take the place of a less convenient, more immediate, truth. Few writers have succeeded, in life no less than in fiction, in confusing the mental and physical realms of experience as thoroughly as Kleist, or in thus provoking more perpetual and indefinite speculation as to the "reality" of events presented in either. Whatever its particular motivation for articulation, the "Kantian crisis" in Kleist's life, since designated as such by literary history and isolated to have been initiated at this moment in his life, finds its most direct expression in the central dilemma outlined in the same letter. Kleist writes: "We cannot decide if that which we name truth is truly truth, or if it only appears to us as such. If the latter, then the truth which we gather here *is*, after death, no longer. And all striving to acquire possessions which would also follow us into the grave is in vain."[6] Apparently speaking out of a desire for immortality already frustrated in its own anticipation, Kleist represents, and seriously misrepresents, the major problem implied by Kant's critical theory as one of cognitive undecidability. If "what we call truth" may "only appear to us as such," then it may also lack all objective validity and be "gathered" to outlive us, as the permanent "possession" after which we have "striven," only "in vain." (It should be noted, however, with respect to the peculiarity of Kleist's formulation here, that since the desired end of "all striving" it indicates is specifically for our "possessions" to "follow us *into* the grave," the particular immortality Kleist despaired of is in its conception already in contradiction, or crisis, with itself.) "What we name truth" will be named for the purposes of this study "representational narrative" or "narrative fiction," and the special relevance of Kant to an examination of narrative can be read in the very terms of the brief and mistaken summary Kleist offers. For in ascribing the situation of an inability to "decide" upon truth to a distinction between, on the one hand, what we perceive as and "name truth," and, on the other, that which would be "truly truth," Kleist demonstrates, far more successfully than if he had intended to, the more correctly Kantian and troubling notion that between "what we name truth" and the "truly true" no distinction can within reason be made.

The dilemma of cognitive uncertainty described by Kleist, while adding to the persuasive tension of his own plea for understanding, in fact reduces, as it divides, the full force and purport of Kant's hypothesis. For the central premise of Kant's critical deduction is that any demonstration of the possibility of knowledge must necessarily and simultaneously be the limitation of knowledge to the apprehension—or in Kleist's words, the "gathering"—of what "appears to us" alone. In order for any object to be understood or even objectified—those mental operations, in strict conformity with Kant's hypothesis, being essentially the same—that object must be made present to us by the formal intuition and relational mechanism composing our perceptions independent of and prior to any material sensation of the object itself. Since those forms and connectives are not inferred from but are instead constitutive of experience, we can never claim to "know," without their mediation, what we may only "think" as "things in themselves": "things" not already represented, and *as* representations, sequentially connected by perception in the mind.[7]

"Representation" (*Vorstellung*), the central term in Kant for the "appearance" (*Erscheinung*) of things our minds construct, thus signifies the antithesis of its aesthetic meaning of *mimesis*, as well as bearing its significance in political practice of a part standing ethically—formally, by synecdoche—for a whole. For we do not "know" reality by a copy we make of it, nor know from one selected member a larger constituency to which it pertains. What we "know" and all that we know *is* representation: the appearances which identify the reality we experience just as discourse, in articulating our understanding of experience, should logically constitute the identity of those appearances by name. Thus to distinguish what "we name truth" from that which would be "truly truth" is to remain tautologically and squarely within the limitations of knowledge deduced by Kant rather than to depart from or transcend them to a knowledge whose "truth" would take no name. In brief, if less than satisfactory response to Kleist's complaint: the "truth" as it "appears to us" is one to which we have no alternative in Kant, most especially that of forgetting that all alternatives imagined must be false. The unashamed repetitiveness, the apparent tediousness of Kant's own discursive style—as compared negatively by Kant himself to the writings he credits with having awakened him from his "dogmatic slumbers," the "subtlety" and "charm" of the "attack" upon metaphysics carried out by his "acute" predecessor, David Hume[8]—the "dry," "longwinded" quality which Kant trusted would preserve his work from wide and rapid "popularity,"[9] is owing in no small measure to his *Critique*'s constant recollection and reminder that the only "truth" separating critical thought from the illusions of all forms of idealism[10] remains a thought to which we may only refer by name.

Thinking in language is in fact the activity Kant defined *as* philosophy, in contradistinction to the form of reason carried out by intuition, mathematics. Kant presents the deduction of the specifically modal difference between mathematics and philosophy in the *Methodenlehre* terminating the first *Critique* as well as in section 2, "Concept of Philosophy in General," of the introduction to the *Logic*. As modes of knowledge, Kant reasons, both philosophy and mathematics propose to understand their objects of investigation through a coordination of concepts and representations. What distinguishes them is not an integral distinction between the objects they study—the separate categories of quantity and quality described instead by Kant to overlap[11]—but, as Kant argues for the first time, the ways in which those objects are formally conceived. The concepts of mathematics, according to the understanding of representation afforded by the *Critique*, are representations of intuitions "constructed a priori," or without the aid of experience, whereas the concepts of philosophy are themselves the representations of experience and thus necessarily a posteriori, or dependent upon empirical perception to be thought.[12] Mathematics, in other words, intuits the forms it investigates "in concreto"—the "concrete" for Kant, however, signifying the negative of precisely that condition with which it is most commonly identified, namely, the empirical.[13] For the forms which *are* the concepts of mathematical reason are in Kant's terms "concrete," are fully synthetic, complete and particular, and thus yield no occasion for discursive speculation, to the extent that unlike "things" empirically experienced they are, exclusively, all that they appear to be—should the term "appearance" still be considered a serviceable designation for the manifestation to the mind of forms which the mind itself constructs. Construed neither mentally from physical sensation nor "conceptually," that is, by way of discursive relations, the cognitions of mathematical reason might best be described instead as "natural," were nature itself "constructed a priori" of purely formal objects reason could "know."

Philosophical knowledge, or knowledge derived *"from* concepts,"[14] is also composed by a priori intuitions, the mental forms of time and space. But those intuitions, rather than being self-sufficient or mentally capable of representing themselves, are only formally constructive insofar as they are practically applied. They represent what they are not—the sensation of matter—to the mind as phenomenon. The concepts of philosophy, according to the *Critique*, are thus grounded no less in sensory experience than in the mental representation of that experience. Consequently, and most decisively, the knowledge derived from those representations, for the reason that the latter are *not* purely or "concretely" intuitional, must in turn be understood to *refer*, as well as to confer form. Since the sources of its cognitions are unavoidably twofold—"springing," as Kant writes, from "zwei Grundquellen," "two fundamental sources"[15]—philosophical reasoning must understand its own referents to refer with certainty solely to representations, rather than to things in their essence, while recognizing the essentiality of referentiality, of an object given by experience, to its mode. "The great fortune" met with by nonempirical reasoning in mathematics "naturally brings about the supposition," Kant cautions in the first *Critique*, that "all concepts" can be considered purely intuitional, and thus reason itself capable of "becoming master over nature."[16] Such a "pure philosophy," however, only "bungles about in nature," Kant continues, without rendering the "reality" of its concepts intuitable, or those concepts themselves thereby "credible."[17]

The difficulties consciously encountered by a *critical* philosophy, by contrast, lie precisely in its recognition of the heterogeneity of its concepts. For the very motive for "criticizing" philosophical reason is that its "representations" are conceived both "a priori in intuition," and "a posteriori" according to the "matter of phenomena" given only "by means of experience."[18] The *name* given by Kant in the *Logic* to this condition of epistemological heterogeneity, inherent in and definitive of philosophy, is specifically that of its linguistic modality, "discourse": ". . . herein . . . mathematics has an advantage over philosophy, in that the cognitions of the former are intuitive, those of the latter, on the contrary, only *discursive*" (emphasis in text).[19]

Knowledge which is "only discursive" is limited by its dependence upon nonformal, sensory perception. Thus the discourses of philosophy and of experience, rather than being held in distinction by the desire for an ideal knowledge, must be recognized as a single discourse subject to critical judgment with as much regard to its referential veracity as to its formal ability to logically convey. The mistaken perception that his own epistemology is ideal or "transcendental," instead of "critical," is forcefully disputed by Kant in his *Prolegomena to Any Future Metaphysics*. Kant is forced, however, in turn, by the power and pervasiveness of that misperception to announce in the *Prolegomena*, his introductory sequel to the *Critique of Pure Reason*, a de facto rewriting of the first *Critique*. He states the wish to replace the term "transcendental"—even as that modifier had been limited in the first *Critique* to describing the mental *Vermögen*, or "faculty," rather than the objective exercise, of cognition—entirely by the single word "critical," hoping thereby to impede future developments of the same mistake.[20] The confusion, which has nonetheless grown to blur all lines of lexical distinction over time, of the negative premise of Kant's *Critique* with a historical apex in the affirmation of idealism, can be seen however to have been more thoroughly refuted before this attempted "retraction" on Kant's part.[21] For Kant's initial determination of the necessarily *discursive* mode of philosophical reasoning is itself the necessary logical condition for an implicitly *critical* theory of knowledge. Departing from formal idealists and empirical skeptics alike, Kant maintains the ultimacy of a structural and thus indismissible bond between philosophy and that matter which is all but philosophy, material sensation. Discourse, the mental intermediary between philosophy and the senses, is also the ground for the limitations to be recognized, the fallibilities to be criticized in both. For Kant, the inherently self-critical dimension of all philosophical reasoning is its own constitution of discursive representation: its constitutional and indispensable link, in other words, to literature.

Kant compared the very rules by which we comprehend and connect experience cognitively to the rules of "grammar" in a language.[22] Similar to the intelligibility of meaning afforded by a regulative grammar, the understanding of "how truth is possible" is declared in the *Logic* to be itself unproblematic, "since here [in the judgment of truth] understanding acts according to its essential laws."[23] For the same reason, however, the one cognitive possibility which understanding must fail to comprehend is its own apparent and autonomous abuse: the mistaking, as if against its laws, of falsity for truth. Kant continues in the *Logic* to explain why such errors cannot actually pertain to understanding itself:

> Now, if we had no power of cognition other than understanding, we would never err. There lies, however, aside from understanding, yet another indispensable source of cognition in us. That is sensibility, which gives us the material of thought and thereby acts according to other laws than those of understanding. From sensibility, viewed in and of itself, error can however also not arise, because the senses do not judge at all.
>
> The ground of the arisal of all error must therefore be sought solely and alone in the *unnoticed influence of sensibility upon understanding*, or, to speak more precisely, upon judgement. This influence, namely, brings about that we hold merely subjective grounds for objective ones in judging, and consequently that we mistakenly exchange the mere seeming appearing of truth for truth itself. For therein consists the very essence of the seeming appearance, which on that account is to be considered as a ground for holding a false cognition to be true.
>
> What makes error possible is therefore the seeming appearance by which the merely *subjective* is falsely exchanged for the *objective* in judgement.[24]

Just as its prerequisite, sensory experience, forces even formal knowledge, that of "appearances," to be represented by discourse rather than made present in intuition, the involvement of sensibility in understanding entails our susceptibility to mistakes. Neither understanding alone, whose rules, like the conventional laws of a language, can no more be broken without notice than misjudged, nor the "senses" themselves, which are not governed formally, and thus as Kant observes, "do not judge at all," is attributed with the "mistaken exchange" of "false cognitions for true." Instead, the convergence, void of reflection, between sensory perception and conceptualization—"the unnoticed influence of sensibility upon understanding"—is given to be the basis for "the arisal of all error": the same basis, that is, given in the *Logic*, for knowledge itself.[25] Furthermore, like "true" knowledge, "false cognitions" necessarily take a discursive form. Kant proceeds to suggest that once the manifestation of error in a *"seeming* appearance" (*"Schein"* as opposed to *Erscheinung*) is recognized, the error itself may be recognized to be confined to its form of appearance alone: "Denn man kann doch vielleicht recht haben in der Sache und nur unrecht in der Manier, d.i. dem Vortrage" ("Then one can perhaps be right in substance and only wrong in manner, i.e., in elocutionary form"). Language may fail to represent knowledge correctly; yet knowledge "in substance," *"in der Sache,"* can never be conceived independently of its "elocution," whether the latter be viewed as a particular "manner" or as the universal regularity of cognition itself. Philosophy which limits itself critically to the representation of experience must commit its representations to the form of valid statements, or definitions; its errors, consequently, are also committed in the course of reason's discursive exposition. It is thus without any promise of foreseeable improvement in the future that Kant may (and must) admit openly, and with remarkable equanimity, in the first *Critique*, that "philosophy swarms with faulty definitions."[26]

Indeed, the near indifference with which Kant indicates the inevitable preponderance of errors in philosophy can itself be seen to indicate the singular radicality of his *Critique*. For Kant's candid treatment of discursive errors, rather than obliquely concealing a problem of cognition by its admission, points directly to the more redoubtable fact that errors in themselves are in no way centrally disruptive of his theory of knowledge. Deceptions stemming from the senses of perception and their representation gain little and detached attention in

Kant—in contrast with the attention given them in the empirical as well as Cartesian tendencies in philosophy Kant followed after, and also when compared with the limitations of reason relentlessly exposed throughout the *Critique* itself. The reason is that within the context of those same limitations cognitive error is a concept of effective inconsequence. The de-emphasis upon the essential epistemological opposition between truth and falsity, within a philosophical project concerned foremost with exposing the foundations of knowledge, is the logical and highly heterodox result of Kant's understanding of the means by which cognition proceeds. As discussed above, Kant deduces those means to belong specifically to discourse. But what we may understand by discourse—employed by necessity, as it is daily, with respect to experience—can only partially correspond to the critical understanding of discourse by which that necessity is independently, or a priori, deduced. For the epistemological criticism of "pure" or idealized reason whose point of departure is the unconditionally discursive nature of knowledge must also identify the articulations of reason with discourse that is independent of any single given experience. Thus, according to the logic of "representational" language informing the *Critique,* the significance of statements in their extension and of the very words they employ to designate sense is severed from any direct equation with their only known subject matter, particular experience. Stated in more familiar theoretical terms, the meaning of the language used in the service of reason submitted to criticism is rather precisely that of the *language* employed, according to the criticism of literature, by concepts of fiction. "Fiction" itself, for the very same reason, while later substituted by neo-Kantians for the concept of "criticism" itself,[27] is a term entirely excluded from the explicit considerations of the *Critique.* The identification of representational narrative, understood as fiction, with reason functioning within the limits of criticism is based instead upon the relationship both share with knowledge. While structured internally upon principles of sequential logic and causality, the individual discourses of narrative fiction and of reason cross at the question of the representationality *and* referential reality of the knowledge they afford. Thus the issue of fictionality is raised in Kant not in terms of fiction itself or of error, but, on the contrary, under the category of reliable statements of knowledge, "definitions." While the abstract clarity of Kant's analysis of definitions may seem immediately to cloud its significance for literary thought, a closer inspection of his examination of this most fundamental form of discursive knowledge may reveal that it describes with disorienting precision the unsuspected premises upon which both the concept and interpretation of "fiction" are built.

Kant's deduction of the status of definitions begins, in sec. 100 of the *Methodenlehre* of the *Logic,* with the distinction between definitions of "analytic" and "synthetic" composition. Analytic definitions correspond to a "given concept," synthetic definitions to a "made concept," and both are further subdivided as either a posteriori or a priori in cognitive origin. The first two of these preliminary oppositions (between analytic and synthetic definitions and their objects, given and made concepts) prove rapidly to be purely formal distinctions. For the sequential mode of investigation carried out in analysis determines that its results, unlike those of synthesis, can never be known to be conclusive; similar to an exclusively metonymic narration, a definition by analysis would be, by definition, necessarily incomplete. Thus sec. 104, the only moment in the *Logic* dealing solely with "analytic definitions," also disqualifies them from further epistemological consideration: "Since there is no test through which one can become certain of whether or not one has exhausted all the characteristics of a given concept through complete analysis: so are all analytic definitions to be considered uncertain." [28]

The distinction between a priori and a posteriori "made concepts" is, however, fundamental, and relates directly to the modal distinction between mathematics and philosophy discussed earlier. A definition which is an a priori synthesis of a concept is again called a "construction" by Kant, since it itself "makes" the object it simultaneously defines. By contrast, a synthetic a posteriori definition would be an "exposition" of appearances, a definition based upon an "empirical" rather than an "arbitrary synthesis," as Kant calls the wholly nonexperiential modality of mathematical conceptualization. Kant insists at first that all definitions, whether of "arbitrarily made," "mathematical concepts," or of "empirically made," "experiential concepts," must be composed synthetically rather than analytically: "then also with respect to . . . the empirical concepts, water, fire, air and the like, I should not itemize what lies within them but learn through experience what belongs to them."[29] In a following moment proceeding from that premise, however, the very possibility of defining an empirical concept is denied. For experience, like its discursive representation in the mind, can never be fully and simultaneously made present. As no word can be considered final in the course of representing experience, no discursive knowledge of experience can be considered sufficient and thus no definition of experiential concepts truly definitive. Since discourse, in other words, is an inexhaustible mode of conveying, its empirical definitions can never exhaust the object they are intended, rather than "arbitrarily" "constructed," to convey. As Kant concludes in sec. 103, "Since the synthesis of an empirical concept is not arbitrary but empirical and, as such, can never be complete (because one can always discover more attributes of the concept by experience): so empirical concepts also cannot be defined."[30]

A definition of any concept relating to experience is thus more accurately called an "exposition" or "description" (sec. 105), whereas a mathematical definition—the only truly synthetical, because nonexperiential, definition—is renamed by Kant a "declaration" of "what one understands under a word": "was man unter einem Worte versteht."[31] The concept of a cognitive definition itself—of the identification of any object for the purposes of knowledge, performed linguistically by the form of equation stored within the grammar of language, predication—is maintained as a working concept by Kant which upon logical analysis is divided and replaced. Like the unrestricted conceptions of reason and experience, which Kant maintains it is the task of philosophy to oppose equally, the articulation of reason by means of definitions is critically determined by Kant to involve *two* activities, each unidentifiable with definitions understood ideally or empirically, and each distinct from the other in both object and mode. Returning to the striking marginalization of the problem of error in Kant, it can now be seen that reason—because of the same discursive nature which relates it to experience in the first place— must be recognized to merely approximate experience through a series of predications rather than to identify its reality with a single definition in the mind. Reason, once criticized, could thus be held accountable for error only insofar as it forgets its limitations as representational discourse and "declares" to be essentially true statements which can only "describe."

Sequential, expository "description" whose conceptual basis represents experience may seem in itself a concisely adequate description of narrative fiction. Definitions which cannot rigorously be considered definitions, which are logically "incomplete," only "a part of a definition," and yet can offer "a true and useful representation of a concept,"[32] are comparable with the statements we understand to compose narrative when viewed from the perspective of its representational realism. The fundamental act of understanding the *story* of a narrative requires that we comprehend and keep in mind its representations. To view narrative with regard to its "realism," however, is to view realism itself as the style or orientation of a work regarded, without apparent paradox, as "fiction." Thus, like the definitions Kant determines to be more precisely "descriptions," mere "approaches" or "approximations" (*Annäherungen*[33]), no epistemological claims—or only self-consciously weak ones—are found to be made by a representational discourse assumed at its outset to be fiction. Finally, the modesty of cognitive purpose ascribed to narrative fiction is in turn attributed twofold to the discourse of narrative analysis, literary criticism.

But what has been called fictionality here is not the fact of faulty definition in Kant, or the result of the uncertainty of discursive cognition. The radical nature of the fiction involved in the critical composition of cognition lies instead in those definitions Kant finds to be necessarily true. For the articulations of knowledge which alone are capable of presenting syntheses, in that they are independent of or "arbitrary" with regard to experience, are deduced by Kant to be entirely, and immodestly, identical with discourse. Fully synthetic definitions may be called "declarations," Kant stated, "in so far as they declare one's thought" not as to the understanding of experience but specifically, as cited above, as to "what one understands under a word."[34] "Was man unter einem Worte versteht" is the only possible object of definitions which "are not only always possible but also necessary."[35] We must always know, and thus be able to define by declaration, what we understand to be represented by a word: a word *as a word,* rather than as a referential marker of experience. For Kant specifies that such knowledge is only "the case with mathematicians"[36] whose knowledge is composed of "concrete *Anschauungen*" (that term of vision best translated into English as "intuitions," since it means to conceive or have a view of that for which no particular empirical experience accounts).[37] Thus the sole object of a definition which must be accurate, by critical definition, is that manifestation we know as a word. The "matter" of knowledge, in terms of Kant's epistemology, is, in other words, a dictionary: discursive declarations of the concepts constructed by discourse; words stating thoughts of what is understood under words. The fictionality Kant's criticism of reason proposes can perhaps be most effectively distinguished from that concept of fiction allowing for its description as "realism" (or for that matter as truly "fictional" fiction, or "fantasy") by the thought of a dictionary read without access to memory or imagination: a dictionary cut off from all sensory visualization, related only within itself and, of course, "concretely," to other books.

The image of such a dictionary and the hypothesis of such a reading—both, incidentally, a posteriori, or referring to experience, and thus no accurate definitions of knowledge in Kant—are merely offered here as antidotes to the confusion of verbal and nonverbal representation most commonly underlying discussions of verisimilitude in fiction: the equation of words with plastic or pictorial rendering which, for the purposes of critical thought, should seem a far greater conceptual shock. But Kant's own understanding of cognitive definitions exceeds the mode of antidotal oppositions, just as his critical project, meant to contribute medicinally to the well-being of philosophical procedure, extended further than the disproof of skepticism at which it initially aimed. For the discussion of definitions in the *Logic* proceeds to distinguish the reality from the facticity of the modes it deduces. Section 106 divides definitions into those whose meaning must be understood to be "nominal" and those whose meaning must be known to be "real." "Nominal definitions" are said to define, as designated, knowledge which is effective in name alone. A "name" here is the "arbitrarily given" designation of the "meaning" a definition itself "contains"; that is, by way of a specifically nominal definition a certain meaning is made known to correspond to a certain name, but no knowledge of any measure is afforded of a non-nominal object. Whether viewed with regard to the individual name defined or with respect to that object's further relations, the meaning of a nominal definition is thus limited to the performance of a purely logical signifying function: it articulates the "logical essence" of its object, "or merely differentiates" that object from other objects or names of meaning.[38] Its own adequacy, like that of any denotation, could only be known based on evidence external to itself. But as a statement of meaning known to have been attributed "arbitrarily," in the absence of any qualitative correlation with its object, the demonstration of the sufficiency of a nominal definition, or "name explanation," arises "merely" in the "particular relation" composed by its own "comparison with other definitums."[39] Thus Kant's understanding of the distinctions of meaning effected by nominal definitions alone fundamentally anticipates the modern semiological analysis of language in its entirety: that of a differential, rule or grammar-generated, and in itself only arbitrarily referential, signifying system.

Yet Kant defines "real definitions," or "explanations of things," to depart from a semiological model in extending to "the knowledge of an object." "Real definitions" do not describe an object empirically but display, according to its "internal determination," its very "possibility."[40] "Explanations of things" define their reality, and the reality of which they provide knowledge is defined in turn by "things" irrespective of names and comparative relations. The identification of the objects of definitions as being either "things" or "names" is itself a conventional distinction made toward the end of securing a non-contradictory method for epistemology, that is, one which would prescribe, on purely logical grounds, the functions of its discourse, or "mode."[41] Its earliest major formulation, in Aristotle's *Posterior Analytics*, relates to the particular emphasis placed upon the epistemological role of definition in his *Metaphysics*. In his refutation—especially relevant to the epistemologies preceding Kant—of what he terms "one-sided theories," those that hold that nothing or everything is "true," Aristotle introduces the concept of definition, or statements of "meaning," as a means of substituting semantic "truth" for questions of "true" being: "we must postulate . . . not that something is or is not, but that something has a meaning, so that we must argue from a definition, viz. by assuming what falsity or truth means" (*Metaphysics* 4.8.1012ª29–1012ᵇ8).[42] Leibniz, preceding Kant, in his *Schriften zur Logik und Methodenlehre,* founds the distinction between "nominal" and "real definitions" upon the sequential analysis ("Aufzählung der Merkmale") carried out in the former as opposed to the exposition, as in a geometrical proof, of the "possibility" of an object given in the latter.[43] Kant, following Leibniz, goes on in sec. 106 of the *Logic* to identify mathematical definitions as "real." But the consequences of that identification, once it has been made within the context of the *Critique,* entail a rupture no less between Kant's and Leibniz's own epistemologies than between the two categories of definition themselves. In terms of the literary, rather than philosophical ordering of the forms of meaning, the separation between kinds of cognitive statements Kant's *Logic* proposes signifies a break between the semantic possibilities of poetry and representational prose. For Kant's analysis of definitions further specifies that "names" attributed "arbitrarily," because only nominally, with definitive meaning are themselves the only objects which may be made known to us through "experience." The second moment of sec. 106 begins: "Erfahrungsgegenstände erlauben bloss Nominalerklärungen"—"Experiential objects allow for merely nominal explanations." All that we know on the basis of experience—which, it is the founding premise of the *Critique* to remind us, *is all that we know*—is restricted to an exclusively nominal significance. The passage in full prohibits any confusion of nominal knowledge with real.

> 2. Experiential objects allow for merely nominal explanations.—Logical nominal definitions of given concepts of understanding are taken from an attribute; real definitions, by contrast, from the essence of the thing, the first ground of its possibility. The latter thus contain that which always pertains to the things—the real being of the same.—Definitions based on mere negation cannot be called real definitions, because negating attributes can serve to distinguish one thing from another just as well as positing real ones, but cannot serve toward the recognition of the thing according to its internal possibility.

In moral matters real definitions must always be searched for—all our
striving must be directed in that direction. There are real definitions in
mathematics; then the definition of an arbitrary concept is always real.[44]

The distinction between "name explanations" and "cognitions of
things" brought forward in Kant's deduction of the only possible epistemology bears with it the formal relation of epistemology itself—lex-
ically, the "discourse of knowledge"—to the discourse known as narrative fiction. For the only certain knowledge discourse affords of all
objects of experience, the "logical, nominal definition" of phenomenal perception, itself reduces those objects to their identification with
a single, defining "attribute." The formulation of empirical perceptions proposed in the *Logic* thus resembles that of literary figurations
already recognized for their "intended" meaning: that gained at the
loss of their reference to a "real" being. In other words, knowledge—
necessarily of experience—in Kant reads like a poetry purified of all
ambiguities: not a "*poésie pure*" but one whose "meaning" *must* be recognized as well as realized to be merely logically and nominally significant. The understanding as well as the critical bracketing of that
"meaning" is assured by its limitation to single tokens of significance
distinguished only in their relation to each other and replacing any
relation between the naming and the "being of a thing." Just as every
known experience in Kant's epistemology is the representation of an
"appearance," the definitions of experience articulate appearances of
meaning rather than articulating meaning itself. They use language as
language is always used in the course of narrating a "fiction": as a relational medium for the representation of experience to which the fiction itself bears relationship only in name.

For the narration of a fiction sets out from the premise of a *full* substitution of representation for experience. Whatever the credibility of
its "content," the sense of sufficiency afforded by a representational
fiction arises first from the coherence of its form: narration appears to
exhaust, or to comprehend, experience by subordinating its representations to its causal structure, or "story." Thus fiction, as opposed to
poetry, can "tell" a story only by designating a single, identifiable
level of meaning; by speaking, so to speak, in names rather than
words. That is, the language of the discourse we "know" to be fiction

may, *as* fiction, do just about anything: it may compose and coordinate complex plots, exploiting the very notion of causality it appears to put into question; it may structure narrative action to imitate the scenes and suspense of drama; it may articulate physical settings as well as personal subjectivities, historical events as well as peculiarities of character; it may describe, develop, speculate, transform, and in so doing instruct and intrigue us, move, confuse or simply amuse us. But in order to compose itself as a fiction of any fashion, the language of fiction must first function like a language of names; that is, it must indicate the referents *meant* by the experience it defines in text. At the same time, the relationship of fiction to its referents, like that of names, is understood to be no less "arbitrary" and artificial in reality than binding in function. Consequently, by definition, one never asks of a narrative called a "fiction," as of a poem, if its representations, even when most "realistic" or "historically" accurate, are true, nor for that matter considers a poem, even when narrative in form and overtly "fictive" or mythological in content, to be precisely an intentionally *nominal* rendering of reality, a fiction.

What we know of all we experience, of all those occurrences de-fined as they are narrated by the essential form of narrative *and* of grammar, predication, is according to the logic of reason submitted to criticism, the nominal or prefigured knowledge afforded by a nar-rative fiction. Experience *is* narration in Kant, already envisioned or formally structured by the "intuitions" of time and space, connected sequentially by the central mental category of causality, and known by no other means than those it names. Mathematical objects, of which we have no "experience" in the Kantian sense of a necessarily a pos-teriori, phenomenal experience, are thus, strictly speaking, not ob-jects of knowledge at all but realities. The "real being" of a thing, that which is "always pertinent to it" and "the first ground of its possibil-ity," is defined in mathematical definitions, it should be recalled, as "what one understands by a word." The cognitive reality of a "thing" is, according to the *Critique*, not a "thing itself" (of which we can have no knowledge), nor its arbitrary designation as an object of experi-ence, but the *word* for the thing itself: the word not as a "referent" or the representation of a referent (that is, in Kant, of another represen-tation), since it is unrelated to experience and not in itself an intuition, nor as a figure arbitrarily standing for a referent and integrating it into a system of nominal meanings, but the word as articulation of the reality we neither "experience" nor narrate; words *as* the reality which pure reason, separated from experience by criticism—in Kant's terms—"constructs."

In Kant, knowledge of reality, rather than of phenomena, is thus simultaneously the disruption of all logical and nominal narration. Discourse, or words, is the critical means of translating between philosophical reason and empirical experience. Yet real knowledge, Kant proposes, is as such neither philosophical nor experiential. It is not a narrative story told through causally connected representations, not the understanding of a narrative at all but of "a word": the means of representation which itself tells no story. Real knowledge, according to the *Critique*, would be to know not what words "mean" but why words *are*—the necessary and necessarily literary medium between cognition and experience. The logic of Kant's *Critique*, like that of any discursive criticism, demonstrates that the real knowledge toward which discursive knowledge inevitably (as Kleist stated) "strives," but which, at the same time, it can never claim to "possess," is precisely what one understands under "discourse" itself: *"was man unter einem Worte versteht."*

## NOTES

1. Heinrich von Kleist, *Gesamtausgabe*, 7 vols. (München: Deutscher Taschenbuch Verlag, 1964), vol. 6, p. 163.

2. Ibid.

3. Immanuel Kant, *Kritik der reinen Vernunft* (Frankfurt: Suhrkamp, 1977), B xxiii, p. 28.

4. Kleist, *Gesamtausgabe*, vol. 6, p. 163.

5. Ibid., pp. 164–65: "Ach, es ist der schmerzlichste Zustand ganz ohne ein Ziel zu sein. . . . In dieser Angst fiel mir ein Gedanke ein. Liebe Wilhelmine, lass mich reisen. . . . Denn ich kehre um, *sobald ich weiss, was ich tun soll*. . . ."

6. Ibid., p. 163: "Wir können nich entscheiden, ob das, was wir Wahrheit nennen, wahrhaft Wahrheit ist, oder ob es uns nur so scheint. Ist das letzte, so *ist* die Wahrheit, die wir hier sammeln, nach dem Tode nich mehr—und alles Bestreben, ein Eigentum sich zu erwerben, das uns auch in das Grab folgt, ist vergeblich—" (all English translations my own).

7. Kant, *KrV:* B xxv–xxvii, pp. 30–31.

8. Immanuel Kant, *Prolegomena zu einer jeden künftigen Metaphysik die als Wissenschaft wird auftreten können* (Berlin: Akademie der Wissenschaften, 1903), pp. 257–60.

9. Ibid., p. 261: "Popularität (darf) folgen, aber niemals den Anfang machen. . . ."

10. See Kant's "Widerlegung des Idealismus," *KrV:* B 274–75, p. 254.

11. Ibid., B 740–54, pp. 612–22; Immanuel Kant, *Logik* (Frankfurt: Suhrkamp, 1977), A 22, pp. 445–46.

12. Kant, *KrV:* B 743, p. 614; *Logik:* A 22, p. 446.

13. Kant, *Logik:* A 23, p. 446.

14. Kant, *KrV:* B 741, p. 613: "Die *philosophische* Erkenntnis ist die *Vernunfterkenntnis* aus *Begriffen,* die mathematische aus der *Konstruktion* der Begriffe. . . ."

15. Ibid., B 74, p. 97.

16. Ibid., B 752–53, p. 621.

17. Ibid., B 753, p. 621.

18. Ibid., B 749, p. 618.

19. Kant, *Logik:* A 23, p. 446: "herein hat also . . . die Mathematik einen Vorzug vor der Philosophie, dass die Erkenntnisse der erstern intuitive, die der letztern hingegen nur *diskursive* Erkenntnisse sind."

20. Kant, *Prolegomena,* p. 293.

21. Ibid.: "nehme ich diese Benennung lieber zurück. . . ."

22. Ibid., p. 323.

23. Kant, *Logik:* A 76, p. 480.

24. Ibid., A 77, pp. 480–81.

25. See note 15 above.

26. Kant, *KrV:* B 759, p. 625n: "Die Philosophie wimmelt von fehlerhaften Definitionen. . . ."

27. I refer primarily to Hans Vaihinger's "Fiktion des Als Ob" ("fiction of 'as-if'"), or fiction as mental analogy from which the consideration of mental representation versus *real* knowledge must diverge.

28. Kant, *Logik:* A 220, p. 574: "Da man durch keine Probe gewiss werden kann, ob man alle Merkmale eines gegebenen Begriffs durch vollständige Analyse erschöpft habe: so sind alle analytische Definitionen für unsicher zu halten."

29. Ibid., A 218, p. 573: "Denn auch bei den Begriffen der letztern Art, z.B. den empirischen Begriffen Wasser, Feuer, Luft u. dgl. soll ich nicht zergliedern, was *in ihnen* liegt, sondern durch Erfahrung kennen lernen, was *zu ihnen* gehört."

30. Ibid., A 219, p. 573: "Da die Synthesis der empirischen Begriffe nicht willkürlich, sondern empirisch ist und, als solche, niemals vollständig sein kann (weil man in der Erfahrung immer noch mehr Merkmale des Begriffs entdecken kann): so können empirische Begriffe auch nicht definiert werden."

31. Ibid., A 249, p. 574.

32. Ibid., A 221, p. 575: ". . . so ist auch eine unvollständige Exposition, als Teil einer Definition, eine wahre und brauchbare Darstellung eines Begriffs."

33. Ibid., A 220, p. 574.

34. See note 31 above.

35. Ibid., A 219, p. 574: "Solche Definitionen willkürlicher Begriffe, die nicht nur immer möglich, sondern auch notwendig sind. . . ."

36. Ibid., A 219, p. 574.

37. Kant, *KrV:* B 741, p. 613: "Zur Konstruktion eines Begriffs wird also eine *nicht empirische* Anschauung erfordert. . . ."

38. Kant, *Logik:* A 221, p. 575.

39. Ibid., A 222, p. 575.

40. Ibid., A 221, p. 575.

41. Ibid., A 223, p. 576.

42. *The Basic Works of Aristotle,* ed. Richard McKeon (New York: Random House, 1941), pp. 750–51.

43. G. W. Leibniz, *Hauptschriften zur Grundlegung der Philosophie,* ed. Ernst Cassirer (Hamburg: Felix Meiner Verlag, 1966), vol. 1, pp. 41, 43.

44. Kant, *Logik:* A 222, p. 576.

*Stanley Corngold*

# Hölderlin's Poetry and the Persistence of the Self

R ECENT LITERARY THEORY has profoundly altered the way in which
English and German Romantic writers are read. The thrust of the
new criticism has been to discredit the self or subject as an origin of
meaning and value. But what is Romanticism if not "an act of reflection on the fundamentally subjective character of the spirit," on "the
isolated self thrown back upon itself"?[1] It is therefore to be expected
that Romantic texts should come in for harsh treatment, including
more than a little aversion and manhandling, with the purpose of
having them turn critic's evidence. The Romantic soul has been asked
to sing in an unheard-of way and suspicions of character remain.
Thus we read in the influential *Neues Handbuch der Literaturwissenschaft*,
"The claim to canonical status, which has been attributed to German
Romanticism for more than a century by its historical reception, has
today been widely forfeited."[2]

To think about Romantic poetry two decades ago was to feel oneself
at the wellspring of modern reflection on the self. It was (wrote Paul
de Man in 1965) to grasp writers like Wordsworth, Keats, and Solger
as furthering "the most audacious and advanced forms of contemporary thought," especially the distinction between a personal and a
"transcendental type of self."[3] To Romantic writers was owed "the experience of an *act* in which, to a certain extent, we ourselves have par-
ticipated," an act "contributing in an immediate way . . . to the constitution of our consciousness of temporality."[4] Today these words have
taken on an odd untimeliness. It is only with a much diminished and
ironical sense of self and time that many readers still maintain a feeling of community with Romantic writers.

A new criticism explores in literary texts a repeated moment of the dispersion of self-consciousness into indeterminate fragments. In the more radical view later espoused by de Man, "no discussion of specific experiences of [Romantic] consciousness is any longer conceivable."[5] The dignity of Romantic literature would then consist in the clarity with which it makes plain this permanently "dürftige Zeit," the time of the mind wanting in meaning. The Romantic text has its incoherence to confess, and if in one view it does indeed admit to self-loss as charged, in "metaphorical vehicle[s] of the imperative toward deconstruction,"[6] in another view, colored by Nietzsche's scorn for the Romantic masquerade, the Romantic confession is made in patent bad faith.[7] Certainly the grounds of poetic and critical authority have shifted.

The once dominant critical discourses of New Criticism and the *critique de la conscience* drew on and acknowledged their filiation from Kant and Hegel, but the new critical theory, in rejecting this older literary criticism, rejects many of the claims of Romantic metaphysics as they bear on a transcendental or any other kind of centering self. The rhetoric of Romantic poetry is implicated in this attack, since the philosophical vocabularies of Kant's third *Critique* and of Hegel's *Phenomenology of Spirit* and *Aesthetics* in turn enriched themselves with subjective key words from European pre-Romantic and Romantic poetry. The "beautiful soul" (*die schöne Seele*), for example, figures in Hegel's *Phenomenology* as an exemplary if aberrant form of narcissistic consciousness, but this figure was inspired in Hegel's mind by Friedrich Hölderlin (1770–1843), by the novelistic character Hyperion, by Novalis, and by the aunt of book 6 of Goethe's *Wilhelm Meisters Lehrjahre*.[8] This connection has its own history: Dilthey noted that "in their systems Schelling, Hegel, and Schleiermacher carry through on logical and metaphysical grounds the view of life and of the world developed by Lessing, Schiller, and Goethe,"[9] and Windelband declared that Kant's third *Critique* justified Goethe's (symbolic) poetry, a justification which might extend to unconscious imitation.[10]

Once Romantic philosophies of idealism are read suspiciously, Romantic poetry is bound to be read suspiciously as well. The truth claims of Romantic poetic fictions and the fictive character of many philosophical texts (for example, the dialogue in Solger, the "conversation" in Friedrich Schlegel, and the journey of the Spirit in Hegel's

*Phenomenology*) make it hard to tell these genres apart. In Hölderlin's poetry, too, "reflection has been assimilated to such a degree that the traditional treatment of the question concerning the relationship of philosophy to poetry in Hölderlin has become obsolete. In the degree of their reciprocal involvement, Hölderlin's poetry occupies a singular position, . . . one in which reflection enters poetry not simply as a thematic but as a structural element."[11] The intimacy of philosophy and poetry is certainly not unique to Hölderlin. Passages from Rousseau's *Nouvelle Héloïse* and the *Promenades* (the *Fifth Promenade* especially) have the rigor and argumentative terminology (anti-Lockean-sensationalist) of Rousseau's explicitly philosophical writing.[12] The same is true of Wordsworth's *Prelude*, whose "words" would "speak of nothing more than what we are," an ambition that, with its "words," "nothing," "we," and "are," diagrams the metaphysical tradition that until recently has been generating our critical vocabularies. Another sort of Romantic poetic authority has been lost with the passing of the German and Swiss existential literary criticism influential in the 1950s and early 1960s. This is the authority of Heidegger's perspective on Hölderlin, which sees as epochal a revelation occurring in the Romantic period—namely, Hölderlin's perception of the ontological difference between Being and beings.[13]

The difficulty of understanding Romanticism lies in the actual intimacy of our relation to it, our whole critical-interpretive enterprise being a sort of unsettled aura surviving the wreck of Romantic hope. Now, however, it is said that, apart from its complicity with modern rhetorical deconstruction, the Romantic mood is gone, and we read Romantic anxiety with post-modern detachment. The conceptual pairs supplied to the older criticism by Romantic poetry—sentiment/sensation; consciousness/nature; imagination/reason—having lost their cogency, are taken as instances of bad binary thinking. It has seemed possible, for example, to show Rousseau, Wordsworth, and Hölderlin valorizing the pole of Subject (Consciousness) and the pole of Object (Nature), alternately and incessantly. The outcome of such readings cannot therefore be a statement about a unified Romantic consciousness—neither one that registers its triumph or its defeat vis-à-vis stubborn materiality and contingency, nor one that finds itself (or benignly loses itself), having been ministered to by Nature, even in negative pleasure.[14]

The deconstruction of the thought of Rousseau, with Hölderlin soon following, arrives in the wake of Jacques Derrida's deconstruction of the "sovereign" authorial subject.[15] Such projects are part of a structuralist and post-structuralist effort to abolish as illusory the presence of the self to itself and to a reader.[16] But the loss of self even at the level of critical and poetic consciousness is not thought of as a disaster; indeed, reimagined as a necessary divestiture, it is defended as the very condition of writing. The loss of self, wrote de Man in 1980, apropos of Rousseau, is entailed by the arbitrary, mechanical character of "performative" language, including the language of fiction, in whose grip the deluded self pursues its justification. Even the cognitive language produced in justification is only the "aberrant, metaphorical correlative" of the self. "Far from seeing language as an instrument in the service of a psychic energy, the possibility now arises that the entire construction of drives, substitutions, repressions, and representations is the aberrant, metaphorical correlative of the absolute randomness of language prior to any figuration or meaning."[17] On this view, neither Romantic poetic nor interpretive language can converge on its own concern; neither creates a field demarking or developing a self.

The critical dissolution of the self is accompanied necessarily by the loss of the categorical dialectic of self and other, which is considered an epiphenomenon of the false consciousness of identity arising from the "mirror-phase" of development, as the negative consequence of resentment, or as an intersubjective instance of a metaphysical shell game.[18] Kant and Hegel have been replaced by the master thinkers of the "third term"—by Marx, Nietzsche, and Freud, who support neither the individual terms of the dialectic nor even this dialectical structure, but rather the textlike system enabling and accommodating them as tropes. Whether society, language, or the unconscious, the system is constituted as an endless and impersonal exchange of negative differential terms.[19]

CERTAINLY this revaluation is occurring too quickly, often without pause or wisdom. Before joining it one needs to know better what has been said on the question of the self by the Romantic poets and by an older tradition of criticism. In the 1920s William Michel described the late "Hesperian turn" in Hölderlin's work and personality as a process of "stabilization" (*Verfestigung*, which can be translated, with attention to its etymology, as "armoring"). This movement, continued Michel,

> leads from longing and self-deception to what actually is: to the self, to present reality, to the forms and themes of the art of Hölderlin's time and country. . . . Hölderlin's experience of life leads . . . to concentration, to a pulling the self together, to greater boldness in holding fast to the self and everything that belongs to the expanded order of the self. What he inclines to by birth and temperament—the anxious or enthusiastic orientation to the other which tends at one moment to weakness and masquerade and at another to the most exalted dispossession of self—is systematically rejected.[20]

This description of Hölderlin's "turn" poses an exemplary challenge to the reader of Romantic literature. The reader, I will be arguing, also must turn from the appearance of universal self-deception and speak of the poetic self as "present reality." The reader must, that is, hold fast to the Romantic understanding of the self as this understanding is given him or her in spite of critical fashion. This urgency can be situated within Romantic writers themselves in the very rhetoric which today shapes a chiefly destructive criticism.

> Der Mensch will sich selber fühlen. . . .
> Sich aber nicht zu fühlen, ist der Tod.
>
> [Man wants to have a sense of self. . . .
> Not to have a sense of self is death.]
> *Hyperion*

THE TERM "self" persists throughout Hölderlin's work. His conception of the self includes the notion of the otherness of the self to itself. The self is not therefore a simple origin. Yet the recognition of the moment of alterity in the self does not imply that the self is only a fiction, a rhetorical figure, or a meaningless because contradictory metaphor. The nonidentity of the self is a given—this is what Hölderlin in the early essay "Judgment and Being " ("Urteil und Sein") calls its "divided identity."[21] In *Hyperion*, Hölderlin conceives of the self mythically as "the marriage of poverty and abundance" and metaphysically as the condition of consciousness. This nonidentity he terms "the profound feeling of mortality, of mutability, of . . . temporal limitations."[22] Such perspectives inform his conception of *Bildung*—of education and self-development—which animates and is reflected in the work, as the field of struggle of a particular self-consciousness to realize the historical fate of Western culture.[23] The moment of development demands a moment of self-estrangement: "One's own being (*das Eigene*) must be as much learnt as what is other. For this reason the Greeks are indispensable to us. But we shall not match them precisely in what is our own, our 'national' being, because . . . the *free* use of *one's very own being* is most difficult."[24] That difficulty is meant to be surmounted. Hölderlin declares, "Put yourself by a free choice in harmonious opposition with an external sphere, just as you are in harmonious opposition with yourself by nature, but in an unknowable fashion as long as you remain in yourself."[25]

The conception of a self that must be learnt through empirical separation from itself (from *em-peiros*, "undergoing a risk") persists into the late hymns.[26] The *Bildung* of a self compels it to develop through moments of alienation and return; it is oriented indeed toward a third term, neither self nor particular other. For Hölderlin, "the crucial interaction no longer takes place between self and world but between that contact and its negation in time," that is, between having and abandoning such moments of contact.[27] *Bildung* is thus oriented away from particular objects, aspects of personality, other persons, and pastoral and social themes toward a heightened experience of temporality. It turns toward historical and sacred objects and finally toward Nature as that generality enabling, sustaining, and enveloping all such particular contacts and negations. Nature is the condition of the possibility of the self that desires to know it. The momentary loss of immediate experience is the cunning of the self that seeks Nature as a "principle in which time is sustained without loss of that movement of dissolution which defines it for those entities subject to it."[28]

Hölderlin himself authorizes the traditional concern with self-development in the criticism of Romantic poetry, a criticism perhaps culminating in de Man's essay "The Rhetoric of Temporality" (1971). There de Man identified an authentic Romantic temporal consciousness as follows: "The dialectic between subject and object does not designate the main romantic experience but only one passing moment in a dialectic, and a negative moment at that since it represents a temptation that has to be overcome." Overcoming this temptation "corresponds to the unveiling of time in a natural world to which in truth it bears no resemblance."[29] Precisely this point is anticipated by the young Hölderlin in his novel fragment *Hyperion's Youth* (*Hyperions Jugend*): "It is need which constrains us to lend eternally mutable nature affinity with what in us is immortal. This need, however, also gives us the right [to do so]. This belief is founded on the confines of finitude; as a result it is general in every being that feels itself to be finite."[30] Hence, "when nature co-operates with you, sympathetically . . . when joyfully surprised, in the realm of the senses your spirit as in a mirror contemplates its likeness, and the forms of nature join with solitary thought, be glad and love . . . but never forget yourself."[31]

I do not hear in these sentences of Hölderlin the ring of delusion, even though time, for him, implies the career of self-development. To feel their force, one could compare them with the caveat of a recent critic of Romantic poetry.

> There can be no consistent progress in the self's process of disabusing itself, because the retrograde tendency of constituting new objects is always at work, continually creating new moments of absolute conviction of "experiences of the real" through interpretative strategies that have not come to be recognized as beliefs because they are (at least temporarily) so deeply held as to be invisible.[32]

Hölderlin also values the moment of insight in which an "interpretative strategy" is unmasked, yet he does not consider as merely retrograde that "tendency of constituting . . . new 'experiences of the real'." The moment of insight also supplies the legitimacy with which experiences are constituted. For if they are based on a belief, the belief is founded on the very "confines of finitude," the condition of being a self. In what unlivable ascesis could a being deplore as an obstacle the condition standing in the way of its entirely "disabusing" itself of itself?[33] "Ought I to be congratulated or pitied," Hölderlin asked, "that nature had given me this irrepressible drive again and again to develop the forces which are in me?"[34] These forces, he wrote to Schelling, require experience:

> Talent (*Genius*), which is without content, cannot exist without experience, and experience, which is without soul, cannot exist without talent. Each contains the necessity of shaping itself (*sich bilden*) and of constituting itself through art and judgment, of producing an order, a live harmo-

nious changing totality. Art, which organizes, and the drive to development (*Bildung*) from whence it comes, cannot exist and are not even
conceivable without their inner element—natural talent, genius—and
their outer element—experience and historical scholarship.[35]

Hölderlin exalts experience: "Viel hat erfahren der Mensch. / Der
Himmlischen viele genannt, / Seit ein Gespräch wir sind / Und hören
können voneinander." ("Man has experienced much. / Named many
of the heavenly beings, / Since we have been a discourse / And can
hear from one another."[36])

The new object ("experiences of the real"), in being organized, constitutes a self. Experience, even if as error, belongs to truth: "Only
that is the truest truth wherein error too becomes truth because truth
places it in the whole of its system, into its time and place. . . . That is
eternal serenity, divine joy, that one puts everything particular in its
place, in the whole where it belongs."[37]

Here "truth"—like "experience" above—is conceived as an act of
writing. Is Hölderlin's truth then subject to the general deconstruction of Romantic writing? In his last works de Man found Rousseau
deconstructing "cognitive" rhetoric itself, for "writing always includes the moment of dispossession in favor of the arbitrary power
play of the signifier."[38] The subject is threatened by the act of writing,
threatened with "the loss of something that once was present and that
it once possessed"—and which it supposed might be carried over into
the poem. Still more it is threatened by an experience of the "radical
estrangement between the meaning and performance of any text."
Earlier de Man stressed a "transition"—a temporal term—between
an inferior blind form of language (the "act") and a superior insightful
form (the "interpretation"). Now the threat of self-loss shifts from the
space between act and reflection to the space "inside" every act and
reflection. An unchanging spatial category of nonconvergence holds
apart the meaning of the referential speech-act from that of its "performative" compulsion.[39] Now there can be no such thing as "transition" from act to interpretation and no distinction in truth-value between act and interpretation. As there could be no self, so there can
be no truth.

I believe, however, that Hölderlin's work is not the record of a sense
of failure of a convergence inside language but rather the record by

language of a struggle to conserve in a superior mode of self what is threatened by loss. "The feeling of the sacred," for example, in the tragic drama "no longer expresses itself immediately, it is no longer the poet and his own experience which appear," yet "every poem, including the tragic, must have come forth from poetic life and reality, from the poet's own world and soul, because otherwise the proper truth is lacking, and if we cannot carry over our own spirit (*Gemüth*) and our own experience into a foreign analogous material, nothing at all can be understood and given life." The tragic poet denies his "person, his subjectivity" but not "the spirit, the sacred, as the poet felt it in his world"; he sustains himself as the "carrying over," the metaphor, of the given immediate feeling. This passage comes from the "Philosophical Basis" of *The Death of Empedocles* (1799). Undoubtedly, the earlier Hölderlin—a Hegelian Hölderlin—comes under the head of a philosophy of renunciation and recovery. This is the Hölderlin of the *Reflection:* "Only that is the truest truth wherein error too becomes truth because truth places it in the whole of its system into its time and place." For a statement of the difference between Hegel and the later Hölderlin, I turn to Michel Foucault:

[With Hegel] we find the developing theme of a thought which, by the movement in which it is accomplished—totality attained, violent recovery at the extreme point of poverty, solar decline—curves over upon itself, illuminates its own plenitude, brings its circle to completion, recognizes itself in all the strange figures of its odyssey, and accepts its disappearance into that same ocean from which it sprang. In opposition to this return, which even though it is not happy is perfect, we find the experience of Hölderlin . . . in which the return is posited only in the extreme recession of the origin—in that region where the gods have turned away, where the desert is increasing, where the *technē* has established the dominion of its will; so that what we are concerned with here is neither a completion nor a curve, but rather that ceaseless rending open which frees the origin in exactly that degree to which it recedes: the extreme is therefore what is nearest.[40]

This region is evidently found in such later poems as the hymns "Andenken" and "Patmos." But here too Hölderlin's question presses for an answer: whose is the activity which ceaselessly rends open and in rending open does not open an abyss but frees "the origin" just as it makes it recede?

The action of rending open and making recede characterizes the poetic activity of a subject vis-à-vis "the sacred." The origin, the sacred, is freed and concealed in a movement of poetic language. This is the responsibility of the poet's self—a responsibility whose history is, in Wordsworth's phrase, "the growth of a poet's mind." It is precisely Hölderlin's increasing distance from Hegel that bears witness to his sense of poetic individuality.[41]

HÖLDERLIN seeks Nature as sustaining time even in the very movement of its dissolution—a form of being that might stay "die reissende Zeit" (time which runs with violent speed, which tears along but also tears what it touches). But Hölderlin also writes that Nature is torn by time and in the tragic moment is "nothing more than time," wholly subject to the "lord of time." If that Nature which encompasses development can itself suffer absence and loss, if in it *"beginning and end* [can] no longer allow themselves to be coupled together like rhymes," then what stability can a self or subject have?[42] Its development would become less the historical enactment of the self than the repeated experience of its death.

Such a perspective gives rise to the view described by Edward Said, that Hölderlin's work reveals an "absolute incompatibility between the realm of totality and the realm of personal interiority." In his desire for totality "Hölderlin personifies an extremism so complete in its heedless articulation of impossible desires as to exclude the possibility of accommodating one man's inner self to it. [His] works deliver naked desire, totally unconditioned by subjectivity . . . it is a pure serialism unraveling itself, for its own sake."[43] This is indeed a very French, surreal, and deconstructed Hölderlin; for Derrida, too, asserts: "Articulation is difference. . . . The relationship . . . is one of seriality without paradigm."[44] At this point, however, the disoriented reader might review Hölderlin's letter to Schelling, beginning, "Talent, which is without content, cannot exist without experience."

Such a conclusion—desire wholly without subjectivity—is paradoxical, Said continues, for how then can poets think like Hölderlin and still retain some semblance of their subjectivity? The answer is that outside of their poetry their subjectivity is indeed only a semblance, and a tortured facsimile of it at that. They turn themselves inside out and in the public sphere choose unreason, alienation. They make themselves exterior to social discourse. Hölderlin is therefore only himself, and then only as desire, in his poetry; for the rest he is mad. But this answer does not respond to the fact that throughout the period of his greatest creativity Hölderlin was by any criterion only infrequently mad—a provocative mix of lucidity, rage, and formalized behavior that has repeatedly suggested Hölderlin's lifelong pretense of being mad. The career of Hölderlin's desire for totality is bound up with his madness, as readers of Maurice Blanchot well know, but both of these themes call first for a description of Hölderlin's self-consciousness.[45]

If you can stand boldly in a chariot with four fresh horses rearing up
spiritedly in the reins, and can direct their forces—whipping in the one that
gets out of line and bringing down the one that rears up, giving rein,
guiding, turning, whipping, stopping and starting again, until all sixteen
hooves are moving in rhythm towards the finishing post—
you have achieved mastery.[46]
—Goethe

THE TERMS "self" and "self-loss" figure often in Hölderlin's work, but not so that either term could be filled with explicit ethical-existential import to mean "Hölderlin encourages a belief in the primacy of the self" or "Hölderlin calls for an abnegation of the self."

He does not encourage self-loss as a testimony to humility in the way that a goal of autobiographical writing has recently been defined—"one's beneficent expropriation in an unconscious circuit of exchange."[47] This latter phrase could not describe a beneficent destiny. It almost literally invokes the end of Hölderlin's poetry—his insanity, his poverty, the state of mind imaged in the second strophe of "The Middle of Life" ("Hälfte des Lebens"): "Die Mauern stehn / Sprachlos und kalt, im Winde / Klirren die Fahnen." ("The walls stand / Speechless and cold, in the wind / Weathercocks clatter.")

The term "self" is not pure humility; neither should it be defined as

an antithetical claim for a strong poetic ego, bent on an extensive totality of experience or bent on originality and ready to wrestle with
nature for it. This error is arraigned early, in *Hyperions Jugend:* "Proudly
I rejected the help with which nature cooperates in every form-giving
activity, the readiness with which the stuff of the spirit proffers itself: I
wanted to tame, to constrain."[48] Hölderlin devalues this sort of superiority as bent on an exorbitant consciousness of separation: the self
divinizes its own sense of finitude. This consciousness at first exalts
the constitutive distance between man and "the gods," then, claiming
strength, attempts avidly to constrain the gods. Hölderlin names and
in his poetry avenges—with vacuousness—the titanic blunder.[49]

These, however, are only two of the implications of the terms "self"
and "self-loss" which recur in cognate forms in Hölderlin's poetry.
They describe a deficient form of the experience of self and of self-
depletion, but these forms have to be paired with their authentic
counterparts.[50]

In its authentic modes, self mediates the moment of self-loss. The
figure of Rousseau in "Der Rhein" illustrates one such mode in his
elected withdrawal from the temptation of self-glorification. By choosing simplicity he shuns the danger in the extreme clarity of his understanding of finitude. He grasped as, say, Locke did not, the constitutive priority of consciousness over the sensory representation,
and his return to an order of pastoral sensation means at once to
remember an innocent "error" and to moderate the force of a truth
that would entitle men to blast open the earth. Rousseau chooses to
forget—to forget self-consciousness at the point where it might be
tempted to call itself a god. Laying on the cloak of forgetfulness is a
gesture preparing for what Cyrus Hamlin calls "the hermeneutic": it
projects the temporal delay enabling interpretation.[51] The wisdom of
such a project is Socratic.

There is, finally, a still stronger mode of self: the self bent on expan-
sion can experience or virtually experience fusion with the god, the
dazzlement of immediate or virtually immediate contact. Thus in "The
Poet's Vocation" ("Dichterberuf"):

> Der unverhoffte Genius über uns
> Der schöpferishe, göttliche kam, dass stumm

Der Sinn uns ward und, wie vom
Strahle gerührt, das Gebein erbebte.

[Divine, creative Genius came over us,
Dumbfounding mind and sense, unforgettably,
And left us as though struck by lightning
Down to our bones that were still aquiver.]

Or in "At the Source of the Danube" ("Am Quell der Donau"):

Da fasst' ein Staunen die Seele
Der Getroffenen all und Nacht
War über den Augen der Besten.

[Amazement then took hold of
The souls of all who were struck, and night
Obscured the eyes of the best men.]

This contact implies a terrible danger, an extinction of personality, like death. From the standpoint of the speaker all life consists in swerving from this moment, in rendering the sacred as a poetic word ("das Heilige sei mein Wort"). The entire foregoing phenomenology is based on the relation of the self to the sacred—the absolute object of desiderative consciousness. In "Homecoming" ("Heimkunft") Hölderlin writes:

. . . denn, was auch Dichtende sinnen
Oder singen, es gilt meistens den Engeln und ihm.

[. . . for whatever the poets may ponder,
Sing, it mostly concerns either the angels or him.]

In "The Poet's Vocation" ("Dichterberuf"):

Der Höchste, der ists, dem wir geeignet sind.

[The Highest, he it is whom alone we serve.]

The sacred figures in this poetry as a desideratum, while the reflective consciousness struggles to grasp its absence as necessary. This dialectic originates a poetry evoking the proximity of the divine in the fervor of the recognition that no pure contact is possible. This fervor develops as the desire for divine names. And if the self (as Jacques Lacan says) is double, involving a "marked" absence, like an empty grave, and a signifier of that absence, like a grave marker—a "ghost" or proper noun—then Hölderlin's poetry of proper nouns is par excellence a poetry of the subject.[52] This subject seeks its place in a symbolic order of names for the absence of the god, which it differentiates as it calls for truer names.

Hölderlin conceives of his desire in both objective and subjective genitive senses as the desire of the absent divinity. Desire exists in a register of fulfillment as felt "degrees of enthusiasm"; the agent of this recognition is the poetic self. "The great poet," writes Hölderlin, "is never abandoned by his self, and he may raise himself as high above himself as he wishes." Thought guards against the dangers of "*falling* upwards as well as into the depths, . . . but feeling is the best poetic sobriety and reflection."[53]

Each articulation of poetic self-consciousness therefore corresponds to a moment of felt desire. Each describes a distinctive relation of the finite subject to its origin. In this sense Hölderlin's poetry of the self is a poetry of thought, a poetry that records a history of *types* of contingency. Thus, typically, the speaker at the close of "Hälfte des Lebens" has suffered a devastating loss of original being. In the grip of its need, a wounding hunger for fullness, such a self, as in "Wie wenn am Feiertage," could approach too near "the tables of the gods." The titanic figure in whom the sense of separation is exultant produces by sheer will the aura of an illusory divinity. Finally, the self that, like the speaker at the close of "Mnemosyne," takes hold of itself in contemplation, does so in the aftermath of a disaster. It reflects on the error, exemplified by the Greeks, of having returned too wildly to the fire of the origin. The experience of a fusion with the god is interiorized as a cautionary example.

This field of forms of self-fulfillment and self-loss is diagrammed in the opening lines of "Patmos":

> Nah ist
> Und schwer zu fassen der Gott.
> Wo aber Gefahr ist, wächst
> Das Rettende auch.

[Near is
And difficult to grasp, the God.
But where danger threatens
That which saves from it also grows.]

The feeling of the nearness of the god keeps the self proof against the two kinds of despair at absence: emptying and fury. The difficulty of grasping the god suggests the self in labor—the labor of the concept, but also the labor, through feats of will and desire, cunning and technique, to lay hold of the god. And so each quadrant of the subject's being harbors a different danger, as shown in the chart.

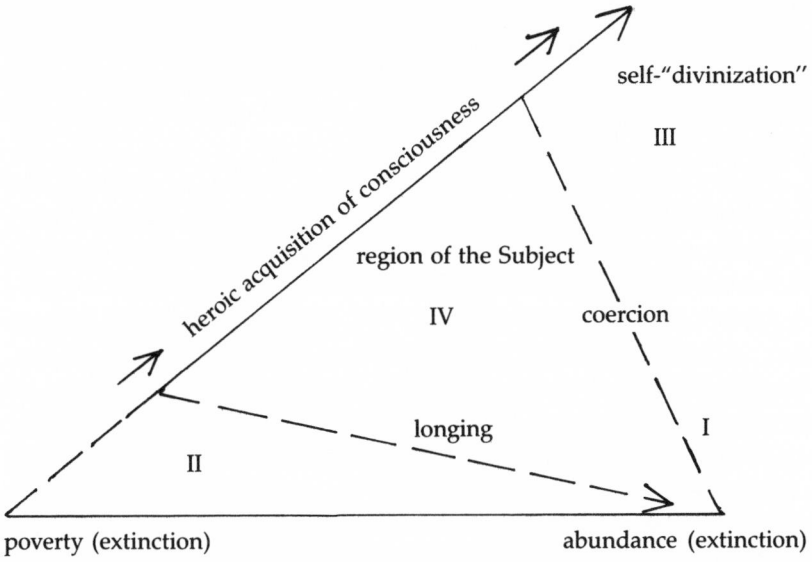

There is danger of invasion by divinity (I), which could consume the self and leave it, after separation, wasted and mute (II). There is danger, too, of a divinization of the self-centered effort to take hold of the god (III). Saving grace is then neither the accession of sobriety nor the accession of the god alone, but the tension sustaining the right ratio of both elements (IV), already given in the initial statement of the predicates of being: its present absence (nearness), its absent presence (the difficulty of its being grasped). This tension is the third term—neither phenomenal subject nor other—and has priority within Hölderlin's

world as the history of the rapport of the self and the god. The tension
is not impersonal:

> Denn nicht vermögen
> Die Himmlischen alles. Nämlich es reichen
> Die Sterblichen, eh an den Abgrund. Also wendet es sich, das Echo,
> Mit diesen.

> [For the Heavenly ones
> Cannot do everything. Namely mortals
> Sooner attain to the abyss. Thus the echo turns
> With them.]

That "the echo turns" is as much the work of man as of "the heavenly
ones" ("Mnemosyne"), as much the work of man in the world of the
hymn "Griechenland" (second version) as of the "terrible" god of "air
and time."

STATEMENTS about the persistence of the self in Hölderlin collide with
the brute fact of Hölderlin's madness, which a writer as thoughtful as
Maurice Blanchot has actually considered evidence of Hölderlin's pur-
poseful extinction of personality.[54] Said, Foucault, and Derrida have
also written on Hölderlin as an exemplary conjunction of an extreme
fidelity to poetry and an extreme of depersonalization. The recent
French author who has written most effectively about Hölderlin's poetry and madness, however, is Jean Laplanche: his book *Hölderlin et la
question du père* inspired Foucault's and Derrida's essays on Hölderlin.
Laplanche was a student of Lacan's, and his work aims to describe
Hölderlin's psychosis as so consistently informing his poetry that both
illuminate the calamitous absence at their source.

For Lacan and Laplanche the schizophrenic unconscious can be
likened to a dysfunctional text-generating system warped by a missing element: this is the "paternal signifier," the *Nom du Père*. This term
counts not only as one signifier among many but as one crucial to the
system's performance of its signifying function. In its absence the
signs belonging to the sign-chains crisscrossing the unconscious cannot be organized or relayed in ways permitting their symbolic juncture
with meanings. Madness is the case of a Word warding off objectifica-

tion, a disaster of the imaginary life inducing a cascade of revisions. Hölderlin's work, however, offers the unparalleled example of a schizophrenic poetry plainly full of meaning and rigorous form. For Hölderlin, then, the empirical practice of poetry literally accomplishes the function of the Name-of-the-Father: the torn unconscious goes over into "an external sphere"; the *Nom du Père* becomes the *Non du Père* of poetic activity. Hölderlin's poetry repeats an unknown, unconscious text, sustaining him, as schizophrenic, for a time. His poetry keeps open this gap, which is not to be accounted a deficiency, because only the openness of poetry could "fill" it; no empirical being could. Indeed Hölderlin's isolation testifies to the inevitability of his separation from any being who could fulfill this function for him. He grasps that for poetry, the issue of an absence in being, "God's absence helps" ("Gottes Fehl hilft").

HÖLDERLIN'S POETRY, according to Laplanche, articulates a certain absence in his unconscious and functions in its place. The work is a long, irregular paraphrase of the ineffable Name-of-the-Father, which defends against vacuousness, exaltation, or rage. But what answer does this picture give to the question of the self? Do we have in this account a falsifiable argument for the absence of the subject from poetic activity? On the contrary, Laplanche's essay constitutes a partly avowed, partly implicit reaffirmation of the continuity of self, conscious subject, and poetic work.

"Consciousness," writes Lacan, "matters only in its relation [to the question] of recentering the subject as speaking in the very lacunae of that in which, at first sight, it presents itself as speaking." [55] This view shifts the place of ("recenters") the subject but does not annihilate it. Laplanche, too, undertakes to recenter Hölderlin's subject in the position of "the true subject," namely, to cite Lacan, "the subject of the unconscious." [56] When it comes to relating this displaced subject to poetry, however, Laplanche employs a mimetic model in which unconscious self and poetry correspond, despite the fact that the use of such a mimetic model endangers more than a methodology. It puts into question any form of the attack on the subject as it has been understood since German Idealism and as that attack might issue from Lacan and Laplanche.

In Laplanche's view Hölderlin's poetry thematizes, mythologizes, reflects on, and enacts *the negative;* in doing so it doubles the absence of "the paternal signifier." But the paternal signifier has precisely the function of guaranteeing signification. Its absence would induce a cascade of revisions. Where, then, in the absence of the Name-of-the-Father does Hölderlin acquire the signifying function allowing him to articulate this very theme? It becomes necessary to posit and attach to this impoverished unconscious another self, another agent, capable of producing an intelligible poetry of absence. And if this self is to be different from the unconscious, it must be conscious. Now, of course, such a self is said precisely to be absent in schizophrenia as anything other than a hapless oscillation of desire. Yet if such a self is posited but also eclipsed, the work becomes a mere doubling imprint of the unconscious in the torn state in which it lacks the paternal metaphor. But this view is inconsistent with Laplanche's, for it returns to an older and naive conception which Laplanche is bent on surpassing—the conception of the psychotic writer as the "living poem," emitter of only "thing-presentations." So we are inevitably brought back instead to a conscious poetic agency endangered by schizophrenia but never absent: the fragile sense of self that seeks to maintain itself in poetry. Only in this way can we imagine Hölderlin seizing the threat to his language, seizing his madness as a question for his poetry: the question of the father, of the absence of the father.

Nothing about the psychoanalytical theory of Laplanche via Lacan controverts the assumption of a mediating subject. Laplanche's account of Hölderlin's psychosis actually constructs such a self around its schizogenic faults. At the outset Laplanche holds to Hölderlin's own governing model of a self bent on the unfolding, the *Bildung*, of its forces and only thereafter identifies gaps in the structure. And when, at the close, Laplanche exalts the self's deficiencies by identifying schizophrenia as "that which opens up the question of the human," he does not annihilate the subject but precisely, rather, "opens it up."

Laplanche introduces such an opening into a clinical and critical dialogue through a curious refinement of mimesis. This moment, however, also identifies the error of a poetics of the unconscious self, defined as "like a text." It is as if, despite the mimetic fallacy—the poem taken improperly as a mimesis of the inner life—Laplanche could achieve a satisfying degree of conceptual refinement by writing of both poem and life as doublings of a form of *absence*, a modality of *nothingness*, the poem of absence being explained as a reflection of the absence constitutive of psychosis; indeed he sees the poem as enshrining *that very absence*. In this way, the crude mimesis of substantial representation is apparently sublated, but actually only deferred. For if we are not now speaking of the poetic presentation of thinglike experiences, we are nonetheless speaking of a presentation of a nonthinglike experience.

The allegedly aberrant model of correspondence is never actually absent from Laplanche's procedure. He first identifies the nucleus of the psychosis as the missing Name-of-the-Father, which is held to guarantee the tolerable, the human functioning of language as signifying-via-absence. Since Hölderlin nonetheless continues to write poetry, the absent signifier reappears in a triad of modalities of absence: "the poetic myth of distancing and of opening—the philosophy of language—the poetic activity as such, this exercise of language in which language comes closest to its own negative essence."[57] It is toward "these three fields of absence, of the negative, [that] Hölderlin's poetry turns." Laplanche then suggests that schizophrenia is itself a turn to the negative, to a field of absence including these three redemptive possibilities. Hölderlin's poetry is thus an exemplary repetition of psychotic negativity, for which one would have to reinvent the word "denegation."

But nothing is gained from solutions by neologism. The representation of schizophrenic being in language continues to imply the existence of an intentional subject. This is stressed in Jean Beaufret's revealing summary of Laplanche's argument:

> If the poetry of Hölderlin is more and more the incorporation in language or, rather, the creation, at the very origin of language, of this negative pole, the absence of which made language itself "the great superfluity" [*Hyperion*], it is because the poet feels more and more the menace which this absence is for him if he does not succeed in considering it, in its turn, as a means of salvation.[58]

Observe that "incorporation" corresponds to a representative theory and "creation" to a constitutive theory, and Beaufret's balancing of both theories to the copresence, in Laplanche's thesis, of these two perspectives. Since, however, "creation" is the recreation of the absence which already exists for the poet, both theories imply the continuity of the poet's conscious being and his poetry, the conversion by a self of its felt poverty into types of negativity. Beaufret's final conjuration of "the poet" is entirely legitimate.

This is indeed a bemusing state of affairs. For where then does the decisive Parisian attack on the self-constituting subject occur? From the outset we have regarded the thinkers of Paris as the main source of this attack. Have we misunderstood them? Or can it be that, faithful to their own logic, these critics owe their perceptions precisely to a blindness to their own theoretical program? We have seen Lacan's and Laplanche's plain or implied reinstitution of the subject. Here now is Foucault's contribution to the same question:

> Hölderlin's experience is totally informed by the enchanted threat of forces that arose from within himself and from others, that were at once distant and nearby, divine and subterranean, invincibly precarious; and it is in the imaginary distances between these forces that their mutual identity and the play of their reciprocal symbolization are constructed and contested.[59]

But who imagines the distance between these forces, who symbolizes their symbols in play and constructs their "identity" if not the poet with his "experience" and "scholarship"? Foucault is describing the activity of a poetic self.

It seems to me that neither Lacan, Laplanche, nor Foucault endangers the venture of showing the persistence of the self both as experience and as privileged function; indeed they actually give it intellectual support. What of Derrida? In *On Grammatology*, Derrida writes:

> Freud says of the dreamwork that it is comparable rather to a writing than to a language, and to a hieroglyphic rather than to a phonetic writing. . . . Saussure says of language that "it is not a function of the speaker." With or without the complicity of their authors, all these propositions must be understood as more than simple *reversals* of a metaphysics of presence or of conscious subjectivity. Constituting and dislocating it at the same time, writing is other than the subject, in whatever sense

the latter is understood. Writing can never be thought under the category of the subject; however it [the category of the subject] is modified, however it is endowed with a consciousness or unconsciousness, it will refer, by the entire thread of its history, to the substantiality of a presence unperturbed by accidents, or to the identity of the selfsame (*le propre*) in the presence of self-relationship.[60]

But it is very dubious to say that the subject must refer to categories of "substance": consider the entire foregoing account of Hölderlin. It is equally dubious to claim that the "identity" to which the subject refers is any more surreptitiously theological than that of other definite beings or indeed that of beings lacking definite identity conditions, as for example the referent of such Derridean categories as "trace," "différance," and "dissémination."

In "La parole soufflée," a work written at about the same time as *Of Grammatology*, Derrida takes away the sweeping claim to expose the barren "ideological" derivation of the subject through the "entire thread of its history." Addressing Laplanche's work directly, Derrida concludes that the effort to think the historical moment that could bring about a discourse at once critical and clinical—the effort to think the relation of history and "the same"—is an effort for which we are not yet ready. "What is entailed," Derrida writes, "by the possibility of a discourse in which these two dimensions—the clinical and the critical—could be spoken?"[61] It is, I hold, precisely the possibility of a discourse on the self. This discourse is the one actually produced by the French attention to Hölderlin, even when the object is his thematics of absence. For the themes of the mythic negativity of the absence of the gods, the rational negativity of language, and the negativity of poetic practice are poetic decisions taken by Hölderlin on the strength of his experience.

Derrida concludes by asserting the impossibility of thinking history and the "same," that is, the historical situation of the unity embedding the difference between the subject viewed clinically and by literary criticism. This situation entails the impossibility of thinking the unity of the subject except as the factitious replica of a theological object. It also entails, however, the impossibility of thinking *away* the subject as a "divided unity" or as a "harmonious opposition." The deconstruction of the subject is a project that therefore lies always ahead of us. It has not been done; and on the evidence of those who are attempting to do it, it cannot be done, either factually or by right.

## NOTES

1. The first quotation is from Georges Poulet, in *Les Métamorphoses du cercle* (Paris: Plon, 1961), p. 136; the second, by Peter Szondi, in *Satz und Gegensatz* (Frankfurt a.M.: Insel, 1964), pp. 9–10. Throughout this essay I give the term "Romanticism" the wide governance it has for many comparatists: the period ranging from French *pré-romantisme* (the generation of the 1750s) to German *Romantik* (up until the 1830s).

2. Karl R. Mandelkow, foreword to vol. 14 of *Europäische Romantik I* (Wiesbaden: Akademische Verlagsgesellschaft Athenaion, 1982), p. ix.

3. Paul de Man, "The Sublimation of the Self," in *Blindness and Insight: Essays in the Rhetoric of Contemporary Criticism*, 2d ed., rev. (Minneapolis: University of Minnesota Press, 1983), esp. pp. 49–50.

4. Paul de Man, "Wordsworth and Hölderlin," in *The Rhetoric of Romanticism* (New York: Columbia University Press, 1984), p. 50. My essay relies explicitly in several places on Paul de Man's writings on Hölderlin. I single out certain texts as more nearly "correct" in their tendency than others. But such distinctions are also made for narrative and polemical reasons and should not obscure my general responsiveness to de Man's deeply thoughtful readings.

5. Paul de Man, "Introduction," *Studies in Romanticism* 18 (1979): 498.

6. David Simpson, *Irony and Authority in Romantic Poetry* (Totowa, N.J.: Rowan and Littlefield, 1979), pp. 57f.

7. The view received a powerful and sustained impetus from René Girard's analysis of "the Romantic lie" in *Deceit, Desire and the Novel: Self and Other in Literary Structure* (Baltimore: Johns Hopkins University Press, 1965), a translation of *Mensonge romantique et vérité romanesque* (Paris: Grasset, 1961).

8. *Materialien zu Hegels Phänomenologie des Geistes*, ed. Hans Fulda (Frankfurt: Suhrkamp, 1973), pp. 256–57. One should recall, too, the presence of Faust in the composition of the *Phenomenology*, an influence much discussed by Lukács, Walter Kaufmann, Rüdiger Bubner, and others (I am indebted to Mark Roche for this point).

9. Wilhelm Dilthey, *Gesammelte Schriften*, 18 vols. (1914–1977: vols. 1–13, Stuttgart: B. B. Teubner; Göttingen: Vandenhoeck and Ruprecht; vols. 14–18, Göttingen: Vandenhoeck and Ruprecht), vol. 5, p. 13.

10. Cited in Ernst Cassirer, *The Philosophy of the Enlightenment* (Boston:

Beacon Press, 1964), p. 278. The entire passage in Cassirer reads, "Windel-band said of Kant's *Critique of Judgment* that it constructs, as it were, *a priori* the concept of Goethe's poetry, and that what the latter presents as achievement and act is founded and demanded in the former by the pure necessity of philosophical thought."

11. Gerhard Kurz, *Mittelbarkeit und Vereinigung: Zum Verhältnis von Poesie, Reflexion und Revolution bei Hölderlin* (Stuttgart: Metzler, 1975), p. 1.

12. De Man's readings of Rousseau in *Allegories of Reading* aim to overcome the separation introduced by Rousseau's commentators between those texts allegedly inspired by intellectual analysis and those inspired by sentiment. See, for example, chapter 10, "Allegory of Reading (*Profession de foi*)," p. 223.

13. Cf. Martin Heidegger, *Erläuterungen zu Hölderlins Dichtung* (Frankfurt: V. Klostermann, 1951).

14. In "Genesis and Genealogy (Nietzsche)," in *Allegories of Reading*, de Man attacks the "genetic pattern" according to which Romanticism has been read. Under the head of such a pattern come at least two models of Romantic historiography. The first and less adequate is "a non-dialectical notion of a subject-object dichotomy, revealing a more or less deliberate avoidance of the moment of negation that coincides, for Hegel, with the emergence of the true Subject" (80). Such a moment in Hegel as the following is presumably meant: "Thinking is, indeed, essentially the negation of that which is immediately before us." This sort of nondialectical system ends up with "an altogether un-Hegelian concept of the subject as an irrational unmediated experience of particular selfhood (or loss of selfhood)" (80).

On the other hand, even "a dialectical conception of time and history [in the manner of Hegel] can very well be genetic" (80). But it may be precisely the Romantic poets who came closest to undermining the authority of any sort of genetic pattern (82). If it can be shown, then, as de Man claims to show apropos of Nietzsche, that "genetic models are only one instance of rhetorical mystification among others," then even such values as "the pan-tragic consciousness of the self . . . are made to appear hollow when they are exposed to the clarity of a new ironic light" (102). The weak options for an understanding of a Romantic self-consciousness, then, are the self as (1) the irrational particularity of immediate experience, (2) a negative illusory Subject engendered by participation in a speciously genetic teleological process. Is there no way out of this double bind, no mediation possible between "irrational immediacy" and the "negative Subject"?

15. I am thinking of the nearly simultaneous publication in 1966 and 1967 of two works of Jacques Derrida. These are, first, the study of Rousseau's "Essay on the Origin of Language" in *Of Grammatology*, trans. Gayatri Chakravorti

Spivak (Baltimore: Johns Hopkins University Press, 1976). Second is Derrida's essay on Freud, "Freud and the Scene of Writing," in *Writing and Difference*, trans. Alan Bass (Chicago: University of Chicago Press, 1978), pp. 196–231. In the latter, Derrida writes, "The 'subject' of writing does not exist if we mean by that some sovereign solitude of the author" (p. 226). See, further, Andrzej Warminski's essay on Hölderlin's "'Patmos': The Sense of Interpretation," in *Modern Language Notes* 81 (April 1976): 478–500.

16. See further, Derrida: "The interval that constitutes in the present [the trace of what is not present] must also, and by the same token, divide the present in itself, thus dividing, along with the present, everything that can be conceived on its basis, that is, every being—in particular, for our metaphysical language, the substance or subject" (*Speech and Phenomena*, trans. David Allison [Evanston: Northwestern University Press, 1973], p. 143).

17. De Man, *Allegories of Reading*, p. 299.

18. Cf. Jean Laplanche, in *Hölderlin et la question du père* (Paris: Presses Universitaires de France, 1961): "How describe as other than *narcissistic* this situation in which the subject defines itself uniquely by its dual relation with the Other, where it posits itself as a subject in a specular relation, being itself the other of this Other" (55). Laplanche does not stop here in his constitution of Hölderlin's subjectivity. He reads this narcissism as an early and deficient condition; in fact it precipitates "schizophrenic" attacks. But other critics— for example, René Girard in *Deceit, Desire and the Novel*—are less tolerant of Romantic narcissism. For them the Romantic subject does not stop here. "Stendhal too finds in the Romantic *vaniteux* not the generous impulse of a being truly prepared to give itself but rather the tormented recourse of vanity at bay, the centrifugal movement of an ego powerless to desire by itself" (15). An interpretation of the Hegelian dialectic as motivated by resentment is put forward by Gilles Deleuze in his *Nietzsche and Philosophy*, trans. Hugh Tomlinson (New York: Columbia University Press, 1983).

19. I owe this formulation to Jeffrey Mehlman's *A Structural Study of Autobiography* (Ithaca: Cornell University Press, 1976).

20. William Michel, *Hölderlins abendländische Wendung* (Jena: Eugen Diedrichs, 1923), pp. 8–9.

21. Friedrich Hölderlin, *Sämtliche Werke* (Stuttgart: Kohlhammer, 1961), vol. 4, pp. 216–17.

22. Ibid., p. 235.

23. Summarizing the account given by Beck and Bertaux of Hölderlin's shift of interest from Kant to Fichte, Laplanche writes, "The Kantian categorical imperative gives way to the side of moral feeling, of belief in a law that is less universal than personal, which requires the individual to unfold, to develop,

his possibilities, his *forces*, rather than burdening him with the task of making his actions conform to a universally valid maxim" (*Hölderlin et la question du père*, p. 39).

The requirement that Hölderlin endure as a *particular* being persists. In a late letter to von Seckendorf (12 March 1804), for example, Hölderlin rejects a certain Romanticism of the picturesque. Jochen Schmidt glosses the letter: "The earth has primacy, because Hölderlin's care is for self-assertion, for the preservation of the individual life. And hence the assertion of the concluding strophe of the ode 'Ganymede,' acutely bent on individuality and particularity: 'And everything blossoms in its own fashion'" (*Hölderlins später Widerruf* [Tübingen: Niemeyer, 1978], p. 181).

24. Friedrich Hölderlin, letter to Bohlendorff, 4 Dec. 1801, *Sämtliche Werke*, vol. 6, p. 476.

25. Hölderlin, *Sämtliche Werke*, vol. 4, pp. 255–56.

26. Cf. H.-G. Gadamer's discussion of *Bildung* in *Wahrheit und Methode*, 2d ed. (Tübingen: J. C. B. Mohr, Paul Siebeck, 1960), pp. 7–16.

27. Mehlman, *A Structural Study of Autobiography*, p. 67.

28. De Man, *The Rhetoric of Romanticism*, p. 56 (translation modified).

29. Paul de Man, *Interpretation, Theory and Practice*, ed. Charles Singleton (Baltimore: Johns Hopkins University Press, 1969), p. 190.

30. Hölderlin, *Sämtliche Werke*, vol. 3, p. 212.

31. Ibid., p. 216.

32. Frances Ferguson, in a review article, *Georgia Review* 31 (1977): 516.

33. Centuries along in the sustained Hölderlinean and Romantic meditation on an "enlightened" reason that would disabuse the self of everything, E. M. Cioran writes: "How match ourselves against ghosts? This is what appearances become when, disabused, we can no longer promote them to the rank of essences. Knowledge . . . produces between them and ourselves a hiatus which is not, unfortunately, a conflict: if it were, all would be well; no, this hiatus is the suppression of all conflicts, it is the deadly abolition of the tragic" (*The Fall into Time* [Chicago: Quadrangle Books, 1970], p. 155).

34. "A passage written at the end of 1793." Cited in Laplanche, *Hölderlin et la question du père*, p. 32.

35. Hölderlin, *Sämtliche Werke*, vol. 6, pp. 347–48.

36. "Friedensfeier" (third version).

37. Hölderlin, *Reflexion*, in *Sämtliche Werke*, vol. 4, p. 234. Hölderlin concludes this aphorism by noting an obstacle in the way of truth's successful placement of error within its "system." This obstacle is the special condition which the thinker must achieve, namely, "schneller Begriff" ("quickness of comprehension"), requiring a "durch und durch organisiertes Gefühl" (a

"thoroughly coherent sensibility"). Indeed, if Hölderlin's thought is dialectical, it is also vertiginously quick; terms cross over with unnerving rapidity. Yet what is crucial here is that where Hölderlin registers a difficulty in the way of truth, the modern critic sees an impossibility. This substitution impoverishes a prevailing Romantic sensibility that continues to desire a goal of plenitude verging on the unexperienceable, while suffering the consciousness of its impossibility. In a word, the newer criticism demystifies or otherwise etiolates Romantic sublimity.

38. De Man, *Allegories of Reading*, p. 296.

39. A similar version of the critique of the separate integrity of act and interpretation reads, "Non-verbal acts, if such a thing were to be conceivable, are of no concern to [Nietzsche], since no act can ever be separated from the attempt at understanding, from the interpretation, that necessarily accompanies and falsifies it" (de Man, *Allegories of Reading*, chap. 6, "Rhetoric of Persuasion (Nietzsche)," pp. 127–28).

40. Michel Foucault, *The Order of Things* (New York: Pantheon, 1970), p. 334. A good deal of recent Hegel criticism rejects a vision of Hegel's *Subjekt* as "bringing its circle to completion." Instead it stresses a pattern of persistent revelation and concealment as the figure of Hegel's thought.

41. "In Hegel the dialectic frequently finishes in an absolute impasse for the individual. If the dialectic picks up again, it is in a 'new figure' in whom the predecessor was only a moment. In Hölderlin the necessity of again taking up the movement toward a synthesis is inherent in the individual; it is as an individual that he is fascinated by the Hen Kai Pan" (Laplanche, *Hölderlin*, p. 117).

42. Hölderlin, *Sämtliche Werke*, vol. 5, p. 220.

43. Edward Said, *Beginnings: Intention and Method* (New York: Basic Books, 1975), p. 312. Said is here referring to Foucault's argument in "La pensée de dehors," *Critique* 22 (1966): 525–27.

44. Cited without source in Michael Ryan, *Marxism and Deconstruction* (Baltimore and London: Johns Hopkins University Press, 1982), p. vii.

45. Maurice Blanchot, "La folie par excellence," *Critique* 7 (1951): 99–118.

46. Johann Wolfgang von Goethe, letter to Herder (Wetzlar, July 1792), discussed in G. Lukács, *Essays on Thomas Mann*, trans. Stanley Mitchell (London: Merlin Press, 1964), p. 52.

47. Mehlman, *A Structural Study of Autobiography*, p. 167.

48. Hölderlin, *Sämtliche Werke*, vol. 3, p. 210.

49. Peter Szondi's reading of "When on a Holiday" ("Wie wenn am Feiertage"), which sees Hölderlin's urge to exalt his impoverished self as the obstacle to hymnic poetry, identifies (at its weak side) this important impulse

("Der andere Pfeil," *Hölderlin-Studien* [Frankfurt a.M.: Inself, 1967], available as "The Other Arrow: On the Genesis of the Late Hymnic Style," in Szondi, *On Textual Understanding and Other Essays*, trans. Harvey Mendelsohn [Minneapolis: University of Minnesota Press, 1986], pp. 23–42).

50. The extremes of Hölderlinean selfhood can be seen to reflect two notions of selfhood deeply ingrained in Germany at the time of Goethe: Fichtean autonomy and the Spinozistic sublation of individuality. But only with Hölderlin do the modes become existentially problematic. For Goethe "the affirmation of self" (*Verselbstigung*, as in "Wandrers Sturmlied" and "Prometheus") and "unselfing" (*Entselbstigung*, as in "Mahomets Gesang" and "Ganymed") represent legitimate modes of selfhood and expression as long as they are recognized as ineluctable modifications of one another. Each is individually valid when seen as a moment in the context of its necessary reversal. For Hölderlin, both the Fichtean and Spinozistic modes lose all legitimacy, be it individually or together, and he is left fighting for another term (I owe this point to a discussion with Mark Roche).

51. Cyrus Hamlin, in his lecture at a special session on Hölderlin at the conference of the Modern Language Association in Chicago, 1977.

52. Stuart Schneiderman, *Jacques Lacan: The Death of an Intellectual Hero* (Cambridge, Mass.: Harvard University Press, 1983), pp. 6–7.

53. Hölderlin, *Sämtliche Werke*, vol. 4, p. 243.

54. Blanchot, "La folie par excellence," p. 112.

55. Jacques Lacan, *The Four Fundamental Concepts of Psychoanalysis* (New York: Norton, 1978), p. 83.

56. Jacques Lacan, "Introduction au commentaire de Jean Hyppolite sur la *Verneinung*," *La Psychanalyse* 1 (1956): 20. Cited in Anthony Wilden, *The Language of the Self* (Baltimore: Johns Hopkins University Press, 1968), p. 142.

57. Laplanche, *Hölderlin*, p. 133.

58. Jean Beaufret, "Hölderlin et la question du père," *Les Temps modernes* 194 (July–Dec., 1962): 152–53. This, according to Renate Böschenstein, is too much said; for her, "the position of Hölderlin's father-term must be sought *between* 'absence' and the 'fault' (*faille*) [left by] an absence" (my italics). See her "Hölderlin auf die Suche nach dem Vater," *Hölderlin-Jahrbuch* 21 (1978–79): 346.

59. Michel Foucault, "The Father's 'No,'" in *Language, Counter-Memory, Practice*, ed. D. F. Bouchard (Ithaca: Cornell University Press, 1977), p. 77.

60. Derrida, *Of Grammatology*, pp. 68–69.

61. Derrida, *Writing and Difference*, p. 170.

*Dorothy Kelly*

# Writing Difference Itself

IN ORDER TO WRITE the difference between philosophy and literature, it would seem appropriate to compare two texts, one philosophical and one literary, which deal with a common problem. Then one could ask the question "What is the difference?" And what better communal problem than that of the concept of difference itself? One then could ask the question "What is difference?" And what better difference to analyze than *the* difference "par excellence," the difference which perhaps could be said to found all other differences, oppositions, and polarities: that of sexual difference ("vive la différence")? It must be said here that the investigation of sexual difference inevitably begins with the difference of woman, woman as that which is *different* from man, and hence on the problem posed by feminine identity. So let us compare two texts which deal with the problem of feminine identity: Derrida's philosophical text *Spurs: Nietzsche's Styles,* and Balzac's literary text *Séraphîta.* (Of course, in so labeling these texts, we are always already caught up in the problem, since Derrida's philosophical text is unmistakably literary, and Balzac's text is largely about Swedenborg. But we will defer this problem for the moment.) In studying the identity of woman, her difference from man, we may learn about difference itself, which is necessary for any understanding of the particular difference between philosophy and literature.

Derrida's text, *Spurs: Nietzsche's Styles,* is an "androgynous" or dialogical text. It is, first of all, a dialogue *inside* of one text, between the French and English versions of the same text. It is also a dialogue (or a "trialogue") among Derrida, Nietzsche, and Heidegger. But most importantly, it is written *about* the "dialogues" or interactions between various styles of Nietzsche's writings and the relation of these styles to a rather radical and unique concept of "woman." The text has no single subject; rather, it intermeshes the investigation of style, of a concept (woman), of interpretation (of Nietzsche by Heidegger), and of an economy (property). It is indeed an androgynous text in that it treats very heterogeneous materials.

To summarize the part of Derrida's text on woman rather briefly, there are three "positions" or stances of women in Nietzsche's texts. There is first what one could consider to be the "conventional" woman who takes the subordinate place in a patriarchal and phallogocentric system which claims that she is powerless: "In the first of these propositions the woman, taken as a figure or potentate of falsehood, finds herself censured, debased and despised. In the name of truth and metaphysics she is accused by the credulous man who, in support of his testimony, offers truth and his phallus as his own proper credentials."[1] The second woman, who is also debased, reverses this order to become the superior element in the hierarchy of male/female (she has/is/uses the truth). In so doing, she perpetuates the repressive system by trying to take over the power: "in order to resemble the masculine dogmatic philosopher, this woman lays claim—just as much claim as he—to truth, science and objectivity in all their castrated delusions of virility" (Derrida, 65). Both of these two types of women remain "nonetheless within the economy of truth's system, in the phallogocentric space" (Derrida, 97) and represent a position of negation.

But the third type of woman is *different*, is, one could say, difference itself. She is not the opposite of the male but is what makes opposition possible. She knows, to quote Derrida, that "castration does not take place" (in Derrida's sense of not having a *proper*, unique place, and in the sense that it has not literally taken place for her, it is a fiction, even though it may be a fiction which grounds the "reality" of the phallogocentric system); yet she also knows that one cannot simply deny the entire system of power, opposition (castration), and phallogocentrism (this would only repeat its repressive gesture): "Woman—her name made epoch—no more believes in castration's exact opposite, anti-castration, than she does in castration itself . . . she knows that such a reversal would only deprive her of her powers of simulation, that in truth a reversal of that kind would, in the end, only amount to the same thing and force her just as surely as ever into the same old

apparatus. She knows that she would only find herself trapped once
again in a phallocentrism" (Derrida, 61). So she *simulates* and *affirms*:
she plays with the system, keeping her distance, and thus affirms difference: "woman is recognized and affirmed as an affirmative power, a
dissimulatress, an artist, a dionysiac. . . . She affirms herself, in and
of herself, in man" ("elle s'affirme elle-même, en elle-même et dans
l'homme") (Derrida, 96–97).

These three positions, however, do not combine to form a comfortable unified system in Nietzsche, because of what Derrida calls "the
hymen's graphic." The impossibility of unity and systematization is
the result of the undecidability between the categories; in order to
have a system, "each term that is implicated in the three schemata
must be *decidable* within an oppositional couple and in such a way that
for each term, such as woman, truth, castration, there should exist
a counter term" (Derrida, 99). The hymen's graphic puts into effect
a loss of control and a blurring of borders: "this graphic, which describes a margin where the control over meaning or code is without
recourse, poses the limit to the relevance of the hermeneutic or systematic question" (Derrida, 99). In Nietzsche's text it is the "inability
to assimilate—even among themselves—the aphorisms and the rest"
(Derrida, 101) which triggers the nonmastery, the "rhythmic blindness" of the loss of control. It is the radical heterogeneity (or androgyny) of Nietzsche's text which prohibits systematization and the
ultimate definition of woman: "The exchange of stylistic blows . . .
confuses sexual identity" (Derrida, 53).

In the works of Honoré de Balzac, we find a rather uncanny embodiment of these three types of woman in Séraphîta. Our study will be
for the most part a literary interpretation of Séraphîta's "identity"
which will carry on an implicit and sometimes explicit dialogue with
Derrida's philosophical text. Derrida's three types of women will help
us to make precise the role of Séraphîta in this Balzac text, and the
example of Séraphîta will make Derrida's abstract concepts more concrete. (Here, we are of course following the traditional distinction between philosophy and literature which sees literature as the example
of a concept in philosophy, a distinction which should not, perhaps,
be dismissed too lightly.) We will find that Balzac's character may give
us some surprising insights into what it is to "be" a woman, "if we
could still say such a thing" (Derrida, 49).

We shall begin by asking *the* question: Who is Séraphîta? This question of identity, specifically of sexual identity, quickly emerges as the center of attention. The title of the story is, of course, *Séraphîta*, and because of the signifying force of titles of texts, we immediately assume that this story is about a woman. But as soon as we move from this title to the first subtitle our assumptions become questionable. From the title *Séraphîta* we proceed to the subtitle, "Séraphîtüs." What happened? Who is this story about? About Séraphîta? Or about Séraphîtüs? Or about two people, perhaps brother and sister? Suddenly, the sure and comfortable assumptions we made about the title of the story are undermined by the second word of the story, and all because of the difference between three letters. Already from the beginning of the story, from the first two words, we are confronted with a question of identity and of sexual difference which is textual difference.[2]

However, as we continue to read, we learn more about the character Séraphîtüs, a young man with whom a beautiful young woman, Minna, is in love. Since Minna, the narrator, and even Séraphîtüs himself all speak of Séraphîtüs as a man and call him by this name, the reader slowly forgets Séraphîta, whose name one expects to be explained later in the story. In the plot of the text, Séraphîtüs takes Minna up to the summit of a mountain, where the two of them overlook the abyss of the beautiful coastline of Norway and where Séraphîtüs refuses Minna's love. They then wind their way back down the mountain, separate, and Séraphîtüs takes a nap (typical Balzacian oddity of plot). This interval of sleep is represented by an interval in the text, a blank space which will be important to us later on.

The second section of the text is entitled "Séraphîta," and here, after a transformation which occurs during sleep, Séraphîtüs becomes a woman who is loved by a young man, Wilfrid, but she refuses his love also. The remainder of the story describes Séraphîta's prodigious grasp of philosophy, and finally describes her transformation into an angel and her ascension into heaven, which is witnessed by Minna and Wilfrid. Obviously Séraphîta's identity is problematic, and a more detailed literary investigation of her character may help us gain a better understanding of her odd nature.

The first step in the study of her identity would logically be the description of the body of Séraphîta herself, the literal determination of her sex. Normally one would think that sexual identity would be easily verifiable *physically* and that this would be the basis of the identification. But Séraphîta poses some interesting problems when it comes to her physical characteristics. Our first glance at her reveals nothing of her sexual identity when she is seen walking at a distance:

> Par une matineé où le soleil éclatait au sein de ce paysage en y allumant les feux de tous les diamants éphémères produits par les cristallisations de la neige et des glaces, deux personnes passèrent sur le golfe, le traversèrent et volèrent le long des bases du Falberg, vers le sommet duquel elles s'élevèrent de frise en frise. (329)[3]

> [One morning, when the sun was blazing down into the heart of this landscape, lighting up the flashes of the ephemeral diamonds produced by the crystallized surface of the snow and ice, two persons crossed the gulf and flew along the shelves of the Falberg mounting toward the summit from ledge to ledge.] (9–10)

Immediately after this the narrator questions their very identity: "Were they two human beings or were they arrows?" (10). Distance makes the pinning-down of identity impossible (this distance perhaps representing, as we shall see later, the distance of language). The language used by the narrator to describe Séraphîta continues to be ambiguous; for example, she is merely "the being on whose arm she [a pale girl] leaned" (10).

Subsequently, we get a *heterogeneous* description of Séraphîta, who is alternately described as very masculine and as very feminine. These opposing perspectives, which we see through the narrator's eyes, show that Séraphîta manifests opposing elements simultaneously. On the masculine side, it is said that Séraphîta "seemed to be a young boy of seventeen" (translation mine), but she has a body "slight and fragile as a woman's" (16). It must be said that the narrator never categorically states Séraphîta's identity but only describes, as in the above quotation, what she *seems* to be, or gives a comparison between her and something else. Her identity appears only in a relational mode of similarity, not in a literal one.

Perhaps the strangest and most revealing manner in which Séraphîta is described has to do with the overall picture which we get of her, or rather the *lack* of one. We see only parts of her body, usually extremities which do not necessarily reveal a person's identity. We see her feet first of all, and these are never described in detail; we then see her hand resting on Minna, again a mere hand with no more detailed description, then her head, which is not described in physical detail but only in the kind of movement that it makes. Then we get the most detailed description of the golden locks of her hair and her pale complexion—again, nothing that can offer us a clue with which to assign an individual and personal physical identity to Séraphîta. We see only very general parts of the body, and isolated ones at that, never united into a clear-cut and unique definition. Séraphîta does not have a physical identity in this story at all, but is almost a mannequin of generalized body parts seen one at a time and never all together. A plurality of different elements, she is a real exception in the corpus of Balzac's works, for Balzac usually takes great pains to give significant physical qualities to his characters.[4] Séraphîta, as plurality, is not "one": she contains difference, distance within.

Finally, the text completely precludes the possibility of any kind of physical identity because, as Minna's father says, "Séraphîta was never seen perfectly nude, as children are sometimes; she was never touched by the hand of man or woman; she lay spotless on her mother's breast, and she never cried" (69). Hence the text tells us that any kind of referential definition of sexual identity is impossible in this case: "there is no truth in itself of the sexual difference in itself, of either man or woman in itself" (Derrida, 103). The sexual identity which the text investigates is not biological: it is not something that one can verify in the "literal" realm. In the psychoanalytical sense, one cannot tell whether Séraphîta has the phallus or not. She then puts into question the very existence of castration, and she suspends the relation with castration, as Derrida says.

So we must turn elsewhere to learn about the identity of Séraphîta, because we cannot find it in the literal, physical realm; and as suggested by the lack of a literal identity, we might investigate a rhetorical identity. We recall that one of the first ways to gain insight into Balzacian characters is to study their environments. The metonymic relationship between the identities of the characters in Balzac's texts and their surroundings is really a metaphoric one, especially in this story where we are forced to make a connection between the two when we leap from the name of Séraphîta in the title to the landscape descrip-

tion in the first paragraph. When we study this first section we find
that the landscape symbols do indeed represent in a surprising way
the problematics of the main characters and that the identity of the
land can give us insights into human identity.

Certain key words in the first paragraph appear to be a condensation of and introduction to the problem of delimitation. We began by
seeing the *coastline* of Norway, the dividing line between land and sea:

> On seeing the Norwegian coast as outlined on the map, what imagina-
> tion can fail to be amazed at its fantastic contours [découpures]—long
> tongues of granite, round which the surges of the North sea are for ever
> roaring? (2)

Our attention is drawn immediately to the "découpures," to the cut-
ting-out and delimiting of land and sea, to the borders between what
will soon be two opposing and conflicting elements.

This opposition is first of all a veritable struggle which gives "a
record of a contest between the ocean and the granite, two equally
powerful elements—one by its inertia, the other by its motion" (3).
The dividing line between these two elements is described as an abyss
or a *chasm*, the place where the land meets the sea: "a gulf [abîme] a
hundred fathoms deep and six feet wide" (3). Hence there is no gradual change from sea to land along a flat and sandy stretch of beach:
there is only the radical and uncommunicative abyss. These coastlines
are actually called "beachless shores" (2), without a gradual and continuous change from one element to another.

Thus the space or division between sea and land is, appropriately, a
*space* (an "abîme"), and a dangerous and uncharted one at that: path-
less gulfs [abîmes sans chemins, 327] (2). In fact, the edge of the abyss
is that which disrupts and defies rules: "the rocks are differently
riven, and their contorted precipices defy the terms of geometry" (3).
In this introduction to the landscape we have a very definite and
clear-cut opposition between two elements which remain separated
by a frightening and dangerous *space* which disrupts. This distance
*between* (the abyss) will be very important in our analysis to come.

In a second moment in the text, however, this initial setup of a clear-
cut distinction between land and sea gives way to a different figure.
As we get farther away from the coast where the bay turns inland, a

new relation between land and sea emerges, and as we approach from the typical Balzacian bird's-eye view closer to the characters' dwellings and finally to the characters themselves, the relation between polarities changes. We are in a special *time*, at the dividing line between two centuries, a time of a very special winter: "The winter of 1799–1800 was one of the hardest in the memory of Europe; the Norwegian sea froze in every fiord, where the violence of the undertow commonly prevents the ice from forming" (7).

Just at the turning point between epochs, in a hazy place where limits are not clearly defined, we encounter an extreme winter where the sea freezes and becomes like the land. Both sea and land are now alike and the polarities have become entangled. From the initial *chasm* which divided land from sea we reach the *chiasmus* which mixes up by crossing over the properties of land and sea:

> At this part the gulf is wide enough to allow the waters flung back by the Falberg to die murmuring on the lowest edge of the hills, where the strand is softly fringed with fine sand, mingled with mica, tiny crystals, and pretty pebbles of porphyry and many-colored marbles brought from Sweden by the river, with waifs from the sea, and shells, flowers of the sea tossed up by storms from the Pole or from the Tropics. (4–5; translation altered slightly)

Here there is a gradual and continuous change from land to sea, from solid to liquid, which mixes together first of all solid pieces of land brought to the sea by the river (liquid) with bits of solid landlike substances (shells) which come from the sea (liquid). There is such a mix-up of solid and liquid elements that the beach becomes the strange union of the opposing elements. The above quotation ends with the metaphor "flowers of the sea," which in an oxymoron joins the flower (a land element) to the sea.

Opposing elements thus relate to each other in two ways. In the narrative temporality of this story, the structure of the *chasm* completely separates one polarity from the other, but this structure evolves into that of the *chiasmus*, which then puts into question the radical split between polarities. In this second moment, there is still a difference between land and sea, but a difference which is simply that and no longer a rigid polarity. The border between the elements has become undecidable: it is "a margin whose very consequences are incalculable" (Derrida, 61). (In Derrida, the border, the split or chasm which separates polarities—masculine and feminine—is castration: here we see "castration's undecidable contours" [Derrida, 63].) This evolution from the structure of chasm to chiasmus is the same as the evolution of the structure of masculine and feminine polarities in the text, as we shall soon see. Furthermore, solid and liquid, active and passive attributes of the land and the sea are themselves conventional attributes of masculinity and femininity which subsequently get mixed up.

The only very detailed physical description relating to Séraphîta is, in fact, a metaphor which identifies her with a hybrid flower whose physical detail represents just what we have seen in the vague physical description of Séraphîta. First of all, it is made up of two distinct colors that change somehow from one to the other, just as Séraphîta displays masculine and feminine traits; and of tiny leaves which are heaped one upon the other to such an extent that they become confused, just as the physical description of Séraphîta is a heap of confused body parts. This symbol thus gives us a physical description of a flower which represents the *structure* of the description of Séraphîta, and once again we see that the closest we come to identity for Séraphîta is a metaphoric one which is essentially linguistic (and distancing or differentiating).

Let us pause a moment here to see what we have learned so far about polarities and identity in this story. We know that the identity of the polarities becomes problematic when borderlines are effaced, when strict and rigid lines of demarcation dissolve. And we can see that identity itself is questioned and investigated in this story *symbolically*, through the metaphors provided by the land and the sea, and by that of the flower. The very necessity of this symbolism is extremely important, for we never get a one-to-one mapping of identity onto things or people: identity is always once-removed by the space of symbolism. There is always a distance (a chasm) between a thing and its definition. Identity, the sameness of the one and the same, is thus paradoxically marked by the distance, the difference, of language, and is thus always represented by tropes, by the structure of language itself: identity is, in a certain way, always linguistic. It is always, then, relational, and this is indeed the only way we really learn of

Séraphîta's identity, through her relationships, which correspond structurally to the rhetorical, linguistic relations which define her identity in this text. Here we must repeat that in the text, Séraphîta is not called by this name alone, and that we actually do not come across this name until the second section of the story. For, as we saw earlier, immediately after the title *Séraphîta* we encounter "Séraphîtüs," the subtitle. Here we find that the identity of Séraphîta/Séraphîtüs is determined by *others*, by the people who know this being. *Women* see Séraphîta as a man; it is Minna who is in love with her, as the text makes explicit, who *names* her Séraphîtüs: "The person whom Minna named Séraphîtüs leaned on his right heel in order to raise the long plank" (translation mine). Minna names *her* in order to name *herself*. When, at one point, she begins to doubt whether or not Séraphîtüs is of this earth, she cries: "'Who and what are you?' said she, with an impulse of delicious alarm. 'But I know. Thou art my life'" (12). As her life, as her being, her existence *is* this other definition. Thus Minna uses Séraphîta as a mirror to construct her own (female) identity by seeing in Séraphîta the "other," the male. The "gouffre," the chasm between the sea and the land, as we saw earlier, represents the line of demarcation between opposing entities, and we recall that Minna and Séraphîta were in the process of walking along the abyss in the beginning of the story. By naming Séraphîta, Minna can place herself on the "proper" side of the abyss. In speaking of the literal abyss she claims, "I would look only at you as we climbed the walls of this abyss; if I had not, what would have become of me?" (10). In the literal sense, if she hadn't looked at Séraphîta, she would have fallen and died, and in the symbolic sense, if she doesn't have Séraphîta as a point of reference, she cannot keep from dying in the figural sense of losing her identity, or of never being able to establish it. She thus cedes the phallus to Séraphîta, accepts her loss, and gives herself a false identity with the result that she truly loses herself (she becomes like the first type of woman in Nietzsche).

Hence Minna gives identity to both Séraphîta and herself, an identity based completely on a relational foundation; one could say a differential identity. And it is a definition in the sense of the naming in language of a "thing" that does not exist in reality except relationally.

Curiously, in the text it is not only Minna who sees Séraphîta from this point of view. The narrator also sees her as male, as we can see in the following passage:

> Minna stood up to take the young man's hand, hoping to draw him down to her so as to press on that fascinating brow a kiss of admiration rather than of love; but one look from his eyes, a look that went through her as a sunbeam goes through a glass prism, froze the poor child. (17)

The narrator refers to Séraphîta as a young man, thus also giving her a masculine identity. And, most surprising of all, Séraphîta also refers to herself in the masculine form. In the following passage, the verb *arriver*, which is conjugated with the verb *être* and whose past participle agrees in gender with the subject, shows that Séraphîta gives herself a masculine identity: "I am disgusted with all things" (20) ("Je suis arrivé au dégoût de toutes choses") (333). Thus Séraphîta actually assumes the identity Minna assigns her. Yet even though Séraphîta assumes this identity for a while, she ultimately refuses it when she refuses to be Minna's partner: "I cannot be your companion" (18). Here, she refuses her love and also refuses to be her masculine counterpart: to seriously assume the masculine identity which she is assigned. She thus suspends the process of identification and does not allow it to solidify into polarities. Immediately after this scene Séraphîta changes from being called Séraphîtüs to Séraphîta, a change represented by a division in the text (and by sleep), which is similar in structure to the chasm.

Again, in the second section, we find that Séraphîta's identity is assigned by others, since all of the men in the story see her as a woman. In this part entitled "Séraphîta," we have the mirror opposite of the first section, for here Wilfrid, a young man, loves Séraphîta. Here also the narrator gives Séraphîta the same identity as does the character who is in love with her, for the narrator refers to her as a woman: "She turned languidly toward him, after tossing back her hair like a pretty woman overpowered by sick-headache and too feeble to complain" (24). And Séraphîta herself changes and refers to herself in the feminine gender: "I am sure of it, Wilfrid" (25) ("j'en suis sûre, Wilfrid" [in French, the feminine ending of "e"]) (334). But again she ultimately refuses this identity also: "You see, my friend, I am not a woman" (26).

She suspends the decidable opposition between polarities, between masculine and feminine, by assuming both, then neither one nor the other. Thus although Séraphîta accepts provisionally, perhaps playfully, the identities which others give her, she ultimately refuses to be labeled either as a man *or* as a woman and affirms her difference from the definition.

In the third section of the story, we find the title "Séraphîta-Séraphîtüs"; Séraphîta is characterized by both genders at once, affirming her heterogeneous, androgynous identity. And curiously, there never really *was* a clear-cut distinction between the genders in the first two sections of the story, for near the place where the genders change, they are all mixed up. In section 1, entitled "Séraphîtüs," in which Séraphîta is male, we find that at the end Séraphîtüs begins to "abdicate his manly strength" (22). Even though she is still called Séraphîtüs, she is referred to by Minna as "chère" (dear), and by Séraphîta herself as "trop lasse" (too tired)—again, words with feminine endings. Hence even the textual identities assigned to Séraphîta are broken down. As Séraphîta says of herself, she belongs in neither realm: "I am an exile far from heaven; like a monster, far from earth!" (21). Thus, as with the description of conflict between the land and the sea which we discussed earlier, here we have an initial polarity which is set up and eventually destroyed when it no longer functions properly, when the opposition between elements becomes ambiguous and the limits between the sexes are suspended indefinitely.

Hence, in her relations with others, Séraphîta assumes the identity that they give her, but only in a "playful" way, not in reality. She plays at being a man and plays at being a woman, but she does not "believe" in either category. This, according to Derrida, is the role of woman: "she who, unbelieving, still plays with castration, she is 'woman'" (Derrida, 61). Thus, in identifying Séraphîta, the others can try to identify themselves, to give themselves a solid, stable, relational identity which they could not perhaps get on their own. Séraphîta is conscious of the fact that those who love her do not love *her*; they only need her as a mirror upon which to erect a self-identity which they can cling to and love: as Séraphîta says, "you love me for your own sake, not for myself" (27). Both men and women use the imaginary self (in the Lacanian sense), the fictional mirror-self, as a basis for their identity. Ultimately Séraphîta wants Minna and Wilfrid to love each other, something the two of them refuse to do. Séraphîta is like a mirror within which the two can see and love an image they create in an odd type of narcissism, but through which they cannot see to the real *other*.[5] The love that they experience is artificial in every way, for they erect the false identity of the loved one in order to create their own false identity and love. In the text, this stage is surpassed only with the *breaking* of the mirror, with the death of Séraphîta. Then Minna and Wilfrid can love each other not because of a fictional sexual difference but because of the experience they share in their difference. In a sense, this is an extremely negative moment because Minna and Wilfrid can be awakened to the "truth" about Séraphîta (and themselves) only through her death, through the death of the playful, affirmative woman who affirms herself as man and woman and as neither man nor woman, as that which puts boundaries into question.

This mirror seems to be necessary, however, because as mirror, Séraphîta always seems to be protecting the two characters from danger. Her way of doing this in particularly dangerous situations is by *breathing* on them (in the religious sense, this is like the breath, the "souffle," of God). Her breath acts as a potion which makes one forget by putting back into the unconscious that which is too difficult to be digested consciously. In one instance, the breath keeps Minna from dying:

> "I am dying, my Séraphîtüs, having loved no one but you," said she, mechanically moving to throw herself down.
> Séraphîtüs blew softly on her brow and eyes. Suddenly, as a traveler is refreshed by a bath, Minna had forgotten that acute anguish; it had vanished under that soothing breath. (12)

Séraphîta also saves Wilfrid from a deathlike swoon: "Wilfrid had fallen half-dead on the floor. Séraphîta breathed on the young man's brow, and he fell calmly asleep, lying at her feet" (29).

Thus, Séraphîta's breath has the role of veiling truths which are too dangerous: "I feel I am not sufficiently shrouded, and fear lest you should see me too clearly; you would quail if you knew me too well" (20). All of the characters want to discover the truth about Séraphîta's identity, as Wilfrid makes explicit, the truth about truth, but she keeps veiling herself and does not permit them to see: "she comes forth and then vanishes like some coy truth" (40). And what is this dangerous truth that she must hide? In Minna's case, as we saw before, it is the "abîme," the chasm itself. And here we find that when we ask ourselves what the abyss is which Séraphîta must veil, we must answer that it is Séraphîta herself. She *is* the abyss, as the text says:

> Séraphîtüs left Minna clinging to the granite, and went as a shadow might have done to stand on the edge of the crag, his eyes sounding the bottom of the fiord, defying its bewildering depths; his figure did not sway, his brow was as white and calm as that of a marble statue—abyss facing abyss. (12; translation altered slightly)

Wilfrid calls the flower which gave us the clearest physical description of Séraphîta an abyss, as we see when Minna shows the flower to Wilfrid and her father, and the following scene ensues:

> "This is supernatural," said the old man, seeing a flower in bloom in winter.
> "An abyss!" cried Wilfrid, fevered by the perfume. (42; translation altered slightly)

The distance of the metaphor reflects the distance (the abyss) in Séraphîta's identity. She causes others to experience the abyss, their own abyss of nonidentity, if she does not carefully veil herself. When Wilfrid sees Séraphîta, the text claims that he falls into the abyss: "For some days past, whenever Wilfrid went to Séraphîta's house, his body there fell as though into an abyss [gouffre]" (34). Here, Séraphîta as woman is not veiling the fact that she does not have the phallus (is castrated) but rather is veiling the fact that castration "does not take place," that identity does not exist in the concrete: "The feminine distance abstracts truth from itself in a *suspension* of the relation with castration. This relation is suspended much as one might taughten or stretch a canvas, or a relation, which nevertheless remains—suspended—in indecision" (Derrida, 59).[6]

Séraphîta as the abyss of separation *is* textual play and difference. Woman (Séraphîta, the title of the story) is difference, the difference between three letters, between "a" and "üs." Séraphîta is always at a distance because we cannot name and possess her. And she is always at a distance from herself: "There is no such thing as the essence of woman because woman averts, she is averted of herself" (Derrida, 51). She *is* distance, the chasm which separates: "Perhaps woman—a non-identity, a non-figure, a simulacrum—is distance's very chasm, the out-distancing of distance, the interval's cadence, distance itself, if we could still say such a thing, distance *itself*" (Derrida, 49). Séraphîta's role in the text is to subvert any definition of identity: "Out of the depths, endless and unfathomable, she engulfs and distorts all vestige of essentiality, of identity, of property" (Derrida, 51). Thus, in this view of woman we have neither man as the top of a hierarchical polarity nor woman at the top as the reversal of the same; rather this initial "habitual" polarity of the opposites of male and female is undermined by the role of the playful, affirmative woman, just as it is in Derrida's third type of woman. Ultimately, then, the questions "What is woman?" and "Who is Séraphîta?" are impossible ones: "Woman (truth) will not be pinned down. . . . That which will not be pinned down by truth is, in truth—*feminine*" (Derrida, 55).

At the end of the story, Minna and Wilfrid finally see each other and love each other in the light of their love for Séraphîta. And Séraphîta becomes an angel (which traditionally is androgynous) and ascends to heaven, ultimately eliminating the previous negative moment of death through rebirth. This ascension (and consequently the entire religious aspect of the story), along with the newfound love between Minna and Wilfrid, symbolize perhaps the overcoming of a repressive and essentially improper polar structure. This overcoming cannot somehow be rid of the fictional polar structure, does not come up with a more proper structure, but instead becomes conscious of it and its error, and with this consciousness can continue to strive for an identity in difference, an identity that, because of its self-reflexivity and playfulness, is "above" the old.

Thus Séraphîta as difference, as an undecidable heterogeneous being, shows us that any investigation of difference, such as the difference between philosophy and literature or between man and woman, will not provide us with a neat systematic answer; instead, once a polarity has been set up (which in Derrida is the operation of a certain type of castration) the investigation will put into question the limits between polarities so that their borders become undecidable and the polarity is undermined. The polarity, and thus castration, cannot simply be negated and suppressed; the difference *remains*, but castration's borders become undecidable.

If we now compare the two strategies of Derrida's and Balzac's texts on women, we can perhaps articulate their differences and the undecidable contours of these differences. First of all, Derrida's text takes woman as its object. The aim of the philosophical text is to construct a metaphor which would express the identity of woman: woman is "X." It seeks the truth about woman, a constative understanding; it seeks to unveil the identity of the woman in Nietzsche and to arrive at a "system" of the three types (even if the system is undecidable). And here we must distinguish between Derrida's text and those of other philosophers, for in Derrida it is clear that the object of this search is unattainable, must be put in quotation marks. Derrida questions the very search as he is searching: "One can no longer seek her, no more than one can search for woman's femininity or female sexuality. . . . Yet it is impossible to resist looking for her" (Derrida, 71).

The philosophical text thus, as Derrida says, keeps its distance from woman by defining her. It keeps its distance from distance (woman). If it did not keep its distance from woman, were seduced by her, siren-like, it would die, would become woman, would become literature: "Yet one must beware to keep one's own distance from her beguiling song of enchantment. A distance from distance must be maintained" (Derrida, 49).

This is perhaps the difference. Literature, Balzac's story, has woman as the *subject*, in the sense of the speaking subject and also of the content. There are three undecidable aspects of one woman, Séraphîta: masculine, feminine, and the undermining of these very categories. The difference and distance in woman speak, woman speaks. And woman is that which can't be pinned down by truth, is that which undermines categorization. She is the space of metaphor: the simultaneous undecidable metaphors in Balzac's text: man = woman, man ≠ woman. The distance is *in* woman, *in* language, *in* sexuality itself. Most importantly, woman is an operation, a performative type of language which puts quotation marks around (or distances) concepts:

"The question of woman suspends the decidable opposition of true and non-true and inaugurates the epochal regime of quotation marks which is to be enforced for every concept belonging to the system of philosophical decidability" (Derrida, 107). For example, after reading *Séraphîta* we cannot speak of woman but must speak of "woman," a "woman" who already has difference (masculinity) within. This distancing is the feminine operation in Derrida's terms. Woman engulfs, puts quotation marks around, property and properness, the truth which is the object of philosophy. Instead of constructing a metaphor, "woman is X," literature is already an impossible metaphor which must be interpreted.

As Derrida realizes, philosophy tries to distance itself from woman but in so doing repeats the feminine operation, that of distancing, and thus falls into the trap: "A distance from distance must be maintained. Not only for the protection . . . against the spell of her fascination, but also as a way of succumbing to it, that distance (which is lacking) *is necessary*" (Derrida, 49). Philosophy is always literary, and after Derrida it must take cognizance of the fact that philosophy creates metaphors, while continuing to pursue the impossible truth, the answer to the question "What is woman?"

What is the difference between literature and philosophy? It is, as Balzac's and Derrida's texts have shown us, ultimately unknowable. But we can observe two different stances, almost grammatical places, of the two discourses. Philosophy is a constative discourse which takes a concept as its object, attempting to construct a metaphor which would adequately describe this concept. In Derrida's case, one could say that philosophy tries to construct unequivocal statements about undecidability.[7] But philosophy, in various degrees, is literature (the borders are blurred), is itself a heterogeneous and multiple text, just as Derrida's text is dialogic. Literature, on the other hand, has a concept as its subject, the concept speaks, and the concept is always already an undecidable metaphor (woman = man). Thus literature makes undecidable statements unequivocally. Literature is to varying degrees a constative discourse on this very subject (and thus is philosophical), just as Balzac's text is ultimately a discourse on woman, has its own subject as its object.

The difference between philosophy and literature is just that: a distance, an abyss which separates but also joins; which differentiates, but not completely; which can never be measured because it is that which makes measurement possible. It is Derrida's *différance* and *hymen*, the chasm of woman's difference. But there *is* still a difference; there is still difference.

Most studies of *Séraphîta* have overlooked the rather "dangerous" questioning of identity in the story. Séraphîta's androgynous nature is accepted and then dismissed in favor of labeling and discussing the text as a philosophical discourse on Swedenborg. The story is in fact *both* of these things, a dry philosophical treatise and a bizarre personal history. It is, one might say, itself androgynous (like Derrida's text), composed of a dialogue between two opposing modes of discourse, just as Séraphîta is composed of a dialogue of opposing elements. And it is, in a sense, the uncanny literary correlative of Derrida's text, a "philosophical" text whose "subject" is woman. As Derrida has shown, the role of the woman, of the "subordinate" element of the polarity, is of capital concern to philosophy. Thus this story, through Séraphîta's story, tells us that we must not neglect either one of the polarities but that we must acknowledge, accept, affirm, perhaps playfully assume, the heterogeneous and undecidable nature of the text and of the character, and perhaps of ourselves.

### NOTES

1. Jacques Derrida, *Spurs: Nietzsche's Styles*, trans. Barbara Harlow (Chicago: University of Chicago Press, 1979), p. 97. All further references to this book appear in the text.

2. Curiously, in the past this story has not been seen as a rather unusual questioning of identity. Rather, it has been viewed as a vehicle through which Balzac was able to express his sometimes erroneous understanding of Swedenborg's philosophy. Of course, a large part of the story is indeed composed of various declamations formulated by the main characters on Swedenborg and on religion. But *one-half* of the story does not deal with philosophy (except in a very oblique way). It deals rather with the personal interactions between a very strange main character and the people nearest to her. In the philosophical and religious context of the story, her strangeness can be explained

to a certain extent by claiming that she is an angel and thus an androgyne, but this does not account for the interesting and unusual way in which her androgyny is presented, and cannot account for the uncanniness of her double nature. We will thus discuss this "other side" of the story of Séraphîta.

3. Honoré de Balzac, *Séraphîta*, vol. 7 of *La comédie humaine*, ed. Pierre Citron (Paris: Seuil, 1966), pp. 327–75. Translations have been taken from Honoré de Balzac, *Séraphîta, A Daughter of Eve, and Other Stories*, trans. Clara Bell and R. S. Scott (Philadelphia: John D. Morris, 1900).

4. Geneviève Delattre, "De Séraphîta à 'La fille aux yeux d'or'," *L'Année Balzacienne* (Paris: Garnier, 1970), pp. 183–226.

5. Shoshana Felman, "Rereading Femininity," *Yale French Studies* 62 (1981): 19–44. Here Felman also recognizes that another Balzacian heroine serves as a mirror for the self-reflection of another character (24).

6. Derrida often plays with the word "voile," which can mean veil or sail, and "toile," which means an artistic canvas.

7. Barbara Johnson, "The Frame of Reference: Poe, Lacan, Derrida," *Yale French Studies* 55–56 (1977): 504. Here Derrida makes "unequivocal statements of undecidability" and Lacan makes "ambiguous assertions of decidability."

*James Mish'alani*

# Kafka:
# Text's Body, Body's Text

L ONG BEFORE it appears in its own life as a bioanatomical object, the body itself is integrally lived; and after it makes its appearance, lying or standing there ready for scrutiny, dissection, examination, it yields itself thus in its objectivity only to kindred bodily probing, wherein the hands that search, press, palpate and the roving eyes, the patient, close-held ear, are not encountered but lived as modes of access to their object. Generally, the lived body is for itself transcendence towards the world as that within which things are to be met. And the world, disclosed in an implicit understanding of what things one can behave towards and how one can variously behave towards them, thus stands in correspondence to the body.[1] As limit, the world determines the specific ways in which things are to be dealt with. As access, the body on its side projects through the lived articulation of limbs and organs those paths towards, by, and about things whereby the very complexion of the world is always revealed.[2] The body is world-revelation. But as the presence of things in the lighting of revelation is not uniform or indifferent, but variegated, so is the body differentiated, articulated, variously organed and limbed, outfitted, equipped and geared. The window lets in the light of day and opens out on scenes only for the seeing eyes of a creature of vistas and distances. The hammer, standing out towards nails and wood, as towards all that they may be nailed together for and all that they may be brought together from, does so only insofar as it is ready for the hand that lifts it.[3] The pair of shoes suited to the earth, gathering about it the doorsill to the country path, the windswept fields, sun, rain, grain, bread, evening, dawn, the hearth and the floorboards by child-bed or deathbed, does all this in its humble reliability for the tread of the peasant woman whose footedness releases her through it to the security of the world.[4] The jug that comes to full presence as jug in the outpouring of the gift in which, be it water or wine, earth and sky together dwell by a marriage of soil and rock to rain and sun in spring or vine—this jug does its manifold-simple gathering of the world's extremities *for* the hand that pours the outpour, *towards* the lips for whom a refreshing drink is given, or *before* the faces lifted up in thanks to the gods for whom a libation is poured.[5] Thus are things in ways most essential rooted in the body; and as primal ground the body in turn remains matrix to the world, not an object found in it.[6]

Nor does the other's body appear in the manner of an object in my encounter with him or her, whose features, glances, gestures and movements all point beyond themselves and thus turn me with them towards that which occupies them and in relation to which I must assume a specific stance if only to reject it or, deciding it does not concern me, pass it by. The other's body lights up the world for me no less than mine does, in a co-transcendence towards a common horizon of meaning consensually confirmed, and ever renewed, laying for us a shared ground of world engagement without which even error, disagreement, and dissension become impossible. As the equipment through which I ordinarily pass in my projects does not stand out as an object until it breaks or is lost, so the other's body and mine do not obtrude and call attention to themselves in pure anatomical objectivity unless a radical breakdown occurs, occasioned by some such disruptions as disease, death, or a chaos of incoordination. Otherwise and until then, the other and I continue to be co-workers at world-disclosure, passing through each other's attitudes and movements as through unobstructed space. The human shape that comes towards me from the opposite direction reveals that part of my path I have left behind. The open hand thrust out from that tattered sleeve turns me towards the money it lacks, cold nights, hunger. The open mouth about to speak, just as the printed page lying before me, a distant product of what a hand once filled an empty sheet with, calls me to a conversation from which I will not emerge the same. I listen. I read.

A vulture was hacking at my feet.[7]

A startling declaration! Whence do these words come to us? From what bodily reality do they emanate? No doubt we are to suppose them coming from someone who has survived the attack of which he tells. But what manner of survivor can he be, having been attacked not by a bird of prey but by a vulture, a scavenger, eater of the dead? What are we to make of a narrator already carrion even before the attack of his narrative?

Every corpse is a desertion. It shuts out the world lit up by the comportment and demeanor of a once-mobile physiognomy. Insofar as the other is my co-worker in disclosing our world, his corpse spells more than his demise, an event among other possible events within the world, but attacks the security of world-disclosure itself. Where once the flash of a glance, the appeal and call of a word or gesture, propelled me towards things, I now find nothing but an insipid, uncomprehending, and incomprehensible density shut in upon itself irrevocably. This death is no mere intimation of my own by analogy, but effectively an actual dimming of my life. Now I must reconvene the conversation of our world elsewhere without his help as interlocutor and point of support. Yet this corpse speaks, or at least writes, and wants to tell a tale. Have we, perhaps, been too hasty in declaring it totally dead? Might there not be a manner of death consistent with language, or a manner of language appropriate to the dead? Was not the vulture only hacking at the feet? And what need have we of feet in a conversation?

> It had already torn my boots and stockings to shreds, now it was hacking at the feet themselves. Again and again it struck at them, then circled several times restlessly around me, then returned to continue its work. A gentleman passed by, looked on for a while, then asked me why I suffered the vulture. "I'm helpless," I said. "When it came and began to attack me, I of course tried to drive it away, even to strangle it, but these animals are very strong, it was about to spring at my face, but I preferred to sacrifice my feet. Now they are almost torn to bits."

A gentleman, with his feet intact, has stepped in for us and asked what we would have liked to ask, were we in speech with an interlocutor rather than reading a text; were we, that is, face-to-face with him. And we get an answer: to save his face he had to lose his feet. Let us repeat this condensed statement of the matter, as we might repeat a dream formula, so revealing in its telegraphic brevity. To save his face he had to lose his feet. It becomes evident that if we are to penetrate further into this text we cannot avoid taking up the matters of facedness and footedness.

In the polarity of face and feet human uprightness comes to its own possibility. Stature is a matter of standing in presence. We stand on the earth and are allotted a place there. With our feet we establish ourselves on firm ground and rise to face our fellow mortals. Thus we are present to each other. To be present we must appear, make an appearance, present a face; and in order to appear we must rise firmly grounded, address and be addressed from a surefooted standing. In this standing we bear a name. In bearing a name we can be called. Being called we can turn and offer our face in coming before the face whence the call came. In this turning and facing the life of the word is secured.

But a shadow falls upon our humanity when the two poles of our standing and facing are sundered. The vulture is the shadow of the death of our humanity in the rupture between face and feet. In a conversation with Gustav Janouch, Kafka once said that it is a characteristic of our times that the animal is closer to us than man. He hastened to add that that was our cage, which is to say that this closeness to the animal does not release us to a different, albeit inferior, association, but binds us into isolation. As nearness to that which, despite its intimacy to the point of bodily assimilation, remains uncannily alien, strange and other, our closeness to the animal seals our fate and shuts us up in irredeemable estrangement. For if in our times one is human only in being as an animal among humans, and the one who is so is anyone whoever, then each one is as an animal among humans, each of whom is as an animal among humans, each of whom is as an animal among humans, ad infinitum: a total disintegration without a remaining fixed point of reference. Humanity has become its own absence, estrangement from a community that is not there, marginality to a nonexistent center, outsideness to which there is no corresponding inside. At such extremity the strange is not strange by its distance from the ordinary, for nothing is ordinary, and everything is strange, yet strangeness is the most ordinary thing of all. In this reign of absence one can of an afternoon sit even in intraspecific conversation, dog to dog, with one's neighbor dog, wondering if he may not have the same burden as oneself but is ashamed to voice it, wanting to confess that one weeps over it when alone and how much sweeter it would be to weep in company, but saying nothing, giving him a prolonged look instead, which he returns with a silent, dull gaze of his own in which one can read nothing clearly, if he is merely wondering at one's silence or in his turn addressing the same silent plea to oneself, and in this regard one is disappointing him no less than he disappoints one.[8]

What is ever and always important for Kafka is that in our times this ubiquitous intimacy of absence as an irrevocably paradoxical way of being (which is not being) in (which is out of) the world (which is nonworld) is lived (or died) bodily. Our embodiment has lost its cementing force, its power to hold us together and hold us to things and things to us and us to ourselves in a world habitation that is whole, holy, and hale. Our embodiment has come to be our estrangement, our strangeness installing itself in our very bodies, not only in forms of animal identification but in a characteristic disjointedness of the human frame itself.

The death of personhood announced in the swoop of the vulture is a radical dissociation of foot and face, a collapse of the center that would hold them towards each other in a coordination indispensable for the attainment of human stature. To suffer the vulture is to suffer a fatal disjunction: either face or feet, but not both. To have one of these two modes of human embodiment the other must be given up. In either case, the very possibility of presence of one self to another self in the dignity of genuine community, wherein an enduring conversation unfolds and discloses a world both hallowed and grounded, is lost. Without the mediation of the human face the foot becomes brute domination. One rises on it to bring under one's power a domain of one's own and establish a sphere of control within which everything stands, or rather lies, in reserve at one's pleasure and whim.[9] Thus the basic movement is a bringing underfoot in willful self-insistence. And what is brought thus underfoot is no longer the ground for one's being towards others, and is no longer itself released in one's free release towards fellow mortals, but becomes rather the guarded sphere of an uncontested and uncontestable will that captures, subdues, keeps, and disposes of things in a centripetal movement of absolute self-assertion. This faceless brutality is a manner of death from which our narrator turned away, preferring to forsake his feet instead. But what is a face without feet? No longer grounded in a surefooted standing, it no longer is presence or appearance in person but mere apparition, a floating, insubstantial, and ghostly visage whose words are mere ineffectual murmurings lacking the authority to answer, claim or promise, a dry rustling in the wind.

We, consigned as we are to the fate of modern individuality, are ever and anew coming up against this futile alternative: either to rise inexorably like a blind force into the midst of things, securing our place as sheer displacement, or else solicitous, displacing ourselves to a vanishing point, to renounce our brutality and turn towards others a wan visage that can at best plead, commiserate, wish or dream in common. But . . .

> "Fancy letting yourself be tortured like this!" said the gentleman. "One shot and that's the end of the vulture." "Really?" I said. "And would you do that?" "With pleasure," said the gentleman. "I've only got to go home and get my gun. Could you wait another half-hour?" "I'm not sure about that," said I, and stood for a moment rigid with pain. Then I said: "Do try it in any case, please." "Very well," said the gentleman, "I'll be as quick as I can."

Perhaps waiting is what is adequate to our plight. But waiting for what? If a vulture is not cause but sign of death, can the gun avert the catastrophe? Can it force life back into the dead or dying? Whenever there is talk of the plight of modern humanity, and heaven knows there is enough of it nowadays, our immediate temptation is to think that what is thus occupying us, if it is anything real or worth talking about, must be a certain problem whose terms can be defined, its causes identified and their susceptibility to our intervention determined in clear and precise ways that would guide our planning and doing to the end of removing it. We think we must be able to mount an assault on our predicament. Pushing through with our problem-solving powers, we are to bring it into our sights, and training on it our intricate machinery of detection and mastery at a safe distance, without compromising ourselves, discharge our energies against it and rid ourselves of it. Thus, the time of our waiting is essentially a time of assessing our prospects, calculating our means, planning our approach, and marshaling our resources. The waiting as waiting becomes inessential, mere concomitant to the fury of our activity, born of the delay necessary in bringing our apparatus of control to bear on that which afflicts us, resignation to the unavoidable lag between our first alarm and final deliverance. It is waiting for the end of our troubles, which when properly targeted can be finally destroyed. But might there not be a more essential waiting, a waiting that does not wait *for* anything but waits *upon*, waiting upon even our afflicted condition itself, listening in it to the voice of our destiny? Such waiting would be radically different from any whiling away the time, that is to say, from any indifferent filling or passing of time, albeit in pain or uncertainty, while our planning teams theorize and deliberate, that is, until the gentleman has brought out the gun from the place of his uneasy and fretful residence he calls home.[10] For . . .

> During this conversation the vulture had been calmly listening, letting its eye rove between me and the gentleman. Now I realized that it had understood everything; it took wing, leaned far back to gain impetus, and then like a javelin thrower, thrust its beak through my mouth, deep into me. Falling back, I was relieved to feel him drowning irretrievably in my blood, which was filling every depth, flooding every shore.

In a final orgasmic shudder, the boundaries we thought separated afflicter, afflicted, and world are broken through and submerged in an all-pervasive flow. The devouring bird enters its devoured victim, devoured by him, becoming one with his life substance, thus doing its devouring from his ownmost element. And the blood in which it is thus irretrievably drowned, the life principle now bearing within itself a craving for the dead, breaks all bounds, inundating the farthest limits of the world. That baneful threat to human stature, both intimate and extensive, is incorporated into ourselves and now pervades the very manner in which the world is world for us. Things can no longer be sheltered with us in an authentically human upright standing and facing, but are consigned with us to the status of disposable matter which in its disposability has a fatal affinity with those indifferent heaps of waste for the scavengers. When neither that which threatens nor that which is threatened is a particular thing within the world but the very revelation of Being entrusted to us in these afflicted times, when, that is, our affliction is none other than the way in which world is world for us, then at what specific source of menace or malignancy can the technological thinking of the gentleman with the gun aim? From what safe distance can it bear down on its supposed target when it itself is mired and held fast within this world affliction? When it in its essence provides the frame determining the very character of our plight, the technological gun and the vulture's beak being ultimately one.

Franz Kafka once described the tuberculosis from which he suffered and ultimately died as his own devouring of himself—an apt description of an affliction in which one's mouth is implicated with one's blood. Is it not possible that in this tale of the vulture he has left us a record of how he himself had become internal vulture to himself, all the more appropriate for his having often spoken of himself as a memory come to life, that is to say, a posthumous being? Indeed, such is not only possible but very likely. Would it not then invalidate the far-flung reflections we have so recklessly followed out here? Not at all. To suppose so would be to assume that by tracing a piece of literary narrative back to a bodily disease we thus arrive at an ultimate and irreducible fact with which we can rest satisfied as source of intelligibility. Let us briefly respond that if the vulture can be really Franz Kafka's tuberculosis, then Franz Kafka's tuberculosis can be really the vulture as we have understood it. Before he ever textualized it with pen and ink, the plight of modern individuality had inscribed itself with its cruel stylus deep into his flesh.[11] His bodily suffering was the first part of the writing he endured. The body of his text, the body that turns up so insistently on his pages, now caged, now maimed, now starved, now tortured, now dilapidated, faint and tottering, now wandering around the earth uninterred, is the text of his own body, testament to the plight of human embodiment in our times.

Both his bodily text and his textual body will remain for us talismans of this world epoch as we rise on our feet again and now bend

our steps in measured pace on our meditative path, which in its movement rests in a silence that listens and waits.

## NOTES

1. Heidegger defines the world as follows: ". . . world 'is' no particular
being but rather that by means of and in terms of which Dasein *gives itself to
understand* what beings it *can* behave toward and how it *can* behave toward
them" (Martin Heidegger, *The Essence of Reasons*, trans. Terence Malick [Evans-
ton: Northwestern University Press, 1969], p. 85).

2. Thus, starting from the side of the body, we may say with Merleau-Ponty,
"My eye for me is a certain power of making contact with things" (Maurice
Merleau-Ponty, *Phenomenology of Perception*, trans. Colin Smith [London:
Routledge & Kegan Paul, 1962], pp. 278–79). Or, starting from the side of
things, we may say with Heidegger, "Presence within the lighting articulates
all the human sense" (Martin Heidegger, "The Anaximander Fragment," in
*Early Greek Thinking*, trans. David Farrell Krell and Frank Capuzzi [New York:
Harper & Row, 1975], p. 36), and "the posture of man is pervasively tuned by
the openness of being as the whole" (Martin Heidegger, as quoted in David
Michael Levin, "The Opening of Vision," *Review of Existential Psychology and
Psychiatry* 16 [1978–79]: 142). But whether we start from body or from world,
their reciprocal answering to each other in the structure of disclosure is
evident.

3. For the hammer, see Martin Heidegger, *Being and Time*, trans. John
Macquarrie and Edward Robinson (New York: Harper & Row, 1962), part 1,
division 1, 3.

4. For the pair of shoes, see Martin Heidegger, "The Origin of the Work of
Art," in *Poetry, Language, Thought*, trans. Albert Hofstadter (New York: Harper
& Row, 1975), pp. 33–34.

5. For the jug, see Martin Heidegger, "The Thing," in *Poetry, Language,
Thought*, pp. 171–74.

6. This is why Heidegger says, "The human body is something essentially
other than an animal organism." For the latter is a thing within the world
(Martin Heidegger, "Letter on Humanism," trans. Frank Capuzzi with J.
Glenn Gray, in *Basic Writings*, ed. David Farrell Krell [New York: Harper &
Row, 1977], p. 204). For the rooting of things in our body, see Merleau-Ponty,
*Phenomenology of Perception*, p. 291.

7. Franz Kafka, "The Vulture," trans. Tonia and James Stern, in *The Complete Stories*, ed. Nahum N. Glatzer (New York: Schocken Books, 1976), pp.
442–43. In the course of this essay, Kafka's "The Vulture" will be quoted in its

entirety. Subsequent quotations from it will not be separately acknowledged by footnote, but will be marked by special indentation in conformity with the opening sentence here cited.

8. Franz Kafka, "Investigations of a Dog," in *The Complete Stories*, pp. 300–301. This is why the configuration animal-among-humans is not a stable one within Kafka's image repertoire and is constantly undergoing transmutations: *animal-among-humans* ("The Metamorphosis," "A Report to the Academy"), *human-among-animals* ("Jackals and Arabs"), *animal-among-animals* ("Investigations of a Dog," "Josephine the Singer"), *human-among-humans* (almost everything else, but most notably "Couriers," "A Common Confusion").

9. Both the Old and the New Testament are instructive about the foot as organ of dominion. To place one's foot on a field is to take possession of it; but usually the foot is shod, and it seems that the appropriative power passes on to the shoe, so that one can claim dominion over a land by throwing one's sandal over it (Ps 60:8; 108:9), or transfer one's title by taking off the sandal and handing it over (Rt 4:7–8), or have one's title disputed or denigrated by the sandal being snatched away, as by one's brother's widow if one refuses to perpetuate the brother's name through her, in which case one must continue to hold the inheritance under the contemptuous epithet "House-of-the-Unshod" (Dt 25:9–10). The shoe seems to mediate a certain tension between foot and ground. One must take off one's sandals at a holy ground that cannot be possessed (Ex 3:5; Jos 5:15), and the apostles, wearing sandals, were to shake the dust from under their feet where they were not well received, as a sign that only where the word had been favorably heard could the ground be suitable for a common standing and facing (Mk 6:11; Mt 10:14). This is a far cry from the triumphalism of crusader and conquistador, both perhaps reverting to Ps 60:8 and 108:9: "I throw my sandal over Edom and shout: Victory! over Philistia." In more recent times, and in accordance with a newer triumphalism, when Neil A. Armstrong planted his booted left foot in lunar dust at 22:56:20 (EDT), on July 20, 1969, the imprint was recorded on film and circulated on television and postcard as the fetish of a giant leap for humanity. Now the word that opens up a territory has become nothing more than mathematical, physical law, giving mastery over things in a highly developed technology. Scientific knowledge, perhaps the sole accomplishment of the spirit really acknowledged among us, becomes both the source of power and the measure of right to possess and bring power herself underfoot. As knowledge, power justifies itself.

10. For different types of waiting see Martin Heidegger, "Conversation on a Country Path about Thinking," in *Discourse on Thinking*, trans. John M.

Anderson and E. Hans Freund (New York: Harper Colophon Books, 1969), especially pp. 62, 68, 72–74.

11. Cf. "In the Penal Colony," where the inscribing machine that was to write the sentence deep into the flesh, and through pain bring about illumination of guilt for the convict, turns into a mad mouth and tears him apart. The whole connection between writing and devouring, as well as the all-pervasive importance of the mouth and its connection with the word, food, the belly, the hand, the eye, and the foot in Kafka's writings have remained unexplored here.

*Deborah Esch*

# "Think of a kitchen table": Hume, Woolf, and the Translation of Example

> No criticism can be instructive which . . . is not full of examples
> and illustrations.
>
> —Hume, *Essays and Treatises on Several Subjects* (1752)

To BEGIN with the question of the example is in effect to cite Aristotle as precedent, as an example of such a beginning. In book 2, chapter 20 of the *Rhetoric*, where he outlines the two kinds of proof common to all branches of that art—the example and the enthymeme—the philosopher writes: "Let us then first speak of the example (παράδειγμα); for the example resembles induction, and induction [as a starting-point and first principle of knowledge] is a beginning (ἀρχή)."[1] The citation from Hume that serves as epigraph articulates a double point of departure: it first of all raises the question of the place and function of the example in a critical argument, and secondly, quite apart from the claim it makes for and about examples, it is itself an example, an illustrative quotation in the treatment of "example" in the Oxford English Dictionary. Hume is cited in support of the first of the word's significations, that of "a typical instance; a fact, incident, quotation, etc., that illustrates, or forms a particular case of, a general principle, rule, state of things, etc.; a person or thing that may be taken as an illustration of a certain quality."[2] What complicates the matter further, and departs from the double beginning in the direction of a potential double bind, is that "example" appears to be an exception to the rule that governs the lexicon's ordering of a given word's range of significations:

> The order in which these senses were developed is one of the most important facts in the history of the word; to discover and exhibit it are among the most difficult duties of a dictionary which aims at giving this history. If the historical record were complete, that is, if we possessed written examples of all the uses of each word from the beginning, the simple exhibition of these would display a rational or logical development. The historical record is not complete enough to do thus. . . . In exhibiting this in the Dictionary that sense is placed first which was actually the earliest in the language; the others follow in the order in which they appear to have arisen. (xi)

In the instance of the word "example," the enumeration of definitions, beginning with the sense just indicated of a typical instance or illustration of a general principle, is uncharacteristically ranged according to what a note in the entry terms "the presumed logical order," which (despite the incompleteness of the historical record because of a shortage of written examples) the editors substitute for the standard chronological order of recorded usage. But according to the second definition of "example" cited in the dictionary—"the species of argument in which the major premise . . . is assumed from a particular instance"—one might expect to arrive at the general rule ("that sense is placed first which was actually earliest in the language") on the basis of the particular case. The fact that Aristotle, who is cited as an illustration for the second signification, defines "example" in the first book of the *Rhetoric* (1.2.9) as "the proof from a number of particular cases that such is the rule," would tend to support this assumption. In this case, however, the example of "example" proves counterexemplary.[3]

As it turns out, the counterinstance of "example" does not so much refute the rule as displace it, in a way that the editors of the *OED* attempt to take into account. Their explanation and justification for the dictionary's procedures make provision for the special case of "adopted or adapted words which had already acquired various significations in the language (e.g. Latin) from which they were taken" (xi).[4] The order in which the senses of these words appeared in English does not correspond to the so-called "natural order" in which they developed in the original language, and is in the editor's view "accidental":

> For it was not in the primary sense that the word was first taken into English, but in a figurative, transferred or specialized use. . . . In such a case it is not possible to make the historical order of the sense in English agree with the logical order in which they arose in Latin or other previous languages; and every such word must be treated in the way which seems best suited to exhibit the facts of its own history and use. (xi)

The disjunction between logical and chronological takes place as an effect of the translation of the word from another language ("e.g. Latin"), in which the senses are yet presumed to have arisen in a logical order, into English. Something is lost in this translation, due specifically to its substitution of a "figurative, transferred or specialized use" for the "primary sense" that is available only in the original (indeed, the designated primary sense of "example" as "something taken out"—from the Latin *eximo, eximere*, "to take out"—is, appropriately enough, taken out, removed from the catalogue of significations). This structure of substitution is similarly marked in another translation of the Greek "original," Aristotle's *paradeigma*, which has been "taken into" English to designate, for example, a particular set of relations among linguistic elements, the function of which is to "determine the possibility of substitution": "Linguistics teaches that two items can be taken as members of a paradigm class only when they can replace one another in a given context. . . . The meaning of an item depends on the differences between it and other items which might have filled the same slot in a given sequence."[5] But as Jacques Derrida's reading of Aristotle's example of the sun in the *Poetics* ($1457^b25-30$) argues, this structure of substitution is built into the "original" before any act of (interlinguistic) translation takes place.[6] Already in the text of Aristotle, the moment of exemplification upon which argument apparently depends is to be read as one of substitution or supplementarity, and not simply of augmentation.

The displacement of the dictionary's rule in the case of "example" is thus associated with an act of translation that entails the replacing by a "figurative, transferred or specialized" sense of a prior usage that is assumed to be free of these attributes. What follows is an attempt to analyze an analogous translation of one example in particular—not from Latin (or Greek) into English, but within the latter, from the language of the philosophical text into that of the literary. At issue is the question, posed at the outset, of the function of examples for a critical argument, and the extent to which a reading of a "literary" text, of a narrative that takes into account its own "figurative, transferred or specialized" translation of the terms of properly philosophical inquiry or proof, can make explicit the potentially destabilizing effect of the example upon the thesis it is supposed to illustrate.

FOR HUME, the need for a categorical distinction between philosophy and literature on the basis of their respective modes of "proof," of argumentation and narration, simply did not arise. His "ruling Passion," as he wrote in his autobiographical essay "My Own Life," was literature; he confessed that "almost all my life has been spent in literary Pursuits and Occupations," and that he "regard[ed] every object as contemptible, except the Improvement of my Talents in Literature." His expectation was clearly that the *Treatise* and the *Enquiries* would establish his "literary Reputation" among his contemporaries (a hope that was sorely disappointed in the case of the earlier work).[7] As his most notable modern biographer maintains, Hume from the beginning "regarded philosophy as part and parcel of literature. To be a philosopher is to be a man of letters: the proposition was received by Hume and the eighteenth century as axiomatic."[8] But for the most part Hume's readers, in this century in particular, have departed from this conventional wisdom. In a reading that is in this respect counter-exemplary, Raymond Williams reflects on this development in the interpretation of Hume:

> In the republic of letters a man can live as himself, but in the bureaucracy of letters he must continually declare his style and department, and submit to an examination of his purpose and credentials at the frontier of every field. The influence of bureaucracy even extends to his readers, nervous under the stare of critics who are conducting what looks like a census of occupations. Is David Hume moralist, logician, historian, es-

sayist? Under which of these categories are you proposing to read him? Remember, before answering, the serious penalties involved, if you get on the wrong side of any of these lines.[9]

The question of the bureaucracy of letters—a bureaucracy that thrives on the failure of translation—is a pressing one, for it is in the institutions of education that these lines are drawn, and the effort is successfully made to establish and reinforce a separation between ways of reading and teaching discursive "as opposed to" fictive texts. A Humean appeal to experience affords countless examples of this practice.

To side with Williams on this issue is to align oneself at the same time with Hume, and to argue that such a separation, at the textual as well as the institutional level, is to a great extent unwarranted. More specifically, one immediate effect of such a division of textual labor is to confine to the field of literary criticism a number of fundamental interpretive techniques, both hermeneutic (or semantic) and poetic (or formal), that are equally indispensable to critical readers of philosophical texts. This enforced separation results as well in curricular practices whereby writers whose oeuvre does not fit neatly into one bureaucratic niche or another are either dissected in such a way that their so-called "fictive" works are appropriated by literature courses, while philosophy departments lay claim to the discursive texts (and here Rousseau is an exemplary instance), or such writers are simply not taught at all (as has frequently been the case with writers like Godwin or de Quincey, whose work, while preserved for scholarship, is often lost for pedagogy). When the techniques of "literary" analysis are brought to bear on philosophical texts, the reader discovers that "philosophy"—even when it makes claims to the contrary—depends upon specific rhetorical operations (both tropological and persuasive) that are necessarily "part and parcel" of the language of its formulations. In these terms, the fact that works like the *Treatise of Human Nature* and the *Enquiry Concerning Human Understanding* narrate what they call a "method" or a "chain of reasoning" (156), rather than a characterization or a story, is of secondary importance. It is here that a reading of the narrative generally designated "literary" can perhaps yield insight into the nature and function of the rhetorical structures and strategies it has in common with philosophical texts.

If such a general claim is to be persuasive, of course, it must be shown to be the case in an exemplary instance.[10] The present focus, then, is Hume's repeated staging of the scene of sense perception, which takes place first (chronologically speaking) in part 4 of book 1 of the *Treatise*, in the section entitled "Of skepticism with regard to the senses." This chapter is in part a rigorous rehearsal of Hume's system as elaborated to this point, in which he attempts to clarify the conditions of perception by narrating increasingly complex versions of ordinary experience. He begins this phase of his inquiry with a question: what causes induce us to believe in the existence of body (188)—a query that divides itself, more precisely, to ask why we attribute a *continued* existence to objects, even when they are not present to the senses, and why we suppose them to have an existence *distinct* from the mind and perception. "These are the only questions," the text asserts, "that are intelligible on the present subject" (188). To pose them, as the reader soon discovers, involves Hume in the staging of an exemplary scene of sense perception: that of the philosopher at work, of Hume himself engaged in writing the *Treatise*. The scene, which effectively cites Descartes's *Meditations* as well as Locke's *Essay*, is narrated in Hume's experimental present-tense:

> To begin with the question concerning the external existence of our perceptions . . . it may be perhaps said, that . . . as several impressions appear exterior to the body, we suppose them also exterior to ourselves. The paper, on which I write at present, is beyond my hand. The table is beyond the paper. The walls of the chamber beyond the table. And in casting my eye towards the window, I perceive a great extent of fields and buildings beyond my chamber. From all this it may be infer'd, that no other faculty is requir'd, besides the senses, to convince us of the external existence of body. (190–91)

The inference proves mistaken, however, and Hume goes on to argue that the senses alone cannot produce the notion of a continued and distinct existence. After correcting several "vulgar" assumptions about perception, he pursues the question of what it is about sensory impressions that encourages us to attribute to them such an existence:

> After a little examination, we shall find, that all those objects, to which we attribute a continu'd existence, have a peculiar constancy, which dis-

tinguishes them from the impressions, whose existence depends upon our perception. . . . My bed and table, my books and papers, present themselves in the same uniform manner, and change not upon account of any interruption in my seeing or perceiving them. This is the case with all the impressions, whose objects are suppos'd to have an external existence; and is the case with no other impressions, whether gentle or violent, voluntary or involuntary. (194–95)

In both instances in the *Treatise*, separated by only a few paragraphs, specific examples are provisionally substituted for the general explanation, as part of the text's attempt to stabilize a shifting set of questions, to make the steps in an abstract argument concrete and intelligible—and indeed these passages come as a relief to the reader struggling to follow the twists and turns of a complex analysis.[11] It was in further deference to this perplexed reader that Hume recast his system in the later *Enquiries Concerning Human Understanding and Concerning the Principles of Morals*, which he describes as an abridgement, a "shortening and simplifying of the questions."[12] In the first of the *Enquiries* he presents an almost purely essayistic version of the abstract argument advanced in the *Treatise*—as one critic judges, Hume "here subordinates philosophy as a project for finding the truth to philosophy as a persuasive manner of talking about the issue of truth."[13] Perhaps as a result, the reliance on analogy and example, on concrete instances (often of the domestic sort), is even more pronounced in the later work. In section 12 of the *Enquiry*, "Of the academical or skeptical philosophy," which sketches in abbreviated form the parallel section in the *Treatise*, Hume carries over the example he employed in the earlier text:

This very table, which we see white, and which we feel hard, is believed to exist, independent of our perception, and to be something external to our mind, which perceives it. Our presence bestows not being on it: our absence does not annihilate it. It preserves its existence uniform and entire, independent of the situation of intelligent beings, who perceive or contemplate it. (151–52)

Yet this "universal and primary opinion of all men," Hume goes on to claim, "is soon destroyed by the slightest philosophy," which instructs us that no object can ever be immediately present to the mind, but only an image or perception conveyed by way of the senses. Again, he has recourse to the particular: "The table, which we see, seems to diminish, as we remove farther from it: but the real table, which exists independent of us, suffers no alteration: it was therefore nothing but its image, which was present to the mind" (152). In other words, according to what Hume terms the obvious dictates of reason, the existence we consider when we say "this table" is only a perception in the mind, a fleeting copy or representation of another existence, another table, which remains uniform and independent. But this argument, in order to convince, has apparently to proceed by way of "experimental observation," of a detailed account of the immediate—that is, this very table. The object common to the three scenes thus begins, naturally enough, as the writing table of the philosopher and becomes, as the example on which he repeatedly relies, the material support for his argument, his attempt to persuade the reader who might be skeptical or simply slow. For the scene of sense perception is, in Hume's text, a scene of persuasion, an effort to render the thesis convincing through exemplification. The example thus occupies a liminal position in the context of a narrative that is at once "a project for finding the truth," as well as "a persuasive manner of talking about the issue of truth."

The function of examples for such a dual project is thematized in *To the Lighthouse*, where Hume's table is translated over a greater distance, this time into a later, literary text that narrates not a chain of reasoning but the history of a number of characters: among them, a philosopher and his reader. At several junctures the reader encounters Ramsay, whom some maintain to be "the greatest metaphysician of his time,"[14] as he reflects on Hume's life and work: first, on the lectures he will give on "Locke, Hume, Berkeley, and the causes of the French Revolution" to the young men at Cardiff,[15] and then on the notorious anecdote about Hume's misadventure in the bog, with his only possibility of rescue contingent upon saying the Lord's Prayer in response to the demand of a pious old woman (a narrative Ramsay finds particularly amusing). Lily Briscoe, who figures the artist as well as the reader, finds herself at intervals thinking about Ramsay's own work and trying to understand it by way of an example:

Whenever she "thought of his work" she always saw clearly before her a large kitchen table. It was Andrew's doing. She asked him what his father's books were about. "Subject and object and the nature of reality," Andrew had said. And when she said Heavens, she had no notion what that meant, "Think of a kitchen table then," he told her, "when you're not there." So now she always saw, when she thought of Mr. Ramsay's work, a scrubbed kitchen table. It lodged now in the fork of a pear tree, for they had reached the orchard. And with a painful effort of concentration, she focused her mind, not upon the silver-bossed bark of the tree, or upon its fish-shaped leaves, but upon a phantom kitchen table, one of those scrubbed board tables, grained and knotted, whose virtue seems to have been laid bare by years of muscular integrity, which stuck there, its four legs in air. Naturally, if one's days were passed in this seeing of angular essences, this reducing of lovely evenings, with all their flamingo clouds and blue and silver to a white deal four-legged table (and it was the mark of the finest minds to do so), naturally one could not be judged like an ordinary person. (38)

By virtue of its concrete particularity, the table suggested by Andrew Ramsay affords Lily Briscoe what it afforded Hume and his reader—a point of stability in a scene of flux, a struggle for comprehension. In the words of the novel, Lily relies upon it, as upon the branches of the tree, "to help her stabilize her position" (169). Yet the deployment of the example in the literary context is marked by a difference: its status as a substitution, a tropological structure, is made apparent. In Woolf's narrative, the table is twice designated by a specifiably rhetorical term: "All of this . . . danced up and down in Lily's mind, in and about the branches of the pear tree, where still hung in effigy the scrubbed kitchen table, symbol of her profound respect for Ramsay's mind" (41). And again, much later in the novel:

> But what a face, she thought, immediately finding the sympathy she had not been asked to give troubling her for expression. What had made it like that? Thinking, night after night, she supposed—about the reality of kitchen tables, she added, remembering the symbol which in her vagueness as to what Mr. Ramsay did think about Andrew had given her. (232)

The literary text, then, calls the example by another name, one that designates it unmistakably as a structure of substitution, and it speculates as well on how such a figure acquires its sense: "Suddenly . . . the meaning which, for no reason at all, descends . . . making them symbolical, making them representative, came upon them, and made them . . . the symbols. Then, after an instant, the symbolical outline which transcended the real figures sank down again . . ." (110). And indeed it is "for no reason at all" that this effigy, the "phantom table" that allows Lily to grasp, albeit figuratively, Ramsay's analytic, loses its symbolical outline to become, in Mrs. Ramsay's mind, simply a piece of the shabby furniture in the summer house, one among the "crazy ghosts of chairs and tables whose London life of service was done" (43). Or again, it turns up as a fixture in another scene, a reverie in which Mrs. Ramsay becomes the phantom who "glides like a ghost among the chairs and tables of that drawing room on the banks of the Thames" (132). The reader of *To the Lighthouse*, inundated with these literal and figurative tables, thus begins to have difficulty keeping them straight, particularly given the phantasmal aspect of the literal table on the one hand, and on the other the attributes of Lily's figure: it is characterized as "something bare, hard, not ornamental," and as "uncompromisingly plain." The desire on the reader's part to control the staging of the example, to fix the scene, is thematized in yet another passage: "One must keep on looking, without for a second relaxing," Lily reflects. "One must hold the scene—so—in a vise and let nothing come and spoil it. One wanted, she thought, . . . to be on a level with ordinary experience, to feel simply that's a chair, that's a table . . ." (299–300).

Woolf's "that" returns the reader to Hume's "this," to his example drawn from the ordinary experience of the philosopher. For Hume, as has been noted, the example is designed to stabilize the "unruly perceptual relationships" he attempts to analyze. Woolf's text, however, makes explicit the status of the example as a rhetorical figure—as Hume's trope, in the *Treatise* and the *Enquiry*, for continuity and distinctness. *To the Lighthouse* narrates the fictive character of that stability and continuity where the figure is concerned, and marks the example as a "necessary fiction" of the kind for which Hume, in the *Treatise*, questions the ability of philosophy itself to account.[16] In these terms, the unreliability of the senses in Hume's scheme becomes a figure for the unreliability of his example. Hume's text freely acknowledges the readiness of the mind to prefer its own fictions of unity and continuity to the isolated data it perceives (*Treatise*, 254); it does so expressly in the crucial section on "personal identity," where Hume links such a propensity with a "literary" impulse.

But Woolf's "fictive" work raises a further question—one that is arguably more properly "philosophical"—that Hume's text fails to address. Put most schematically, it is the question of whether an example can, in the final analysis, be said to support the general proposition it provisionally replaces. Lily Briscoe's meditation on the table in *To the Lighthouse* suggests that the particularity on which the example depends for its apparent intelligibility is a function of a structure of substitution that does not, despite appearances, provide a stable, secure foundation on which an argument can come to rest, but that may on the contrary undermine the general truth it is supposed to endorse. The fate of Hume's example as translated in Woolf's text suggests that the concrete illustration in an abstract argument such as Hume's—commonly regarded as the moment in the text that affords a handle by which to grasp the general problem—may in fact confound the reader, unless account is taken of the rhetorical status of the structure of exemplification. If the text of philosophy forgets that a substitution has taken place, literature can perhaps serve as a reminder. *To the Lighthouse*, understood as a reading of Hume, cautions against such a forgetting in exemplary fashion.

The novel may thus be said to narrate the possible discrepancy between an example and the proposition it is supposed to fit, to recount it as an allegory in which the effigial table becomes, to borrow a phrase from Coleridge's reflection on that rhetorical structure, a "phantom proxy." This allegory, which narrates the questionable epistemological status of narrative itself, whether literary or philosophical, inscribes as well a moment of doubt about the example:

> But Mr. Ramsay kept always his eyes fixed upon [the table], never allowed himself to be distracted or deluded, until his face became worn too and ascetic and partook of this unornamented beauty which so deeply impressed her. . . . He must have had his doubts about that table, she supposed; whether the table was a real table; whether it was worth the time he gave to it; whether he was able after all to find it. He had had his doubts, she felt, or he would have asked less of people. (232)

Hume, like Ramsay, has his doubts about that table as an instance of the "experimental method" by which he attempts to transform cognitive inquiry. In the well-known conclusion to book 1 of the *Treatise*, he formulates those reservations in a voice that is difficult to distinguish from Ramsay's:

> But before I launch out into those immense depths of philosophy, which lie before me, I find myself inclin'd to stop a moment in my present station, and to ponder that voyage, which I have undertaken, and which undoubtedly requires the utmost art and industry to be brought to a happy conclusion. Methinks I am like a man, who having struck on many shoals, and having narrowly escap'd a ship-wreck . . . has yet the temerity to put out to sea in the same leaky weather-beaten vessel. . . . The wretched conditions, weakness, and disorder of the faculties, I must employ in my enquiries . . . reduces me almost to despair, and makes me resolve to perish on the barren rock, rather than venture myself upon that boundless ocean, which runs out into immensity. (263–64)

Ramsay's voyage out to his barren rock, accompanied by tales of storm-tossed vessels and shipwrecks and punctuated by his incantatory "we perish, each alone," in a sense literalizes Hume's allegory of the trials of the philosopher. But while Hume's voyage is a solitary one—"everyone keeps at a distance," he writes, "and dreads that storm, which beats upon me from every side"—Ramsay is accompanied on his excursion to the lighthouse by his daughter and son, whose Oedipal resentment and resistance to his tyranny the father tries to overcome. His strategy is to begin by saying "some simple, easy things. . . . But what? For, wrapped up in his work as he was, he forgot the sort of thing one said" (250). Then he hits upon an example of the sort of thing one said: "There was a puppy. Who was looking after the puppy today? . . . And what was she going to call him?" (250–51).

A translation of Ramsay's example is readable in another narrative of the philosopher-father and his offspring, one that resists the categories of the bureaucracy of letters and is to that extent exemplary. In one of his *cartes postales*, Derrida alludes, in the context of a reflection on and profession of fidelity, to Ryle's example, in *The Theory of Meaning*, of the dog named Fido. Derrida speculates about why Ryle might have chosen this name for his dog: "because one says of a dog that it responds to its name, to the name 'Fido,' for example—because a dog is the figure of fidelity, and that it better than anything responds to its name, above all if it is Fido?" The philosopher asks his son why he thinks Ryle decided on the name of a dog, Fido, and Pierre Derrida responds, "so that the example will behave" (*pour que l'exemple soit docile*).[17]

The attempt to domesticate the example (in the words of Woolf's text, to "tame" it, to "rest in contemplation of it") may be understood as a gesture performed by the text of philosophy, a gesture that the text we call "literary" enables us to reach as such. Perhaps this accounts for the fact that, as far as the philosopher as well as the reader is concerned, the exemplary dog in *To the Lighthouse* remains nameless, and thus cannot respond, and cannot be made to behave.[18]

## NOTES

1. Aristotle, *'Art' of Rhetoric*, trans. J. H. Freese (Cambridge, Mass.: Harvard University Press, 1975), p. 273 and note b.

2. *Oxford English Dictionary* (Oxford: Oxford University Press, 1933), vol. 3, p. 914.

3. When faced in *A Treatise of Human Nature* with the conversion of an example for his argument into a counterexample, Hume dismisses the problem summarily: ". . . the instance is so particular and singular, that 'tis scarce worth our observing, and does not merit that for it alone we should alter our general maxim" (*A Treatise of Human Nature*, ed. L. A. Selby-Bigge [Oxford: Oxford University Press, 1978], p. 6. All subsequent references to the *Treatise*, indicated parenthetically by page number in the text, are to this edition).

4. In their note on the use of illustrative quotations, the editors remind the reader that "it is to be distinctly borne in mind that the quotations are not merely examples of the fully developed use of the word or special sense under which they are cited: they have also to illustrate its origin, its gradual separation from allied words or senses, or even, by negative evidence, its non-existence at the given date. It would have been desirable to annotate the quotations, explaining the purpose for which they are adduced; but the exigencies of space render this impossible, and they are therefore left to speak for themselves" (xi).

5. Jonathan Culler, *Structuralist Poetics: Structuralism, Linguistics and the Study of Literature* (Ithaca: Cornell University Press, 1975), pp. 13, 45. See also

the use made of the category by Hans Blumenberg in "Paradigma, grammat-sich," in *Wirklichkeiten in denen wir leben* (Stuttgart: Reclam, 1981), pp. 157–61.

6. Jacques Derrida, "La mythologie blanche: La métaphore dans le texte de philosophie," in *Marges de la philosophie* (Paris: Éditions de Minuit, 1972), pp. 247–324; trans. Alan Bass, in *Margins of Philosophy* (Chicago: University of Chicago Press, 1982). On Hegel's reading and rewriting of Aristotle's ex-amples in *De anima*, see Andrzej Warminski, "Pre-positional By-play," *Glyph* 3 (1978): 98–117.

7. David Hume, "My Own Life," Appendix A in Ernest Campbell Mossner, *The Life of David Hume* (Oxford: Oxford University Press, 1980), p. 611.

8. Mossner, *Life of David Hume*, p. 63.

9. Raymond Williams, *Writing in Society* (London: Verso, 1984), p. 121.

10. In paragraph 31 of the first *Enquiry*, Hume asserts unequivocally that one example is as good, philosophically speaking, as a hundred (*Enquiries Concerning Human Understanding and Concerning the Principles of Morals,* ed. L. A. Selby-Bigge [Oxford: Oxford University Press, 1975], p. 36). Aristotle is more exacting in this regard; he counsels in the *Rhetoric*, "If the examples stand before the general principle, they resemble induction, which is suitable to rhetorical speeches only in a very few cases; if they stand last they resemble evidence . . . wherefore also it is necessary to quote a number of examples if they are put first, but one alone is sufficient if they are put last; for even a single trustworthy witness is of use" (279).

11. Paul de Man attributes this function to the example in his reading of "Über das Marrionettentheater," in *The Rhetoric of Romanticism* (New York: Co-lumbia University Press, 1984), p. 276.

12. David Hume, in a letter to Gilbert Eliot, March or April 1751, quoted in John Richetti, *Philosophical Writing: Locke, Berkeley, Hume* (Cambridge, Mass.: Harvard University Press, 1983), p. 254.

13. Richetti, *Philosophical Writing*, p. 255.

14. Gillian Beer characterizes Ramsay as "a possibly major, though self-debilitated philosopher" in an essay on the anxiety of influence vis-à-vis the philosopher-father articulated in Woolf's narrative ("Hume, Stephen and Elegy in *To the Lighthouse*," *Essays in Criticism* 34 [January 1984]: 39). For S. P. Rosenbaum, it is not Leslie Stephen but rather G. E. Moore whose influence in this regard is most notable ("The Philosophical Realism of Virginia Woolf," *Philosophy and Literature* 6 [1982]: 33–44, and "Railing against Realism: Philos-ophy and *To the Lighthouse*," *Philosophy and Literature* 7 [1983]: 89–91).

15. Virginia Woolf, *To the Lighthouse* (New York: Harcourt, Brace, 1927), p. 70. All subsequent references to the novel, indicated by page number in the text, are to this edition. The biographical connection between Ramsay (read

as a figure for Woolf's father, Leslie Stephen, who wrote extensively on eighteenth-century philosophy) and Hume has resonances as well on the side of the latter: Hume's most intimate friend during his student days at Edinburgh was Michael Ramsay of Mungale; Allan Ramsay (the Younger) was a close associate who painted the best-known portraits of the philosopher in 1754 and 1766; the Chevalier Andrew Michael Ramsay, a disciple of Fenelon, was an acquaintance and philosophical antagonist of Hume: the author of the *Philosophical Principles of Natural and Revealed Religion Unfolded in a Geometrical Order* (published in 1748–49) called Hume's *Treatise* (before having read it) "an obscure, dark, intricate performance" (quoted in Mossner, *Life of David Hume*, p. 95).

16. Richetti, *Philosophical Writing*, p. 205.

17. Jacques Derrida, *La carte postale: De Socrate à Freud et au-delà* (Paris: Flammarion, 1980), pp. 260–61.

18. Cf. Woolf's biography of Eliza Barrett's dog Flush, particularly the transformations of the "ordinary drawing room table" in the final chapter (*Flush: A Biography* [New York: Harcourt, Brace, 1933], pp. 98–108).

*Alphonso Lingis*

# Seppuku

Yukio mishima found himself in words. Consumed by words.
"Any art that relies on words makes use of their ability to eat away—of their corrosive function—just as etching depends on the corrosive power of nitric acid. . . . It might be more appropriate, in fact, to liken their action to that of excess stomach fluids that digest and gradually eat away the stomach itself" (*Sun and Steel*, trans. John Bester [Tokyo: Kodansha International, 1970], pp. 8–9).

If words can be the medium of artistry—and Mishima was a master of words at a prodigiously early age, publishing his first novel at the age of thirteen—it is because words are a medium that reduces reality to abstraction. In psychoanalytic terms, a medium that displaces the libido from pleasure-surfaces to phallic objects, idealities or absences. Words fix objects, objectives, termini. They themselves die away at these termini.

In doing so they have the ability to eat away at, disintegrate, time. Prisoners under death sentence, we have to wait for the end, for the moment when the gates will be opened and we will step forth to do what we have to do, each of us: go face our death, ourselves, with all our own strength and weakness. But meantime we have to wait, twenty-four more hours, twenty-four more days, twenty-four more years.

It is this void of the present progressive tense with which [words] deal. . . . [I]n marking the void, [they] dye it as irrevocably as the gay colors and designs of Yuzen fabrics are fixed once they are rinsed in the clear waters of Kyoto's river, and in doing so consume the void completely moment by moment, becoming fixed in each instant, where they

277

remain. Words are over as soon as they are spoken, as soon as they are written. Through the accumulation of these "endings," through the moment-to-moment rupture of life's sense of continuity, words acquire a certain power. At the very least, they diminish to some degree the overwhelming terror of the vast white walls in the waiting room where we await the arrival of the physician, the absolute. And in exchange for the way in which, by marking off each moment, they ceaselessly chop up life's sense of continuity, they act in a way that seems at least to translate the void into a substance of a kind. (68–69)

This verbal existence, this corroded, castrated, decomposing verbal existence, comes to long for the flesh; this word longs for incarnation.

The body-mind split is not simply a categorical distinction made within discourse, in particular within Platonic, metaphysical discourse. Discourse posits the body as its ideal opposite. But first, what is meant—what is first meant—by body? The body that arises as the ideal of discursive existence, the body that the one who finds himself in words longs for, can be summed up, Mishima says, in taciturnity and beauty of form. This body-fetish or body-ideal is counterposited to the negativity of words as "existence."

Mishima found that the more one finds oneself in words the more one idealizes the body, the more one seeks the body with the words. The sensations die away, the words fade out as soon as they are proffered or imagined, leaving the mind in the presence of the signified, the ideal. The nitric acid, after having eaten away the copper plate, corrodes itself. With words one constitutes ideal objects, in Husserl's terminology; one constructs fictions, in Mishima's. Husserl, however, identified these ideal identities with the reality of the phenomena. Husserl did not really bracket metaphysics but, Derrida says, formulated its structure most rigorously; Mishima became not a metaphysician but a man of letters—but the difference is perhaps only a *distinctio formalis a parte mentis.*

My composition teacher would often show his displeasure with my work, which was innocent of any words that might be taken as corresponding to reality. It seems that I had an unconscious presentiment of the subtle, fastidious laws of words, and was aware of the necessity of avoiding as far as possible coming into contact with reality via words if one were to profit from their positive corrosive function and escape their negative aspect—if, to put it more simply, one was to maintain the purity of words. I knew instinctively that the only possibility was to maintain a constant watch on the corrosive action lest it suddenly come up against some object that it might corrode." (9–10)

Constantly aware of the corrosive effect of the words, Mishima used words positively only to construct fictions, vigilant always to avoid touching reality with words. This practice maintained reality, and the body, as an ideal region at an absolute distance from words. And this ideal in turn gave its telos to the only possible positive usage of words; the ideal in the verbal arts must lie solely in the imitation of the formal beauty of the taciturn and statuesque body. It is what made Mishima a classicist in literature.

BUT WHAT WAS IT that drove Mishima to words? What was it that drove him to find himself, in the corrosion, the castration, the disintegration of words? The world, whose shrouds were lifted by the sun.

My first—unconscious—encounter [with the sun] was in the summer of the defeat, in the year 1945. A relentless sun blazed down on the lush grass of that summer that lay on the borderline between the war and the postwar period—a borderline, in fact, that was nothing more than a line of barbed wire entanglements, half broken down, half buried in the summer weeds, tilting in all directions. I walked in the sun's rays, but had no clear understanding of the meaning they held for me.

Finespun and impartial, the summer sunlight poured down prodigally on all creation alike. The war ended, yet the deep green weeds were lit exactly as before by the merciless light of noon, a clearly perceived hallucination stirring in a slight breeze; brushing the tips of the leaves with my fingers, I was astonished that they did not vanish at my touch.

That same sun, as the days turned to months and the months to years, had become associated with a pervasive corruption and destruction. In part, it was the way it gleamed so encouragingly on the wings of planes leaving on missions, on forests of bayonets, on the badges of military caps, on the embroidery of military banners; but still more, far more, it was the way it glistened on the blood flowing ceaselessly from the flesh, on the silver bodies of flies clustering in wounds. Holding sway over cor-

ruption, leading youth in droves to its death in tropical seas and coun-
trysides, the sun lorded it over that vast rusty-red ruin that stretched
away to the distant horizon." (19–20)

It was about the year that Mishima was writing those words that I,
one evening, went to a performance of Bach's St. Matthew Passion
with a friend. When it was over, we stood outside the hall, in the
night, with the epic depiction of the crucifixion of God still thunder-
ing about us, the powers of the orchestra writhing with the storm
clouds, volcanic eruptions, and earthquakes with which all nature
had, in Bach's conception, agonized over the death of its creator. And
then my friend, who is Dutch, said to me how alien all that had become to the Europe he had fled. He had been in primary school, in
second grade, when the Nazi blitzkrieg overran the Netherlands. During the first years, the Nazi authorities were irreproachably correct
with the Hollanders, whom they regarded not as a conquered people
but as Low Germans being reunited into Greater Germany; only the
Jews were in danger. In the small town where my friend lived, one
merchant's home was a station of the underground railway through
which Jewish children, hair bleached, were passed secretly out of the
Netherlands on the way to southern France. The merchant's son occasionally carried messages on his bicycle, the merchant and his accom-
plices thinking no one would think to suspect this third-grade child of
anything. One afternoon in early spring my friend was sitting in his
classroom when the school assembly bell rang. All the classes filed out
into the courtyard and lined up in rows with their teachers. When
everyone was assembled, the school principal appeared, accompanied
by two SS officers, and the merchant's son. It was the first really warm
day at the end of winter, and my friend remembered now the sunlight
flooding over the budding trees and the already yellow forsythia
bushes, in which glittered and chattered the birds that had returned.
Then the black boots of the officers flashed in the sun, again and
again, striking with muffled thuds the soft body of the boy long after
he was dead.

Mishima wrote twenty-five years after Hiroshima and Nagasaki, remembering the sun over the blood and flies. Our nation has now
stockpiled two and a half tons of nuclear explosives for every man,

woman, and child on the planet, and the current administration has budgeted three trillion dollars for a new nuclear buildup. Israel, South Africa, Pakistan, the most unscrupulous political regimes, now have nuclear arsenals; thirty nations are now working to create nuclear arsenals. We who read and write this know that it is improbable that there will be anyone to read what we write twenty-five years from now, to see the wings of the flies glittering over the blood of humankind.

THE SUN that in 1945 streamed over the defeat, the blood, and the flies illuminated the space of a meanwhile. General MacArthur had forced Emperor Hirohito to declare that he was not the divine pivot of all Japanese heroism but a man, and in fact quite a stupid man. Between Hiroshima, Nagasaki, and the final bomb, an interim. In which what was destined for Japanese was to screw in the little screws in transistor radios and computers and accumulate capital. Yet one day, in this interim, Mishima ran to his window to see young Japanese men, brawny and shouting, flooding down the street, eyes turned to the sun.

They were bearing an old and heavy shrine on their shoulders. Bodies gleaming with sweat, struggling under its weight, which seemed to compress power into them, they crashed through the gates of the Mishima home and trampled the courtyard to ruins.

They were intoxicated with their task, and their expressions were of an indescribable abandon, their faces averted; some of them even rested the backs of their necks against the shafts of the shrine they shouldered, so that their eyes gazed up at the heavens. And my mind was much troubled by the riddle of what it was those eyes reflected.

As to the nature of the intoxicating vision that I detected in all this violent physical stress, my imagination provided no clue. For many a month, therefore, the enigma continued to occupy my mind; it was only much later, after I had begun to learn the language of the flesh, that I undertook to help in shouldering a portable shrine, and was at last able to solve the puzzle that had plagued me since infancy. They were simply looking at the sky. In their eyes there was no vision: only the reflection of the blue and absolute skies of early autumn. Those blue skies, though, were unusual skies such as I might never again see in my life—like a fierce bird of prey with wings outstretched—one moment strung up

high aloft, the next plunged to the depths; constantly shifting, a strange
compound of lucidity and madness. (12–13, 14)

What spoke to Mishima so eloquently was the massed bodies of the
shrine bearers. It is an eloquence one believes—one does not believe
the intoxication of feeble or debauched bodies; what they say one con-
signs to pathology and compensations. One believes the eloquence of
health and power. The body insists on correspondence and fitting-
ness—strength in the body is this insistence. The shrine bearers
shared something. A communication not through words, signs ex-
changed, but in the burden and violent physical stress. As they bent
under the weight they sustained together, their eyes were open and
intoxicated—by what? Not by an idea, from the old religion, that
would have its own consistency, maintained through a verbal construction, and that would justify the world laid bare under the skies.
Is there any such idea that could redeem the ashes and the blood of
Hiroshima and Nagasaki? Not by a religious image or participationist
myth—Buddhism has never secreted such things. Mishima's mind,
his imagination, or his verbal speculations were not able to join the
ecstatic vision of the shrine bearers. When his body had become massive enough to shoulder the shrine with them, he discovered that
what they saw with such intoxication was the skies, the empty skies
that illuminate all that is real, illuminate *anicca*, the impermanence.
"Glory was surely a name given to just such a light—inorganic, super-
human, naked, full of perilous cosmic rays" (101).

THE POSSIBILITY, then, of existing in the sun, in the sun that poured its
perilous light over the impermanence, had spoken to Mishima in the
carnal eloquence of the shrine bearers. But to open one's eyes to the
skies it was necessary to find for oneself not the taciturn form of
the ideal body one seeks with words, but such an eloquent body.

This body Mishima went to find in the tempering of his organism
by steel—"heavy, forbidding, as though the essence of the night had
in [it] been still further condensed" (25). He fitted his arms, legs,
torso to the inertia, dense opacity, mineral death of the steel.

This is not gearing into the world of implements—the inhabiting of
one's body as an intentionally conducted functional system—which

existence philosophy declared to be the primary form of comprehension and the fundamental form of selfhood. The eloquent body Mishima sought was an excess beyond the intentionally structured organism Merleau-Ponty had isolated and distinguished from the body as an objective form and substance. Body-building, which was unknown in traditional Japan, is introduced now that massive musculature has become superfluous both for productive labor—where every body limit is relayed by machine power—and even for warfare, now mechanized. Mishima did not undertake building musculature in order to appropriate a world of instrumentalities but in order to exist in the tragic light of the sun.

How strange to seek in death and night the body that could open to the sun and the skies! If what one is seeking is the open skies and the universal light that illuminates all reality, all impermanence, is not this ascent to the universal necessarily through words, all generic, all universals? Is it not language that Being inhabits, that discloses earth and skies, mortals and immortals as such? Does not the body, as all Western classicism has understood, represent the particular, the here-and-now, that which is to be transcended in order to accede to the universal?

But Mishima had found that all the artistry of words, all the appropriation of words, all the appropriation of oneself in words, consisted in using words in singular, deviant ways. There once existed, to be sure, essentially impersonal and monumental words with which epic art was composed. But the conditions for their functioning are lost to us today, and Mishima will come gradually to divine the reasons for this.

> As the relentless pressure of the steel progressively stripped my muscles of their unusualness and individuality (which were a product of degeneration), and as they gradually developed, they should, I reasoned, begin to assume a universal aspect, until they finally reached a point where they conformed to a general pattern in which individual differences ceased to exist. The universality thus attained would suffer no private corrosion, no betrayal. That was its most desirable trait in my eyes. (30–31)

The night and death of the steel drove out the psychic penchants that had materialized in the body in the form of habitus—indolence incarnated in a slovenly posture, sensuality or impressionability materialized in dry, lusterless skin and flaccid abdomen—it brought out, empowered, affirmed, the generic, the racial type, the animal, in the individual body.

> Ideas are . . . essentially foreign to human existence; and the body-receptacle of the involuntary muscles, of the internal organs and circulatory system over which it has no control—is foreign to the spirit, so that it is even possible for people to use the body as a metaphor for ideas, both being something quite alien to human existence as such. And the way in which an idea can take possession of the mind unbidden, with the suddenness of a stroke of fate, reinforces still further the resemblance of ideas to the body with which each of us, willy-nilly, is endowed, giving even this automatic, uncontrollable function a striking resemblance to the flesh. It is this that forms the basis of the idea of the enfleshment of Christ and also the stigmata some people can produce on their palms and insteps. (16)

The flesh, divested of its individuality, its eccentricity, by the steel, the night and death of steel, the universalized body, is the locus of ingression of ideas, is ideal.

In the coupling of organism with steel, the vital substance with the extreme condensation of night and death, there was not intentional function being transmitted through the inertia of implements, but a transference of properties. The properties that come to compose the excess musculature came from the steel, and were its own properties; the flesh becomes ferric.

But once Mishima found himself within this ferric substance, this body was no longer the taciturn and resplendent ideality of form which discourse posits and opposes. "Muscles, I found, were strength as well as form, and each complex of muscles was subtly responsible for the direction in which its own strength was exerted, much as though they were rays of light given the form of flesh" (28–29). There was not a unitary intentional arc mobilizing and activating a postural or motor diagram, as in the body that operates equipment; there was distribution of multiple seats of power-vectors, each activating itself. "Nothing could have accorded better with the definition of a work of art . . . than this concept of form unfolding strength, coupled with the idea that a work should be organic, radiating rays of light in all directions" (29).

There arose then a new artwork ideal—an existent formed into splendor not by virtue of the proportions it fixed but by its distribution of rays of power. This carnal ideal was to counterpoise itself to the words, to replace Mishima's first classical writing with a muscular style. Whereas Mishima's first classicism was animated by a constant and vigilant sense of the corrosive effect of words, his art now is purged of the morbid and voluptuous imagination that dreams of an efficacy in fictive constructions. The juxtaposition of action and art in one life makes each dissipate the dreams of the other. ". . . I was conceited enough to believe that my technique in dealing with words was sufficiently practiced for me to choose impersonal words, thereby enhancing their function as a memorial and putting an end to life of my own free will. This—it would be no exaggeration to say—was the only revenge I could take on the spirit for stubbornly refusing to perceive 'the end'" (84–85).

The idea of art is justified not only because this mode of radiant and depersonalized power came to figure as an ideal for the artifice of words to imitate, but also because this body abstracted itself from mundane dependence—and one day from the steel itself—to figure as an absolute—"transparent, peerless power that required no object at all" (23).

> . . . [t]he sense of existence by which strength cannot be strength without some object represents the basic relationship between ourselves and the world, and on that I depended on steel. Just as muscles slowly increase their resemblance to steel, so we are gradually fashioned by the world; and although neither the steel nor the world can very well possess a sense of their own existence, idle analogy leads us unwittingly into the illusion that both do, in fact, possess such a sense. . . . Thus our sense of existence seeks after some object, and can only live in a false world of relativity. . . . Away from steel, however, my muscles [now] seemed to lapse into absolute isolation, their bulging shapes no more than cogs created to mesh with the steel. The cool breeze passed, the sweat evaporated—and with them the existence of the muscles vanished into thin air. And yet, it was then that the muscles played their most essential function, grinding up with their sturdy, invisible teeth that ambiguous,

relative sense of existence and substituting for it an unqualified sense of transparent, peerless power that required no object at all. Even the muscles themselves no longer existed. I was enveloped in a sense of power as transparent as light. (32–33)

The relationship with steel, to which the sun had driven Mishima, had resulted in a displacement of his sense of himself. One that had, the summer of the defeat, fled the sun in horror, Mishima had become an intellectual, had fled into the intellectual's cave, that dark, amorphous, warm, visceral inwardness. Now the steel had routed the self from this retreat, displaced its locus onto the surfaces. Onto the contours of the musculature, whose ridges and reliefs he does not feel from within, out of his visceral ego, but contemplates in the gleaming surfaces of mirrors and feels in the expanses of pain. The self had become a surface self, a self no longer in inwardness but in distension, exposure, and exhibition. Whose sense of the world exposed to the sun is a surface thought. For whom thought no longer means identifying the inwardness beneath the dispersion, the substrates beneath the phenomena, the principles behind the appearances.

> Yet why must it be that men always seek out the depths, the abyss, why must thought, like a plumb line, concern itself exclusively with vertical descent? Why was it not feasible for thought to change direction and climb vertically up, ever up, toward the surface? Why should the area of the skin, which guarantees a human being's existence in space, be most despised and left to the tender mercies of the senses? I could not understand the laws governing the motion of thought—the way it was liable to get stuck in unseen chasms whenever it set out to go deep; or whenever it aimed at the heights, to soar away into boundless and equally invisible heavens, leaving the corporeal form undeservedly neglected.
>
> If the law of thought is that it should search out profundity, whether it extends upwards or downwards, then it seemed excessively illogical to me that men should not discover depths of a kind in the "surface," that vital borderline that endorses our separateness and our form, dividing our exterior from our interior. Why should they not be attracted by the profundity of the surface itself?
>
> The sun was enticing, almost dragging my thoughts away from the night of visceral sensations, away to the swelling of muscles encased in sunlit skin. And it was commanding me to construct a new and sturdy

dwelling in which my mind, as it rose little by little to the surface, could live in security. That dwelling was a tanned, lustrous skin and powerful, sensitively rippling muscles. I came to feel that it was precisely because such an abode was required that the average intellectual failed to feel at home with thought that concerned itself with forms and surfaces. (22–23)

We have seen first the fission and polarization that posited the ideal taciturn and formal body in opposition to the discursive existence; now we have seen the self come to inhabit the eloquent and surface body which opposes itself to the verbal artistry. This body seeks words—impersonal and monumental words that depersonalize and conduct one to the fields of death illuminated by the perilous rays of the sun. The thought that now conducts this search does not seek an origin, principle, or cause prior to the split of words from flesh, the split of inwardness from exposedness, the splintering of the forms and surfaces under the absolute dispersion of the light; it is also not a dialectical thought that seeks at each moment to return the one back into the other. The surface thought rather pushes on to the outlying regions, the farthest edges of body and of spirit, seeking there the point of contact. The point of contact—and this was the ultimate principle of this Buddhist metaphysical thought—was not at the origin, the base, the summit nor even the end, the telos. It was at the outer limits. "Things that are farthest removed from each other, by increasing the distance between them, come closer together" (91). The great serpent coiled back upon itself at the outermost sphere of the cosmos.

THE GREAT SERPENT of Buddhist metaphysics Mishima saw not in participating in a traditional religious ritual, but on the day he flew the F104, the most advanced supersonic jet fighter of the Japanese air force.

Pushing on his mind, not back into his body, but toward his mind's own outer limits was to push it outward across the most remote surfaces of the universe; it was also, Mishima knew, to push it to its own death. "Motionless before his desk, [the thinker] edges his way closer, ever closer, to the borders of the spirit, in constant mortal danger of plunging into the void" (92). Death itself is not just a negative operator of the dialectical mind; the earth is physically surrounded by death, and Mishima resolved to take his body to this locus of death.

First he had to undergo physiological flight training. His body was immobilized, strapped to the apparatus of the pressure chamber. Even the movements of the lungs were pushed toward immobility. He felt the panicky brain crave desperately the air that was being sucked out of the chamber; death stuck fast to his lips.

Finally came the day of the first flight. "Erect-angled, the F104, a sharp silver phallus, pointed into the sky. Solitary, spermatozoon-like, I was installed within. Soon, I should know how the spermatozoon felt at the instant of ejaculation."

The plane was fired like a dagger into the stratospheres of death, ascended to thirty-five thousand feet, passed the speed of sound. "For a moment, my chest was empty, as though a cascade of water had descended with a great rush and left nothing behind it. . . . Everything was quiet, majestic, and the surface of the blue sky was flecked with the semen-white of clouds" (100).

At the summit: Mach 1.3, at forty-five thousand feet:

"Nothing happened.

"The silver fuselage floated in the naked light, the plane maintaining a splendid equilibrium. Once more it became a closed, motionless room. The plane was not moving at all. It had become, simply, an oddly-shaped metal cabin floating quite still in the upper atmosphere."

In the pressure chamber the body had been immobilized to the point that it pushed up against the limits of motionlessness of the mind, to the point where its lungs had to be forced by the mind. Now, encased in the fastest engine for motion the technological mind had invented, Mishima found the outer limits of supersonic speed rejoining the absolute rest of the pressure chamber.

There was even no suffocating sensation. My mind was at ease, my thought processes lively. Both the closed room and the open room—two interiors so diametrically opposed—could serve equally, I found, as dwellings for the spirit of one and the same human being. If this stillness was the ultimate end of action—of movement—then the sky about me, the clouds far below, the sea gleaming between the clouds, even the setting sun, might well be events, things, within myself. . . .

This silver tube floating in the sky was, as it were, my brain, and its immobility the mode of my spirit. The brain was no longer protected by unyielding bone, but had become permeable, like a sponge floating on water. . . . Anything that comes into our minds even for the briefest of moments, exists. Even though it may not exist at this actual moment, it has existed somewhere in the past, or will exist at some time in the future. This simple realm of cloud, sea, and setting sun was a majestic panorama, such as I had never seen before, of my own inner world. At the same time, every event that occurred within me had slipped the fetters of mind and emotion, becoming great letters freely inscribed across the heavens.

It was then that I saw the snake.

If the giant snake-ring that resolves all polarities came into my brain, then it is natural to suppose that it was already in existence. . . . It was a ring vaster than death, more fragrant than that faint scent of mortality that I had caught in the compression chamber; beyond doubt, it was the principle of oneness that gazed down at us from the shining heavens. (102–3)

The body—"transparent, peerless power that required no object at all"—was seeking what lay on its own farthest edges. It breaks through the taciturn splendor of the formal body imagined by the words—that dream of immortality. The eloquence of the surface body, the musculature, that is what feeds the imagination. The imagination of others does not feed on one's visceral inwardness or on one's functional body—or even on one's orgasmic carnality. But musculature had come to eat away at itself, leaving only the pure transparent complex of radiating vectors of power. "It was a special property of muscles that they fed the imagination of others while remaining totally devoid of imagination themselves. . . ." Mishima sought an existence, an exposedness that dissipated all imagination, whether of the self or of others. That situation was pure action—combat. Mishima trained in karate and kendo. "It was natural that my rephrasing of the pure sense of strength should turn in the direction of the flash of the fist and the stroke of the bamboo sword; for that which lay at the end of the flashing fist, and beyond the blow of the bamboo sword, was precisely what constituted the most certain proof of that invisible light given off by the muscles" (34).

The confrontation with the other occurs in the world of the seen, that of exposedness. Wherever one looks one is seen, and what one sees is the other's power galvanized into a look fixed on oneself.

We might think that the world, its trees, mountains, and clouds are

arrayed for our look without guile or clandestinity. But in fact the surface that we view in the world, and that does not return our scrutiny,
is the presumptive outcome of a series of profiles already passed by;
the tree or mountain we face is a fact, factum, trace of a passage.
There is no contemporaneousness between it and ourselves; there is a
distance of time, and the imagination that fills in that interim. There is
time for the word that names the object, about which the objectification settles, about which images accumulate like barnacles on the
rusting hulk of a wreckage. With people, too, there are always con-
tractual rules that govern every exchange of smiles, words, gestures,
goods, pleasures—rules, and the scum of the imagination that col-
lects on them. With time, even the morning face one confronts is
a mask.

> In most people, alas, the unsophisticated habit of exposing the face,
> quite unconsciously, to the dazzling light of the morning persists to the
> end. The habit remains, the face changes. Before one realizes it, the true
> face is ravaged by anxiety and emotion; one does not perceive that it
> drags last night's fatigue like a heavy chain, nor does one realize the
> boorishness of exposing such a face to the sun. It is thus that men lose
> their manliness.
>
> The reason is that once it has lost the natural brightness of youth, the
> manly face of the warrior must needs be a false face; it must be manufac-
> tured as a matter of policy. The army, I found, made this quite clear. The
> morning face presented by a commanding officer was a face for people to
> read things into, a face in which others might immediately find a crite-
> rion for the day's action. It was an optimistic face, designed to cover up
> the individual's private weariness and, no matter what despair he might
> be plunged into, to encourage others; it was thus a false face full of en-
> ergy, spurning and shaking off the bad dreams of the previous night.
> And it was the only face with which men who lived too long could make
> obeisance to the morning sun. (70–71)

In combat there is immediacy. One knows the bulk, position, momentum, rhythms, nerves, insight, foresight of the opponent with
one's own eloquent body. There is contemporaneousness, no interval
of time between oneself and the opponent, no time for the scum of
imagination to form.

Victory, of course, does not consist in assaulting the opponent to destroy him with the superior quantity of one's own force and momentum. One combats not with those weaker than oneself but with equals, and through combat one becomes the equal of ever more powerful opponents. One's own blow, then, is not a direct onslaught on the substance of the other; it is shot off as a provocation for a certain kind of blow on the part of the opponent. Victory proceeds out of perfect nonverbal knowledge—the knowledge one has, in the power of one's own body, of the power in the perfectly matched body of one's opponent. One's own blow creates a kind of hollow in space into which the fatal blow it provokes on the part of the opponent fits perfectly. Then one has absolutely mastered the power of the other.

The victory occurs in pure eloquence.

> At the height of the fray, I found the tardy process of creating muscles, whereby strength creates form and form creates strength, is repeated so swiftly that it becomes imperceptible to the eye. Strength, that like light emitted its own rays, was constantly renewed, destroying and creating form as it went. I saw for myself how the form that was beautiful and fitting overcame the form that was ugly and imprecise. Its distortion invariably implied an opening for the foe and a blurring of the rays of strength. . . . [T]he form itself must have an extreme adaptability, a matchless flexibility, so that it resembles a series of sculptures created from moment to moment by a fluid body. The continuous radiation of strength must create its own shape, just as a continuous jet of water will maintain the shape of a fountain. Surely, I felt, the tempering by sun and steel to which I submitted over such a long period was none other than a process of creating this kind of fluid sculpture. (40–41)

One does not see, look at, the opponent—if one waits to see where and how the other positions himself it will be too late; one must foresee where he will be in a fraction of a second. One also does not observe the figure of one's own power; every distance from it taken to see it subtracts from that power. The victor is one who reserves nothing for a life after, casts himself totally, absolutely, into the present, into the unseen hollow he makes of himself.

The victor was the subject of the highest art in Greek classicism. This art was necessary to make a spectacle of what is a spectacle only through art—victory, understood only by combatants, where neither oneself nor the opponent can be a spectacle at the moment victory occurs. This necessary art formulates the classical judgment that the moment of victory is the supreme moment of existence; there is nothing after it or beyond it. What we sense "in the bronze charioteer of Delphi, where the glory, the pride, and the shyness reflected in the moment of victory are given faithful immortality—is the swift approach of the spectre of death just on the other side of the victor" (42).

Victory, then, issues in nothing. That excess, that superfluity which is the peerless power of the musculature, achieves a sovereignty which is itself gratuitous. Victory is only in unconditional combat, in which everything was cast, but it is not a conquering of death. Its glory is a purely worldly glory, this side of death—which is never defeated by any human prowess, and which always overcomes.

And it is indeed this pressing contiguity with death that saves the creation of an artwork—the highest form of art, which, according to Nietzsche, is made of the most precious clay and oil, flesh and blood—from being absurd. This excessive preoccupation with one's own body, on the part of a male, would otherwise be only comical. "A strict rule is imposed where men are concerned. It is this: a man must under normal circumstances never permit his own objectification; he can only be objectified through the supreme action"—the absolute exposedness to "another sun quite different from that by which I had been so long blessed, a sun full of the fierce dark flames of feeling, a sun of death that would never burn the skin yet gave forth a still stranger glow" (46).

That which lay at the end of the flashing fist and beyond the blow of the bamboo sword, reality without images, was death in person. Aristotle listed courage as the first virtue; it is not one virtue among others on the list, for without courage no virtue is possible. Socrates claimed for himself none of the intellectual virtues; the sole virtue he claimed for himself, citing the proofs at the trial, was courage. In the *Phaedo* he argues not only that courage is the specific virtue of the philosopher but that only philosophers are courageous, utterly fearless, for warriors show no fear of death and are courageous only because they fear something more—dishonor or the enslavement of their families and kin. "However much the closeted philosopher mulls over the idea of death, so long as he remains divorced from the physical courage that is a prerequisite for an awareness of it, he will remain unable even to begin to grasp it." In the tensity of physical courage, "the flesh beats a steady retreat into its function of self-defense, while it is clear consciousness that controls the decision that sends the body soaring into self-abandonment. It is the ultimate in clarity of consciousness that constitutes one of the strongest contributing factors in self-abandonment" (44).

This highest acuity of consciousness that sends the body into self-abandonment is, however, not the surface of inscription of words; it is suffering. At its limits, consciousness becomes suffering when it invades the body. "For I had begun to believe that it was the muscles— powerful, statically so well organized and so silent—that were the true sources of the clarity of my consciousness. The occasional pain in the muscles of a blow that missed the shield gave rise instantly to a still tougher consciousness that suppressed the pain, and imminent shortage of breath gave rise to a frenzy that conquered it" (46). It was thus the power of the body that provoked this supreme lucidity in the suffering consciousness.

When one turns to witness the eloquence of the flesh, one's own flesh or that of another, one senses this inner agon, which stills the comedy of a man objectifying himself. This inner agon by which consciousness, whose extreme limits are resolutely extended into the physical substance in the form of suffering, sending the body in self-abandon to its mortal limits. This intuition of an agon with death that is being waged in the gravity and dignity of the body.

Victory is a purely worldly glory this side of death; death is not defeated. Death is also the master of its own meaning. One shall not be able to make one's death serve one's own cause, this side of death. "Here must always arise a discrepancy between the absolute concept of death and the man-made, relativistic concept of righteousness. . . . We do not possess the standard for choosing to die. The fact that we are alive may mean that we have already been chosen for some purpose, and if life is not something we have chosen for ourselves, then maybe we are not ultimately free to die" (*The Way of the Samurai: Yukio Mishima on "Hagakure" in Modern Life,* trans. Kathryn Sparling [New York: Basic Books, 1977], p. 104).

"AND NOW, kept in reserve for the end," Marguerite Yourcenar wrote at the end of her book written after Mishima's seppuku,

> the last and most traumatizing image: so overwhelming that it has rarely been reproduced. Two heads on the rug, surely acrylic, of the General's office, placed alongside of one another like ninepins, almost touching. Two heads, inert balls, two brains that the blood no longer irrigates, two computers stopped in the midst of their job, no longer sorting out and decoding the perpetual flux of images, impressions, incitements and responses which by the millions pass every day through a being and form what we call the life of the mind and even that of the senses, motivating and directing the movements of the body. Two severed heads, gone on to other worlds where another law rules, that, when one contemplates them, produce more stupor than horror. Judgments of value, whether moral, political or aesthetic, are in their presence, momentarily at least, reduced to silence. The notion that forces itself upon us is more disturbing and simpler: among the myriads of things that are, and that have been, these two heads have been; they are. What fills these eyes without any look is no longer a banner unfurled in political protest, nor any other intellectual or carnal image, nor even the void that Honda had contemplated, and which suddenly seems to be nothing but a concept or a symbol that is in the end all too human. Two objects, already quasi-inorganic debris of destroyed structures, and, once passed into the fire, will they too be but mineral residue and ashes; not even subjects for meditation, because the data are lacking for us to meditate on them. Two pieces of wreckage, rolling on the river of action, which the immense wave has left for a moment dry on the sands, before washing them on. (*Mishima, ou la vision du vide* [Paris: Gallimard, 1981], pp. 124–25)

*Jane Marie Todd*

# The Philosopher
# as Transvestite:
# Textual Perversion in *Glas*

IN THE FIRST PAGES of *Glas*, Derrida poses the problem of philosophy in terms of the anxiety of influence.[1] In a passage from the *Aesthetics* that comes to serve as an emblem of sorts for *Glas*, Hegel describes the "phallic column of India" that over the course of centuries evolves from a solid mass of rock to a hollow, carved sepulcher. Derrida suggests that his task is to hollow out Hegel's text, make it a tomb for its author "so as not to be imprisoned by the colossus."[2] To counter or escape the law of the father, the phallic law represented by Hegel, Derrida takes his cue from the homosexual Genet, whose essay "What Has Remained of a Rembrandt" is, like *Glas*, arranged into two columns, and erects a fetishistic column that doubles the first one. At the same time, he erects a tomb, or transforms the monolith of Hegel's writing into a sepulcher, staging the death and burial of the imposing philosopher.

As a figure for this second activity, this work of mourning for Hegel, Derrida turns to *The Phenomenology of Spirit* itself, taking on the role of mourner that Hegel assigns to *women*. For in Hegel it is the daughter, the wife, the sister, or the mother—woman in general—who performs the rites of burial. As we shall see, Derrida is this woman also; or at least he dresses himself as a woman in order to achieve his goals, in order to bury Hegel but also to seduce, to play at and with philosophy. Thus, in order to escape the philosophy of law, Derrida enlists two outlaws, the woman and the homosexual, and takes on their roles in writing *against* Hegel.

*Glas* traces the passage in the *Phenomenology of Spirit* from the family to the state, that is, from the "singularity" of the family unit to the "universality" of the state. This passage is brought about through the son who, having been educated, leaves the family unit and becomes a citizen. Yet in this operation, someone remains behind: the mother, wife, or daughter, the woman who guards the hearth. Derrida explains that Hegel posits a tension between "the law of singularity" and "the law of universality." These two laws organize a series of oppositions: divine law/human law, family/community, woman/man, night/day, and so on. Human law, produced and administered by men (males), is public, visible, and universal: it regulates the state rather than the family and is associated with daylight. Divine law is a hidden, nocturnal law; it governs the family and is proper to women. It is more natural than human law but is also in conflict with it, since it works against universality. "Natural, divine, feminine, nocturnal, familial, such is the predicative system, the law of singularity. . . . The goal proper to the family, to woman who represents it, is, strictly speaking, the singular as such." The problem is that "in its essentiality, singularity can only disappear" (161); according to the Hegelian dialectic, singularity must be overcome, sublated into universality. Yet woman remains in contradiction to this dialectical progression: as guardian of the hearth, she obeys a contradictory law, works against universalization, against the male law: "The government—the head —authorizes and organizes familial right, the element and natural being-there of the community, [but] it is also threatened by it. The family puts the head in peril" (165).

Hegel writes that the "essential object" of the family is not the citizen, since he does not belong to the family but to the government, nor is it the individual who is not yet a citizen but will become one; if the goal of the family is "the singular as such" (a goal in contradiction with the goals of the government), the family's proper object can only be "that singular being belonging to the family, but captured as universal essence, stripped of its effectivity." That is, the family is not concerned with a living being but with "the dead man who, from a long succession . . . of his dispersed being-there is gathered together . . . into a *single* completed figuration . . . and from the worries of contingent life has been raised into the calm of simple universality.—

Since it is only as citizen that he is *effective* and *substantial*, the singular being, inasmuch as he is not a citizen . . . and belongs to the family, is only the ineffective and hollow [*marklose*] shadow" (Hegel, quoted p. 162). The only moment when the individual belongs completely to the family, not as contingent, empirical being but as a "simple universality" is when he or she is dead; otherwise, the individual belongs to the universality of the government, as a citizen.

The activities proper to the family, then, are "preparation of the dead, institution of death, wakes, monumentalization, archives, heritage, genealogy, classification of proper names, graving on tombs, wrapping of the corpse, burial, funeral chants, etc" (162). The family perpetuates itself by remembering those who have died, by granting the human remains a place in the genealogy of the family, by engraving the proper name in the family archives. Thus, concludes Derrida, "the family does not yet know the productive work of universality in the community, only the work of mourning" (162).

As we have seen, it is women who guard the hearth, remaining behind after men have become citizens; women are the representatives of the family. Derrida concludes that, since men belong to the family only in death, "it falls to espoused femininity to care for, strictly speaking, a corpse. When a man *attaches himself* to a woman it is always a question of entrusting his death to her. . . . Entrusting his death, the guarding of a body without marrow, grants woman the duty of erecting his sepulcher after binding his rigid corpse (unction, wrappings, etc.), keeping him in a living, monumental, interminable erection" (161–62). When a man marries, what he offers his wife is not himself as a living subject (since that still belongs to the government) but his dead body, the only part of himself that belongs essentially to the family. In some sense, the wedding night is already a wake; the image of the rigid penis entering the woman's body blends with that of the corpse entering the earth, since "the night of the subterranean world is woman, explains Hegel" (162). In addition, the dwelling that the woman oversees is already in some sense a sepulcher. Thus, if Derrida is burying Hegel, hollowing out the phallic text so that it may serve as a dwelling or sepulcher for Hegel's proper name, he is acting as (or like) a woman.

In the passage from the *Aesthetics* that Derrida quotes in the first pages of *Glas*, Hegel alludes to certain Dionysiac rites, where women adorn themselves with a false phallus and pull on a string in order to erect it "almost as big as the rest of the body." Describing his own project in *Glas*, Derrida writes: "To work in the name of Hegel, to erect it, for the space of a ceremony, I have chosen to pull on a string. . . . It is the law of the family" (10). Thus, Derrida disguises himself as woman, adorned with a fetish object, in order to erect the false phallus in the name of Hegel. It is in *becoming woman* that he escapes Hegel's influence, or rather, in pretending to be a woman—who is pretending to be a man.

This image suggests his later discussion of Kant and the problem of sexual difference. For Kant, "woman wants to be a man, man does not want to be a woman. . . . Kant does not develop this last proposition, dropped at the end of a paragraph" (148). This leads Derrida to speculate: "What would it mean, for a man, to want to be a woman, when woman wants to be a man to the precise extent that she is educated? [That] would then mean, except for an apparent detour, that he would want to be a man, want to be—that is, to remain—a man" (148). For Kant, man is the goal toward which woman strives; limited in her powers, she wishes to become a man "in order to be able to give to her inclinations a greater and freer space for play [*Spielraum*]" (Kant, quoted p. 148). Thus, the man who wants to be a woman would, like every woman, want to be a man; the desire to be a woman would simply be a detour on the way to becoming what both sexes want to be—male.

In the next paragraph, Derrida revises and complicates this first schema:

> Is it so simple? Does Kant say that woman wants to be a man? He says more exactly that she would like, in certain situations, to adorn herself with male attributes in order to realize her female designs: to be better in the position to have all men. She pretends to want to be a man or to be a man in order to "extend the space of play for her inclinations." (148)

Woman does not really want to *be* a man; she merely wants to appropriate a certain "maleness," male power or prowess, in order to achieve her female aims. What, then, would a man who wants to be a woman desire?

> Everything is reversed: either the man who only wants to be a man wants
> to be a woman inasmuch as woman wants to be a man; he thus wants to
> be a woman in order to remain what he is. Or else the man who wants to
> be a woman wants to be only a woman since woman only wants to be a
> man in order to attain her female designs. Man, that is. Etc. (148)

The first instance is simply the logical consequence of the *first* paradigm: the man who wants to remain a man shares with woman his
desire, since she too wants to be a man. His desire to be a man puts
him in the same position as woman, who also wants to be male.

This is not entirely accurate, however, since, for Kant, woman does
not really want to be a man but merely to simulate maleness in order
to better accomplish her designs, in order to seduce men. A man who
wanted to be a woman would thus want to be a woman who merely
*simulated* maleness. That, of course, is precisely how Derrida characterizes himself in the passage cited earlier: he has become a woman,
but a woman adorned with a false phallus. The possibility that Derrida does not consider in his discussion of Kant (or that he merely subsumes under an "etc.") is that of a man who wants to be a woman
(simulating maleness) in order to achieve his *male* designs, whatever
those might be.

Continuing to paraphrase Kant, Derrida links this transvestism of
women to both fetishism and *reading*:

> In fact, even if she really wanted to, which she does not, woman could
> never be a man. The male attributes with which she adorns herself are
> never anything but paste [*toc*], signifiers without signification, fetishes.
> For show [*De la montre*]. Out of sync with the movement of the sun. To
> illustrate the fact that woman can in no case appropriate the male at-
> tribute, by way of example or substitution, science, culture, books, Kant
> denounces a sort of travesty: "Concerning woman scholars: they use
> their books as they use their *watches*; they display them to show that they
> have one, even though ordinarily they are stopped or not set according
> to the sun. (149)

By writing "male attribute" in the singular form and suggesting that
science, culture, and books are *substitutions* for that attribute, Derrida
is hinting that what women lack is a penis, and that their attempts to

appropriate male power amount to fetishism, the merely ornamental use of a false phallus. In the same way, a woman wears a watch simply as an ornament, not attending to its true function of telling time. The equivalent of displaying a watch that is not set to follow the movement of the sun would be treating books only as ornaments, or attending only to the ornaments of the book—the images, metaphors, figures, or verbal expressions—without looking past the words for the ultimate meaning or truth of the book that is presumed to lie outside language. A reading that is regulated by the sun is one that recaptures the author's intentions, that considers the author to be the father or source (as the sun is the source of light) of his writings, a reading that believes the author's intentions "center" the text.[3]

It is not difficult to read Kant's comments about women readers as a characterization of Derrida, who has long mounted an assault on the notion that the author's intentions govern or control the text and, as a reader, has often stressed the decentering effect of language. We begin to suspect that he has taken on the role of woman in order to escape the pervasive influence of the father Hegel, developing a method of reading that does not inherit the father's name and that does not simply replicate the father's text.

In his essay on Nietzsche, *Spurs*, Derrida addresses the question of woman, linking the notion of truth as unveiling (*alétheia*) to the Freudian notion of the castration complex. According to Freud, the little boy recognizes the threat of castration when he sees the female genitals and concludes that girls have been castrated. Derrida explains that "truth-castration is precisely a male *affair*" and that woman believes neither in castration nor in truth. He adds that

> woman . . . no more believes in castration's exact opposite, anti-castration, than she does in castration itself. Much too crafty for that . . . she knows that such a reversal would only deprive her of her powers of simulation, that in truth [it] would amount to the same thing. . . . Unable to seduce or to give vent to desire without it, "woman" is in need of castration's effect. But obviously she does not believe in it. "Woman" is what does not believe in it but plays with it. Plays with it: from a new concept and a new structure of belief aiming at laughter.[4]

Here again, woman adorns herself with a phallus, knowing that it is false, in order to produce desire and to seduce. She manipulates a "truth effect" without believing in truth. Unlike the male fetishist, for whom the fetish commemorates his belief in the mother's phallus, a belief he cannot bring himself to give up entirely, woman knows that the fetish stands for no lost object, no ultimate signified.[5]

In characterizing himself as a woman who erects Hegel's name "for the space of a ceremony," Derrida suggests that his object is to seduce, to feign a philosophical discourse, a discourse on truth, in order to produce desire. Genet, the bastard within/outside the Hegelian family, provides a quotation that serves as a description of this fetishistic writing. In the right column, Derrida quotes Genet's question to his friend Stilitano: "Do you want me to dress as a woman?" (249). The question appears in *The Thief's Journal*: Stilitano has proposed that Genet earn money for them by working as a prostitute out of a nearby bar. Whereas in Kant's paradigm it is women who take on male attributes in order to be better able to seduce men, here it is a man who dresses as a woman in order, once more, to seduce *men*. The possibility that is *left out* of Derrida's consideration of Kant, the very figure of his own textual fetishism, is provided by Genet.

The quotation from *The Thief's Journal* appears in *Glas* at the moment Derrida turns to Freud's essay on fetishism. The question at hand is whether Freud's theory of fetishism is sufficient as a mode of interpreting the sexual fantasies that Genet records in his writings. In another passage from *The Thief's Journal*, a work much quoted by Derrida, Genet describes how he became emotionally attached to Stilitano:

> With a gesture of his vivid hand, he motioned to me that he wanted to undress. As on other evenings, I got down on my knees to unhook the bunch of grapes. Inside his trousers was pinned one of those imitation bunches of thin cellulose grapes stuffed with cotton wool. . . . I still think that it was by virtue of the insidious power of these grapes that I grew attached to Stilitano.[6]

Derrida poses the hermeneutic question: "Is the stylus in question, the fake held by a safety pin, a fetish?" adding that his form of question assumes that "one knows of the fetish at least that it is something" (250). At first glance, the bunch of grapes seems to function as a fetish: "substitute for the penis adored by the child who does not want to give up the mother's phallus, monumental erection of triumph over the threat of castration, denial, compromise, etc. Is not all of that quite recognizable?" (250).

Things are not so simple, however; for Freud, the fetish "saves the fetishist from becoming a homosexual, by endowing women with the characteristic which makes them tolerable as sexual objects" (*Standard Edition*, vol. 21, p. 154). Genet is a homosexual and Stilitano already has the penis that the fetish is supposed to substitute for. The fetish is, then, a *supplementary* penis as well as a "fake wound." This supplementary castration also serves to "re-mark-compensate another substitute for castration," Stilitano's missing right hand. As both a supplementary penis and a supplementary wound, the bunch of grapes compensates for the lost hand and, at the same time, symbolizes it. But in order for the bunch of grapes to symbolize the lost hand, it must act as supplement of a supplement, since for Freud "castration" is the ultimate meaning that mutilated members, missing eyes and teeth, and decapitation signify.

"Castration" is the signified that is not itself a signifier, that which cannot represent something else. Derrida shows, however, that the phallus and castration can be brought into the play of signification. Stilitano's bunch of grapes does not simply signify an absent phallus, and his missing arm actually seems to make him more virile. In fact, Genet writes that "when one member is lost, they tell me, the one that remains becomes stronger. I hoped that the vigor of the missing arm had been captured in Stilitano's organ" (quoted in *Glas*, 156). Thus, the penis itself seems to compensate, supplement the lost member. But if the penis functions as a supplement, it is in the position of the fetish. Derrida concludes that

> as soon as the thing itself, in its revealed truth, finds itself engaged . . . in the play of supplementary difference, the fetish no longer has any rigorously decidable status. Knell of phallogocentrism. . . . The economy of the fetish is more powerful than that of the—decidable—truth of the thing itself or of a discourse deciding about castration (*pro aut contra*). The fetish is not opposable. (252)

The bunch of grapes signifies both castration and noncastration; by adorning himself with it, "Stilitano seems to affirm himself as a male as well as a bashful woman or a 'queer who hates himself'" (252). Adorned with the bunch of grapes, Stilitano has, as it were, a supplementary phallus, like the man disguised as a woman adorned with a false phallus or like the double-columned *Glas*. This fetishism is undecidable: Stilitano is both male and female; the fetish object both represents and guards against castration; the "thing itself," the penis, may also function as a fetish; and "phallogocentrism," which posits that the phallus and its absence, castration, are the ultimate signified of fetishism, is called into question, decentered by that very fetishism. A fetishistic *reading*, then, would escape the author's influence, would decenter the reading that tries to recuperate intentions or locate an extratextual truth.[7]

"If I write two texts at the same time," writes Derrida, "you will not be able to castrate me." He continues:

> If I delinearize, I erect. But at the same time, I divide my act and my desire. I—mark(s) the division and in always escaping you I simulate constantly and never come. I castrate myself—I remain to myself in that way—and I 'play at coming.'
>
> Well almost.
>
> (Ah!) you can't be taken (well then) remain(s). (77)

This passage alludes to Freud's claim that the multiplication of phallic symbols in dreams is a device that the unconscious uses to guard against the threat of castration. But the multiplication also reveals the underlying fear of castration that it guards against: it both protects against and represents the threat.

In this case, the threat of castration is the fear of having one's discourse "cut off," reduced to a single, ultimate signified. This is in fact Hegel's model of reading: the signs ought to disappear, consumed altogether by the reader. It is the father Hegel's law that poses the threat of castration, and it is his law that Derrida tries to escape.

His means of escape: the fetishism or transvestism that consists in adorning himself with a supplementary phallus. As we have seen, this fetishism is associated with both male homosexuals and women: in fact, the phrase "play at coming" is used by Genet to describe one

of his lovers (see p. 32), but it also suggests the women in *Spurs* who
" 'give themselves as' even when they—'give themselves' " (59, translation modified). Thus, Derrida's means of escaping Hegel's influence,
of escaping the law of reading that would castrate his text, is to engage
in a textual fetishism, to pervert Hegel's phallocentric law by becoming a woman or a homosexual. "Each column rises up with an im-
passive adequacy and yet the element of contagion . . . relates every
sentence, every word, every scrap of writing to every other, in each
column and from one column to another of *what has remained* infinitely incalculable" (7). This last quotation describes Genet's short essay, but it can just as easily refer to *Glas*. The form of the text is a
triumph of sorts, but a triumph caught up in the double bind of
fetishism itself: the text is untouchable and not, as Hegel would have
it, consumed without remains, but at the same time it "simulates constantly and never comes." Derrida can only mock the father Hegel by
practicing a textual perversion.

## NOTES

1. For the role of the father in the "ancestral rite" of *Glas*, see also Gayatri
Spivak, "*Glas*-Piece: A Compte-Rendu," *Diacritics* 7 (1977): 22–43. I have also
benefited from a lecture by Spivak entitled "Woman in Derrida" that was delivered at the School of Criticism and Theory, Northwestern University, Summer 1982.

2. Jacques Derrida, *Glas* (Paris: Galilée, 1974), p. 8. All quotations from *Glas*
are my translations.

3. See Derrida's "La mythologie blanche," in *Marges de la philosophie* (Paris:
Minuit, 1972), pp. 247–324, for further discussion of the sun as metaphor for
truth.

4. Jacques Derrida, *Spurs*, trans. Barbara Harlow (Chicago and London:
University of Chicago Press, 1978), p. 61, translation modified.

5. In fact, according to Freud, girls as well as boys believe that women have
been castrated (Sigmund Freud, *The Standard Edition of the Complete Psychological Works of Sigmund Freud*, trans. and ed. James Strachey [London: Hogarth
Press, 1953–74], vol. 19, pp. 252–53). Derrida grafts Nietzsche's comments on
women's scepticism onto Freud's theory of female sexuality in order to provide
himself an escape route from phallogocentrism (that is, the escape of becoming woman) not provided by Freud alone.

6. Jean Genet, *The Thief's Journal*, trans. Bernard Frechtman (New York: Grove Press, 1964), pp. 52–53.

7. On the question of textual fetishism in *Glas*, see also Sarah Kofman, "Ça cloche," in *Les fins de l'homme*, ed. Jean-Luc Nancy and Philippe Lacoue-Labarthe (Paris: Galilée, 1981), pp. 87–117.

*Walter A. Strauss*

# Tournier's Quest for Sophia

T HE AUTOBIOGRAPHICAL and autocritical volume by Michel Tournier
entitled *Le vent Paraclet* (1977) concludes with a strange essay entitled "Les malheurs de Sophie." (The title of the essay is a playful reminder of the Countess Sophie de Ségur's novel for children, published in 1864.) It is a lamentation for the disappearance of wisdom in
our time and a critique of science and philosophy. "We are living
under the terrorism of abstract, half-experimental, half-mathematical
knowledge, and of formal rules of life defined by ethics. . . . What's
happened to wisdom? Sophia, sapientia, wisdom, Weisheit" (VP
283).[1] It is surprising but not unusual to have a declaration like this
one coming from the pen of an author who has had extensive training
in philosophy and whose novels are often philosophical elaborations
or meditations. The argument that Tournier pursues in the essay is
relatively simple: in antiquity Sophia represented the Supreme Deity,
a way of life: "Knowledge which is all at once a rule of conduct, action
made identical with the mind, an effective light" (VP 284). His examples are Socrates, Plato, and Aristotle, and the last "sage" in this
lineage is Spinoza. After Spinoza, there is deterioration and romantic
corruption: Exhibit A—Jean-Jacques Rousseau, particularly in *Émile*
(1762) and the exaltation of morality and instinct; exhibit B—Immanuel
Kant, *Foundations of the Metaphysics of Morals* (1785), the exaltation of
morality and the will. In Tournier's view this degradation is threefold:
ancient wisdom has been corrupted by the mathematical and physical
sciences into a system of Newtonian authoritarianism; action, hence-
forth disconnected from wisdom, has degenerated into categorical
imperatives; and, as a second method of education, the former "ini-
tiative" *paideia* has become a mere vehicle for utilitarian and profes-

306

sional "information." This triple attack—against Knowledge, morality, and utilitarian pedagogy—needs to be examined in greater detail.

On first glance, Tournier's distempered judgment of the last three
hundred years would appear to be "obscurantist" and possibly anti-
Christian, and indeed Tournier has been criticized as "reactionary."
Perhaps he is, but in another sense only. In his lament for the decline
of *sophia* he is actually defending the major Greek philosophers—
wisdom-lovers, literally—against modern questers after mere Knowledge. But if one raises the issue of wisdom versus knowledge in this
form, at least two questions arise. The minor one concerns the problematic position of Aristotle in Tournier's perspective, since Aristotle
stands between the Presocratic/Socratic/Platonic "dispensation" and
the medieval and modern world of *scientia*. The more crucial question
has to do with the monotheistic tradition as a counterpoise to the
Greek world view. Is it not true that Scripture seeks, and demands of
us that we seek, wisdom? Sapientia, not scientia; *patience* rather than
*science*, if Rimbaud's gnomic statement—or at least inspired pun—in
"L'Éternité" is valid in this present context:

> Science et patience   Science and patience [science and not science]
> Le supplice est sûr   The torment is certain.

Or perhaps we are simply back to Rabelais' engaging formula of "science without conscience (i.e., consciousness)." Whatever the case,
Tournier does not reject Greek philosophy in favor of Scriptural wisdom. Rather, his critique pays tribute to Catholicism as a former "very
vigorous avatar of wisdom" (VP 291) and then proceeds to characterize Marxism as "another form of modern wisdom" (VP 292). Both
Catholicism and Marxism have resulted in a sort of disjunction of
thought and action, a "sentimental quietism." "As a matter of fact,
wisdom is living knowledge; it is almost biological, a joyous growth; a
successful approach to the blossoming forth of body and mind. . . .
Wisdom is change, ripening, a shedding of the skin" (VP 290). The
cleavage that has occurred since the end of the eighteenth century,
and for which Romanticism is held primarily responsible (here surely
Tournier has a point), is that between two kinds of experience, one of
the body, the other of the intellect: "two levels of knowing, one pro-

found, obscure, all mixed up with the heart, the nerves and sexuality; the other abstract, cerebral, light-weight, portable" (291). Dare we think of this contrast as Dionysian-Apollonian? It certainly has affinities with Nietzsche's early distinction; in a wider sense, it would appear that Tournier is again calling for a transcendence of the old dualism that grows out of Descartes (why is Descartes not mentioned in this essay?) and that has played havoc with post-Cartesian philosophy (with the exception of Spinoza, as Tournier himself reverentially notes).

"A choice has to be made, the great ancient wisdom being dead, and no one has yet been able to give it a life in tune with the modern world. At least a person can always offer the mind two or three truths which help him to conduct life better." What are these rules of conduct (an oddly Cartesian phrase!)? I think it may be argued that Tournier's fiction is an attempt to articulate something of the sort: an effort to recover the absolute—and here Tournier means literally the absolute as "that which is cut off, that which no longer stands in relation."

Tournier has written six works of fiction so far (*Vendredi; Le Roi des Aulnes; Les météores; Gaspard, Melchior et Balthazar; Gilles et Jeanne*—all novels; and one collection of stories, *Le coq de bruyère*). The most impressive of these, in some ways, is *Vendredi, ou les limbes du Pacifique* (1967; trans. as *Friday*, 1969), primarily because it is a reinterpretation of the Robinson Crusoe–Friday relationship and in some ways a corrective to Jean-Jacques Rousseau's *Émile*. Tournier's objective in this first novel, as in the subsequent work, is to explore what he calls a "mythological dimension," since Robinson Crusoe has clearly fascinated the Western imagination more or less continuously since the publication of Daniel Defoe's classic novel of self-reliance in 1719. Tournier applauds Defoe's notion of juxtaposing and combining two separate episodes that occurred on the island Más a Tierra, off the coast of Chile (Defoe transposed the location of his novel to the Caribbean), one involving an Araucanian Indian in the late seventeenth century, the other involving a certain Alexander Selkirk, abandoned around 1704 on the island for mutinous behavior (not as the result of a shipwreck!). The principal elements of Defoe's novel are well known to most readers: Robinson's ingenious capacity for survival by self-reliance and self-confidence, and the subsequent master-servant camaraderie with Friday. And then, ultimately, the rescue—Defoe stretches Selkirk's four years into twenty-eight. Tournier, while admitting (with a nod toward Lévi-Strauss and *The Savage Mind*) that Robinson is "the patron saint of all the open-air tinkerers (*bricoleurs*)" (VP 226), sees him also as the victim of solitude, also the hero transcending solitude by raising it to the level of an art of living. Thus Robinson becomes not only a "mytho-logical" figure, like Faust or Don Juan, but a character demanding a modern metamorphosis. Tournier's Robinson is not merely the technologically resourceful individual of Western civilization—that is to say, the product of science and exact knowledge—but also the embodiment of the vice and curse of Western culture, namely colonialism and loneliness. And here we move with Tournier in the direction of "sagesse": Robinson learns to "go beyond" all this and thus becomes the sketch of a potentially new type of man. The result is a fascinating *anthropological* novel, in the widest sense of the term: an ethnographic confrontation between modern civilization and a totally different culture (formerly labeled as "savage"), as well as a metaphysical meditation on the possible redemption of modern man (as an individual).

Tournier's Robinson registers the historical, political, and ethnological changes that have taken place in the 250 years that separate Defoe's novel from his own. The condescending and arrogant assumptions of Western man are no longer valid today after the dissolution of colonial empires and the emergence of the Third World, and after the insights that anthropologists have given us since the end of the nineteenth century. It never occurred to Defoe to think of Friday as anything other than a savage to be civilized by Robinson Crusoe; it never occurred to him that Robinson might have been well advised to rely on the expertise of the Indian in order to carve out an existence appropriate to the island, rather than trying to make the island an extension and replica of England. But we are wiser (or at least more melancholy—witness Lévi-Strauss' *Tristes tropiques*) about these matters today; and so Tournier ingeniously reverses the situation in the following manner. Robinson, after surviving the rigors of adaptation on his island Speranza (note the name!) and being joined by Friday, first lapses into a swinish and self-indulgent hedonism, from which he finally liberates himself by becoming the technological entrepreneur-

bricoleur that he was in Defoe's novel: he civilizes the island, West-
ernizes it (for no apparent purpose other than a sort of occidental
habit), administers it. Friday goes along with this alien management,
without much understanding or enthusiasm, and at last accidentally
blows up Robinson's powder kegs. Out of this symbolic devastation
the need to survive grows imperative once more, this time on a culturally more sensible basis, that is to say along the lines of Friday's
wisdom. From this point until close to the end, Friday is the hero of
the narrative. He represents an "elemental" antithesis to Robinson:
Robinson is the child of the soil, Friday is "aerial." The dynamics of
the story are, as it were, polarized into a dialectic of earth and air,
seeking its center of energy in the sun: the novel becomes a solar
myth. Friday brings another kind of culture to the island: kite-flying,
Aeolian harp sounds—the activity of the wind. The problem for
Robinson now is to learn how to combine earth-Knowledge with
wind-wisdom: his principal occupation becomes agriculture. And as
the new elemental mystique invades him (Tournier has obviously led
us from a Cartesian universe into a Bachelardian universe), his sexuality also undergoes fascinating transformations. There is, first, a
symbolic retreat into the womb of the earth (a cave); then there is actual copulation with the ground and a symbolic marriage of man and
vegetation, producing the mandrake root and its archetypal associa-
tions. But the final phase of this cosmic symbolism occurs when an
English ship rescues Friday and Robinson: in this instance, Friday
goes to Western civilization (as a reverse "missionary"?), whereas
Robinson opts to remain on Speranza in his solitude, which is now no
longer a solitude but a growth toward union with the sun, a symbolic
reconciliation of man and cosmos. This is not accomplished in the
novel, but the way, the direction, is sketched out. In a commentary on
the novel, Tournier offers the formula of a "double question,"

Earth + Air = Sun
Robinson/earth-bound + Friday/air-borne = Robinson sun-oriented.
(VP 235)

At this point Tournier notes that these three stages in Robinson's
evolution correspond to the three stages of Knowledge as described

in Spinoza's *Ethics:* (1) Knowledge derived from sense experience; (2) rational and scientific Knowledge; (3) Knowledge of the absolute, which "is an intuition of its essence."/"It goes without saying," he says later, "that this parallel was not intentional. But besides the fact that the *Ethics* is in my view the most important book since the Gospels, and since its lesson is very deeply inscribed in my mind, I note that these three stages correspond most certainly to a very classical schema which can be found in more than one religious or philosophical doctrine" (VP 236). Has there ever been higher praise accorded to Spinoza? But that is not really the point here. Michel Tournier has absorbed Spinoza so thoroughly that Spinoza's metaphysics can easily serve as an infrastructure to his novel: it is not a question of "illustrating" a philosophy or exemplifying it by superimposition; Tournier's reflections are molded by his cohabitation with the philosophers and find their "natural" outlet in the creative activity of the novelist, which in this instance is a quest for wisdom beyond mere knowledge. Something of this is implied in the subtitle of the novel under discussion, "the limbo of the Pacific," a state of suspension between past and future, between the old cosmos and the cosmos envisaged. "Three ways are open in the life of each man and of each woman: 1) purely passive and degrading pleasures—alcohol, drugs, etc.; 2) work and social ambition; 3) pure artistic or religious contemplation. Robinson's three lives thus provide a bridge between our everyday existence and Spinoza's metaphysics" (VP 236). And, in a sense, one might have to admit that this bridge, though important, is narrow, since it has room only for man's solitude. But, as John Donne had noted, "no man is an island intire to itselfe"; so indeed in Tournier's treatment Robinson and Friday are teacher and pupil (reciprocally), not merely master and servant, and thus constitute a true couple within their shared solitudes.

Tournier's next two novels, *Le Roi des Aulnes* (1970; trans. as *The Ogre*, 1972) and *Les météores* (1975; trans. as *Gemini*, 1981), move into the world of the twentieth century and recycle some motifs and legends dealing with human relationships, this time set in a wider social spectrum. *The Ogre* (actually the Erl-King or King of the Alders) audaciously superimposes the Erl-King motif with the St. Christopher legend in a fable that may be called "phoric," paidophilic, and—finally—pedagogical (in the literal sense of the term: leading children;

that is, educative, didactic). It seems that the next novel, *Les météores*, had been projected to be Tournier's magnum opus but somehow fell short of its mark. But that does not prevent the work from being altogether remarkable. The English title, *Gemini*, comes somewhat closer to what the novel actually *is*; the French title, implying a general complex of meteorological conditions (not merely meteors)—climate, weather, the elements, but particularly the "aerial" forces impinging on the other elements—comes closer to the novel's intended mythological scope. Concerning this mythological and religious dimension, Tournier has this to say:

> It was to have been the major dimension and to justify the original title *The Paraclete Wind* announced at the time of the publication of *The Ogre*. My initial project aimed for a resacralization of celestial phenomena by a fusion of theology and meteorology; the one was to contribute spirit, the sacred, the divine, the other was to contribute the very concrete poetry of rain, snow and sun. It was a question of eradicating the difference between the two meanings of the word heaven—air, atmosphere and dwelling-places of God and the blessed—and to make contact with the solar cult outlined at the end of *Friday*. (VP 260)

The fact that this attempt at "resacralization" did not succeed, and that Tournier admits that "the novel has developed in a much too profane direction" (VP 261), seems to me largely to have deferred, not abolished, the question—which in my view is how to make the modern novel once more into a vast symbolic-mythological structure of meanings. (One thinks of Cervantes, Balzac, Proust, Joyce, and Mann in this connection, and, if one looks for parallel tendencies among Tournier's contemporaries, why not Günter Grass and Gabriel García Márquez and possibly Milan Kundera?) Tournier's problem is similar to Proust's, Mann's, Musil's, and Broch's: how to make the novel "philosophical" without sacrificing its identity as a narrative genre? Anthropology, meteorology, philosophy, and theology all have their impact on *Les météores* without bringing about a satisfactory synthesis. Thus, the notion of the "ideal" existence of twins as "intercessors" between earth and sky, between female and male—much of this derived from Sir James G. Frazer and possibly from Mircea Eliade—was originally intended as the ground from which this resacralization would proceed, and it clearly points in the direction of a mediation by the Holy Spirit, which, in Tournier's projected theology, more and more takes the place of Jesus Christ.

> I was expecting the Paraclete wind (the Holy Spirit restored to meteorology) to become doubly metamorphosed into flesh and speech. The third person of the Trinity in effect assumes the fecundation of the Virgin Mary, then the gift of languages to the apostles, these interventions being commemorated respectively by the feasts of the Annunciation and Pentecost. (VP 261)

The problem of *Les météores*, it seems to me, is that the synthesis is not achieved in this work: the characters become too absorbing and too imperious for their author; the book loses focus; and its second half, an initiatory voyage of one twin in search of the other, never quite manages to regain the momentum of the earlier part of the novel. Tournier was right to withdraw the title *Le vent Paraclet* and transfer it to his volume of essays.

The fourth novel, *Gaspard, Melchior et Balthazar* (1980; trans. as *The Four Wise Men*, 1984) does not attempt to correct the shortcomings of *Les météores* but appears to move in a somewhat different direction from the three earlier novels; it may be that this direction is the complement of the world view sketched out in those novels. The story is that of the journey of the three Magi—another kind of initiatory motif—but with a curious difference: a fourth *magus* is added to the three, and he is the one on whom everything hinges. His name is Taor (although he hails from the Malabar Coast, his name is surely intended to resonate with the Hebrew *tahor*, meaning "pure"), and he arrives too late for the Nativity. He then allows himself to be sent to the Dead Sea salt mines in order to pay a laborer's debts; he spends thirty-three years there in the most wretched and abysmal conditions, where to be the "salt of the earth" becomes a curse—but not without its compensations: even the descent into the hell of Sodom brings with it an understanding of the dark aspects of human destiny, as if to demonstrate the paradox enunciated earlier: "Salty sweetness is sweeter than sweet sweetness" (FWM, 167). And so, after thirty-three years of servitude, Prince Taor sets out for Jerusalem, following, so to speak, the promptings of his destiny. He arrives too late for the Last Supper, but the modest banquet table is still set for him, and for him alone, for he has become through his experience an Adam made whole once again.

> Taor's head reeled. Bread and wine! He reached for a goblet and raised it to his lips. He picked up a piece of unleavened bread and ate it. He then toppled forward, but he did not fall. The two angels, who had been watching over him since he left the salt mines, gathered him into their great wings. The night sky opened, revealing a sea of light, and into it they bore the man who, after having been last, the eternal latecomer, had just been the first to receive the Eucharist. (FWM, 249)

It should be reasonably clear from all this that Tournier's conception of creative activity—and especially his conception of the novel—is mythological, contemplative, and points toward possibilities of spiritual redemption. If philosophy since 1700 has been generally speaking merely scientific and utilitarian—a point that can certainly be disputed—Tournier seems to think that the search for universal Knowledge *sub specie temporis* is not enough: wisdom exists *sub specie aeternitatis*, as Spinoza said; it reaches for the absolute. The fact that the novel is Tournier's chosen instrument for metaphysical and mythological reflection is not at all a contradiction; despite the novel's need to remain anchored in the concrete, it works very much like Spinoza's three stages of Knowledge (to which Tournier is so devotedly attached), which is anchored in sensation and passes through reason to a wisdom of essences. In the same way the novel moves from the concrete into the abstract and beyond that into "vision." That, after all, is the great tradition in fiction, whether we are dealing with Don Quixote, the great creators of the nineteenth century, the marvelous synthesizers of the twentieth century (Mann, Proust, Joyce), or even the "deconstructors" of these syntheses (Musil, Kafka, Beckett). Tournier places himself in this grand tradition, over against the artificial productions of the "new novelists"; and in this renewal he resembles writers such as Malcolm Lowry (also because of his openly "personal" touch) and Gabriel García Márquez, mentioned previously.

And so we return to *Sophia*, with which we began. Roger Shattuck wittily observed, "Tournier courts an old maid called Sophie who may be much younger than she looks."[2] At least she is capable of being reborn. There are, according to Tournier, essentially two ways: (1) the island-man, "l'homme-île" alone with his "femme-île," *absolute* in the fullest sense of the term, and eternal: Robinson-Speranza; and (2) "l'homme-jardin," man of the continent, subject to the cycle of seasons. "The garden-man by vocation digs the soil and interrogates the heavens"—just as Robinson had done toward the end of his evolution. But there is a difference: the gardener's "absolute" is not an eternal duration but a mystical instant. Yet there is still a fourth dimension, and Tournier refers to it as "metaphysical"; it is an awareness "that time contracts, that space limits itself to these few square feet, a stone enclosure, that a being—my garden, in fact—blooms forth alone in an exorbitant immobility which is the same as the immobility of the absolute. . . . The present moment becomes eternalized in a divine improvidence and amnesia" (VP 301–2). But here, it seems to me, we are even beyond metaphysics, in some sacred precinct of *hagia sophia*, soothed and comforted by the Paraclete wind, and all this strangely and seductively irradiated by a solar myth. "Novelist with a slight metaphysical suntan" (VP 195) is Tournier's amusingly apt characterization of himself. But is it only the metaphysical sun? Is it not also a theological wind, the *ruach* of Genesis and of the Old Testament, Claudel's "esprit créateur," the Holy Spirit of the New Testament; and a historical wind proceeding from Joachim of Floris' (twelfth-century) notion of a triple unfolding of history culminating in the age of the Holy Spirit? As I noted before, a whole section of *Les météores* (150–61) is given over to a lengthy "pentecostal" disquisition, which at least proposes the need for a Third Testament—a pneumatocentric theology—to supersede the other two testaments, not by abrogating them but by fulfilling them. The book on the "four" Magi suggests the ground out of which this theology grows—Tournier's notion that the fall of man is a disjunction of the divine "image and likeness" (Genesis 1:26) in which Adam and Eve were created: ". . . their profound resemblance or likeness to God was gone, but they retained a trace of it, a face and a body which remained the indelible image of the divine reality. Ever since then a curse has weighed on that false image, which fallen man carries around with him . . ." (FWM 193). If this interpretation is valid, then Michel Tournier's novelistic enterprise may ultimately appear to us as an attempt to reintegrate poetry (language) and thought (metaphysical as well as theological) into a grand synthesis, as the great philosophers, poets, and novelists had done in the past. It is no small compliment to Michel Tournier to say that he appears to be a traveler on that glorious highway.

## NOTES

1. In-text references are as follows: VP: Michel Tournier, *Le vent Paraclet* (Paris: Gallimard, 1977), translations mine; FWM: Michel Tournier, *The Four Wise Men*, trans. Ralph Manheim (New York: Random House, 1984).

2. Roger Shattuck, in *The New York Review of Books,* 28 April 1983, p. 15.

*Herman Rapaport*

# Forecastings of Apocalypse:
# Ashbery, Derrida, Blanchot

Il y a là cendre.
—Jacques Derrida, "Feu la cendre"

And this is one of the principal goals of the film: to have done with the
description of horror by horror, for that has been done by the Japanese
themselves, but make this horror rise again from its ashes by incorporating
it in a love that will necessarily be special and "wonderful," one that will be
more credible than if it had occurred anywhere else in the world,
a place that death had not *preserved*.
—Marguerite Duras, "Synopsis" of *Hiroshima mon amour*

Here it comes, I said to myself, the end is coming; something is happening,
the end is beginning. I was seized by joy.
—Maurice Blanchot, *La folie du jour*

*All life*
*Is as a tale told to one in a dream*
*In tones never totally audible*
*Or understandable, and one wakes*
*Wishing to hear more, asking*
*For more, but one wakes to death, alas,*
*Yet one never*
*Pays any heed to that, the tale*
*Is still so magnificent in the telling*
—John Ashbery, "Litany"

A N APOCALYPTIC TONE. . . . It is a memory of what was and a
prophecy of what will be, and in postmodern philosophy and
literature it can be heard from within a texture of voices where one can

317

perceive faint overtones suggesting an ethical urgency releasing its grip on the self. For such overtones are merely very displaced residues of a holocaust, faint premonitions of an apocalypse. Of them, Jacques Derrida has remarked, "Il y a là cendre," meaning that the cinders and ashes mark our human condition as that which exists against the horizon of "une incinération," of a burn-all in which can be detected the echo of a distant screaming, an echo which has itself scattered like ash, has blown all too lightly on the wind.[1] For Derrida it represents a purity of the word, a clarity of voice, the transparency of a historical and ethical condition. "Il y a là cendre" suggests that given the terrifying greyness of ash, the substance of ash is, curiously, all too buoyant, light, flimsy, or blithe.

It is a breeziness that I will take up at some length with respect to John Ashbery's poetry, an ashen levity, perhaps, whose significance touches on an apocalyptic disclosure that, as in the writings of Jacques Derrida and Maurice Blanchot, is constituted as an unrepresentable "event" which has, nevertheless, left its impression or traces on language, a trace-work that is communicated as a weightless tone, a disembodied echoing. Yet, however insubstantial, it is still an ethical tone recalling what was and what will be; only, its resonance resists the kind of focusing that would result in a moral or ideological tone, the kind that is so movingly conveyed in a religious context by Elie Wiesel when he examines Cain and Abel as participants in the first genocide.[2] "La cendre n'est pas ici mais il y a là Cendre."[3] It is always already over there, *là*. "La cendre," that is to say, "là: cendre." Ashes, holocaust, apocalypse—it is always there where the subject is not, dis-placed, deported, pushed out of view. "Là: cendre . . ."—it is the napalm holocaust of Vietnam shown in the living room, as if always to say, "there . . . over there . . . not here . . . not now. . . ."

Through the tele-communication holocaust reveals its catastrophic displacements, its inaccessibility to a metaphysics of presence or presentation. The "shots" of the holocaust are, like postcards, "ni lisibles ni illisibles, ouvertes et radicalement inintelligibles," and, to this degree, they overlap with the reports of the rifle.[4] The catastrophic is accessible only in terms of those aftershocks whose sources are never clearly disclosed, never wholly "there," but concealed, muffled in undecidability. Yehuda Amichai, an Israeli poet, realizes the immensity of the unfocused resonances of an end when he writes,

> Everything here is busy with the task of remembering:
> the ruin remembers, the garden remembers,
> the cistern remembers its water and the memorial grove
> remembers on a marble plaque a distant holocaust.[5]

It is not that anything is really thinking, but that traces of a distant holocaust can be recollected or gathered together, however faintly, by one sensitive to the quietude of an apocalyptic tone, to its displacements in a Middle Eastern city, or from within a pastoral, idyllic setting. Perhaps the most unsettling example of this in America is the Vietnam Veterans' Memorial in Washington, D.C., for there again, the power of the dark marble, sloping, as it does, into the ground, is one of quiet recollections, of "letters," traces, echoes, at once anonymous and intimate, which murmur ashenly, "il y a là cendre." They are the ditched names, remembering a distant holocaust.

Maurice Blanchot writes in *Après coup* that the limpidness of narrative style is an "idylle" in prose, the seduction of horror. The quietude, the remembering, the collusions of idyllic restfulness make up "une belle forme qui ruinerait nécessairement l'horreur de toute vérité tragique" ("a beautiful form which necessarily will disturb the horror of all tragic truth"). One might recall, for example, a film like *Apocalypse Now*, with its inviting *mises en scène* achieving false verisimilitude, an approaching of the catastrophic which discloses the wish of being touched by it at a remove. "Hiroshima mon amour," one of Marguerite Duras's characters calls it. Echoing Duras, Blanchot has written:

Mais, avant toute distinction d'une forme et d'une contenu, d'un signifiant et d'un signifié, avant même le partage entre énonciation et énoncé, il y a le Dire inqualifiable, la gloire d'une "voix narrative" qui donne à entendre clairement, sans jamais pouvoir être obscurcie par l'opacité ou l'énigme ou l'horreur terrible de ce qui se communique.

[But before all distinctions between a form and a content, a signifier and a signified, before even the division between enunciation and enunciated, there is the unqualifiable Saying, the glory of a "narrative voice" which allows itself to be clearly heard, without ever being obscured by the opacity or the enigma or the terrible horror which it communicates.][6]

Citing Theodor Adorno, Blanchot says there cannot be narrative after Auschwitz, because there cannot be a narrative capable of witnessing or testifying to what has happened without recovering it as an aesthetic construct betraying the historical truth whose nausea escapes stylistic mastery. The ethics of telling is at every point contaminated by the idyllic, and Blanchot cites Styron's *Sophie's Choice* as evidence for this banal recovery of sentiment.[7] For Blanchot the writer must engage in an "unqualifiable Saying" whose clarity and truth are triumphant, a Saying encumbered by opacity, and by a withdrawal or retreat from narrative itself which marks the horror of the unspeakable. This is the unspeakability marking an unswearable relation between victim and persecutor, a fracturing of the obligatory within which the light of reason announces itself as at once most determinate and indeterminate, as a madness of day.

The invocation of cinders and ash, it is a Saying encumbered by the opacity of the residues of violence, a Saying which draws attention away from a ground-zero of catastrophe even while it talks about it. Blanchot is especially aware of how the metaphors by means of which an ethical relationship between people is described at once bring out the catastrophic while leading away from it, perhaps entirely eliding it. Derrida's choice of the phrase "Il y a là cendre" suggests, similarly, that even the residues of holocaust disclose a very disconcerting flimsiness or flakiness. For if the cinders and ashes become a metaphor standing in for the "object" of an ethical relationship, they implicate the victim in an evasion of objectivization, recollection, or presence. "Mais l'urne de langage est si fragile. Elle s'effrite et tu souffles aussitôt dans une poussière de mots qui sont la cendre même." ("But so fragile is the urn of language, it decomposes and suddenly you breathe a dust of words which is itself ashes.")[8] It is less a question of establishing an ethical system than an understanding that language itself (that is, the name, slangs, dialects, neologisms, tongues) is what remains of those who die, that the ashes are words. And this ashiness of language, whatever it is, remains unfocused, powdery, diffused, unsettled, suspended. It is perhaps less important, from this perspective, that an apocalyptic or holocaustic tone can be focused on the difference between the just and the unjust—though this is by no means forgotten or considered insignificant—but that it intuit the aftermaths and premonitions of catastrophe, and that it do so through the remains of the dead, that ash with which we write—ashes of words, tongues, phrases, tonalities, sensibilities. Perhaps more than words, it is the inflections, manners, habits, senses, feelings which accompany words or saturate them that allow us to remember those who have experienced the collapse, the end. Arnold Schönberg's *Survivor of Warsaw*, with its hobbled rhythms, its Hebrew melody, its murderous shouting, performs the tonalities of a terrible apocalypse, and it is in this performance that the ethical is disclosed in the sound-shapes of a liquidated culture.

Schönberg, of course, makes a direct address to the Warsaw ghetto's destruction, but in the work of figures like Blanchot and Derrida the approach is very much toward an extremely attenuated and oblique consideration of such events, for both writers suggest that the tonalities of the end are not simply localizable to particular historical events but, in fact, leak out from them into Western culture generally and thereby become very much like a constant background noise against which other kinds of tonalities are heard. John Ashbery is perhaps even more acute in his ability to hear these faint catastrophic tonalities, which in his poetry often blend in with more comic locutions. As we will notice much later, Ashbery, too, acknowledges the holocaust, though like Amichai, he senses it as something enormously quiescent and remote, even if in his work this quiescence is absorbed by the decor of suburban tameness rather than by the illusion of a peaceful and benign nature. More odd, perhaps, is that Ashbery's poetry is so understated and matter-of-fact that often the distinctions between gravity and levity are difficult to determine, as if in postmodern culture the difference were unlocatable in a vernacular tongue. The effect is that cataclysmic events sound commonplace and even silly, that, conversely, faintly whimsical occurrences sound menacing. Ashbery, like Blanchot, is suspended between consciousness whose tonalities are decentered, an "Echo divisé," as Derrida has remarked about such styles. It is through such tonal unfocusings that ethical considerations are raised, for such tonalities reveal the collision and collusion of attitudes as they are found in the tonalities of a discourse which belongs to no one and everyone, a discourse in which the ethical floats like so many echoes which refuse to take on a stable identity or point of view. And it is within this wash of ethical nuance, this tolerance for every conceivable attitude, that the question of victimization is posed. This is evident in one of Ashbery's greatest poems, "A Wave."

> Enough to know that I shall have answered for myself soon,
> Be led away for further questioning and later returned
> To the amazingly quiet room in which all my life has been spent.
> It comes and goes; the walls, like veils, are never the same,
> Yet the thirst remains identical, always to be entertained
> And marveled at. And it is finally we who break it off,
> Speed the departing guest, lest any question remain
> Unasked, and thereby unanswered. Please, it almost
> Seems to say, take me with you, I'm old enough.[9]

These lines occur at the close of "A Wave" and comprise but one of the vast number of sea changes—sudden scenic shifts—in the poem. Here the speaker is momentarily disclosed, as in some other parts of the poem, as a prisoner whose consciousness is suspended in a texture of attitudinizing and intoning through which a disaster is recollected. It is not so much that a victim is making ethical determinations or has merely gone mad, but that this consciousness is always already beyond good and evil and inhabits the waviness of unfocused ethical nuances, finds its home in an unsynthesized and multiple texture of verbal tones flattened only by an anonymous colloquialism which gives the English language an informal appearance, one that is, of course, posed and itself indicative of a society which permits an ethical latitude. It is this latitude which Ashbery reflects as a neutrality, as the beach of consciousness where the shocks of the waves can be felt:

> And the mind
> Is the beach on which the rocks pop up, just a neutral
> Support for them in their indignity.

The whole of "A Wave" could be read as this neutral plain or beach on which are felt the effects of catastrophe or indignity. The rocks, themselves inert, unsignifying, thingy, are washed up on a sandy neutrality, "A luminous backdrop to ever-repeated / Gestures, having no life of their own, but only echoing / The suspicions of their possessor." It is, at best, the effect left by an average, everyday scatter of thoughts. "And the issue of making sense becomes such a far-off one." For the issue is not focusing the scatter of thought into a point of view but of inhabiting far-less-decided "suspicions" which surround the indignity of the things about which nothing can be properly said, about those "unsayable" rocks thrown up on the beach.

The waves are "the reflexive play of our living and being lost / And then changed again," a reflexive play which makes up a passive intoning and attitudinizing that acquiesces to the voicing of its discomfort at the changes brought by the waves so rich in monotony. This is the same monotony of cinders and ashes, and it is of a similar flakelike structure, of a certain peeling off, a decomposition and scattering. It is perhaps not merely coincidental that the book jacket for "A Wave" presents the reproduction of Vija Celmins' "Untitled (Big Sea #1)," whose ashen and almost silvery waves manifest a luminous and yet flat hyper-reality whose monotony suggests collapse into mere greyness, an agoraphobia of dullness. As if to say, with Ashbery, "No, the / Divine tolerance we seem to feel is actually in short supply," or "All those days had a dumb clarity."

If there is an "apocalyptic tone" in works like "A Wave," it is the reflexive play of tonal saturations as they mediate sudden changes of thought, an attitudinizing which makes up suspicions concerning the end, an end which is itself not something and does not occur at some time but an end whose violence consciousness always already lives through as an unfocused sensitivity that marks the horizon of a day-to-day living with others. It is an ethical attitudinizing through which our relation to others is derived from the casualness of speech rather than from direct encounter, as if it were the faint tonalities embedded within language that determined our inconsistent and undecidable relationship with others. It is this dictation by language itself which Derrida has called *télé-pathie*, a dictation concerning the end. "L'apocalypse a lieu au moment où j'écris ceci." [10] That is to say, expression is relayed through the writer by means of language and its intonations of the end, its wish and dream of apocalypse, the "il y a là cendre."

Such "writing" is not the effect of those firm Sartrian supports, self and other, addresser and addressee, but is far more unlocalized, dissipated, open, scattered. In a Sartrian context language is expressed by someone in order to establish the "about to become myself," an expe-

rience present to hand of a me in relation to an other through which
the two recognize one another as a "being-with." Even if the self and
other are by no means reified consciousness—not fully self-given or
present—they are nevertheless focused as ethical agencies with the
capacity to negate and affirm one another and in so doing are capable
of establishing well-defined value structures. Indeed, in *L'Etre et le
Néant* terms such as "guilt," "freedom," "enslavement," "alienation,"
and "admiration" are thematic markers delimiting what are essentially
ethical confrontations between self and other.

In Derrida's *La carte postale* it is precisely the identity and possibility
of an addresser and addressee which is called into question. "Au nom
de quoi, au nom de qui publier, divulguer. . . ?" [11] In whose name,
publish, divulge, in the name of what? Unlike Sartre, who has absolutely no doubt about the stability of his fictional Pierre in *L'Etre et le
Néant*, Derrida at every point questions the determinations of the
name, the univocity of its properness, the consistency of its address
to a readerly horizon which is itself awash in a wear and tear of linguistic tolerance inhibiting the proper reception of the proper name.
"En vue de qui, auprès de qui accepter de divulguer?" [12] That is, with
whom can one allow oneself to tell all? But more appropriately, is it
possible to conceive of an addressee for whom one can indeed write,
one who is not, in any case, oneself? And if one receives one's own
postcards, is the recipient at one with the sender? Is it a "me" or "self"
who is the stable ground for the delimitation of what the postcard
says? Derrida suggests that even a closed circuit in which cards are
sent to oneself is no insurance against the divisibility of the writer and
the name, for the arrival of the letter always discloses something else
of the writer's destiny, an event in which the written says something
else about the name which has preceded its coming and which is not
easily recoverable by even a reader who has authored the message.
But what is this something else the message says? It is, among other
things, the tone the message accrues in its arrival or coming, the resonance it takes on after having passed through the mail, through its
*being sent*, its *transmission*.

> dès qu'il y a, il y a différance . . . et il y a agencement postal, relais, re-
> tard, anticipation, destination, dispositif télécommunicant, possibilité et

donc nécessité fatale de détournement, etc. Il y a strophe (il y a strophe en tous sens, apostrophe et catastrophe, adresse à tourner, l'adresse [toujours vers toi, mon amour], et ma carte postale ce sont des strophes).

[as soon as there is, there is difference . . . and there is the postal system, relay, slow down, anticipation, destination, telecommunicative device, the possibility and hence fatal necessity of mis-routing. There is a strophe (strophe in all senses, apostrophe and catastrophe, the directing of an address [always toward you, my love], and my postcard: these are of strophes).] [13]

As soon as one can assert the arrival or thereness of the postcard one has undecidability or *différance*. There is rather a complex play with the notion of turning words like "détournement," "à tourner," and "strophe" which suggest that the relationship between addresser and addressee is subordinated to the inclinations or directions established through the process of a message's transmission, its sending. The ancient Greek term, "strophe," itself means literally to turn, and it is here that from within the inclination of a routed message strophe takes on apostrophic or catastrophic inclinations. Addresser and addressee are but the effects of such erratic turnings and routings, effects of the inclinations of messages en route. Part of Derrida's interest in talking at length about the postal network is that through it the existential assumptions about dialogue between selves and others are put into question by the medium of something as trivial as a postcard whose routings alter the manner in which the messages are to be taken, affect the tone of the strophe, a tone made up of the inclinations or turns which the text achieves by the directions afforded it by the postal service, its physical journey through the mail, the telegraph, or, in another sense, over the telephone lines. Such a transmission of tone, what is it but the condition of any text's receptivity?

Such receptivity is perhaps itself the major topic of many of Ashbery's poems. For example, in "I Might Have Seen It," a poem from the collection *As We Know*, Ashbery writes,

> The person who makes a long-distance phone call
> Is talking into the open receiver at the other end
> The mysterious discourse also emerges as pointed
> In his ear there are no people in the room listening

This poem forecloses the relationship of an addresser/addressee while, on the other hand, heightening the sense of a mysterious discourse characterized as pointed, emergent, distant, and audible in the openness of the receiver at "the other end." But this end, is it not always already the final end, too?

> As the curtain bells out majestically in front of the starlight
> to whisper the words This has already happened
> And the footfalls on the stair turn out to be real
> Those of your neighbor I mean the one who moved away[14]

Abruptly the poem ends, like a conversation that has been "hung up" at the "other end." The starlight, whispering, the recognition "This has already happened," all suggest the mood of an apotheosis reinforced by the thought of a neighbor who has moved away (died?). Too, the lines run on like phone conversation lines, though here they are not framed by dialogue, only dissipated through the open receiver at the other end. Apostrophe and catastrophe modulated in an ordinary long-distance call.

This living through of the end in both Derrida and Ashbery is what in Maurice Blanchot's "L'Apocalypse deçoit" becomes as that day-to-day awareness marking the withdrawal of the end.[15] For Blanchot notes that as a community with the capacity to annihilate all living things we always already live beyond the horizon of mortality, a living beyond which eludes closure, ending, finality. The end is not something to come but something whose realized potential we have philosophically passed through, an apocalyptic moment which postmodern consciousness survives as a "turning" between apostrophe and catastrophe. Perhaps for Derrida "il y a strophe" means "il y a là cendre." For it is a living through to the end of a rationalism concerning the ground of addresser and addressee, a living through which gives way linguistically to tonal resonances whose saturations play havoc with traditional values or syntaxes, like voices talking through an open receiver.

Indeed, it is through an apocalyptic tone that values are not merely revalorized but scandalously inhabited by delicate attitudinal transgressions. Ashbery demonstrates the scandal within informal English, a suburban and decorous scandal. And in Derrida and Blanchot the scandal is reflected in the ambiguity of resonances from a slightly more academic clime. Still, all these writers are sensitive to the conduit of a neutral voice which has always already passed through the catastrophe to the hitherside of the end, "Those of your neighbor I mean the one who moved away." This scandal, buoyant like ash, is also heard in Blanchot's *La folie du jour*.

> Peu après, la folie du monde se déchaîna. Je fus mis au mur comme beaucoup d'autres. Pourquoi? Pour rien. Les fusils ne partirent pas. Je me dis: Dieu, que fais-tu? Je cessai alors d'être insensé. Le monde hésita, puis reprit son équilibre.

> [Shortly afterward, the madness of the world broke out. I was made to stand against the wall like many others. Why? For no reason. The guns did not go off. I said to myself, God, what are you doing? At that point I stopped being insane. The world hesitated, then regained its equilibrium.][16]

The scandal of the text is that the voice or voices who speak in *La folie du jour* are unable to decide ethically the difference between good and evil, the just and the unjust. For all values are blended in a collaboration or collusion of ethical differences which accompany one through the end and surface in a series of calm or peaceful moments about which attitudes, feelings, memories, scenes are recollected without being able to coalesce. "Un récit? Non, pas de récit, plus jamais." Given this going beyond of the end, one has also gone beyond narrative, story, telling. One has gone beyond the construction of a text that can present the ethical in the form of a tale. And this, it seems to me, is what most characterizes the tonality of apocalypse, that it is a narrative beyond narrative, a poetry beyond poetry. And it is for this reason that its moral saturations will be somewhat disturbing in their deliberate calm and, as I will show, their strategic levity. For the cinders and ashes blow lightly on the wind and their scription is similarly buoyant, perhaps to the point of a profoundly unethical laughter, or a comedy beyond comedy, the frivolity of words, the "il y a là cendre," the "il y a strophe."

ONE DOES NOT have to read far into John Ashbery's poetry to recognize that a system is usually collapsing if not always already disarticulated.

And Ashbery himself is quite obliging in discussing this feature of his work. At one point in *Three Poems* he admits:

> The system was breaking down. The one who had wandered alone past too many happenings and events began to feel, backing up along the primal vein that led to his center, the beginning of a hiccup that would, if left to gather, explode the center to the extremities of life, the suburbs through which one makes one's way to where the country is.[17]

Although addressing a conceptual system, Ashbery analogically refers us inside of what appears to be an urban space as well as a living body, and it is, oddly enough, the levity of a hiccup which threatens to annihilate the entire system, as if an occurrence in one analogical register bore upon the others. In Ashbery, one can only suppose, analogues somehow do not metaphorically refer to one another but inhabit each other and hybridize. But rather than describe this peculiar use of catachresis at length, I will focus merely upon the hiccup itself, since this little explosion or outburst, at least in the very beginning, has an apocalyptic tone, a ring that can be heard yet once more in the syllables of Jacques Derrida's *Glas*.

In *Glas* the *gl* is an example of a syllable neither voiced entirely nor voiceless either. Derrida says of the *gl* that it is

> une voix sans voix étouffant un sanglot ou un caillot de lait dans la gorge, le rire chatouillé ou le vomi glaireux d'un bébé glouton, le vol impérial d'un rapace qui fond d'un coup sur votre nuque, le nom gluant, glacé, pissant froid d'un impassible philosophe teuton, au bégaiement notoire, tantôt liquide et tantôt gutturo-tétanique, un goître enflé ou roucoulant, tout ce qui cloche dans le conduit ou dans la fosse tympanique, le crachat ou l'emplâtre sur le voile du palais, l'orgasme de la glotte ou de la luette, la glu clitoridienne, le cloaque de l'avortement, le hoquet de sperme, l'hiatus rythmé. . . .

> [a voiceless voice stifling a sob or a clot of milk in the throat, the aroused laughter, or the vomit filled with the phlegm of a ravenous baby, the imperial theft of a rapacious person who lands a blow on the nape of your neck, the name sticking, frozen, the cold pissing of an impassive teuton philosopher, of a notorious stammering, sometimes liquid and sometimes guttural-tetanic, a swollen or gurgling goiter, everything that clogs

in the eustachian tubes or the tympanic pit, the spit or scum on the velum, the orgasm of the glottis or of the uvula, the clitorian glue, the cloaca of abortion, the spurts of sperm, the rhythmic hiatus. . . .][18]

*Gl*, the occasion for a Rabelaisian catalogue which quickly dispossesses itself of humor, the sticking in the throat of a sound, the death rattle, the last gurgling noises of the dying man who bleeds, vomits, spits, and tries to speak at the same time, the sounds of a baby choking on its mother's milk, a baby who vomits on the breast, but too of the choked-up lover or the *chanteuse.* This sound, this almost inaudible murmuring, is carried not on the breath but on or in the body's fluids and becomes the channel or current for the *gl*, that sticky syllable which makes us laugh even while a protagonist drowns to death between glugs. The *gl* is the result of a spasm, like laughter, maybe, or like that of the body's response to asphyxiation, as in a gas chamber. It is a syllable whose death knell is spasmatic, like the urination of an icy person, perhaps a German who at one time bothered to piss against the cattle cars as people were hauled out to extermination sites during World War II. The *gl*, a peculiar reminder or remainder of genocide, haunts *Glas* with inappropriate and yet unrelieved hilarity, as if the sound itself were not simply a curse, intended and executed, but a far more subtle kind of humiliation on the order of a bodily symptom.

It is in terms of this *gl* that we must bear witness to the approach of an apocalyptic tone, a spasm of the ethical which is mundane, automatic, inevitable, and often hardly noticed, like a hoquet or hiccup. But can we hear it? Can we sense this death knell, this *gl* directed at our being and which passes beyond our ability to separate mind from body, speech from biology, *eros* and *thanatos?* This knell which we cannot properly mourn?

In both *Glas* and *Three Poems* we ought to hear the spasm of the text and the breaking down of the system, what in both Derrida and Ashbery appear as textual fractures, explosions, catastrophes.

Ce que je cherche à écrire—gl—ce n'est pas une structure quelconque, un système du signifiant ou du signifié, une thèse ou un roman, un poème, une loi, un désir ou une machine, c'est ce qui passe, plus ou moins bien, par la stricture rythmée d'un anneau.

[That which I try to write—gl—is not any kind of structure, a system of signifier and signified, a thesis or a novel, a poem, a law, a desire or a machine: it is that which passes more or less through the rhythmic stricture of a ring or sphincter.][19]

The spasm neutralizes, makes impossible any text which would accede to be something particular, nullifies the attempt to write within a particular genre or type of writing. It is the corporeality and the premeditated rhythms and outbursts which impede the production of a classical or systematic text, an outburst which produces its own kind of systematic discourse, its own kind of analytic. If we see this in Derrida and Ashbery, we have seen it before: in Milton's *Lycidas*, with its curious outbursts or interruptions, or in George Herbert's quiet, muffled "ejaculations." Derrida's *Glas*, of course, takes the notion of spiritual outburst rather far, but not without good reason. Derrida calls this notion "le spasme saccadancé d'une éructojaculation, le clapet syncopé de la langue et des lèvres" ("the jerked spasm of a belched ejaculation, the syncopated clap of tongue and lips").[20] Here the tolling of the bell is grafted onto metaphors of the body, and here too a curious hybrid is the result. Derrida's term for it is "invagination." What is relevant for us, however, is not so much this type of condensation or catachresis but the sense of catastrophe, violence, or cataclysm which is aroused in the reader.

Ashbery's poems, of course, have a flat and insouciant tone, something inherited from Frank O'Hara but which owes considerable debt to the weightlessness of American conversational style, what amounts to an evasiveness masked by a casual "what me worry?" delivery. It is this false neutrality, this mastery of the insincere that Ashbery does not mock so much but exploits for the purposes of producing a limpid zero-degree of writing which he calls a "calm world." Yet, in this even-tempered style whose voice does not, perhaps cannot rise, there is an involuntary disquietude or spasmatic outburst like the beginning of a hiccup. It is

a jagged kind of mood that comes at the end of the day, lifting life into the truth of real pain for a few moments before subsiding in the usual irregular way, as things do. These were as much there as anything, things to be fumbled with, cringed before: dry churrings of no timbre, hysterical staccato passages that one cannot master or turn away from. These things led into life. Now they are gone but it remains, calm, lucid, but weightless, drifting above everything and everybody like the light in the sky, no more to be surmised, only remembered as so many things that remain at equal distances from us are remembered. The light drinks the dark and sinks down, not on top of us as we had expected but far, far from us in some other, unrelated sphere. This was not even the life that was going to happen to us.[21]

In such passages the remoteness of the effect becomes an index of how ubiquitous and massive is the catastrophe which goes unnamed but into whose ambit we are, as Ashbery says, "slurped up." The jagged mood is not produced so much as sustained, and the real pain subsides and is irregular. It is "as much there as anything." What we must consider above all is the distance or farness which allows the voice to say, "This was not even the life that was going to happen to us." As if experience and discourse were somehow incommunicable.

In *La folie du jour* by Maurice Blanchot, the narrator or voice is at once embodied and disembodied.

Parfois, je me disais: "C'est la mort; malgré tout, cela en vaut la peine, c'est impressionnant." Mais souvent je mourais sans rien dire. A la longue, je fus convaincu que je voyais face à face la folie du jour; telle était la vérité: la lumière devenait folle, la clarté avait perdu tout bon sens; elle m'assaillait déraisonnablement, sans règle, sans but.

[At times I said to myself: "This is death. In spite of everything, it's really worth it, it's impressive." But often I lay dying without saying anything. In the end, I grew convinced that I was face to face with the madness of the day. That was the truth: the light was going mad, the brightness had lost all reason: it assailed me irrationally, without control, without purpose.][22]

Not unlike Ashbery's voices, his "us" which speaks in the passages from the *Three Poems*, the voice in *La folie du jour* is trying to determine what life might be involved with it; but for the moment there is only the sense of distance, and of lights and darks. If in Ashbery the light drinks the dark and sinks down, and if that light participates in an unrelated sphere, in Blanchot's *récit* the light is itself the madness of day, an unrelatedness into whose ambience the voice is uncontrollably caught up.

There is not simply a stream of consciousness at work in these texts but spasmatic—or as Ashbery says, irregular—movements, words, and expressions which disappear and protrude in a limpidity neither prose nor poetry, voice nor writing. The hysterical staccato passages and direct encounters in Ashbery are muffled in the eerie calm of mind and text, the sedation of words. The outbursts and spasms lead into life only to be dissipated there, leaving in their wake a calm, drifting, and genreless writing which turns into light, distance, farness, difference, otherness. The subject or cogito is not so much a center or locus where identifications are resolved or counterpointed but a pervasive field or saturation of vocal and attitudinal densities conveyed through a calm or limpid style. One might say that through the tone of the writing the subject is evacuated or dissipated, the voice estranged or made remote to itself. In this way the voice achieves a passivity at the same time that it asserts itself most clearly and lucidly in what Blanchot has called the madness of the day.

What has happened? The "I" has achieved what Emmanuel Levinas calls a difficult liberty, a break in participation with the life-world as world. We are on the brink of infinitude, since in the negativity of nonparticipation the difference between selfhood and otherness is given up, and intelligibility too gives way to a certain madness or disequilibration. Whatever holds the life-world together is by means of a difficult freedom unhinged and the subject vertiginously swept into an abysm or catastrophe of relations where no word serves to reobjectify or systematize what has been unloosened. This is the moment which Levinas terms the ethical. It is the silent moment, though words can be uttered there, since the word stops before that which is radically other, prostrating itself before the *Autrui*. It is at this passive moment, this articulated silence, that the ethical manifests itself and gives shelter to meaning. "To have meaning," Levinas writes, "is to be situated relative to an absolute, that is, to come from that alterity that is not absorbed in its being perceived. Such an alterity is possible only as a miraculous abundance, an inexhaustible surplus of attention arising in the ever recommenced effort of language to clarify its own manifestation."[23] It is the voice or tone which addresses the absolute from this liberated aspect, this catastrophic horizon which Derrida calls the apocalyptic. Its tone is part of a plural which cannot be unified or centered or institutionalized, however much postmodernism and deconstruction will operate as recuperative code words to the vulgar for such purposes. Moreover, the apocalyptic tone is irregular, wavering, jagged, spasmatic, like the burst of a *gl* or the beginning of a hiccup.

In "D'un ton apocalyptique adopté naguère en philosophie," Derrida writes:

Si de façon très insuffisante et à peine préliminaire, j'attire votre attention sur l'envoi narratif, l'entrelacement des voix et des envois dans l'écriture dictée ou adressée, c'est que dans l'hypothèse ou le programme d'une démystification intraitable du ton apocalyptique, dans le style des Lumières ou d'une *Aufklärung* XX^e siècle, et si on voulait démasquer les ruses, pièges, roueries, séductions, machines de guerre et de plaisir, bref tous les intérêts du ton apocalyptique aujourd'hui, il faudrait sans doute être très attentif à cette démultiplication différentielle des voix et des tons qui les divise peut-être au-delà d'une pluralité distincte et calculable. On ne sait pas (car ce n'est plus de l'ordre du savoir) à qui revient l'envoi apocalyptique, il saute d'un lieu d'émission à l'autre (et un lieu est toujours déterminé *à partir* de l'émission présumée), il va d'une destination, d'un nom et d'un ton à l'autre, il renvoie toujours au nom et au ton de l'autre qui est là mais comme avant été là et devant encore venir, n'étant plus ou pas encore là dans le présent du récit. Et il n'est pas assuré que l'homme soit le central de ces lignes téléphoniques ou le terminal de cet ordinateur sans fin.

[If, in a very insufficient and only just preliminary way, I draw your attention to the narrative sending, the interlacing of voices and envois in the dictated or addressed writing, I do so because great attention no doubt would have to be given this differential reduction or gearing down of voices and tones that perhaps divides them beyond a distinct and calculable plurality—at least in the hypothesis or the program of an intractable demystification of the apocalyptic tone, in the style of the *Lumières* or of an *Aufklärung* of the twentieth century, and if we wanted to unmask the ruses, traps, trickeries, seductions, the engines of war and pleasure,

in short, all the interests of the apocalyptic tone today. We do not know
(for it is no longer of the order of knowing) to whom the apocalyptic dispatch returns; it leaps from one place of emission to the other (and a
place is always determined *starting from* the presumed emission); it goes
from one destination, one name, and one tone to the other; it always refers to the name and to the tone of the other that is there but as having
been there and before yet coming, no longer being or not yet there in the
present of the *récit*. And there is no certainty that man is the exchange
(middle) of these telephone lines or the terminal of this computer without end.][24]

The apocalyptic tone comes unannounced, out of nowhere or, more
accurately, that somewhere unmoored from sender and receiver. In
this context the apocalyptic tone can be considered not only to be
spasmatic, like the *gl*, but extremely violent, sudden, unassimilable.
Hence its difficult liberty, that break in participation with the life-
world that concerns Levinas. It is the infinitude or negativity of nonparticipation, that difference between self and other, I and you. It is
also, to recall Levinas, the ethical moment and precisely because it
concerns a violent emission whose dispatch escapes our ability to
comprehend it in terms of day-to-day communication in whose speech
acts we often invest an uncritical trust.

Ashbery reflects these ideas on tone with admirable effortlessness,
or at least stylistic relaxation, when he writes in *Three Poems*:

> Such particulars you mouthed, all leading back into the underlying ques-
> tion: was it you? Do these things between people partake of themselves,
> or are they a subtler kind of translucent matter carrying each to a com-
> promise distance painfully outside the rings of authority? For we never
> knew, never knew what joined us together. Perhaps only a congealing of
> closeness, deserving of no special notice.[25]

Certainly there is an indeterminateness about the relationship of a self
and an other, but it is not so much the vagueness of the attachment as
the tone itself which is significant. For this tone (the writing's pose,
rhetorical staging, manner of informality, precision, and so on) quietly
establishes through the interaction of small, almost imperceptible
shocks, a difficult liberty, one that articulates the relationship to alterity uncovered in the familiar and the intimate. Here, as in Derrida,

the voice disembodies itself, recovers itself as always already disembodied, uninvested in a specific sender or a specific receiver. "Was it you?" Ashbery asks. Did "you" say these "particulars"? And more ambivalently, "Do these things between people partake of themselves," that is, the people themselves or the things themselves, so hard to tell which? Or are we subjected to something subtler, something "outside the rings of authority," something which establishes a "compromise distance"? "For we never knew, never knew what joined us together." We never can know, because the what is not recoverable as someone's speech or intention or affection, because the what is not recuperable as anything but Ashbery's curious tone which evades sources and destinations, a tone of what Derrida above calls ruses, traps, trickeries, seductions, the engines of war and pleasure, or "all the interests of the apocalyptic tone today." Like Derrida, Ashbery admits that we cannot know to whom the *envoi* returns. Rather, it just seems to leap and refers to the tone of the other "that is there but as having been there and before yet coming, no longer being or not yet there in the present of the *récit*," as Derrida says above.

What is of most importance, perhaps, is that in Ashbery, as in Levinas and Derrida, the tone does address apocalypse and within an ethical context. However, as has been stressed, we are not talking about the kind of apocalyptic address which moralizes, but of apocalypse we now can see in its Levinasian ethical perspective. "For the ethical relationship which subtends discourse," Levinas writes, "is not a species of consciousness whose ray emanates from the I; it puts the I in question. This putting in question emanates from the other." This discourse, or apocalyptic tone, emanates *as* language, and "language," Levinas insists, "is perhaps to be defined as the very power to break the continuity of being or of history."[26] In Levinas, Blanchot, Derrida, and Ashbery this thought is not only considered but is, as I have suggested, thematized in terms of holocaust.

In *Three Poems* Ashbery writes:

There was however, a residue, a kind of fiction that developed parallel to the classic truths of daily life (as it was in that heroic but commonplace age) as they unfolded with the foreseeable majesty of a holocaust, an unfrightening one, and went unrecognized, drawing force and grandeur from this like the illegitimate offspring of a king. It is this "other tradition" which we propose to explore. The facts of history have been too well rehearsed (I'm speaking needless to say not of written history but the oral kind that goes on in you without your having to do anything about it) to require further elucidation here.

Later, Ashbery adds, "From the outset it was apparent that someone had played a colossal trick on something."[27] There are two holocausts of which Ashbery speaks: the one is foreseeable, recognizable, plain, and political; the other is fantastic, imagined, visceral, but also extremely remote, like something hard to remember. The historical is a kind of inaccessible reality or otherness which we know but cannot conceive outside of objectified facts which, like things, resist penetration. The "other tradition" is what is achieved by a difficult liberty, what goes on inside one without one's having to do anything about it. The latter, not unlike the hiccup, threatens the coherence of the system. Moreover, like the oral tradition or voice in Blanchot's texts, the "other tradition" in Ashbery does not recoil at the foreseeable majesty of a holocaust: for with the recognition of a difficult freedom an indifferent tone emerges, one that is unfrightened. The catastrophe is neutralized, sopped up, forgotten, muffled, understated. "It was apparent that someone had played a colossal trick on something," the voice says about the vanishing of millions of people. Here catastrophe inclines to what Blanchot terms the *passé passif*, an apocalyptic passivity which makes up the banality of historical process, the calm, regular movements of industrial genocide.

Blanchot speaks of this in terms of the disaster of writing and comments on the *passé passif* in this way:

> Comment avoir rapport avec le *passé passif*, rapport qui lui-même ne saurait se présenter dans la lumière d'une conscience (ni s'absenter de l'obscurité d'une inconscience)?
>
> [How can one have a relation with the *passé passif*, a relation which itself cannot present itself in the light of consciousness (nor absent itself from the obscurity of an unconscious)?][28]

The *passé passif* is that which can neither be remembered or presented as such, nor forgotten completely and absented. It is what Blanchot terms the *limitrophe*, the threshold that one obscurely experiences as a distant happening which is painfully intimate. It is this *passé passif* which the writer struggles to bring forward out of the dark into the hyper-luminosity of day, the forum of consciousness, and yet it is a bringing forth which is by definition impossible. It slurps up, Ashbery says. For Blanchot the holocaust is precisely the light which cannot be rescued from the shadow of a certain existential and phenomenological obscurity; it is the disaster in the midst of which the subject is cast as a voice among a chorus of voices, a tone which slips in through writing, hence the *écriture du désastre.*

Both Blanchot and Derrida recognize that the *envoi* of the apocalyptic tone exceeds naming, a point Ashbery implicitly shares when he talks about the colossal trick "someone" played on "something." In *L'écriture du désastre,* Blanchot considers this in the following manner:

> *Le nom inconnu, hors nomination:*
>
> *L'holocauste, événement* absolu *de l'histoire, historiquement daté, cette toute-brûlure où toute l'histoire s'est embrasée, où le mouvement du Sens s'est abîmé, où le don, sans pardon, sans consentement, s'est ruiné sans* donner *lieu à rien qui puisse s'affirmer, se nier, don de la passivité même, don de ce qui ne peut se donner. Comment le garder, fût-ce dans la pensée, comment faire de la pensée ce qui garderait l'holocauste où tout s'est perdu, y compris la pensée gardienne?*
>
> *Dans l'intensité mortelle, le silence fuyant du cri innombrable.*
>
> [*The unknown name, beyond nomination:*
>
> *The holocaust,* absolute *event of history, historically dated, this burn-all where all history was itself set ablaze or clarified, in which the movement of meaning was swallowed up, where the gift or offering, without knowing pardon or consent is destroyed without* giving *place to anything which could affirm itself, annihilate itself, the offering of that very passivity, offering of that which cannot be offered. How can it be preserved even by thought? How can thought be made the preserver of the holocaust where all was lost, including a guardian thought?*
>
> *In mortal intensity, the fleeing silence of an innumerable cry.*][29]

To Blanchot, the holocaust is an absolute event of history, an otherness, an unnamable event which in itself recognizes its own estrangement by forcing a denial of the name (genealogy, race, paternity) by means of a reinscription, the tattooing of numbers on arms: *l'écriture du désastre.* This expression, this inscription of otherness, breaks the continuity of being and history, and it is here that the ethical projects itself, that a curious genealogy of morals reveals itself in the midst of cataclysm. Yet, if the ethical intrudes upon its own veiling, it maintains its withdrawal in terms of the radicality of a break whose facticity eludes thought, and whose morality is eclipsed by the innumerable, the unnamable, the unspeakable, the unrecuperable. Hence "the movement of meaning is swallowed up," even if its trace still makes itself known to us.

Derrida refers to holocaust and the disaster of writing in *La carte postale* when he notes:

Le symbole? un grand incendie holocaustique, un brûle-tout enfin où nous jetterions, avec toute notre mémoire, nos noms, les lettres, les photos, les petits objects, les clés, les fétiches, etc. Et s'il n'en reste rien. . . .

[The symbol? a great holocaustic fire, a burn-all finally into which we will be thrown, with all our memory, our names, letters, photos, small objects, keys, fetishes, etc. And if nothing remains of it. . . .][30]

Elsewhere he writes,

                          Depuis toujours je sais
que nous sommes perdus, et que de ce désastre très initial
une distance infinie s'est ouverte
                     cette catastrophe, tout près du commencement,
ce renversement que je n'arrive pas encore à penser fut la
condition de tout, n'est-ce pas, la nôtre, notre condition même,
la condition de tout ce qui nous fut donné ou que nous nous soyons
l'un à l'autre destiné, promis, donné, prêté, je ne sais plus
            nous nous sommes perdu—l'un l'autre
tu m'entends?

                     [I have always known that we are lost,
and that this very initial disaster opens an infinite distance
                this catastrophe, so near the beginning,
this turning upon itself which I cannot contemplate anymore may have
been the condition of everything, is it not so?, of us, of even our
condition, the condition of everything in which we may have been
given over or in which we are destined, promised, handed over to,
lent, I don't know what more

we are lost—the one in the other
you understand?][31]

Ah shucks, Ashbery might reply. "The great careers are like that: a slow burst that narrows to a final release, pointed but not acute, a life of suffering redeemed and annihilated at the end, and for what? For a casual moment of knowing that is here one minute and gone the next, almost before you were aware of it?"[32] In *Three Poems* the shock of collapse is over; in fact, Ashbery is most at home with the apocalyptic tone, having domesticated it, or cultivated it in his own backyard among the rutabagas. He too realizes that the end has always already happened. Like any good psychologist or "crazyologist" (an apt bop term), the poet must recognize that the problem with people is that they fear the very thing that has already occurred to them: the collapse is past history, a trivial or banal occurrence which the subject still fears, like bill collectors after the bankruptcy. In *Three Poems* the voice comes from on high, *le très haut*. It is flat and absolute, all-knowing, yet obnoxiously cute and abrasive. It is what Derrida might call synthesized. It is an irregular and sometimes tenuous tone which admits that "in the end it falls apart, falls to the ground and sinks in."[33] That is, something is swallowed up, imperceptibly, automatically almost. It is in this sense that Ashbery writes in "Litany" a remark touching so apocalyptically on the *passé passif*, this engulfing passivity.

> Yet somehow it doesn't bode well that
> In your sophistication you choose to disregard
> What is so heavy with potential tragic consequences
> Hanging above you like a storm cloud
> And cannot know otherwise, even by diving
> Into the shallow stream of your innocence
> And wish not to hear news of
> What brings the world together and sets fire to it.[34]

## NOTES

1. Jacques Derrida, "Feu la cendre," *Anima*, no. 5 (1985).
2. Elie Wiesel, *Messengers of God* (New York: Summit, 1976).
3. Derrida, "Feu le cendre," p. 51.

4. Jacques Derrida, *La carte postale* (Paris: Flammarion, 1980), p. 88.

5. Yehuda Amichai, *Great Tranquility* (New York: Harper & Row, 1983), p. 21.

6. Maurice Blanchot, *Après coup* (Paris: Minuit, 1983), pp. 97, 98.

7. Ibid., p. 98.

8. Derrida, "Feu la cendre," p. 75.

9. John Ashbery, *A Wave* (New York: Viking, 1984), p. 89.

10. Jacques Derrida, "Télépathie," *Confrontation*, no. 10 (1983): 202.

11. Derrida, *La carte postale*, p. 89.

12. Ibid., p. 89.

13. Ibid., p. 74.

14. John Ashbery, *As We Know* (New York: Penguin, 1979), p. 83.

15. Maurice Blanchot, *L'Amitié* (Paris: Gallimard, 1971).

16. Maurice Blanchot, *La folie du jour*. Translated by Lydia Davis as *The Madness of the Day* (Barrytown, N.Y.: Station Hill, 1981), pp. 20, 6.

17. John Ashbery, *Three Poems* (New York: Penguin, 1972), p. 53.

18. Jacques Derrida, *Glas* (Paris: Galilée, 1974), pp. 137b–138b.

19. Ibid., p. 125b.

20. Ibid., p. 138b.

21. Ashbery, *Three Poems*, p. 54.

22. Blanchot, *La folie du jour*, pp. 25, 11.

23. Emmanuel Levinas, *Totality and Infinity*, trans. Alphonso Lingis (Pittsburg: Duquesne University Press, 1969), p. 97.

24. Jacques Derrida, "D'un ton apocalyptique adopté naguère en philosophie," *Les fins de l'homme* (Paris: Galilée, 1981), p. 470. Translation, John P. Leavey, "Of an apocalyptic tone recently adopted in philosophy," *Semeia, An Experimental Journal for Biblical Criticism*, no. 23 (1982): 87.

25. Ashbery, *Three Poems*, p. 10.

26. Levinas, *Totality and Infinity*, p. 195.

27. Ashbery, *Three Poems*, pp. 55–56.

28. Maurice Blanchot, *L'écriture du désastre* (Paris: Gallimard, 1980), p. 51.

29. Ibid.; see *The Writing of the Disaster*, trans. Ann Smock (Lincoln: University of Nebraska Press, 1986), p. 47. I have adapted Ann Smock's translation of this very difficult passage, whose resonances are perhaps impossible to capture in English. "Cri innombrable" strongly suggests "cri innomable" (the unnamable cry). Also, Blanchot's use of "le don" is difficult to render because it alludes to Heideggerian postulations of the "gift" as well as to anthropological meanings in which a "gift" is very much a sacrificial offering. I have chosen the term "offering" because of the sacrificial resonances, but also because an offering is a proffering of something, or, to put it another way, an "appeal." We could approximate Blanchot's passage by pointing out to

English-speaking readers that a word like "appeal" provides the kind of ambiguity Blanchot prefers. For example, one might ask, "What is the *appeal* of the holocaust?" To what does it *appeal*, both in the sense of protesting to some-one and in the sense of being attractive to someone? And how does this *appeal* at once disclose and foreclose meaning, understanding, comprehension? Blanchot himself takes up this line of questioning in *Après coup* (Paris: Minuit, 1983), pp. 85–100.

30. Derrida, *La carte postale*, p. 46.
31. Ibid., pp. 23–24.
32. Ashbery, *Three Poems*, p. 69.
33. Ibid., p. 15.
34. Ashbery, *As We Know*, p. 41b.

# Notes on Contributors

CLAUDIA BRODSKY is assistant professor of comparative literature at Princeton. Her book *The Imposition of Form: Narrative Representation and Knowledge* will be published by Princeton University Press in 1987. She has published articles on Kant, Faulkner, Goethe, Richardson, and narrative theory.

KEVIN L. COPE is assistant professor of English at Louisiana State University. He recently completed a book on the philosophical foundations of judgment in the Enlightenment and has published articles on Restoration and eighteenth-century literature. He is working on a book about the institution of genre.

STANLEY CORNGOLD is professor of German and comparative literature at Princeton. *The Fate of the Self: German Writers and French Critics* appeared in 1986 and *Franz Kafka: The Necessity of Form* is forthcoming. He is currently at work on the topic of wit, judgment, and imagination in eighteenth-century German literature.

DEBORAH ESCH is Andrew W. Mellon Assistant Professor of English at Princeton. She is author of *The Senses of the Past: The Rhetoric of Temporality in Henry James,* and co-editor and co-translator of two volumes of essays by Jacques Derrida. She has also published articles on Kant, Kleist, Wordsworth, Benjamin, and de Man.

STEVEN FULLER is assistant professor of philosophy at the University of Colorado, Boulder. Author of *Knowledge Disciplinized: The Foundations of Social Epistemology* (D. Reidel, 1987), he is also founder and editor of *Social Epistemology: A Journal of Knowledge, Culture, and Policy.*

His work locates meeting points between analytic and continental philosophy, especially in the philosophy of science.

WALTER GLANNON is assistant professor of Spanish and Portuguese at Smith College. He has published papers on Cervantes, Galdos, Unamuno, and Wittgenstein, and is currently writing a book on Unamuno.

DOROTHY KELLY is assistant professor of French at Boston University. She has published articles on Balzac, Nodier, Genette, and Barthes, and is completing a book on gender identity in nineteenth-century French fiction.

ANTHONY LABRANCHE is associate professor of English at Loyola University (Chicago). He has published articles on the existential grounding of autobiography in the *Review of Existential Psychology and Psychiatry* and is currently working on ethnological autobiography.

ALPHONSO LINGIS is professor of philosophy at Pennsylvania State University. He is the author of *Excesses: Eros and Culture* (SUNY Press, 1983), *Libido: The French Existential Theories* (Indiana University Press, 1985), and the forthcoming *Phenomenological Explanations* (Martinus Nijhoff). He has translated five books by Merleau-Ponty and Levinas and published numerous articles on issues in contemporary philosophy.

T. R. MARTLAND is professor of philosophy at SUNY Albany. Former chair of the Executive Committee of the International Association for Philosophy and Literature, his articles have appeared in leading journals in philosophy and aesthetics. His most recent book is *Religion as Art* (SUNY Press, 1981).

KEVIN MCGINLEY is assistant professor of philosophy at Seattle University. He completed his doctorate at Boston University in 1982 and works in the area of ethics.

JAMES MISH'ALANI is associate professor of philosophy at the University of Washington. He works in the areas of philosophy and literature, contemporary continental thought, psychoanalysis, and ethics.

Louis Nicholas Raphael has taught French and French literature at Reed College and the University of Texas at Austin. He has also published on Baudelaire and is currently working as a securities analyst in New York.

Suresh Raval is professor of English at the University of Arizona. He is the author of *Metacriticism* (1981) and *The Art of Failure: Conrad's Fiction* (1986).

Herman Rapaport is associate professor of English and comparative literature at the University of Iowa. His *Milton and the Postmodern* (University of Nebraska Press) appeared in 1983, and he has just completed a book on *The Temporal Clue: Heidegger and Derrida*. His research and teaching are in critical theory, contemporary culture, video art, and the Renaissance.

Carl Rapp is associate professor of English at the University of Georgia. His *William Carlos Williams and Romantic Idealism* won the Brown University Press First Book Prize Award in 1984. He is currently working on the relationship between philosophy and poetry in the early modernist period.

James LeRoy Smith studied aeronautical engineering and philosophy at Pennsylvania State and completed a doctorate in aesthetics at Tulane. He has taught at East Carolina University since 1969, where he is currently professor and chair in the Department of Philosophy. He has published essays on criticism, ethics, aesthetics, and political and social philosophy.

Walter A. Strauss is Truehaft Professor of Humanities at Case Western Reserve University. Author of *Proust and Literature: The Novelist as a Critic* (Harvard, 1957) and *Descent and Return: The Orphic Theme in Modern Literature* (Harvard, 1971), he works in the areas of contemporary French literature and nineteenth- and twentieth-century comparative literature.

Jane Marie Todd is visiting assistant professor at the University of Illinois at Chicago. She has published articles on Derrida, Freud, Paul de Man, and feminist theory, and is currently working on a book, *Women Reading Freud*.

STEPHEN H. WATSON is assistant professor of philosophy at the University of Notre Dame. He specializes in contemporary continental philosophy and has published articles on topics in hermeneutics, deconstruction, and phenomenology.

JOEL F. WILCOX is an academic adviser at the Undergraduate Academic Advising Center of the University of Iowa. He works chiefly in Renaissance literature, particularly Chapman's translations of Homer and Milton.